'Cities are playing an increasingly large role in environmental policy making. *Urbanization and Climate Co-benefits* comprehensively lays out how cities can use the co-benefits approach to plan for environmentally responsible cities, which meets the needs of both people and the planet. The innovative structure of the book, combining theory and planning as well as on-the-ground experiences makes it highly relevant to both scholars and practitioners at a time when the future of cities is recognized as crucial for global sustainability.'

Kazuhiko Takemoto, *Director, United Nations University Institute for the Advanced Study of Sustainability, Japan*

'*Urbanization and Climate Co-Benefits* provides much needed insights through examination of both the technical and non-technical aspects of co-benefits. The book stimulates the reader to think about how such an approach may be implemented across the urban sectors. This book is a very timely contribution as discussions on co-benefits are becoming increasingly prominent at all levels of policymaking.'

Shobhakar Dhakal, *Associate Professor, Asian Institute of Technology, Thailand*

'This book offers a framework to understand climate co-benefits in cities based on in-depth empirical research carried out by an interdisciplinary team of researchers. It offers an important guide to advance our knowledge on how to develop sustainable cities and to design a road map for achieving the Sustainable Development Goals (SDGs) and implementing the New Urban Agenda adopted at the 2016 Habitat III Conference in Quito.'

Govindan Parayil, *Mark and Melody Teppola Presidential Distinguished Professor, Willamette University, Salem, Oregon, USA, Former Vice-Rector, United Nations University, Tokyo, Japan and Professor, University of Oslo, Norway*

Urbanization and Climate Co-Benefits

Urban areas are increasingly contributing to climate change while also suffering many of its impacts. Moreover, many cities, particularly in developing countries, continue to struggle to provide services, infrastructure and socio-economic opportunities. How do we achieve the global goals on climate change and also make room for allowing global urban development? Increasing levels of awareness and engagement on climate change at the local level, coupled with recent global agreements on climate and development goals, as well as the New Urban Agenda emerging from Habitat III, present an unprecedented opportunity to radically rethink how we develop and manage our cities.

Urbanization and Climate Co-Benefits examines the main opportunities and challenges to the implementation of a co-benefits approach in urban areas. Drawing on the results of empirical research carried out in Brazil, China, Indonesia, South Africa, India and Japan, the book is divided into two parts. The first uses a common framework to analyse co-benefits across the urban sectors. The second part examines the tools and legal and governance perspectives at the local and international level that can help planning for co-benefits.

This book will be of great interest to students, practitioners and scholars of urban studies, climate/development policy and environmental studies.

Christopher N.H. Doll is a research fellow at the United Nations University Institute for the Advanced Study of Sustainability in Tokyo, Japan. He is active across many areas of sustainability research, including urban development, biodiversity governance and the diffusion of low carbon technologies. He holds a Masters and PhD in remote sensing from the University of London.

Jose A. Puppim de Oliveira is a faculty member at the Getulio Vargas Foundation (FGV/EAESP and FGV/EBAPE), Federal University of Rio de Janeiro (COPPEAD-UFRJ) and Fudan University (Shanghai). He is also a researcher affiliated to the United Nations University (UNU-IIGH) in Kuala Lumpur and MIT Joint Program on Science and Policy of Global Change, Cambridge (USA).

Routledge Advances in Climate Change Research

Urbanization and Climate Co-Benefits

Implementation of Win–Win Interventions in Cities

Edited by Christopher N.H. Doll and Jose A. Puppim de Oliveira

LONDON AND NEW YORK

from Routledge

First published 2017 by Routledge

2 Park Square, Milton Park, Abingdon, Oxfordshire OX14 4RN

711 Third Avenue, New York, NY 10017

Routledge is an imprint of the Taylor & Francis Group, an informa business

First issued in paperback 2018

British Library Cataloguing in Publication Data
A catalogue record for this book is available from the British Library

Library of Congress Cataloging in Publication Data
Names: Doll, Christopher Hideo, editor. | Oliveira, Jose Puppim de, editor.
Title: Urbanization and climate co-benefits: implementation of win–win interventions in cities / edited by Christopher Hideo Doll and Jose Puppim de Oliveira.
Description: Abingdon, Oxon; New York, NY: Routledge, 2017. |
Series: Routledge advances in climate change research
Identifiers: LCCN 2016030751 | ISBN 9781138953444 (hb) |
ISBN 9781315667300 (ebook)
Subjects: LCSH: Sustainable urban development. | Urban ecology (Sociology) | City planning–Climatic factors. | Urbanization–Environmental aspects.
Classification: LCC HT241.U743 2017 | DDC 307.1/216–dc23
LC record available at https://lccn.loc.gov/2016030751

ISBN: 978-1-138-95344-4 (hbk)
ISBN: 978-0-367-02690-5 (pbk)

Typeset in Goudy
by Wearset Ltd, Boldon, Tyne and Wear

Contents

Figures

Tables

Boxes

Contributors

Editors

Christopher N.H. Doll is a research fellow at the United Nations University Institute for the Advanced Study of Sustainability in Tokyo, Japan. He is active across many areas of sustainability research, including urban development, biodiversity governance and low carbon technology diffusion. He holds a Masters and PhD in remote sensing from the University of London.

Jose A. Puppim de Oliveira is a faculty member at the Getulio Vargas Foundation (FGV/EAESP and FGV/EBAPE), Federal University of Rio de Janeiro (COPPEAD-UFRJ) and Fudan University (Shanghai). He is also a researcher affiliated to the United Nations University (UNU-IIGH) in Kuala Lumpur and MIT Joint Program on Science and Policy of Global Change, Cambridge (USA).

Contributors

Kaoru Akahoshi is a programme officer at the Institute of Global Environmental Strategies. Kaoru's research focuses on a co-benefits approach and integrating environment and social consideration (ESC) into development projects.

Osman Balaban is an associate professor in the Department of City and Regional Planning at the Middle East Technical University in Ankara, Turkey. His research and teaching interests include urban politics, environmental politics and policies and low-carbon urbanism. He currently serves as the Editor-in-Chief of the METU *Journal of the Faculty of Architecture*.

Tomás Bredariol holds a MSc from the Public Policies, Strategy and Development Program from the Federal University of Rio de Janeiro. He is an environmental engineer and has been working with climate change since 2011 at the Center for Integrated Studies on Climate Change and the Environment – Centro Clima/COPPE/Federal University of Rio de Janeiro – Brazil.

Anthony Capon is the inaugural professor of planetary health at the University of Sydney. A former director of the global health institute at United Nations University (UNU-IIGH) in Malaysia, Tony is a public health physician and an authority on environmental health and health promotion.

Flavia Carloni is a consultant of the World Bank and of the Center for Integrated Studies on Climate Change and the Environment, at COPPE/Federal University of Rio de Janeiro, Brazil. She holds a PhD in Energy and Environmental Planning at COPPE/UFRJ. She is currently supporting the City of Rio de Janeiro in implementing a monitoring system for GHG emissions and climate mitigation actions.

Amit Chatterjee is an assistant professor with the faculty of Planning, School of Planning and Architecture, Bhopal, India. He has over a decade of combined experience in teaching, research and industry. His research interest is primarily focused on urban environment and future cities.

Jining Chen heads the Ministry of Environmental Protection in the People's Republic of China. Prior to that, he was the President of Tsinghua University. His research interests include, but are not limited to, environmental policy design and implementation.

Mehrnoosh Dashti is a post-doctoral fellow in the United Nations University, Institute for the Advanced Study of Sustainability (UNU-IAS). She has focused on sustainable urban waste management and climate change mitigation, particularly in the area of low carbon technology transfer and to Asian developing countries. She holds a MSc and PhD in Energy Systems Engineering.

Puspita Dirgahayani is an assistant professor in the Urban and Regional Planning Department, Institute of Technology Bandung (ITB), Indonesia. Her research interests are urban public transportation planning and policy, including Transit-Oriented Development. She earned her doctoral degree from Urban Transportation Research Unit, Department of Urban Engineering, University of Tokyo, in 2009. She then joined the United Nations University as a UNU-IAS Postdoctoral Fellow.

Huijuan Dong is an associate professor at Shanghai Jiao Tong University in Shanghai, China. She is also a former research associate of the National Institute for Environmental Studies in Tsukuba, Japan. Her research interest is to study the environment and energy-related problems by adopting different environmental economic methods, focusing particularly on China.

Wenbo Dong is a professor at the Department of Environmental Science and Engineering, Fudan University, Shanghai, China. His research interests are in the areas of environmental photochemistry and radical chemistry of organic pollutants, theory and methodology of pollutant control, and development and planning of low-carbon society.

Magali Dreyfus is a CNRS (French National Centre for Scientific Research) researcher, based at CERAPS – Lille University. Her research interests focus on environmental and energy law, climate multi-level governance and local governments' sustainable development policies.

Fábio Duarte is a professor at the Pontifícia Universidade Católica, in Curitiba, Brazil, and scholar at the Massachusetts Institute of Technology, working on the interface between technologies and cities. His new book is *Space, Place and Territory: A Critical Review on Spatialities* (Routledge).

Hooman Farzaneh is currently a junior associate professor at the Institute of Advanced Energy, Kyoto University, Japan. He has expertise on a broad spectrum of issues related to quantitative and qualitative analysis focusing on developing research patterns of low carbon scenarios and policy implementations designed to tackle air pollution problems in regional and local scales.

Tsuyoshi Fujita is the Director/Professor of Center for Social and Environmental System Research, National Institute for Environmental Studies in Tsukuba, Japan. He is also an Alliance Professor of Nagoya University and a visiting professor of the United Nations University. His research focus is mainly on industrial ecology, eco-towns and low-carbon cities.

Tatiana Gadda is a professor at the Universidade Tecnológica Federal do Paraná, in Curitiba, Brazil. She has developed research in a number of topics, including urban revitalization, urban transportation system, sustainable consumption, material flows, urban food system and urban ecosystems analysis. She is also an expert member of the Intergovernmental Panel on Biodiversity and Ecosystem Services (IPBES).

Yong Geng is the Dean and a distinguished professor in the School of Environmental Science and Engineering at Shanghai Jiao Tong University. His research interests include environmental management, energy analysis, low carbon policies and integrated water resource management.

Andreas Jaeger has worked as a policy researcher at the Institute of Global Environmental Strategies since 2013. In addition to his engagement in policy processes related to the Sustainable Development Goals (SDGs) and Habitat III, Mr Jaeger has conducted research and coordinated projects on low-carbon transport, low-carbon development policy frameworks and multi-level governance, as well as subnational data issues in Asia.

Ping Jiang is an associate professor of Fudan Tyndall Centre and the Department of Environmental Science and Engineering of Fudan University in Shanghai, China. His research is in the area of environmental management.

Momoe Kanada is a consultant at the World Bank Environment and Natural Resources Global Practice Group. She is a former assistant fellow at the National Institute for Environmental Studies in Tsukuba, Japan. Her research interest is in effective policy design for pollution prevention and control.

Manmohan Kapshe is a professor in Architecture and Planning at the Maulana Azad National Institute of Technology (MANIT), Bhopal, India. His research areas are low carbon development actions, regional and sectoral analysis of emissions, and impacts of climate change on human settlements. He has served as lead author, contributing author and expert reviewer for various reports of Intergovernmental Panel on Climate Change (IPCC).

Paulose N. Kuriakose is currently serving as an assistant professor at the School of Planning and Architecture, Bhopal, India. His research interest lies in the domain of travel behaviour and sustainable transport policies in the context of the global south.

Emilio La Rovere is currently a professor in the Energy Planning Program at COPPE/UFRJ, and Coordinator of the Center for Integrated Studies on Climate Change and the Environment. He has been serving as Lead author of IPCC, Intergovernmental Panel on Climate Change reports, and is author of several reports prepared for the Secretariat of the United Nations Framework Convention on Climate Change (UNFCCC).

So-Young Lee is a senior policy researcher at the Institute for Global Environmental Strategies. Dr Lee specializes in environmental sociology, especially ecological discourses and practices, and environmental justice. Her current research focuses on governance in sustainability transitions and co-benefits for the underprivileged.

Wanxin Li is an associate professor at the Department of Public Policy, City University of Hong Kong. Her research interests include policy design, policy experimentation, policy evaluation, information transparency, environmental and social governance, inequality, and subjective well-being.

Zhixiao Ma is a post-doctoral researcher at the National Institute for Environmental Studies in Japan. His research focuses on climate change mitigation and environmental risk assessment, particularly those involving the water–energy–air–health nexus. His recent research has analysed the characteristics of air pollutants in China through big data.

Nirmala Menikpura is a research fellow at the Institute for Global Environmental Strategies (IGES). She holds a PhD in Environmental Technology and MSc in Bio-Systems Engineering. Her research interests are in the areas of waste management and climate change, development of indicators and quantitative tools/models for life cycle sustainability assessment, sustainability assessment of the waste electrical and electronic equipment (WEEE) process flow, and socio-economic and environmental Life Cycle Assessment (LCA) of products and processes.

Retno W.D. Pramono is Secretary of the Graduate Urban and Regional Planning study programme in Gadjah Mada University, Indonesia. Research interests include place quality and well-being, environmental management and spatial planning implementation-evaluation.

Csaba Pusztai earned his PhD in Environmental Sciences and Policy at the Central European University. Between 2012 and 2014, he was a UNU-IAS Postdoctoral Fellow at the United Nations University Institute of Advanced Studies in the Sustainable Urban Futures programme studying problems at the intersection of urban governance and sustainability. Currently he is a postdoctoral researcher at the New Zealand Forest Research Institute (Scion) focusing on forestry value chain optimization and sustainability.

Hitomi Roppongi studied environmental governance at the United Nations University, where she focused on local climate policy for her thesis. She is interested in the role local governments may play in tackling global environmental problems. She is a prospective doctorate student at the Bartlett School of Planning, University College London.

Wan-yu Shih is an assistant professor of the Department of Urban Planning and Disaster Management at Ming-Chuan University, Taiwan. Her research interests lie in exploring the interdisciplinary nature of ecological planning and climate change adaptation in urban areas, with a special focus on Green Infrastructure.

Norihisa Shima is an associate professor of urban and regional planning at the Department of Regional Development Studies, Toyo University, Japan. He received a PhD from the Department of Urban Engineering, University of Tokyo, awarded by the City Planning Institute of Japan. He was at UNU-IAS from 2010 to 2013.

José Gabriel Siri is a research fellow at the United Nations University's International Institute for Global Health in Kuala Lumpur, Malaysia. His work focuses on systems thinking to improve decision-making around urban health and well-being, including research on the role of cities in health, and input on the central place of health in global policy processes for urban development.

Leksono P. Subanu currently teaches at the Department of Architecture and Planning, Faculty of Engineering, Gadjah Mada University, Yogyakarta, Indonesia. His primary research interest is in social and cultural processes that uniquely influence the political and economic aspects of spatial and development planning in Indonesia.

Aki Suwa took a professor position at Kyoto Women's University in 2014 after being a research fellow at the United Nations University Institute of Advanced Studies. Her interests include renewable energy and the local governance to promotion of renewables. She is a Japanese national, holding a Master's degree in environmental technology from Imperial College, and a

PhD degree in Planning Studies from University College London, University of London.

Bing Xue is a principal investigator at the Research Center for Industrial Ecology and Sustainability at the Institute of Applied Ecology of the Chinese Academy of Sciences. His research interests mainly focus on the interactions analysis on human-environmental system and climate change governance.

Eric Zusman is a senior policy researcher at the Institute for Global Environmental Strategies (IGES). His research focuses on air pollution regulation, climate policy, transport policy and co-benefits in Asia. He is a political scientist by training with nearly two decades of work and research experience in Asia.

Acknowledgements

This book is the result of a four-year research programme entitled 'Urban Development with Co-Benefits Approach', which was hosted and run by the United Nations University Institute for Advanced Studies (UNU-IAS) from 2010–2014. The project built a wide network of academics and practitioners around the world. Many of the contributors to this book have kindly hosted us on field visits to China, India, Brazil, Japan and Indonesia. Besides the academic outputs, the project generated a series of tools to assess co-benefits and ran several workshops with academics and practitioners to disseminate the tools and discuss the idea of climate co-benefits.

The project was funded and initiated by the Ministry of Environment Japan (MOEJ). We thank the continuous support of MOEJ, in particular Kazuhiko Takemoto, Takeshi Sekiya, Masako Ogawa, Osamu Mizuno, Sachio Taira, Keiko Kuroda and Takahiro Yanagida. The research was guided by the advice of the Scientific Steering Committee formed by Professor Keisuke Hanaki from the University of Tokyo (chair), Professor Tsuyoshi Fujita from the National Institute of Environmental Studies (NIES), Professor Atsushi Sunami from the National Graduate Institute for Policy Studies (GRIPS), Dr Akio Takemoto from MOEJ and Asia-Pacific Research Network for Global Change Research (APN) and Professor Govindan Parayil from UNU-IAS. We also appreciate the support of UNU-IAS staff: Yukie Shibata, Harumi Akiba, Ayuko Fujikawa and Bou Ty, as well as the inputs from many researchers, particularly Aki Suwa, Raquel Moreno-Peñaranda, Joni Jupesta, Joana Portugal-Pereira from UNU-IAS and Keiko Hirota, Eric Zusman, Jane Romero, Nirmala Menikpura and Magnus Bengtsson from other institutions.

Over the years, our project also benefited from the work of many students and interns from around the world who passed through UNU-IAS in Yokohama over the course of the project: Abdul Jalal, Erin Kennedy, Sybille Berger, Non Okamura, Franziska Ferdinand, Hitomi Roppongi, Tim Smith and Yukiko Kamio.

Finally, we are grateful to Kenichi Tsusaka, Christopher O'Malley and Tamara Luisce for their timely contribution to the preparation of the manuscript and last but not least to Annabelle Harris and Margaret Farrelly at Routledge for their understanding, guidance and encouragement through this process of taking our ideas and realizing them in this book.

1 Climate co-benefits in urban areas

Jose A. Puppim de Oliveira and
Christopher N.H. Doll

Introduction

How do we achieve the global goals on climate change and also make room for allowing urban development in countries around the world?

The United Nations 2030 Sustainable Development Agenda (UN 2015) calls for a transformation in development processes in order to achieve the Sustainable Development Goals (SDGs), of which goal 11 is to 'Make cities and human settlements inclusive, safe, resilient and sustainable' (UN 2015). Development processes in cities have generated many social and economic benefits in the last decades, but patterns of urban development have shown themselves to be deficient in a number of areas. Many cities are not able to provide services, infrastructure and/or socio-economic opportunities to all, which puts tremendous pressure on the local resources. Others have good urban services and infrastructure but generate impacts on other parts of the world and on the global environment because of the unsustainable consumption patterns. Consequently, urban areas contribute increasingly to climate change, as well as suffer many of its impacts (McGranahan *et al.* 2007). Thus, the achievement of any meaningful development goals needs to change how we develop and manage our cities.

Future rapid urbanization in developing countries demands a massive provision of sanitation infrastructure, public transportation, housing and jobs for citizens, as well as safeguarding a healthy environment. The climate co-benefits approach we propose in this book refers to policies and other initiatives that simultaneously contribute to addressing climate change and solving local environmental problems, which also have other developmental impacts. The co-benefits approach is especially important for developing countries, which have to overcome many urban challenges simultaneously with limited capacities and resources. This book integrates themes of climate change and local development at the urban level through an analysis of the constituent urban sectors to explore where and how co-benefits may be found. It takes an explicitly transdisciplinary approach to provide insights to a wide audience on lessons for suggesting ways to promote, design and implement the co-benefits approach in urban areas.[1]

This book examines the main opportunities and challenges for generation of climate co-benefits in cities and how we could promote co-benefit interventions in urban areas, including concepts and tools based on empirical studies. It focuses primarily upon sub-national processes, particularly in cities in developing countries, but the research also looked into the links of local and sub-national processes to national and international regimes. This book is divided into two parts. In the first part, we use a common framework to assess co-benefits and apply it across the urban sectors. These chapters make an in-depth analysis of the sector and are supplemented by a series of cases (denoted by the chapter number followed by a section number, e.g. 2.1) to draw valuable lessons on implementation for that sector. These cases derive from the results of empirical research conducted in different parts of the world between 2011 and 2015. Part II then looks at what it will take to bring about such changes in urban development. It examines a wide range of processes, such as international governance and law, that can help and hinder co-benefits, as well as the tools that can help uncover urban co-benefits. Finally, we consider how integrated thinking about urban processes can generate wider societal co-benefits.

Defining climate co-benefits

Although, there are many definitions of co-benefits (Mayrhofer and Gupta 2016), they all reflect the notion that one initiative can result in at least one other benefit in terms of economic, social and/or environmental improvements beyond the main intended outcome. For example, if the main intended outcome is local development or environmental control, the intervention may also have implications for reducing emissions of greenhouse gases (GHGs), and consequently for combating climate change. The roots of co-benefits in climate policy are in the discussions of ancillary benefits of environmental improvements (win–win opportunities for environment protection and economic benefits) that were brought to climate discussions (Pearce 1992). In environmental policy, climate co-benefits were important to advance air pollution initiatives as a way to mitigate climate change, particularly in places where the regulation of GHGs through domestic legislation was difficult to pass politically. The United States is a prominent case but many developing countries also did not want to have their emissions capped. In this context, as climate mitigation could not be pursued solely, or even as the main purpose of public policies, climate goals would have to come as co-benefits of other goals.

Climate co-benefits can be generated when one outcome of an intervention is a benefit in terms of climate change mitigation or adaptation. On the one hand, climate co-benefits could occur as the benefits of certain development interventions in tackling climate change as compared to other viable development alternatives (including doing nothing or business as usual). On the other hand, the co-benefits can arise when purposely mitigating climate change leads to development benefits at the local or regional level, such as reduction in air pollution, creation of jobs or energy cost savings. The latter may be considered to be developmental co-benefits generated by climate action, and the former the climate co-benefits generated by a climate-friendly development option.

Sometimes it is difficult to determine which benefit should come first in terms of policy priority or results. For example, the Delhi Metro was envisioned to give better public transportation access to the local population, but the project was also qualified as a climate mitigation project (see Chapter 2.1). The co-benefits approach can especially fit the development needs of developing countries, which have to overcome many challenges with limited capacity and resources. In terms of climate policy, co-benefits refer to the development and implementation of policy responses that align different goals, simultaneously addressing global (e.g. GHG emissions), local environmental (e.g. various forms of pollution) and/or socio-economic issues (e.g. jobs, energy security and income) (Puppim de Oliveira *et al.* 2013).

In urban areas, climate co-benefits can be an important policy approach to bring about reduction in many aspects of environmental degradation that affects the well-being of the local population. Climate co-benefits can emerge in two major forms. First, there are the climate co-benefits of solving a local environmental problem. For example, climate co-benefits of a cleaner environment, such as cleaner air and water. In the case of air pollution, there are strong linkages between global climate change (GCC) and local air pollution (LAP). These key environmental issues are discussed extensively in the international political arena, notably in the United Nations Framework Convention on Climate Change (UNFCCC), and the relevance of this approach for urban areas has been noted by the Intergovernmental Panel on Climate Change (IPCC; Seto *et al.* 2014). Emissions from the combustion of fossil fuels contribute significantly to both GCC and LAP. Pollution could be reduced by adding end-of-pipe technologies to abate local air pollutants (SO_2, NO_x, NH_3, or particulates), but this would not mitigate much climate change; so co-benefits are limited. Alternatively, a co-benefit initiative could be the reduction in the combustion of fossil fuels in the first place, which would mitigate local air pollutants and the emission of GHGs. Second, there are clear co-benefits in many climate policies (NEAA 2009). Mitigating global climate change by cleaning the air from short-lived climate forcers, some pollutants, such as black carbon, have a short-term effect on climate (MOEJ 2014) and also local environment and health, as do climate policies aimed at cleaning waterways (e.g. avoiding methane formation in open sewage) or making cities more resistant to extreme weather events. However, this is not always the case in climate policy. GHG emissions can be reduced through Carbon Capture and Storage (CCS) technology applied to fossil fuel power plants, but it mainly addresses greenhouse gases but not necessarily air pollutant emissions. CCS equipment installed in isolation therefore alleviates GCC but not LAP.

The co-benefits approach can be assessed at various levels. Sometimes, the co-benefits do not happen where the action was taken, or only materialize over an extended period of time. For example, reducing energy intensity in a building may not necessarily reduce the air pollution in or around the building (unless the building had its own gas or oil generator), but it will reduce GHG emissions and the total air pollution elsewhere (assuming that part or all of the electricity generated comes from fossil fuels). Besides the reduction in GHG emissions and development impact, the assessment should take into account various other impacts in terms of the institutional changes that occurred because of the initiatives. Therefore, in order to understand how the co-benefits approach can be effectively implemented, we have to analyse beyond projects and urban policies, particularly at the city level, and also look at the links beyond the cities (higher levels of governments) or international initiatives (bilateral, multilateral and global, governmental and non-governmental).

Why are co-benefits in urban areas important?

Developed countries faced tremendous local environmental problems during their urbanization process. Even though some urban environmental problems were generally minimized (e.g. local sanitation), as they industrialized, the environment was degraded heavily, sometimes with consequences for the local population. Japan's experience with heavy pollution in Minamata and Yokkaichi severely affected local communities in the 1960s, and serve as examples of how environmental pollution can affect local development. The costs of solving those problems were huge and responsibility was contested in the courts over many years (Puppim de Oliveira 2011).

The relationship between development and pollution is often described using the so-called environmental Kuznets curve, shown in Figure 1.1a. It describes a general pattern that pollution increases as countries develop, until such time that they are rich enough to afford to invest in cleaner technologies and change the course of this pollution curve in the opposite direction. However, this is not uniform across all types of pollution. In particular, the contribution to global environmental problems, such as climate change, keeps increasing with rising incomes. Presently, many countries face the challenge of reducing those emissions. Some developing countries have rapidly urbanized and industrialized in the last decades following similar paths of environmental degradation. Some of these cities are among the most polluted in the world and increasing their contributions in terms of GHG emissions.

The co-benefits approach can help developing countries to avoid the same urban development path as today's industrialized countries by tackling both local environmental problems and global environmental problems at the same time, so cities in developing countries can be wealthier and keep environmental quality, which is important for the well-being of local citizens. In doing so, the aim is to affect the pollution profile such that local pollution peaks at a lower level, whilst global emissions grow more slowly and stabilize at a lower level (Figure 1.1b).

This is appealing because tackling environmental problems, both local and global, can help cities to save financial and natural resources in the long run. Second, it has a political appeal. Many developing countries blame developed countries for causing climate change because of historical emissions and argue that it is the latter's sole responsibility to pay and solve the problem. Co-benefits have a strong local benefit component in terms of improvements in the local

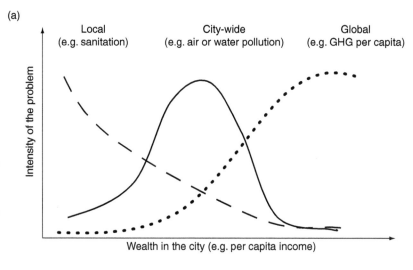

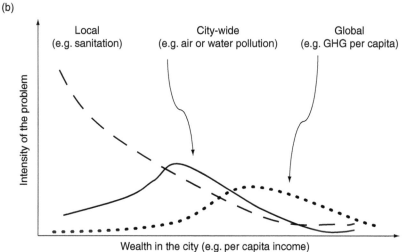

Figure 1.1 (a) The traditional view of environmental pollution under economic development and (b) the changes required to positively impact local and global
pollution.

Source: from Puppim de Oliveira 2013.

environment and the social and economic (as well as political) consequences
that come with this improvement, such as reducing inequality (Garg 2011;
Urge-Vorsatz and Tirado Herrero 2012). Setting cities on the path of good
public transportation, clean and secure energy sources and low waste generation
can have important long-term implications for cities of developing countries,
which can avoid many problems and costs of the wealthier cities. Despite

growing efforts to introduce urban management practices and systems, the environmental quality of cities in most developing countries remains unsatisfactory or is even deteriorating in terms of both local and global environmental problems. Despite a large number of interesting projects, their effects are not enough to change the course of the curves significantly.

Indeed, both theoretical and empirical models of development show that an increase in per capita income and other development indicators (such as the Human Development Index) leads to an increase in both the emissions of greenhouse gases and the ecological footprint (UNDP 2007). Thus, the future of the climate depends not only on developed countries reducing their emissions to open up an ecological space for developing countries, but also on developing countries not following the same development path of today's richer countries.

Moreover, there are other factors that influence the emission of GHGs. For example, the urbanization rate is more strongly correlated to the per capita emissions of carbon dioxide than GDP per capita. As a result, more urbanized countries tend to emit more carbon dioxide than less urbanized countries (Sethi and Puppim de Oliveira 2015). It means that for two countries with similar per capita income, the CO_2 emissions tend to be higher in the more urbanized country. Thus, it is fundamental that we change urbanization patterns to move towards different development paths, so that urbanization is not a synonym of unsustainable development. In order to address these shortcomings, a more comprehensive approach is required to tackle the multiple, often competing, policy environments in which urban management takes place. We therefore present this collection of cross-sectoral, interdisciplinary research and analysis of urban environmental management focusing on opportunities for co-benefits.

The research approach

This book develops a conceptual approach based on empirical evidence to help to understand what kinds of policies can yield co-benefits in different sectors. The evidence comes from cases which seek to explain how and why projects and policies related to climate co-benefits have succeeded in cities around the world, even though sometimes the climate benefit was not the main goal.

The empirical analyses

The cases that were researched examined a situation where co-benefits have either happened or are projected to occur in the future. The strategy uses interdisciplinary analyses in a case-study-based methodology to identify the magnitude and type of co-benefits and/or how and why initiatives related to co-benefits have taken place (Figure 1.2). Therefore, the cases variously focus on the reduction in pollution from an intervention or how and why a city improved pollution levels. In Figure 1.2, a city would move from Situation A to Situation B because of a planned intervention. The approach then aims to understand the type and level of co-benefits generated, how they were generated

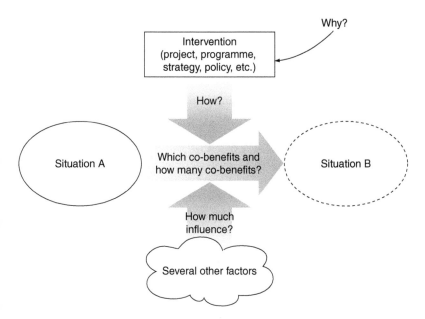

Figure 1.2 The approach to understanding co-benefits interventions.

and what factors influenced the results of the intervention. This includes factors beyond the immediate scope/control of the project as well as unintended consequences. Hence, the cases reveal lessons on both the positive and the negative factors that influence how climate co-benefits can occur. This provides a broad knowledge base for understanding how intentional co-benefits can be enabled through policies and management initiatives.

The Avoid-Shift-Improve framework

The cases and interventions presented in this book are classified following a framework that considers interventions in terms of how they enhanced a particular sector and made climate co-benefits happen. Co-benefits approaches can address development and climate change using the following approaches:

- Avoid – affect demand (i.e. can avoid) without affecting the final wellbeing of citizens;
- Shift – shift from one mode of operation to another;
- Improve – improve the performance of current operations.

The Avoid-Shift-Improve (A-S-I) framework emerged in the 2000s (Dalkmann and Brannigan 2007) as a pragmatic way of framing policies. It originated in the transport sector and grew out of a growing reconceptualization of that sector to a deeper consideration of the role that transport plays in society, rather than as a subset of the energy sector (Huizenga 2012; Schipper *et al.* 2000). That the somewhat obvious realization that the transport sector is primarily concerned with moving *people* rather than vehicles was considered to be a paradigm shift bears testament to entrenched disciplinary modes of thinking that guide much of our analysis of pressing human problems.

The framework is pertinent to co-benefit analysis because it matches closely the way in which emissions are produced. This book extends the A-S-I framework to consider how this can be incorporated into sectors other than transport. Each sector-based chapter in Part I describes the framework for that sector, identifying different elements of A-S-I strategies that can yield co-benefits.

It is also a way of understanding a policy in the broader context of the sector and how it relates to technologies and behaviour. Many policies are a combination of both, but have different challenges and timescales for implementation. They can also be characterized by a range of metrics, which help policymakers monitor progress, examples of which are given below. In general, these factors map onto the framework as follows:

- Avoid – principally behavioural. Example: residents in Yogyakarta, Indonesia, avoided generation of garbage to be taken to the landfill by composting domestic organic waste. This was mainly due to change in their behaviour in discarding waste (Chapter 6.1).

    Key metric: amount of waste generated

- Shift – combination of behaviour and technology. Example: the co-benefits of the Delhi Metro depended on the deployment of the technology (metro system) and the change in behaviour of commuters to shift from car to metro (Chapter 2.1).

    Key metric: mode share

- Improve – principally technological. Example: the co-benefits of changing technologies in the industries in Kawasaki, Japan (Chapter 5.1).

    Key metric: efficiency measures

Sectors tend to favour certain types of interventions over others. Engineering approaches will favour efficiency measures, in part because they are well understood and easier to model. The utility of A-S-I as a way of thinking about how to combine technology and behaviours means it presents a broader set of policy options that can be used to develop a package of interventions, which can look beyond individual projects. It also forms the conceptual framework for the set of tools presented in Part II. Building on the work done in the sector chapters, quantitative evaluation tools in the transport, waste and energy sector use this approach to calculate co-benefits (Chapter 9). The explicit inclusion of a more qualitative approach embedded within the methodology highlights the importance of implementation; more sophisticated quantitative assessments may have little bearing on the actual outcomes if policies are not implemented effectively (Chapter 10). These two chapters should be seen as complementary, loosely interactive tools for determining the co-benefits of interventions and determining the issues around policy selection and implementation.

Understanding policy drivers and implementation of co-benefits

Co-benefits policies come from a series of drivers and obstacles at the local, national and international levels. Understanding the different aspects of project and policy that lead to co-benefits' effectiveness is important to promote co-benefits as an alternative for a sustainable developmental path. The chapters identify several important drivers and obstacles related to urban co-benefits. The factors can be broadly summarized as follows:

- Project level design and management. Some cases investigate the main factors related to project design or management (e.g. finance, training) that explain the effectiveness of co-benefits at the project level. Many of the cases show the important role some projects play to spur larger effects in other cities and other sectors in the same city. For example, the Delhi Metro Corporation (Chapter 2.1) is advising other cities in India on metro systems.
- Policy making and implementation. The chapters analyse under what conditions co-benefits policies can be effective to achieve significant results. Some of the co-benefits initiatives are the result of larger policies, such as national policies for Bus Rapid Transit (BRT) in the case of Indonesia (Chapter 2.3).
- Public administration and management. Some cases in the book explain how the public sector works and what the main drivers are for government effectiveness in pushing for co-benefits. Governments need to develop the capacity to promote co-benefits projects, as they need to be more effective and engage non-governmental actors, as well as spur innovation in society. For example, Surat Municipal Corporation went through a process of decentralization in urban management to be closer and more responsive to the citizens, and as a result became much cleaner (Chapter 6.3).
- Law and institutions. The cases also analyse the role of certain laws and institutions (e.g. informal rules or norms) to promote co-benefits. The cases in Delhi show how the law, and alignment of the law in different levels of government, can spur the development of co-benefits (Chapter 8).
- Urbanization processes. Opportunities for urban co-benefits emerge when new urbanization processes are taking place. There are windows or opportunities for transformation. Shenyang went through an urban regeneration process by moving the industrial area of Tiexi District out of the city centre. This led to improvements in the local environment and efficiency through technological upgrading (Chapter 5.4).

- Urban governance. The analyses in the book look beyond the government sector, understanding the interaction among the different stakeholders in the urban planning process. In most of the cases, non-governmental actors play an important role in the promotion of the idea and implementation of co-benefits initiatives, such as in Yogyakarta, where neighbourhood associations and NGOs started the transformation process and worked together to scale up the community-based solid waste management initiatives (Chapter 6.1).
- Development processes. Governments in developing countries are under pressure to promote economic development in order to generate income and jobs. Initiatives that have an important economic development component can be attractive and receive policy support. The case in Durban is one example of how urban co-benefits can be integrated into job-generating policies (Chapter 3.1).
- International mechanisms. Some global mechanisms have been important in spurring on some of the co-benefits initiatives. Many of the projects listed benefited from the Clean Development Mechanism (CDM) of the Kyoto Protocol, such as the case of Delhi Metro (Chapter 2.1; see also Chapter 7 for a general discussion on international mechanisms, including city-level cooperation).

Understanding innovation for co-benefits

Another dimension in designing effective interventions is to improve the capabilities in cities to generate co-benefits. Small, incremental changes in co-benefits, such as those at the project level, are important. However, radical changes are needed in order to achieve projected carbon reductions, as well as improve local conditions. Thus, besides the effective implementation of co-benefits projects, cities have to create local innovation capacities in order to generate and scale up different innovations for the A-S-I initiatives to have larger impacts. Urban systems have to be able to adopt the best local technologies, absorb new technologies and create the institutional mechanisms to scale up the benefits. Cities need to mobilize resources for implementing those initiatives, but also manage those resources to achieve the expected outcomes and continue innovative processes. The final capacity for large-scale changes is a combination of capabilities and resources. National governments and international organizations could support many of those initiatives and possibly foment similar initiatives in other cities.

This book adopts a comprehensive approach to innovation as a process which involves a spectrum of activities with differing degrees of novelty, from simply copying and improving an existing system to a new urban initiative to the world. We focus on distinctions in terms of the technological 'novelty' of the innovation – the extent to which it differs from existing technologies, ranging from innovations that are close to being pure imitations to those that are fundamentally different from anything currently in existence (Figueiredo 2001). Thus we will consider the building of capabilities for undertaking 'new-to-the-city', 'new-to-country' and 'new-to-world' innovative activities. Innovation involves the recombination of existing knowledge and there is no distinction between innovation and diffusion, and invention and imitation, as they all have potential local impacts.

Technological capabilities include a stock of knowledge-related resources that permit cities to undertake *differing degrees* of operation and innovation activities. Such capabilities involve both the nature of human capital (e.g. specialist professionals, knowledge bases and skills/talents that are formally and informally allocated within specific organizational units, projects and teams) and organizational aspects in the city's internal and external organizational arrangements, such as their routines and procedures, and managerial systems, as well as interaction with actors within and outside the city.

The book also tries to understand the socio-technical transitions which lead to co-benefits cities. In some of the cases (Chapters 2.3, 2.4, 3.2 and 6.2), authors looked at how city organizations (both governmental and non-governmental), or specific sectors in a city, learn and build technological capabilities to generate co-benefits. The cases analysed the following points:

- functioning of the socio-technical systems (Geels 2005)[2] in that city in a particular sector;
- the level of technological capabilities for managing a certain technological function in that sector;
- the learning process and mechanisms to acquire the technological capability over time;
- the enabling or constraining factors to the learning process and to the final results of the application of the technology in terms of co-benefits.

The chapters in the book

The objective of the book is to understand the barriers that hinder an integrated approach to management of the different sectors, and look beyond particular projects. More broadly, the book aims to answer and provide insights into the following questions (see also Figure 1.2):

> What are the main sources of emissions in urban sectors and how can we reduce them?
> What are the links and synergies between different urban sectors?
> How do institutional factors affect the implementation of the initiatives?

Understanding these links is the key to reducing emissions on a system-wide level. Thus, the first part of the book analyses several urban sectors, having one comprehensive chapter per sector followed by empirical studies of co-benefits in that particular sector. The chosen sectors are treated individually because this is how cities are largely still managed. Deciding how to arrange the sectors in this book, one could take many routes. We start with transport (Chapter 2) as it is the sector in which the key organizing framework for this book originated. From this departure, the role of transport is both strongly influenced by and influences land use (Chapter 3) in a city, such that two of the cases (notably, Delhi and Curitiba) have strong links between the sectors. The building sector (Chapter 4) fits neatly here as a link between the land they occupy and the energy they consume. Their role in the urban energy system is formalised in Chapter 5, as part of a broader consideration of the supply and demand of energy in cities. The final sector to be analysed is the waste sector (Chapter 6). One emerging component of a diversified energy mix comes from the waste sector but, again, this forms only one part of a broad sector with many options on waste treatment methods and technologies. The supplementary cases that follow each chapter touch on various aspects mentioned above and can be categorized as shown in Table 1.1.

The cases provide a more detailed examination of projects and analyses that mainly describe co-benefits after the fact, but what is necessary to achieve co-benefits by design? Part II deals with the institutional aspects of planning for

Table 1.1 Summary of cases in the book

Theme	Chapter	Country	Case	A-S-I factors
Model-based analysis	Energy	Japan	Japan's historical pollution control	Improve
	Energy	China	Co-benefits of Chinese megacities	Improve
	Waste	Indonesia	Community-based solid waste management in Yogyakarta	Avoid, Shift
Descriptive	Land use	South Africa	Green infrastructure	Shift, Improve
	Buildings	China/Japan	Building/district efficiency	Improve
	Buildings	Japan	Tokyo's cap and trade system	Avoid
	Energy	China	Industrial relocation, Baoshan	Avoid, Improve
	Energy	China	Industrial relocation, Teixi	Avoid, Improve
Innovation and learning	Transport	Brazil	Rio de Janeiro's Bus Rapid System	Improve
	Transport	Indonesia	Trans-Jogja Bus Rapid Transit	Improve
	Transport	Brazil	Curitiba's transport and land planning	Shift, Improve
	Waste	India	Surat's clean-up	Improve
Governance and political economy	Transport	India	The Delhi Metro	Shift
	Land use	Indonesia	Municipal cooperation, Yogyakarta	Improve
	Waste	China	Suzhou	Improve

co-benefits and starts with an overview of the international efforts to promote a co-benefits approach (Chapter 7). This is expressed through both the formal intergovernmental fora as well as the informal alliances of city networks. Chapter 8 then examines how these long-term goals and visions that are agreed at the international level can be formalised in law as a basis for implementation. We then present two sets of tools that were developed in the project. Quantitative tools were developed in the areas of transport, waste and energy/buildings (Chapter 9), whilst a complementary set of more qualitative 'governance' tools (Chapter 10) were also developed for the same sectors. Given the synergies between the sectors, there is great potential to re-orient our management of key urban systems for wider co-benefits. One research field that is growing in attention from the scientific community is that of human health and well-being. We therefore close the book with a chapter on how governance can integrate the sectors for wider co-benefits, notably health and well-being.[3] The scope of this book, though wide-ranging, is not exhaustive. Areas for further investigation include, for example, looking at the broader role of ecosystem services in poverty reduction and food provision.

Governance and co-benefits

The co-benefits approach is based on the understanding that multiple benefits should be intentionally internalized at the conception of a policy or a project, as opposed to the accidental benefits (ADB 2009). In order to design such an intervention, there is a need to provide the institutional environment where the key governance mechanisms and policy drivers are responsive to the co-benefits approach.

Climate co-benefits assume that the win–win outcomes (climate + development) are possible. However, many obstacles exist to achieve co-benefits in all areas (Puppim de Oliveira 2013). Understanding the impacts of influencing factors and policy drivers on the extent of co-benefits is of key importance to derive policy implications to eliminate the barriers to promote co-benefits as an alternative developmental path. In practice trade-offs between climate change and development outcomes occur in many cases (Mayrhofer and Gupta 2015), particularly in urban areas in developing countries where there is an urgent need to provide all kinds of infrastructure with competing demands and weak governance. Nevertheless, there are many opportunities to achieve climate co-benefits in urban areas by simple means, such as prioritizing existing public transportation and recycling waste. In this sense, 'urban governance' as a general framework for policy making at the local level could significantly influence the effectiveness of co-benefits policies.

Policy responses to urban issues are the combination of efforts and interactions of various actors at the local, national and international levels. As co-benefits interventions are new to the policy arena, institutional innovations have to take place to advance the co-benefit approach in practice. The effectiveness of developing co-benefits interventions depends upon the legal, institutional and technical capacities of the actors involved in urban govern-ance. National and local governments are of critical importance in this respect, as co-benefits policies, just like most environmental and development policies, necessitate the public sector's involvement and guidance. Governments and other stakeholders should ensure good governance at all levels but especially at the local level, which is closest to urban policy making and implementation, and create an urban policy environment that stimulates the development of effective co-benefits initiatives.

Local and sub-national governments could play a crucial role in tackling global and local environmental problems by means of climate co-benefits pol-icies. First, local and sub-national governments have a unique position to tackle environmental problems due to their proximity to the causes and effects of these problems (Puppim de Oliveira 2009; Deri and Alam 2008). Second, local and sub-national governments in many countries are responsible for developing and implementing the regulatory frameworks on urban sectors, such as land use, infrastructure and buildings, which have significant influence on the environ-mental agenda (Satterthwaite *et al.* 2007). Third, local and sub-national gov-ernments have greater opportunities to keep close and direct contacts with the society, and hence could lead changes in local communities and influence the attitudes of citizens (Deri and Alam 2008). Finally, city-wide actions can more effectively be done by local and sub-national governments offering large eco-nomies of scale and multiple benefits when compared to the individual actions by households and enterprises (Satterthwaite *et al.* 2007).

Four 'modes of governing' by local governments can be identified to strengthen climate policies, and consequently co-benefits, in cities; namely *self-governing, provision, regulation* and *enabling* (UN-HABITAT 2011). In the 'self-governing mode', actions to address climate change are taken by local governments per se, as in the example of measures to reduce GHG emissions in municipal buildings or facilities, such as in the case of Durban (Chapter 3.1) and the close link between transport and land use in Curitiba (Chapter 2.2). On the other hand, in the 'enabling mode', local governments introduce mech-anisms to support and enable other actors to undertake the necessary actions to tackle the climate problem, as in the example of solid waste management in Yogyakarta (Chapter 6.1). In the 'provision mode', the role of local govern-ments is to provide the necessary infrastructure and services that have the potential to mitigate climate change and its impacts, such as the case of Delhi Metro (Chapter 2.1). The fourth mode, the 'regulation mode', refers to the introduction of various forms of regulation by local authorities, such as incen-tives, standards and taxation, as in the case of the building sector in Tokyo (Chapter 4.2). Moreover, along with these distinct modes, 'private modes of governing', in which non-governmental actors take part in service delivery and policy implementation across different sectors, are also gaining importance in developed and developing countries (UN-HABITAT 2011).

Local governments could also open entry points with initiatives for actors who are willing to take action. However, the self-governing mode may not suffice for a wider implementation of climate change activities and co-benefit policies as there may not be enough municipal facilities in some cases, or the local government may not have the necessary resources to invest in changing the facilities. Likewise, in the enabling mode, local governments undertake a passive role in terms of addressing climate change through the actions of other local actors who are willing to participate (UN-HABITAT 2011). In cases where local actors are reluctant or ignorant to undertaking actions to address environmental problems, the enabling mode of governing will not help much in pushing the co-benefits agenda forward. On the other hand, provisioning could be an important mode of governing, especially in the context of climate co-benefits. This is because a significant part of actions to tackle climate change is in the form of structural measures (i.e. infrastructure provision) and public goods and services, which cannot be widely provided without government support and intervention. Similarly, regulations are fundamental to set the right institutional framework to promote co-benefits (Chapter 8). New forms of regulations can spur collaboration among different actors and boost urban innovation for co-benefits. In this sense, the regulation mode of governing can be very effective in terms of enhancing the capacities of local actors and facilitating their actions.

No matter which governing mode or likely combinations of modes are dominant in particular contexts, coordinated action among all actors, including public, private and non-governmental ones, are necessary to maximize efforts. Better coordination of efforts and actions at the local level could spur the effectiveness of co-benefits policies and avoid overlapping or counterproductive actions. However, coordination and cooperation should not be limited to the local and national levels and actors. International mechanisms and cooperation should also be taken into account and mainstreamed into urban policy making (Chapter 7). There is a great imbalance in the technological capacity among countries, or even regions within a country. Therefore, communication and cooperation with the wider international community could help national and local governments to obtain the necessary technology and know-how to promote co-benefits policies and projects. Some global mechanisms have already been important to spur some of the co-benefits initiatives. Many of the current co-benefits projects in different parts of the world benefited from the CDM of the Kyoto Protocol, such as the Delhi Metro.

Climate governance has become polycentric in the sense that the axes of the discussions and influential actors and centres of power have dispersed. First, the North–South divide in climate emissions has become less clear, as some developing countries have increased their emissions significantly and have higher emissions than their richer counterparts. Sharp increases happen particularly in large cities (Dhakal 2009) and some Chinese cities have per capita emissions larger than cities in rich countries, such as Tokyo. Second, the disparity between urban and rural in terms of GHG emissions seems to have widened in some developing countries. Thus, the North–South axis is moving to an Urban–Rural axis of emission inequality (Sethi and Puppim de Oliveira, 2015). There is a need to improve climate governance between national and sub-national levels in order to balance the urban–rural disparities. Also, cities should have a more relevant role in formal climate regimes, as they have to play a larger role in solving the climate change crisis.

There are many challenges and opportunities that influence the governance capacity at the local level to generate climate co-benefits. The key aspect of governance for climate co-benefits is the interactions among different governmental and non-governmental stakeholders. Connecting various actors helps to align their different priorities and outcomes of the policies. For example, a transport policy would tend to incorporate environmental aspects in its planning when the stakeholders in government are in charge of environmental issues and non-governmental actors are involved in the policy process. The participation of different stakeholders can also be a driver for policy change and support in the implementation. They can bring pressure to put in place the right legal and institutional environment to boost climate co-benefits.

The four distinct modes of governance could be employed by local governments to address local and global environmental problems. Each mode has its own advantages and disadvantages in tackling problems by motivating local actors and ensuring the participation of local communities. Moreover, the case studies of the co-benefits research demonstrate that there is a good match between certain modes of governing and certain sectors or fields of urban policy. For instance, the effectiveness of co-benefit policies in the building sector could be increased by means of interventions and mechanisms in line with the enabling and regulation modes of governing. On the other hand, intervention appears to be the most appropriate mode of governing when it comes to policy initiatives and projects in the urban transport sector. Nevertheless, instead of adhering to any of these modes, local governments should aim to employ a good combination of these modes considering the local needs and opportunities in their jurisdictions.

Another important aspect of urban governance is related to innovation capabilities. The policy process should facilitate innovations by bringing together outside ideas that have not been tried in that specific location. Urban services and infrastructure should be provided differently from the 'business-as-usual' approach. The Delhi Metro is a good example of a new organizational environment: The Delhi Metro Corporation is a partnership between the national and sub-national governments. This partnership made possible the construction of the Metro (Chapter 2.1).

No matter which governing mode or likely combinations of modes are employed in particular contexts, coordinated action among all local actors, including public, private and non-governmental ones, need to be ensured. In cases where competition rather than coordination is the dominant dynamic at the local level, opportunities might be lost and a positive outcome of a policy area might be offset by the negative progress in another. Furthermore, coordination and collaboration should not be limited to the local and national actors but include the international agencies and donors. International donors not only bring monetary sources to target countries, but also provide know-how in the course of project development and management. Such a process could help target countries to build and enhance local institutional capacity and knowledge. The Delhi Metro Project is a good manifestation of how international cooperation can facilitate local capacity development.

Co-benefits and the New Urban Agenda (Habitat III)

Climate co-benefits is a fundamental component to achieve the goals of the Paris Agreement on climate change and fulfil the commitments agreed at the United Nations Conference on Housing and Sustainable Urban Development (commonly known as Habitat III), held in Quito (Ecuador) from 17–20 October 2016. Habitat III was the third of the large UN conferences to discuss urbanization, which happens every 20 years (previous conferences were held in Vancouver, Canada, in 1976 and in Istanbul, Turkey, in 1996). The main output of the conference was the 'New Urban Agenda', which is a document stating a series of principles and commitments shared among the national governments aiming to make urbanization more sustainable (UN, 2016). There are three overall 'transformative' commitments: (i) Sustainable Urban Development for Social Inclusion and Ending Poverty; (ii) Sustainable and Inclusive Urban Prosperity and Opportunities for All; and (iii) Environmentally Sustainable and Resilient Urban Development.

The New Urban Agenda builds on previous initiatives that have been spawned over the 40 years of the Habitat meetings. These were initially focused on specific issues such as provision of basic services (housing and sanitation) and healthy cities, and culminated with Local Agenda 21 at the UN Earth Summit in 1992, which took a broad look at local sustainable development. Satterthwaite (2016) notes that whilst we move forward on these agendas, it does not presume that old problems are solved and there is much to learn from looking at the failures in delivery of previous initiatives. Whilst the New Urban Agenda lacks the specific metrics and concrete implementation means to make urbanization processes more sustainable, it sets a positive path, but it is more a wish list than a road map. Thus, our hope should be less in the output document and more in the outcome of the process that has involved thousands of stakeholders. This process has stimulated sharing of knowledge and alliances that can improve urban and climate governance for making urbanization more sustainable, which in turn can generate more climate co-benefits. The cognitive effects of Habitat III can also impact urban development, if it is disseminated widely (like the effects of Rio-92 on the international, national and local agendas).

Even though climate change is not among the explicit commitments of the New Urban Agenda, it is mentioned across the document several times. Many of the Agenda's goals are centred on offering more economic opportunities, energy, housing and transportation to urban dwellers. Harnessing massive urban climate co-benefits will be the only way to achieve those goals without threatening the health of the planet and its inhabitants.

Urban development that generates climate co-benefits can also tackle inequality, another key point of the New Urban Agenda. Current urbanization trends are core drivers of inequities and inequalities, and climate change exacerbates them. Climate co-benefits can reduce inequality by addressing the patterns of unsustainable urbanization in the North, and more recently in the South. The core of the problem is the capacity of cities to concentrate massive amounts of consumption, and expel their unwanted residues to other places, with negative consequences not only for the local urban population but also for people living much further afield. Achieving the multiple goals of the Agenda will require taking a different view of the role of cities and their main long-term development objectives, moving urban development from being based on consumption and infrastructure to focusing on quality of life, resource conservation and sufficiency. Resources and services will have to be better shared, generating climate co-benefits and reducing inequalities in access to them, and giving more opportunities to all. As our ambition to simultaneously tackle ever more complex inter-related problems grows, so must our approaches to looking at them from new and integrated perspectives.

Lessons and the way forward to transformation

Cities are at the centre of initiatives to achieve the Sustainable Development Goals (SDGs) of the United Nations 2030 Development Agenda (UN 2015). Not only do they contain most of the world's population, as microcosms of society in general, they bring the connections between different areas of sustainable development into sharper focus (Doll 2015). Urban areas are also key in reducing carbon emissions globally as they are responsible for more than three-quarters of emissions (Seto *et al.* 2014). Thus, in order to achieve the SDGs and the goal of keeping the increase in the average Earth's surface temperature below 1.5–2.0°C, as recognized in the Paris Agreement, we have to drastically rethink the way we build and manage our cities. There is a need for a big transformation in the way we approach urban development policy and the co-benefits approach can play a fundamental role in this large transformation needed in cities.

First, cities need to harness maximum opportunities for innovation in technologies and management in order to use resources efficiently. There are tremendous opportunities for co-benefits by reducing emissions in the various sectors (chapters in Part I). It is incumbent on not only governments but civil society and a combination of governmental and non-governmental actors to generate innovations to solve urban problems.

Second, we need to combine top-down with bottom-up approaches to promote urban co-benefits. Cities, national governments and influential actors in civil society should identify and promote local innovation capabilities and learning. Niches of good practices and innovation in cities should be supported in order to be replicated and thus have a larger effect on urban development. The initiatives of community-based solid waste management in Yogyakarta and other cities in Indonesia had a large effect because they received support from the city government (Chapter 6.1). Similarly, larger co-benefit initiatives should be promoted from the top by sub-national or national governments, with local support from civil society in order to be sustainable in the long term. The Delhi Metro was just possible with the combined efforts from the city and the national government (Chapter 2.1). This can also help to replicate the niches of good practice beyond a particular city.

Third, even though technological and management innovations have tremendous potential for urban co-benefits, as shown in the cases of Kawasaki and Baoshan (Chapters 5.1 and 5.3), their limits for reducing carbon emissions and other pollutants in absolute terms should be acknowledged. The case of mandatory carbon emission capping in Tokyo (Chapter 4.2) illustrates how sub-national governments can innovate and start their own urban policies that set limits to carbon emissions. Policy-making frameworks should recognize ecological limits at the different scales, from local to planetary. Whilst the logic of co-benefits sounds reasonable, one of the drawbacks to the approach in a practical sense is that the benefits are often public goods and therefore do not make immediate financial sense to project developers. The role of the public sector is crucial here to support benefits which would otherwise be neglected. This book focuses on the more tangible co-benefits like air pollution, but some key benefits cannot easily be monetized or even discerned a priori. Adopting the co-benefits approach helps mainstream the notion that there may be other kinds of benefits and that these should be looked for when evaluating alternative interventions.

Governance has a critical bearing on the effectiveness of the framework that is presented here as governance mechanisms effectively act as an enabling factor on whether the technical aspects can be achieved, and ultimately the utility of the co-benefits approach. Hence, the co-benefits approach proposed here encourages a more synergistic multidimensional approach, which suggests that the impact of a specific initiative can be greater by addressing both local development and global environmental issues; and governance is an important aspect to make this happen.

Recognition of this position has been slow to gain traction at the international level. The Kyoto Protocol's main flexibility mechanism for developing countries, the CDM, allowed little space for the sectoral approach to reduce GHGs, concentrating on project specific reductions from a baseline perspective based on rigid methodologies with strict MRV (Measurable, Reportable and Verifiable) for counting of carbon credits. Such requirements greatly reduced the viability of more complex, multidimensional projects in certain sectors, such as urban transport or housing, where carbon reductions are difficult to precisely MRV. However, international attention is moving to integrate ever wider areas and measures to optimize the policy effects, including those related to urban planning and land-use management, particularly for developing counties. The international frameworks coming after the Paris Agreement tend to become less project specific and have opportunities for a broader range of scope, such as the sector or multi-sectoral approach (Chapter 7). Those international frameworks tend to be based on voluntary actions and commitments, such as the Nationally Determined Contributions (NDCs). Although they still fall short of the agreed target, greater flexibility of supported projects which comport with local development objectives will help build ambition to bridge the gap. Thus, there is a need to find ways that national and local development goals can be compatible with reduction of GHGs, which is the primary objective of the urban co-benefits approach. Co-benefits offer a range of opportunities to reduce emissions based on future frameworks, making important the development of methodologies that can help countries to move their development agenda forward with limited impacts on the environment.

Thus, urban co-benefits offer an immense opportunity for developing countries to mitigate damaging actions more quickly and to avoid the unsustainable path of urbanization followed by some developed countries, which has caused tremendous environmental and social harm. Moreover, it offers the chance to avoid becoming locked into an unsustainable path, which then becomes expensive or unfeasible to remedy.

Nevertheless, our understanding of co-benefits and how to generate them on a large scale is limited. The assessment of co-benefits can be challenging in most of the initiatives, even in a qualitative way, due to several factors. First is the lack of, or difficulty in collecting, baseline data. In many cities around the world, basic data are not available, or not available at the scale needed for assessing certain interventions, or data collection is prohibitively expensive and troublesome to collect or estimate, such as mode shifts in the transportation sector (Chapter 2). Second, the causality links between the intervention and co-benefits are difficult to understand. For example, urban forests can clearly bring co-benefits to cities, but in some cases, under certain conditions, trees can exacerbate air pollution, emitting high amounts of volatile organic compounds (VOCs), which in turn contribute to the formation of ozone and carbon monoxide (Cardelino and Chameides 1990). However, this does not impede the development of a co-benefits approach, as many of the benefits are clear, though sometimes not easy to precisely assess. Thus, the cases analyse co-benefits that can be quantified or others that could potentially happen. Future research should identify methods that can better assess co-benefits as well as the institutional arrangements that generate them. Further conceptual clarification and consensus on co-benefits could help disseminate the concept and align sectoral policies to pursue more co-benefits. This could be done by reaching an agreement among different researchers, governments, organizations and stakeholders on an operational definition of co-benefits which is relevant for policy (Puppim de Oliveira et al. 2013).

Despite the excitement at the first global agreement on limiting the average global temperature increase, the Paris Agreement falls short in mentioning sufficiency (the backbone of the Avoid approach for co-benefits) as a fundamental part for achieving the absolute reductions in carbon emissions, preferring to focus on efficiency (Improve) and the shift to renewable energy instead. Whilst each strategy is undoubtedly important and may even be more relevant in certain sectors, without a culture of sufficiency the long-term goals of limiting emissions will be almost impossible to achieve. Decoupling the economy from emissions is very unlikely in practice, as we would have to improve the efficiency of our economy in terms of carbon intensity (tonnes carbon/GDP) 130 times in 35 years (Hoffmann 2016), assuming the developing countries would be offered the ecological space to grow their per capita income at the levels of the European Union (EU).

The history of urban management has been one of solving specific problems through isolated responses often derived from linear thought processes, but this is no longer fit for purpose in a world of multiple and emergent challenges. The combined global agreements of climate and development opens a critical window of opportunity to develop an urgently needed new kind of urbanization; one which is based on the axiom that city activities have both local and global impacts and explicitly recognizes the connection between component urban systems in their technological, social and organizational configurations. This book is a contribution to that vision.

Notes

1 The genesis of this book was a four-year research project undertaken at the United Nations University Institute of Advanced Studies (UNU-IAS) funded by the Ministry of the Environment Japan. The project examined the main opportunities and challenges to implementation of co-benefits related policies in urban areas. A number of outputs resulted from the project and this book presents the key findings, including a set of tools for planning co-benefits (see more at http://urban.ias.unu.edu). This introduction is based on some of the publications that resulted from the project, such as Puppim de Oliveira *et al.* (2013) and Puppim de Oliveira (2013).
2 A socio-technical system consists of a cluster of elements that affects the technological dimension of a society, including technology, regulation, user practices and markets, cultural meaning, infrastructure, maintenance networks and supply networks (Geels 2005).
3 A major international ten-year research programme co-sponsored by the International Council of Science Unions, the United Nations University and the Interacademy Medical Panel (ICSU-UNU-IAMP) has recently been launched on the issue of urban health and in particular the systems approaches that can drive research and understanding in this area.

References

Asia Development Bank (ADB) 2009, *Rethinking Transport and Climate Change, Asian Development Bank Sustainable Development Working Paper Series*, e-book, Asia Development Bank, Metro Manila, Philippines, viewed 6 June 2016, www.adb.org/sites/default/files/publication/28489/adb-wp10-rethinking-transport-climate-change.pdf.

Cardelino, CA and Chameides, WL 1990, 'Natural hydrocarbons, urbanization, and urban ozone', *Journal of Geophysical Research*, vol. 95, no. D9, pp. 13971–13979.

Dalkmann, H and Brannigan, C 2007, *Transport and Climate Change: Module 5a, Sustainable Transport: A Sourcebook for Policy-makers in Developing Cities*, e-book, Deutsche

Gesellschaft für Technische Zusammenarbeit (GTZ), Eschborn, viewed 6 June 2016, http://siteresources.worldbank.org/EXTAFRSUBSAHTRA/Resources/gtz-transport-and-climate-change-2007.pdf.

Deri, A and Alam, M 2008, *Local Governments and Climate Change*, Commonwealth Secretariat Discussion Paper: One Pager, No. 2, London.

Dhakal, S 2009, 'Urban energy use and carbon emissions from cities in China and policy implications', *Energy Policy*, vol. 37, no. 11, pp. 4208–4219.

Doll, C 2015, *Cities Should Be at the Heart of the SDGs*, United Nations University, viewed 9 June 2016, http://unu.edu/publications/articles/cities-heart-of-sdgs.html.

Figueiredo, PN 2001, *Technological Learning and Competitive Performance*, Edward Elgar Publishing, Cheltenham, UK.

Garg, A 2011, 'Pro-equity effects of ancillary benefits of climate change policies: A case study of human health impacts of outdoor air pollution in New Delhi', *World Development*, vol. 39, no. 6, pp. 1002–1025.

Geels, FW 2005, 'Processes and patterns in transitions and system innovations: Refining the co-evolutionary multi-level perspective', *Technological Forecasting & Social Change*, vol. 72, no. 6, pp. 681–696.

Hoffmann, U 2016, *Can Green Growth Really Work? A Reality Check that Elaborates on the True (Socio-) Economics of Climate Change, Part 1 Contradictions of Green Growth*, Green Growth: Ideology, Political Economy and the Alternatives, Zed Books, London.

Huizenga, C 2012, *International Climate Change Initiatives and Low Carbon Transport in Asia: Perspectives and Prospects, Part 4, Section 12, Low Carbon Transport in Asia – Strategies for Optimizing Co-benefits*, e-book, Earthscan, Abingdon, UK, viewed 6 June 2016, http://samples.sainsburysebooks.co.uk/9781136576393_sample_521922.pdf.

Mayrhofer, JP and Gupta, J 2015, 'The politics of co-benefits in India's energy sector', *Environment and Planning C: Government and Policy*, 10 December, 0263774X 15619629.

Mayrhofer, JP and Gupta, J 2016, 'The science and politics of co-benefits in climate policy', *Environmental Science & Policy*, vol. 57, pp. 22–30.

McGranahan, G, Balk, D and Anderson, B 2007, 'The rising tide: Assessing the risks of climate change and human settlements in low elevation coastal zones', *Environment and Urbanization*, vol. 19, no. 1, pp. 17–37.

Ministry of Environment Japan (MOEJ) 2014, *Asian Co-benefits Partnership (ACP) White Paper 2014: Bringing Development and Climate Together in Asia*. Ministry of Environment Japan, Tokyo, viewed 21 September 2016, www.cobenefit.org/publications/images/ACPwhitepaper_FY2013.pdf.

Netherlands Environmental Assessment Agency (NEAA) 2009, *Co-benefits of Climate Policy*, Bilthoven, Netherlands.

Pearce, D 1992, *The Secondary Benefits of Greenhouse Gas Control*, Centre for Social and Economic Research on the Global Environment (CSERGE), Norwich, UK.

Puppim de Oliveira, JA 2009, 'The implementation of climate change related policies at the subnational level: An analysis of three countries', *Habitat International*, vol. 33, no. 3, pp. 253–259.

Puppim de Oliveira, JA 2011, 'Why an air pollution achiever lags on climate policy? The case of local policy implementation in Mie, Japan', *Environment & Planning A*, vol. 43, no. 8, pp. 1894–1909.

Puppim de Oliveira, JA 2013, 'Learning how to align climate, environmental and development objectives: Lessons from the implementation of climate co-benefits initiatives in urban Asia', *Journal of Cleaner Production*, vol. 58, pp. 7–14.

Puppim de Oliveira, JA, Doll, CNH, Kurniawan, TA, Geng, Y, Kapshe, M and Huisingh, D 2013, 'Promoting win–win situations in climate change mitigation, local environmental quality and development in Asian cities through co-benefits', *Journal of Cleaner Production*, vol. 58, pp. 1–6.

Satterthwaite, D 2016, 'Editorial: A new urban agenda?', *Environment & Urbanization*, vol. 28, no. 1, pp. 3–12.

Satterthwaite, D, Huq, S, Reid, H, Pelling, M and Romero Lankao, P 2007, *Adapting to Climate Change in Urban Areas: The Possibilities and Constraints in Low- and Middle-Income Nations, Human Settlements Discussion Paper Series: Climate Change and Cities 1*, e-book, International Institute for Environment and Development, London, viewed 6 June 2016, http://pubs.iied.org/pdfs/10549IIED.pdf.

Schipper, L, Marie-Liliu, C and Gorham, R 2000, *Flexing the Link Between Transport and Greenhouse Gas Emissions: A Path for the World Bank*, e-book, International Energy Agency (IEA), Paris, France, viewed 6 June 2016, www.ocs.polito.it/biblioteca/mobilita/FlexingLink1.pdf.

Sethi, M and Puppim de Oliveira, JA 2015, 'From global "North–South" to local "Urban–Rural": A shifting paradigm in climate governance?', *Urban Climate*, vol. 14, no. 4, pp. 529–543.

Seto KC, Dhakal, S, Bigio, A, Blanco, H, Delgado, GC, Dewar, D, Huang, L, Inaba, A, Kansal, A, Lwasa, S, McMahon, JE, Müller, DB, Murakami, J, Nagendra, H and Ramaswami, A 2014, *Human Settlements, Infrastructure and Spatial Planning. In: Climate Change 2014: Mitigation of Climate Change. Contribution of Working Group III to the Fifth Assessment Report of the Intergovernmental Panel on Climate Change*, Cambridge University Press, Cambridge, United Kingdom and New York, NY, USA.

UNDP 2007, *Human Development Report 2007/2008: Fighting Climate Change*, UNDP, New York, viewed 3 October 2016, http://hdr.undp.org/sites/default/files/reports/268/hdr_20072008_en_complete.pdf.

United Nations (UN) 2015, *Transforming our World: The 2030 Agenda for Sustainable Development, Resolution A/RES/70/1 Adopted by the General Assembly at its Seventieth Session on 25 September 2015*, e-book, United Nations (UN), USA, viewed 6 June 2016, www.un.org/ga/search/view_doc.asp?symbol=A/RES/70/1&Lang=E.

United Nations (UN) 2016, *Draft Outcome Document of the United Nations Conference on Housing and Sustainable Urban Development (Habitat III), Document A/CONF.226/4*, e-book, United Nations (UN), USA, viewed 10 November 2016, www.habitat3.org/the-new-urban-agenda.

United Nations, Human Settlements Programme (UN-HABITAT) 2011, *Cities and Climate Change: Policy Directions*, Global Report on Human Settlements 2011, Earthscan, London and Washington DC.

Urge-Vorsatz, D and Tirado Herrero, S 2012, 'Building synergies between climate change mitigation and energy poverty alleviation', *Energy Policy*, vol. 49, pp. 83–90.

Part I

Co-benefits in the urban sectors

2 Transport

Christopher N.H. Doll

Introduction

The rapid urbanisation of the developing world presents numerous challenges to policy makers both locally and globally. Urban transport in both developed and developing cities poses environmental problems for their residents. Most obviously, the cities themselves face the pressing problem of efficiently delivering mobility to increasing numbers of inhabitants, which is critical for economic development. Concerns over access, safety, congestion and air pollution are uppermost on their agendas, yet at the global level, carbon emissions continue their upward trend. Almost a quarter of energy-related carbon emissions attributable to the transport sector, accounting for two-thirds and a half of oil consumption in OECD/non-OECD countries respectively (IEA 2009). Widespread urban expansion with its associated increase in consumption is a direct threat to efforts being made to curb greenhouse gas (GHG) emissions (Kahn-Ribeiro *et al.* 2007) and the road sector in particular is a source of fast-growing emissions, accounting for three-quarters of transport emissions in 2013 (IEA 2015). Innovative approaches are therefore needed to tackle effectively the myriad of urban transport issues which arise across levels of development. Greater awareness of environmental issues and their interconnected nature combined with an array of technological options presents a range of options in this endeavour. These are not only technology related, but also in the field of policy modernisation and institutional reform.

The co-benefits concept is an approach for aligning climate change with local development issues at the local level. A greater recognition of these factors is appearing in the development of Nationally Appropriate Mitigation Actions (NAMAs – see Chapter 7), which gives more emphasis to co-benefits and the development agenda more broadly. Moreover, it is essential to mainstream climate change into local development by encouraging the implementation of climate-friendly measures in developing cities which are not obliged to reduce their carbon emissions but where much progress can be effectively made. In the context of sustainable urban mobility, there are ever increasing numbers of approaches and innovative practices across the world. However, given that most of these activities are discrete projects and of an incremental nature, it is

challenging to understand how they all fit together and assess the degree of contribution they made in tackling larger environmental problems or whether they
have the potential to scale-up and stimulate systemic change in urban development processes.

This chapter explores how to conceptualise the transport system from a co-
benefits standpoint. It primarily focuses on two environmental benefits that can
be gained from sustainable urban mobility measures: air quality (AQ) improvement and GHG emission reductions. The rest of the chapter is organised into
four further sections. The next section presents a conceptual framework for
understanding urban mobility co-benefits and how intended benefits trace pathways through this framework. The ASIF methodology is introduced, which
forms the basis of the transport tool described in Chapter 9. The subsequent
section discusses how different policies can fit into the derivative Avoid-Shift-
Improve (A-S-I) framework and includes considerations on data and policy
formulation. This is followed by examples of co-benefits achieved in cities
around the world before a final conclusion on trends and future directions in
transport and, more broadly, on how to extend this framework in an institutional context, linking to other chapters in the book in order to gain an insight
into the effectiveness of delivering co-benefits for better planning and management of sustainable urban transport.

Co-benefits from urban mobility: a conceptual framework

Transport was traditionally seen as part of the energy sector, which leads to a
focus on energy-efficiency technologies as the primary mitigation strategy.
Creutzig's (2015) assessment of low-carbon transport narratives identifies three
main classes of models, namely the integrated assessment models (IAM)
favoured by economists, transport models favoured by engineers and place-based
models often used by geographers and public health professionals, each having
its own solution focus, analytical approach and limitations. These essentially
relate to the level of detail that can be accommodated in the model and therefore the general applicability of the model. Transport is considered to be difficult in IAMs because it requires change of billions of users rather than a few key
actors in the power sector and therefore focuses on efficiency and fuels, whilst
place-based models look more at behaviour at the expense of wider applicability
(see the discussion of top-down vs. bottom-up models in Chapter 5.3,
pages 136–137).

Figure 2.1 provides a conceptual framework for understanding how environmental co-benefits can be identified in the transport sector (Doll *et al.* 2011).
The main objective of the framework is to identify the spectrum of elements
which measure the effectiveness of a transport initiative and trace a pathway
from the origination of a policy to the emissions it creates by first identifying the
main driver which prompted the policy or project. The framework reflects a
broader conceptualisation of the sector amongst stakeholders, including policy
makers, international organisations and civil society groups, that began to

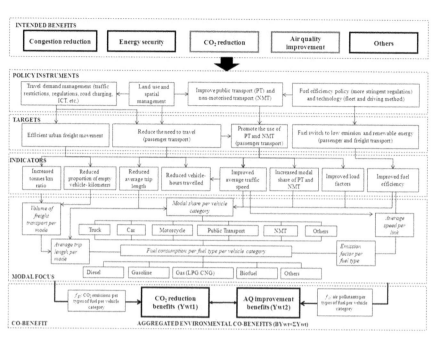

Figure 2.1 Conceptual framework for measuring co-benefits in the transport sector.

promote the notion that transport is fundamentally about moving people and goods rather than vehicles themselves (Huizenga 2012). The implication of this is that any given travel demand can be met by a broader range of strategies that include looking at why people need to travel, how they travel and what technologies and fuels are used.

The original formulation, which focused on environmental co-benefits, identified transport initiatives aimed at tackling one, or a combination, of diverse policy concerns, such as traffic congestion reduction, energy security, GHG emissions and ambient air quality improvement. These are termed 'intended benefits' in the first section of the framework. The need to address an intended benefit comes from a diverse array of actors. It can be initiated by local government itself, central government, non-governmental organisations, the private sector or other parties. For example, traffic decongestion attempts are usually driven by local governments and are mainly associated with the economic benefits that accrue from the minimisation of the time lost during the commuting of passengers and the transport of goods. On the other hand, ambient air quality improvement and GHG emission reductions are concerted efforts of national and local governments. Air quality improvement strategies aim to ameliorate the negative impacts of primary and secondary ambient air pollution on health and ecosystems (e.g. $PM_{2.5-10}$, O_3, heavy metals, tropospheric ozone, etc.). GHG emissions reduction is rarely, if ever, the primary intended benefit for actions in developing countries, though it is moving up the agenda as attempts to tackle anthropogenic global climate change gain momentum and spread to more sectors. Finally, despite energy security having certain economic overtones (e.g. foreign exchange savings due to reduced fuel imports), it is mostly associated with broader resource security considerations and the availability of a substitutable local resource (see the Brazilian bioethanol example later in this chapter, pages 34–35). In contrast to the other types of intended benefits, energy security policies are largely driven by national governments, with local governments having at best limited power during their formulation and implementation. The discussion in Chapter 8 (page 236) also touches on the motivation behind many laws which promote co-benefits.

In order to meet these intended benefits, a combination of different policy instruments that target passenger and freight transport can be devised, which in turn are related to a set of targets and indicators. The achievement of these indicators should result in some combination of a shift in mode of transport, a reduction in travel demand or technological improvement from which the co-benefits can be quantitatively measured by taking into account the average trip length, fuel consumption and average speed of each mode. These factors can then be parsed through the appropriate modal focus and their respective emission factors and/or combined with other ancillary or direct observations to arrive at a calculation of GHG and air pollutant emissions.

The framework is in some ways analogous to the ASIF framework developed by Schipper *et al.* (2000). The ASIF approach is a bottom-up estimate that decomposes a seemingly complex transport system into constituent parts, which not only relate directly to emissions but importantly are closely connected to the different policies that can be deployed in the transport system. The acronym ASIF stands for Activity – Structure (mode and/or fuel shares) – Intensity (efficiency) – Fuel (emission factor) and is explained in more detail in Chapter 9 (pages 248–251).

Different types of transport are known as modes, of which some are motorised and some are not (non-motorised transport – NMT). Each mode has a certain level of activity associated with it (passenger.kilometres), which refers to one passenger travelling one kilometre (the equivalent metric for freight would be tonne.kilometres). Understanding that a certain mode can have a range of technologies which result in different efficiencies and use different fuels with different pollution coefficients (known as emission factors) completes the picture of where emissions originate. Such a formulation means that all conceivable transport policies should be able to be reflected in some component of this framework. Therefore, data on fleet size and fuel structure of that fleet, vehicle activity (vehicle kilometres), average occupancy and fuel economy are required in order to build a complete model that is responsive to all policies. The way in which these factors calculate emissions is given in greater detail in Chapter 9 (pages 250–251).

Operationalising the framework

How do parameters in the ASIF framework translate into actual policies?

The policy-level generalisation of the ASIF framework classifies interventions in terms of the Avoid-Shift-Improve framework (Dalkmann and Brannigan 2007), which is the central organising concept for this book. With respect to the transport sector, the framework implies policies under the following three measures:

1   reducing the need to travel through travel demand management (TDM) and land-use/spatial management (*Avoid*);
2   promoting shift to public transport (PT) and NMT (*Shift*); and
3   improving fuel efficiency through policy and technology. Such measures target both passenger and freight transport (*Improve*).

The implication of the A-S-I approach is that a broader range of competencies are required to fully understand and operationalise the approach that will include *inter alia* planning, community development and lifestyle change; elements contingent on both city government and residents alike.

Naturally, different interventions will mean different levels of co-benefits. Table 2.1 shows how a range of intended benefits will qualitatively result in different levels of co-benefits. By thinking in terms of the rows rather than the columns of this table we can begin to see how co-benefits can be achieved through the implementation of a single policy. What should also become apparent is that combining different sets of strategies can also enhance the level of co-benefits available.

Even though ideal integration may not occur in most circumstances, each type of policy instrument usually articulates a series of targets and indicators that need to be met before the intended benefit materialises. The combination of TDM and land-use and spatial management aims to produce efficient urban freight movement and further increase the tonne/km ratio, reducing the

Table 2.1 Relative assessment of potential benefits from different types of policy

Policy instruments	Intended benefits			
	Congestion improvement	Energy security	CO_2 reduction	Air quality improvement
A: Travel demand management	++	+	+++	++
A: Land-use – behavioural change	++		+++	+++
S: Improvement of PT and NMT	+++	++	++	+++
I: Fuel efficiency policy and technology		++	+	++
I: Fuel switch		++*	+	++

Source: based in part on IGES (2011, p. 6).

Note
* If fuel is locally sourced.

proportion of empty vehicle.km and reducing vehicle hours travelled. As for passenger transport, land-use and spatial management is expected to reduce the need to travel and, thus reduce the average trip length and improve the average traffic speed as congestion is relieved. Promoting the use of PT/NMT aims to improve the system as a whole. Therefore, modal share of PT/NMT will be increased and the load factor of PT will also improve. Lastly, fuel efficiency and technology policies aim to promote the switch to lower emission fuels or renewable energy as well as more efficient vehicle technologies.

Whilst it is apparent from Table 2.1 that not all transport policies will yield the same benefits, it can be seen that they also have different levels of implementability. In simple cases, this can be supported through due diligence measures of monitoring programmes to ensure emission standards are adhered to, but this often requires a wise choice of complementary policies (a policy package approach) so policies reinforce rather than contradict each other. These are generally more important in the range of policies operating over longer timescales and dealing with lifestyle change. An overview of these is presented in Table 2.2.

Fuel switching and efficiency improvement policies are arguably the easiest to conceptualise and evaluate. As they relate quite closely to the energy system and technological change, they are also the ones which predominantly feature in transport/energy models. Modal shift and demand reduction can both be seen as behavioural change (Creutzig 2015), which is more prone to local contexts and requires a different set of skills to estimate the impact.

For example, Salon et al. (2012) identify 14 specific measures that could affect vehicle kilometres travelled; these are grouped under five categories: planning, pricing, PT, NMT and information. Each contributes something but by themselves would be insufficient to effect a major transition. Nonetheless, the precise impacts of each of these policies are highly place dependent and remain unclear beyond broad estimates. A preliminary review by Creutzig (2015) suggests that the aggregate GHG benefits could be between 20 and 50 per cent from activity reduction and modal shift over time to 2050. Notably urban planning could account for around a 5–10 per cent reduction but is likely to be far greater in rapidly growing cities. Estimating these effects remains a big uncertainty and therefore the use of scenarios can be useful to visualise the envelope of co-benefits that a policy can yield subject to certain assumptions (Figure 2.2).

Whilst transport portfolios differ from city to city, the general policy prescription for urbanising cities is to expand the provision of public transport and hope for a shift of people from private vehicles. However, this policy can be hard to achieve if not planned early on, since rising incomes makes personal transport easier to obtain and more attractive if there is an absence of or poor-quality public transport, not to mention the desire for motorisation implicitly linked to notions of modernisation (Wright and Fulton 2005).

Table 2.2 Pertinent considerations amongst each type of policy intervention

Policy option	Example	Practical challenge	Ease of implementation
Reduce travel demand	Shift to non-motorised transport (NMT), absolute reduction in trips and distance travelled	Large scale re-structuring of city layout to make trips short enough to be done on foot/bicycle or eliminated completely	**Harder** Need to get incentives right not just for the new mode but to change entrenched behaviours, which may be politically difficult
Shift modes	More ridership on public transport, or new public transport infrastructure like mass rapid transit (MRT) and bus rapid transit (BRT) rather than use of private modes	Must be implemented such that the new desired mode is more attractive in cost (time, money and physical convenience) than a private mode	**Harder** Need to get incentives right not just for the new mode but to change entrenched behaviours, which may be politically difficult Requires substantial public expenditure
Improve efficiency	Mandating (stricter) standards for new and existing vehicles	High proportion of old vehicles in the fleet	**Easier** Requires effective monitoring and enforcement Requires less public expenditure
Switch fuel type	Mandate certain fuels for certain vehicles	Subject to appropriate fuel availability and delivery infrastructure	**Easier** Can be deployed first amongst a centralised fleet of public vehicles (e.g. buses) Requires less public expenditure

Examples of co-benefits from urban transport

Whilst policy options can be focused on one or more of these categories, transport initiatives implemented in cities commonly aim for a single objective and GHG emission reduction is not a key driver (IGES 2011). Increasing CO_2 mitigation targets can result in a deeper penetration of alternative and cleaner transportation options (CNG, battery-operated three-wheeler, four-stroke vehicles). One of the likely reasons is that measuring fuel switch is relatively simple since the project scopes are more precisely defined. By contrast, other measures encounter complex issues of project boundaries and 'leakage' (Zegras 2007) since significant results can only be achieved by the implementation of a package of measures (Dalkmann and Brannigan 2007). However, some projects have sought to incorporate climate relevant components under the Clean

Development Mechanism (CDM). Although not explicitly a climate project, the Delhi Metro is awarded credits for recovering energy from its braking system (Chapter 2.1). In the context of developing countries, they usually focus on solving local issues, such as reducing congestion, tackling air pollution and reducing fuel dependency.

Much of the initial thinking on co-benefits came from the transport sector and there are a growing number of studies estimating the local and global quantitative environmental impacts of sustainable transport measures, including a collected volume focusing on Asia alone (Zusman *et al.* 2012). Some studies show that GHG mitigation policies have had a positive effect on regional air quality (Rypdal *et al.* 2007; Williams 2007; Vuuren *et al.* 2006), while other studies show that air quality measures have also resulted in carbon emission reductions, among other co-benefits in a wide range of cities, such as Mumbai (Yedla *et al.* 2005), Durban (Thambiran and Diab 2011), Seoul (Chae 2010), Beijing (Creutzig and He 2009), Mexico City (McKinley *et al.* 2005) and London (Beevers and Carslaw 2005), as well as at the country level in Thailand (Shrestha and Pradhan 2010). These studies have shown that the magnitude of AQ co-benefits of climate change mitigation is not trivial. In the case of Mumbai, it has been argued that the transportation projects need to be looked at from the perspective of local air-pollution improvement rather than the CO_2 mitigation (Yedla *et al.* 2005).

Fuel shifting and efficiency improvements

In the case of Seoul (Chae 2010), fuel switch to LNG/CNG for buses are most effective for NO_x and PM_{10} emission reduction, as well as GHG emission reductions. Taxi fleet renovation in Mexico City (McKinley *et al.* 2005) is estimated to reduce approximately 0.4 Mt of CO_2 equivalent emissions per year and, considering the local and global benefit–cost ratio, this measure ranked highest compared to metro expansion and hybrid buses. Another study also concluded that emissions from road transport were shown to be most sensitive to distance travelled and vehicle technologies (Chae 2010). Accordingly, interventions that promote improved efficiency are important, anticipating the continuing growth of private vehicles and road freight transports, through implementation of more stringent standards as well as adoption of efficient fleet and driving method technologies.

As a response to the mounting energy security concerns on the aftermath of the first oil crisis, the Brazilian government promoted policies that aimed to harness local renewable resources (sugarcane) for the production of a new type of fuel type that could substitute conventional transport fuel and which was initiated with the 1975 Pró-Álcool programme. Since then the Brazilian government has progressively enacted a string of biofuel policies, culminating with the current 20–25 per cent mandatory blending mandate of ethanol into gasoline. Given its location in the heart of the country's sugarcane producing region and its status as the country's largest city and economic powerhouse,

São Paulo was the main initial market for bioethanol. Bioethanol constituted 20.4 per cent of the total energy consumed in the transport sector in 2009 (MME 2011), with this role expected to increase given the projected biofuel expansion in the country (Gasparatos *et al.* 2012). Whilst contributing substantially to the intended benefit, the Brazilian bioethanol programme had two other environmental co-benefits: GHG emission reduction and local air quality improvement. Due to a set of interconnected factors, Brazilian bioethanol offers significant GHG emission savings when compared to conventional transport fuel (Gasparatos *et al.* 2012; Zah *et al.* 2007; Menichetti and Otto 2009). As a result of such high GHG savings, which are consistently over 50 per cent (when including direct/indirect land use change emissions), bioethanol has been designated as an advanced biofuel by the US EPA (EPA 2010). This suggests that bioethanol use has been responsible for significant CO_2 emission reductions from the city's transport system in the past decades. Additionally, bioethanol penetration has been partly credited for air quality improvement in the city (Goldemberg 2008). These environmental co-benefits were to a large extent possible due to the rapid introduction of Flex-Fuel-Vehicles (FFV) in 2003, which has led to the gradual phasing out of older, more polluting and less energy efficient vehicles.

Demand management and mode shift

The combination of TDM, land-use/spatial management and PT/NMT improvement is essential. TDM measures include, among others, traffic restrictions, regulations, road charging and the use of information and communication technologies (ICT). Land-use/spatial management measures consist of an array of concepts such as smart urban growth, urban villages, mixed town centres and transit-oriented development (TOD), coupled with green spaces, walkable communities and so on. Specifically for freight transport, measures such as out-of-hours deliveries, construction consolidation and retail/office consolidation are options for establishing a more efficient urban freight movement, as stated in the London Freight Plan (Zanni and Bristow 2010).

Fiscal measures such as road charging can be quite effective in reducing private vehicle use and promoting mode shift to PT/NMT. However, only a few cities worldwide have adopted it. The experience of London's Congestion Charging Scheme shows that the charging area benefit of a reduction in vehicle. km combines with the benefit of increased speed, giving a reduction of 19.5 per cent in CO_2 emissions (Beevers and Carslaw 2005). Furthermore, it indicates that congestion charging channels modal transitions to buses, not to subways (TFL 2007). Similarly, Singapore's Area Licensing Scheme (ALS), started in 1975 and later superseded by an Electronic Road Pricing (ERP) system in 1998, has reduced road traffic flow by 20 per cent and increased speed by 33 per cent (Chin 1996).

Modal shift to public transport is indeed influenced by many factors. A faster public transportation service is one of these factors (McKinley *et al.* 2005). In

Seoul, for example, a 10 per cent increase in speed of public transport induces 5 per cent of car drivers to switch to bus and subway (Lee *et al.* 2003). A comprehensive Bus Rapid Transit (BRT) can double operational speed from 10 to 20 km/h, potentially adding eight million passengers per day.

More significant modal shifts can be gained by integrating one measure with another. In Bogota, a complex project, one of the few transportation projects formally validated through CDM, combined BRT, TDM and NMT measures. It is estimated that, over a four-year period, for two (out of 22 planned) routes the percentage of trips by private cars and taxis decreased by 2.2 per cent, public transport increased by 1 per cent, and bike trips increased by 3.5 per cent, resulting in daily CO_2 emissions savings over 300 tonnes per day of which approximately 90 per cent are related to mode shift and 10 per cent from efficiency gains within the public transit system (Dalkmann and Brannigan 2007). The relative effect of measures on GHG emission reductions from the Transmilenio BRT phase II project were 14 per cent from higher occupancy rates, 18 per cent from mode switch, 19 per cent from bus renewal and 49 per cent from larger units (Grutter 2007). Besides the GHG benefit, air quality benefits in the year 2006 compared to the baseline bus system were reductions of around 900 tonnes of particulate matter (12 per cent reduction), 170 tonnes of sulphur dioxide (43 per cent reduction) and around 6,800 tonnes of NO_x emissions (18 per cent) (Grutter 2007; Labriet *et al.* 2009).

Another example is Santiago de Chile. In an attempt to develop the CDM possibilities of its transport measures, a switch to advanced hybrid diesel electric-buses in a Transantiago feeder area is estimated to have reduced CO_2 emissions by just 0.2 per cent. Additionally, the city-wide bicycle network, under a 'conservative' scenario of 3 per cent bicycle mode share, will see an approximate 0.4 per cent reduction in CO_2 emissions per year (27,000 tonnes per year). A 'moderate' scenario of 6 per cent share will result in a 1.5 per cent reduction (100,000 tonnes per year). For the location efficiency case, under the education-oriented scenario (which located educational facilities directly proportional to residential location patterns), 7.5 per cent of reductions can be gained per year (500,000 annual tonnes of CO_2) (Zegras 2007). The examples above suggest that urban mobility strategies have the potential to yield both AQ improvement and GHG emissions reductions simultaneously. It is further shown that fuel efficiency improvement is effective in reducing both local and global environmental impacts in the short term, but in the longer term more significant reductions can only be achieved by a package of measures that aims to achieve a larger modal shift from motorised private modes to PT/NMT.

Working out the level of co-benefits attainable from these mode shifts is facilitated by tools such as those described in Chapter 9. Such a tool was used to construct a range of scenarios for the Delhi Metro. Doll and Balaban (2013) developed a series of scenarios that looked not only at co-benefits (CO_2 + air pollution) of increased ridership of the metro but, crucially, at where those riders would be coming from. Such projects are often touted to simultaneously increase access to public transport and reduce congestion by reducing the number of motorised trips. Figure 2.2 shows how different assumptions affect not just the magnitude of emissions reductions but also the type of co-benefits available. Each line in the figure represents the level of a CO_2 emissions reduction from a metro use level (50–75–100 per cent) for a given mode contribution. Three mode shift scenarios were examined: a predominant car-based one, an equal contribution and a predominant bus-based one (metro users composed of different ratios of former car and bus users). These were then plotted against emissions reductions of different air pollutants (the co-benefits). As is to be expected, one sees greater CO_2 emissions reductions coming from a greater contribution of private vehicles than buses but what is also apparent is that, whilst there are co-benefits in every scenario, certain air pollution emissions are more sensitive to mode shift. Carbon monoxide (CO) and particulate matter (PM) are more sensitive to the mode contribution than nitrogen oxides (NO_x) and hydrocarbon (HC) emissions. Such an analysis is useful if there are certain pollutants of interest (e.g. ones more prevalent in human health or smog creation), which can help target or refine broad-based policies on mode-shift to target certain user groups.

Transport initiatives have struggled in the CDM for a number of reasons, mainly to do with the strict reporting required to generate certified emission credits. Unlike stationary sources, travel demand results from a large combination of factors; these are harder to accurately model and it is more difficult to collect baseline data. The additionality requirement (the condition that the emission reduction would not have happened without the CDM project) is also

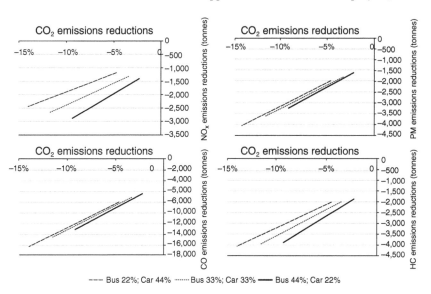

Figure 2.2 Potential range of co-benefits (disaggregated by pollutant) from the Delhi Metro under different ridership and mode contribution scenarios.

Source: reprinted from the *Journal of Cleaner Production*, 58, Doll, CNH and Balaban, O, 'A methodology for evaluating environmental co-benefits in the transport sector: Application to the Delhi Metro', 61–73. Copyright (2013), with permission from Elsevier.

challenging because transport projects are primarily undertaken for reasons of local development rather than carbon reduction. This is especially true in developing countries where the most obvious problems caused by transport are congestion and air pollution. It is for this reason that the co-benefits approach is considered to be a promising method for integrating climate change into urban development strategies. The ultimate outcome is that these factors add to the costs of a project, which in turn make them unattractive for investors.

Connections, trends and future directions

The co-benefits approach is a concept by which a number of desirable outcomes in both local and global domains can be simultaneously realised. For the purpose of this chapter, these are considered largely in terms of air quality and GHG emissions reductions, but as a concept, the reach of co-benefits is far wider, including benefits from increased mobility and health benefits accruing not just from reduced air pollution but also from active (non-motorised) travel (Kwan and Hashim 2016; Chapter 11). It is a potentially useful approach for city administrations in the developing world, who often find themselves addressing multiple challenges with limited resources. Recognising that co-benefits can result by accident or (ideally) design, this chapter has presented a conceptual framework to identify co-benefits in the transport sector. By initially identifying the original intended benefit of an intervention and then tracing this through the policy instruments, targets and mode emission factors, the framework conceptualises how to measure co-benefits either at the project level or during policy design in more advanced cases where data are available.

Given the central importance of the transport sector, it is imperative to broaden our understanding of the role it plays for both emissions and society. In order to do this, we have begun, first, to see transport as the act of moving primarily people rather than vehicles, and second, to consider its links to other sectors rather than a component of the energy sector. In doing so, it has opened up a larger range of policy options for dealing with emissions in the transport sector, most notably the urgent need to deploy high-quality public transport ahead of the diffusion of personal mobility. These have a bearing on issues like land use (Chapter 3) and health (Chapter 11), as well as broader issues of urbanism and the fundamental liveability of cities (Gehl 2010).

The cases presented in the following sections come from Asia and South America and relate to governance issues of implementing transport projects in large cities. In each case, an explanation of the implementation barriers is given. The Curitiba case (Chapter 2.2) also contains a strong transport component and more explicitly makes the connection between land use and transport.

The transport sector is one of the most dynamic, with new technologies emerging both directly for vehicles themselves (such as hydrogen, electric and self-driving cars; enhanced personal mobility options such as electric bicycles and self-balancing scooters) and in wider society, which determine how we interact with existing modes. The role of on-demand car services and ride-sharing schemes that are enabled through smartphone apps and their ability to co-locate drivers and riders could either reduce or increase emissions depending on how we use them. Increasing rider occupancy would make cars more efficient but it would only reduce emissions if those riders switch from their use of a single-occupancy private vehicle. However, it could have a more beneficial effect if, as a mode of paratransit, it facilitates the greater use of public transport (the so-called 'last mile problem'). Such services are already causing controversy as they disrupt the established service providers (taxis) who lobby city authorities to ban their operation. It therefore remains to be seen what role these services will play and whether cities will regulate them for emissions reduction rather than protecting established groups such as taxi drivers. The rise of bike-sharing and car-sharing shows that increasingly, people view transport as they view energy – as a service to access. Ultimately it is mobility rather than its form with which people are most concerned. There are now more options than ever to deliver this to an urban population in a just (available to all sections of the population), efficient, secure and low-polluting way. Finding effective policies to realise this vision is a key challenge for cities in the twenty-first century.

Interestingly, whilst such services are rapidly diffusing across both developed and developing cities, divergent trends appear to be emerging. The concept of car ownership may be losing its appeal in developed countries and fewer young people are applying for driving licences (Haslett 2013); meanwhile, the massive desire for car ownership in China arguably reflects the attitude of 1950s' USA, as a recent report claims that the desire for cars among the young in China remains undented, even in the presence of greater environmental awareness (FIA 2015).

The framework presented here is a tool to help understand how co-benefits may be realised in the transport sector. Although not discussed in detail here, data availability could be a serious limitation in the analytical process if cities do not commit resources to the systematic collection and utilisation of relevant data for the co-benefits approach. In some cases, the data are simply not there, but often the data are present in some form, held by a range of different stakeholders (police, bus companies), and need to be collected and synthesised. Further work on how to operationalise the approach at the city level needs to examine the wider issues of policy formation and coordination, including urban governance, multi-level governance, project implementation and local legal and regulatory capacities. More broadly, the role of international cooperation (Chapter 7), particularly in the field of funding and technology transfer, will also be critical in developing cities. Taken together, these form an orthogonal dimension to the co-benefits discussion. It has a critical bearing on the effectiveness of the framework that is presented here, as they effectively act as an enabling mechanism to whether or not the technical aspects can be achieved and, ultimately, the utility of the co-benefits approach.

Acknowledgements

Parts of this chapter are reproduced from a paper published in the Proceedings of the 2011 Congress of the Asian Planning Schools Association 2011 (Doll *et al.* 2011) and Doll and Balaban (2013).

References

Beevers, SD and Carslaw, DC 2005, 'The impact of congestion charging on vehicle emissions in London', *Atmospheric Environment*, vol. 39, no. 1, pp. 1–5.

Chae, Y 2010, 'Co-benefits analysis of an air quality management plan and greenhouse gas reduction strategies in the Seoul metropolitan area', *Environmental Science & Policy*, vol. 13, pp. 205–216.

Chin, ATH 1996, 'Containing air pollution and traffic congestion: Transport policy and the environment in Singapore', *Atmospheric Environment*, vol. 30, no. 5, pp. 787–801.

Creutzig, F 2015, 'Evolving narratives of low-carbon futures in transportation', *Transport Reviews*, vol. 36, no. 3, pp. 341–360.

Creutzig, F and He, D 2009, 'Climate change mitigation and co-benefits of feasible transport demand policies in Beijing', *Transportation Research*, vol. 14, no. 2, pp. 120–131.

Dalkmann, H and Brannigan, C 2007, *Transport and Climate Change: Module 5a, Sustainable Transport: A Sourcebook for Policy-makers in Developing Cities*, e-book, Deutsche Gesellschaft für Technische Zusammenarbeit (GTZ), Eschborn, viewed 8 May 2016, http://siteresources.worldbank.org/EXTAFRSUBSAHTRA/Resources/gtz-transport-and-climate-change-2007.pdf.

Doll, CNH and Balaban, O 2013, 'A methodology for evaluating environmental co-benefits in the transport sector: Application to the Delhi Metro', *Journal of Cleaner Production*, vol. 58, pp. 61–73.

Doll, CNH, Dirgahayani, P and Gasparatos, A 2011, 'Urban mobility co-benefits and their contribution to sustainable urban development: A developing country perspective', *Proceedings of the Asian Planning Schools Association Congress 2011*, Tokyo, 19–21 September, pp. 1308–1317.

Environmental Protection Agency (EPA) 2010, *EPA Lifecycle Analysis of Greenhouse Gas Emissions from Renewable Fuels*, e-book, Environmental Protection Agency, USA, viewed 8 May 2016, www.epa.gov/sites/production/files/2015-08/documents/420f10006.pdf.

Foundation for the Automobile and Society (FIA) 2015, 'Chinese car desire "echoes 1950s' USA"', viewed 8 May 2016, www.fiafoundation.org/blog/2015/may/chinese-car-desire-echoes-1950-s-usa.

Gasparatos, A, Borzoni, M, and Abramovay, R 2012, *The Brazilian Bioethanol and Biodiesel Programmes: Drivers, Policies and Impacts, Chapter 6, Socioeconomic and Environmental Impacts of Biofuels, Evidence from Developing Nations*, Cambridge University Press, Cambridge, UK.

Gehl, J 2010, *Cities for People*, Island Press, Washington, USA.

Goldemberg, J 2008, 'The Brazilian biofuels industry', *Biotechnology Biofuels*, vol. 1, no. 1, pp. 1–6.

Grutter, JM 2007, *The CDM in the Transport Sector: Module 5d, Sustainable Transport: A Sourcebook for Policy-makers in Developing Cities*, e-book, Deutsche Gesellschaft für Technische Zusammenarbeit (GTZ), Eschborn, viewed 8 May 2016, www.sutp.org/files/contents/documents/resources/A_Sourcebook/SB5_Environment%20and%20Health/GIZ_SUTP_SB5d_CDM-in-the-transport-sector_EN.pdf.

Haslett, A 2013, 'Report: Cost, economy keep many teens from driving', *Washington Post*, viewed 9 May 2016, www.washingtonpost.com/local/trafficandcommuting/report-cost-economy-keep-many-teens-from-driving/2013/10/23/1f9cb768-3b4a-11e3-a94f-b58017bfee6c_story.html.

Huizenga, C 2012, *International Climate Change Initiatives and Low Carbon Transport in Asia: Perspectives and Prospects, Part 4, Section 12, Low Carbon Transport in Asia – Strategies for Optimizing Co-benefits*, Earthscan, Abingdon, UK.

Institute for Global Environmental Strategies (IGES) 2011, *Mainstreaming Transport Co-benefits Approach: A Guide to Evaluating Transport Projects*, e-book, Institute for Global Environmental Strategies (IGES), Japan, viewed 8 May 2016, http://pub.iges.or.jp/modules/envirolib/upload/3209/attach/transport%20co-benefits%20guideline.pdf.

International Energy Agency (IEA) 2009, *Transport, Energy and CO_2 Moving Toward Sustainability*, International Energy Agency, Paris, France.

International Energy Agency (IEA) 2015, *CO_2 Emissions from Fuel Combustion Highlights 2015*, International Energy Agency, Paris, France.

Kahn-Ribeiro, S, Kobayashi, S, Beuthe, M, Gasca, J, Greene, D, Lee, DS, Muromachi, Y, Newton, PJ, Plotkin, S, Sperling, D, Wit, R and Zhou, PJ 2007, *Transport and its Infrastructure, In Climate Change 2007: Mitigation. Contribution of Working Group III to the Fourth Assessment Report of the Intergovernmental Panel on Climate Change*, e-book, Cambridge University Press, Cambridge, UK, viewed 8 May 2016, www.ipcc.ch/pdf/assessment-report/ar4/wg3/ar4-wg3-chapter5.pdf.

Kwan, SC and Hashim JH 2016, 'A review on co-benefits of mass public transportation in climate change mitigation', *Sustainable Cities and Society*, vol. 22, pp. 11–18.

Labriet, M, Caldes, N and Izquierdo, L 2009, 'A review on urban air quality, global climate change and CDM issues in the transportation sector', *International Journal of Global Warming*, vol. 1, no. 1/2/3, pp. 144–159.

Lee, S, Lee, YH and Park, JH 2003, 'Estimating price and service elasticity of urban transportation demand with stated preference technique: A case in Korea', *Transportation Research Record: Journal of the Transportation Research Board*, vol. 1839, pp. 167–172.

McKinley, G, Zuk, M, Hojer, M, Avalos, M, Gonzales, I, Iniestra, R, Laguna, I, Martínez, MA, Osnaya, P, Reynales, LM, Valdés, R and Martínez, J 2005, 'Quantification of local and global benefits from air pollution control in Mexico City', *Environmental Science Technology*, vol. 39, no. 7, pp. 1954–1961.

Menichetti, E and Otto, M 2009, 'Energy balance and greenhouse gas emissions of bio-fuels from a product life-cycle perspective', in RW Howarth and S Bringezu (eds), *Biofuels: Environmental Consequences and Interactions with Changing Land Use. Proceedings of the Scientific Committee on Problems of the Environment (SCOPE) International Biofuels Project Rapid Assessment*. Cornell University, Ithaca.

Ministério de Minas e Energia (MME) 2011, *National Energy Balances*, Ministério de Minas e Energia, Brasilia.

Rypdal, K, Rive, N, Åström, S, Karvosenoja, N, Aunan, K, Bak, JL, Kupiainen, K and Kukkonen, 2007, 'Nordic air quality co-benefits from European post-2012 climate policies', *Energy Policy*, vol. 3, no. 12, pp. 6309–6322.

Salon, D, Boarnet, MG, Handy, S, Spears, S and Tal, G 2012, 'How do local actions affect VMT? A critical review of the empirical evidence', *Transportation Research Part D: Transport and Environment*, vol. 17, no. 7, pp. 495–508.

Schipper, L, Marie-Liliu, C and Gorham, R 2000, *Flexing the Link Between Transport and Greenhouse Gas Emissions: A Path for the World Bank*, e-book, International Energy Agency, Paris, France.

Shrestha, RM and Pradhan, S 2010, 'Co-benefits of CO_2 emission reduction in a developing country', *Energy Policy*, vol. 38, no. 5, pp. 2586–2587.

Thambiran, T and Diab, RD 2011, 'Air pollution and climate change co-benefit opportunities in the road transportation sector in Durban, South Africa', *Atmospheric Environment*, vol. 45, no. 16, pp. 2683–2689.

Transport for London (TFL) 2007, *Central London Congestion Charging, Impacts Monitoring, 5th Annual Report July 2007*, e-book, Transport for London, UK, viewed 8 May 2016, http://content.tfl.gov.uk/fifth-annual-impacts-monitoring-report-2007-07-07.pdf.

Vuuren, DP, Cofala, J, Eerens, HE, Oostenrijk, R, Heyes, C, Klimont, Z, Elzen, MGJ and Amann, M 2006, 'Exploring the ancillary benefits of the Kyoto Protocol for air pollution in Europe', *Energy Policy*, vol. 34, no. 4, pp. 444–460.

Williams, ML 2007, 'UK air quality in 2050 – synergies with climate change policies', *Environmental Science and Policy*, vol. 10, no. 2, pp. 169–175.

Wright, L and Fulton, L 2005, 'Climate change mitigation and transport in developing nations', *Transport Reviews*, vol. 25, no. 6, pp. 691–717.

Yedla, S, Shrestha, RM and Anandarajah, G 2005, 'Environmentally sustainable urban transportation – comparative analysis of local emission mitigation strategies vis-à-vis GHG mitigation strategies', *Transport Policy*, vol. 12, no. 3, pp. 245–254.

Zah, R, Böni, H, Gauch, M, Hischier, R, Lehmann, M and Wäger, P 2007, *Life Cycle Assessment of Energy Products: Environmental Impact Assessment of Biofuels*, e-book, Swiss Federal Laboratories for Materials Science and Technology – EMPA, Switzerland, viewed 8 May 2016, http://publicationslist.org/data/zah/ref-6/070524_Bioenergie_ExecSumm_engl.pdf.

Zanni, AM and Bristow, AL 2010, 'Emissions of CO_2 from road freight in London: Trends and policies for long run reductions', *Energy Policy*, vol. 38, no. 4, pp. 1774–1786.

Zegras, PC 2007, 'As if Kyoto mattered: The clean development mechanism and transportation', *Energy Policy*, vol. 35, no. 10, pp. 5136–5150.

Zusman, E, Srinivasan, A and Dhakal, S 2012, *Low Carbon Transport in Asia: Strategies for Optimizing Co-benefits*, Earthscan, Abingdon, UK.

2.1 Delhi, India

Governance-related opportunities and barriers towards effectiveness of co-benefits policies: the case of the Delhi Metro Project

Osman Balaban

Introduction

In terms of climate policy, the co-benefits approach refers to policy options that simultaneously mitigate GHG emissions along with a particular local problem. Whilst most policy responses could generate ancillary benefits in a coincidental manner, such benefits are not targeted at the outset. However, the co-benefits approach is based on the understanding that multiple benefits should be intentionally internalized at the conception of a policy, as opposed to accidental benefits (ADB 2009).

Policy responses to pursue the co-benefits approach do not take place in a political vacuum. Instead, they are the output of the interaction among various actors at all levels of governance. The local or sub-national level is of particular importance here, as most policies are formulated and applied at the local level (Puppim de Oliveira 2009). Good governance has to be ensured at the local level, which is closest to policymaking and implementation, so as to create an urban policy environment that stimulates effective co-benefit initiatives.

This case discusses the links between co-benefits initiatives and (local) governance issues with a particular focus on a large-scale urban transportation investment, namely the Delhi Metro Project (DMP). The Delhi Metro is not only an interesting urban transport investment but also a comprehensive urban policy initiative that reveals key lessons for understanding the governance-related opportunities and barriers towards effectiveness of co-benefits policies.

Four modes of governing in climate policymaking

A report by the UN-HABITAT highlights four distinct 'modes of governing' that can be followed by local governments to address climate change. They are classified as (a) *self-governing*; (b) *provision*; (c) *regulation*; and (d) *enabling* (UN-HABITAT 2011).

In the *self-governing mode*, local governments take direct action to reduce their energy consumption and carbon footprints, by such operations as renovating and retrofitting the municipal HQ and other related offices, and the use of electric vehicles for municipal operations. Local governments that follow the *enabling mode* aim to introduce policies that encourage local businesses and communities to undertake actions for tackling climate change on behalf of the local government. The *provision mode* is based on the direct provision of the necessary infrastructure and services to mitigate climate change by local governments. Finally, in the *regulation mode*, local governments introduce various forms of regulations, such as incentives, standards and taxation, in order to encourage and enable private sector and civil society actors to take action (UN-HABITAT 2011).

Among the four governance modes, the *provision* and *regulation* modes are more promising for addressing climate change. The benefits of the first two modes, namely *enabling* and *self-governing* modes, might be limited to awareness-raising and agenda-setting. The *self-governing* mode, for instance, could raise awareness of a local community to climate change through the leadership of a local government. Local governments could open entry points for actors who are willing to take action through demonstration projects. However, both the *enabling* and *self-governing* modes may not suffice to pursue more strategic approaches and structural policies such as co-benefits policies. On the other hand, the *provision* mode could be a more effective means of governance for tackling climate change, considering that city-based responses to climate change usually take the form of structural measures (i.e. infrastructure provision) and public goods and services, which cannot be provided without government intervention. Likewise, legal and institutional regulations and reforms are among the necessary actions to address climate change. In this sense, the *regulation* mode of governing can help enhance the capacity of local actors as well as facilitate their actions. No matter which mode or likely combination of modes is dominant in a particular context, coordinated actions among all actors, including public, private and non-governmental ones, need to be ensured. Better coordination of efforts and actions at the local level could spur the effectiveness of co-benefit policies a few levels up. Otherwise, it may cause ineffectiveness and lost opportunities.

Co-benefits of the Delhi Metro

Delhi, the Indian capital, is the second biggest city of India with a population around 17 million people, rising at a compound rate of 4 per cent per annum (Sahai and Bishop 2010). The rapid pace of urbanization in Delhi has had significant outcomes, such as high motorization and its associated problems (Thynell et al. 2010). The increase in the number and use of motorized transportation in Delhi has resulted in air and noise pollution, traffic congestion, fatal road accidents and, last but not least, GHG emissions (Sen et al. 2010; Siemiatycki 2006).

The DMP as an example of the *provision* mode of governing provides substantial lessons to understand the governance-related opportunities and barriers towards widespread application of the co-benefits policies. The DMP can be characterized as a joint project of the national and local government through international cooperation and funding. As of 2014, a metro network with a length of 193 km and six lines has been put into service, presently carrying 2.4 million passengers daily. One important feature of the Delhi Metro is the regenerative braking system installed on the rolling stock. The system generates electricity when brakes are applied by trains in decelerating mode and feeds it back into the system to support the trains which are in accelerating mode. It has been shown that almost 35 per cent of the electricity consumed in the Delhi Metro is (re)generated by this system, which also helps to reduce 41,160 tonnes of CO_2 emissions per year (Sreedharan 2009). However, the co-benefits generated by the use of the metro in urban transport in terms of reductions in GHGs and air pollution have been limited to date, mainly due to low ridership levels and low modal shift from private modes (Doll and Balaban 2013). Most of the current metro riders are former bus riders, not car users. Only one fifth of metro users shifted from cars. Therefore, the metro has so far become a competitor for buses more than for cars. Doll and Balaban (2013) found that, as of 2011, the Delhi Metro reduced 115,658 tonnes of CO_2 per year, along with 1,443 tonnes of NO_x, 163 tonnes of PM, 6,545 tonnes of CO and 1,951 tonnes of HC annually. The authors also noted that the actual emissions reductions by the DMP are significantly lower compared to other scenarios, which, for instance, showed a potential reduction of 700,000 tonnes per year for CO_2 reduction (see Figure 2.2 in Chapter 2).

Low ridership and low modal shift from private modes are outcomes of the weak integration between the metro system and other transport modes, as well as critical land uses in the city. It is verified in some surveys that metro users complain about the difficulties in reaching the stations from homes and workplaces by using other transport modes (Yagi and Nagayama 2010). Even pedestrian access is also referred to as challenging at some stations due to flaws in design and organization of the superstructure. This shows that, in the *provision* mode of governing, local authorities should not limit their activities to provision of certain infrastructure and services but also work to ensure the integration between relevant policies, infrastructure and services. If such integration is ensured at the local level, both scope and level of co-benefits of urban policy initiatives may be enhanced.

Coordination and cooperation among relevant actors at all levels

Good urban governance is key to increasing the effectiveness of co-benefits polices. An essential component of good governance is the proper coordination and harmony among activities of all relevant actors at the local level. Lack of coordination and collaboration may prevent the consistent implementation of policies, or worse, end up with competing or even conflicting policies or projects (see Chapter 8, page **000**, for examples of this in law). In a sense, this has been the case in Delhi. A privileged corporation, namely Delhi Metro Rail

Corporation (DMRC), has been established and given various lawful exemptions and exceptional authorities to carry out the fast-track implementation of the DMP. Having such an agency with exceptional powers has accelerated the implementation of the project but at the same time increased the competition among various institutions in the transport sector. Currently in Delhi, there are several institutions working to improve the transport infrastructure by building BRT lines, monorail and light rail systems along with the metro. However, instead of coordination, there seems to be competition between these institutions and the Metro Corporation. In case of limited coordination and increased competition between alternative policies, there is a risk of limiting or offsetting the co-benefits generated by policy options.

The debate on coordination and cooperation among relevant actors is not only limited to the national or local agencies. The Delhi Metro case indicates the importance of cooperation with international agencies and highlights how such cooperation could help enhance local institutional and technical capacity. Collaboration with international donors is a main governmental policy in India, where several international donors have already been involved in various projects. Among them, Japan is the largest bilateral funder to the Indian Government, particularly in the field of transport infrastructure. Around 65 per cent of the costs for Phase I and II of the DMP were covered by Official Development Assistance (ODA) loans from the Japanese government based on loan agreements signed between India and Japan in 1997. International donors do not limit their focus only on developmental projects. Several climate change-related projects have recently been initiated in India based on international funding. Particularly after the National Action Plan for Climate Change was introduced, certain entry points were opened up for international agencies like the World Bank and the International Council for Local Environmental Initiatives (ICLEI) to develop projects on climate change (Sharma and Tomar 2010).

International donors not only bring monetary sources but also provide know-how in the course of project development and management. As donors usually implement the best models or the most advanced technologies relevant to the project in question, national and local agencies in touch with the donors get hands-on experience based on successful cases. Thus, collaboration with international organizations enables capacity-building and enhancement at the local level. This is clearly seen in the Delhi Metro case. The DMRC now provides consultancy to metro projects in some neighbouring countries like Pakistan and Bangladesh, as well as in several Indian cities, such as Jaipur and Bangalore. International cooperation could also help push the environmental agenda forward in developing countries, where policymakers are interested more in developmental co-benefits rather than in environmental ones. International donors who pursue environmental procedures strictly throughout their collaboration in target countries could lead the national and local agencies to follow environmental safeguards. For instance, the Japan International Cooperation Agency (JICA) has strict environmental regulations that have to be followed throughout the projects funded by the Japanese Government. This has been the case with the DMP from the outset. As per the legal framework in India, an Environmental Impact Assessment (EIA) was not required for railway projects, including the DMP. However, JICA, as a partner, insisted on conducting EIA for the metro project and several assessments of this kind have been made to date.

Therefore, there is a potential to expand the focus of co-benefits policies to wider organizational and institutional domains. To do so, good coordination and cooperation should be established among all relevant actors of policymaking. Vertical and horizontal relationships among a range of relevant actors need to be established and strengthened in the *provision* mode of governing especially. However, as this case shows, collaboration with international agencies can result in somewhat less tangible co-benefits that include capacity-building and transfer of know-how from international level to national and local levels, rather than purely environmental ones.

Good leadership for effective co-benefits policymaking

Good leadership, as an essential component of good governance, has been one of the key factors behind the success of DMP in terms of effective project management and rapid implementation. Mr E. Sreedharan, the former managing director of the DMRC, is known to be instrumental in the development of the DMP, as an experienced expert on large-scale transportation projects. The key staff of the corporation, for instance, were selected carefully by the managing director so as to build sufficient in-house capacity and competence. The DMRC now is known to have a strong in-house technical team and executive officers who are experienced in carrying out effective decision-making. Critically, the managing director showed no tolerance to any kind of outside interference with the project.

Concluding remarks

In summary, government at all levels is of key importance in promoting the mainstreaming of the co-benefits approach into policymaking in both developed and developing countries. Local governments deserve special attention in this respect, as they are the closest units to policy implementation. Four distinct modes of governance could be employed by local governments to address environmental problems, particularly climate change, bearing in mind that each mode has its own advantages and disadvantages. Besides, there may be a good match between certain modes and certain sectors of urban policy. For instance, co-benefits policies might be mainstreamed into the building sector via regulatory frameworks in line with the *enabling* and *regulation* modes of governing. However, direct intervention might be the most appropriate option when it comes to policy initiatives in urban infrastructure due to high initial investment cost. Cities that are in need of infrastructure development should thus consider the *provision* mode of governance. Instead of adhering to any of these modes, local governments should rather aim to employ a good combination of them considering local needs and opportunities. No matter which mode or likely combination of modes is employed, integration of relevant policies and coordination among all relevant actors, including the public, private, international and non-governmental ones, are of vital importance. Otherwise, opportunities might be lost, co-benefits may remain limited and the positive outcome of a policy might be offset by the negative outcome of another.

Acknowledgements

Much of the information gathered for this case came from expert interviews with representatives of JICA and the DMRC in India and Japan.

References

Asian Development Bank (ADB) 2009, *Rethinking Transport and Climate Change*, *Asian Development Bank Sustainable Development Working Paper Series*, Metro Manila, Philippines.

Doll, CNH and Balaban, O 2013, 'A methodology for evaluating environmental co-benefits in the transport sector: Application to the Delhi Metro', *Journal of Cleaner Production*, vol. 58, pp. 61–73.

Puppim de Oliveira, JA 2009, 'The implementation of climate change related policies at the subnational level: An analysis of three countries', *Habitat International*, vol. 33, no. 3, pp. 253–259.

Sahai, SN and Bishop, S 2010, 'Multi modal transport in a low carbon future', in *India Infrastructure Report 2010*, pp. 310–330, viewed 21 September 2016, www.idfc.com/pdf/report/Chapter-19.pdf.

Sen, AK, Tiwari, G and Upadhyay, V 2010, 'Estimating marginal external costs of transport in Delhi', *Transport Policy*, vol. 17, pp. 27–37.

Sharma, D and Tomar, S 2010, 'Mainstreaming climate change adaptation in Indian cities', *Environment and Urbanization*, vol. 22, no. 2, pp. 451–465.

Siemiatycki, M 2006, 'Message in a metro: Building urban rail infrastructure and image in Delhi, India', *International Journal of Urban and Regional Research*, vol. 30, no. 2, pp. 277–292.

Sreedharan, E 2009, 'Climate change – an opportunity for sustainable development: The DMRC experience', *RITES Journal*, pp. 81–88.

Thynell, M, Mohan, D and Tiwari, G 2010, 'Sustainable transport and the modernisation of urban transport in Delhi and Stockholm', *Cities*, vol. 27, pp. 421–429.

United Nations, Human Settlements Programme (UN-HABITAT) 2011, *Cities and Climate Change: Policy Directions*, *Global Report on Human Settlements 2011*, e-book, Earthscan, London and Washington DC, viewed 10 May 2016, www.citiesalliance.org/sites/citiesalliance.org/files/CA_Images/UNH_GRHS2011_CitiesClimateChange.pdf.

Yagi, S and Nagayama, K 2010, 'Opinions of intermodal transfer functions of urban railway systems: A case study of Delhi Metro', *Proceedings of the World Conference on Transport Research*, Lisbon, Portugal, 11–15 July.

2.2 Curitiba

The intended/unintended co-benefits of investing in public transport

Fábio Duarte and Tatiana Gadda

In the 1960s, Curitiba began its journey to become one of the most successful cities in expanding the benefits of public transport to other urban sectors in a quite unfavorable environment. At this time, Curitiba was a relatively unknown city of 400,000 inhabitants. However, its population was growing fast, the city center was crowded and traffic had become a major issue. Projects to crisscross downtown with flyovers were under preliminary discussion. In 1965, the City Council approved a new master plan that would guide the development of the city for the next 50 years. It has been updated several times, but its core principles remain the same.

In the shadow of the modernist success of Brasilia, inaugurated in 1960, with its mono-functional districts, avenues and flyovers designed for a booming automobile industry, Curitiba proposed linear growth along transport corridors principally designed to accommodate a bus system which mimics the performance of a metro. The core idea, which would become a hallmark of sustainable urban plans in the 2000s, is based on the co-benefits of mixed and dense land use areas with full access to public transport. Recently, a growing literature on the co-benefits related to public transport has emerged, ranging from climate change mitigation and air pollution to active modes and health (Lee and van de Meene 2013; Xia *et al.* 2013). Similar benefits have been experienced in Curitiba, and will be discussed in this chapter. But if co-benefits are understood 'as a means to achieve more than one outcome with a single policy' (Puppim de Oliveira *et al.* 2013, pp. 2), in the case of Curitiba we argue that these benefits were sometimes the result of unintended consequences of the planning process, when innovation in one field triggered innovations in another. Co-benefits aim to achieve certain outcomes, whereas sometimes the consequences of planning and design measures have unexpected positive and/or negative results. Urban innovations, even if well planned, will likely profit from a combination of both – reacting to and correcting negative outcomes, whilst building upon the positive ones, as happened in the case of Curitiba.

By the time the first of the five original bus corridors was implemented, in the early 1970s, the city's population had already reached 700,000 and the logic was quite simple: on the one hand, providing high-capacity and reliable bus services in segregated corridors with specially designed bus stops would attract more users to the system, and would also appeal to the incoming population to live along these corridors. On the other hand, for this high-capacity bus service to have enough riders living close by the system, the new land-use zoning exclusively allowed high-density and high-rise buildings in the adjacent two blocks of either side of the corridor. Furthermore, in order to achieve an even trip distribution during the day, it was mandated that commercial activities would occupy the ground and first floor of the buildings facing the bus corridors. In addition, bus lines from less dense neighborhoods would not cross the downtown, but rather feed terminals along the corridors, where passengers would change to express buses.

This core concept remains in place today even as the city population reaches two million inhabitants. The declared co-benefits were mostly between transport and land use: increasing the use of public transport, reducing the use of cars and the consequent traffic congestion, and concentrating the growing population along four main urban axes.

The unexpected adverse results of co-benefits

The co-benefits of linking public transport and land use were clear to those who conceived Curitiba's master plan in the 1960s. Nonetheless, perhaps they were too confident to see collateral effects of this logic and, at the same time, too humble to dare to anticipate other benefits it would bring to the city.

One adverse effect is directly related to increasing the floor-area ratio (FAR) along the corridors. As soon as the City Council designated the higher FAR zones in the city, those areas with higher FAR saw their real estate value increased substantially. If a landowner had two plots, one along the corridor and another a few blocks away, the former had its building potential increased up to four times overnight. At first glance, it would simply indicate that a developer could build four times as much along the corridors, but it also created an unfair situation in the real estate market (private landowners were benefiting from a public policy, without giving anything back). From the public transport standpoint, however, that was the desired effect: more people living close to the bus corridors.

It is noteworthy that in Brazil high-rise buildings have a special connotation: security. With urban violence escalating in recent decades, living in gated communities or in high-rise buildings became the goal for part of the urban upper and middle class. Importantly, in Brazil, the upper and middle classes do not ride buses. Consequently, the areas along bus corridors, where some blocks have 150 inhabitants/ha (Danni-Oliveira 1999), also have some of the highest motorization rates in the city.

High-rise buildings along Curitiba's bus corridors would also bring another unpredicted consequence: the 'urban canyon effect', which affects sunlight (see below), temperature, wind direction and speed and, consequently, air quality. In Curitiba, these 'walls' of buildings on both sides of a street (the valley) can be 80 meters high, effectively providing a new topography for the city (Danni-Oliveira 2000). They either act as a corridor for the wind or prevent the dispersion of air pollutants (such as NO_x or PM, which are mostly related to motor vehicle emissions) within the canyons.

The unexpected positive co-benefits

When the project of Curitiba's bus corridors was launched, no mention was made of air pollution, greenhouse gases emissions or public health – co-benefits currently linked to investments in public transport and mixed and dense land-use zoning. Still, Curitiba shows good results in general and performs better in terms of emissions than similar cities in Brazil. The city ranked second in the world of cities with the most improved air pollution emissions during the first decade of the new millennium (IAP 2012).

A combination of zoning, street design, transportation management, technology and geo-ecological features seem to have been the main reasons for this accomplishment. For example, the industrial district of Curitiba was strategically located where the dominant winds would move pollutants away from the city. In fact, in Curitiba, as is the case of most cities, the main source of air pollution is traffic. Rabinovitch and Leitmann (1993) argue that Curitiba's good performance in terms of air quality is partially the result of the average age of the bus fleet: about three years old. Fleet renovation alone in Curitiba accounted for a reduction of 35,341 tonnes of pollutants between 2005 and 2014 (Zottis 2015). The replacement of regular buses (diesel) by hybrid buses (electricity and biofuel) will reduce PMx emissions by 89 percent, NO_x emissions by 80 percent and CO_2 emissions by 35 percent (URBS n.d.).

By adopting segregated bus lines Curitiba's buses encounter little congestion (IPEA and ANTP 1998) and therefore have a higher average bus speed that produces fewer emissions. The segregated bus lines have also inadvertently functioned as an unofficial but popular cycle route (Leal 2015). Since 2014,[1] in order to improve road safety for cyclists, part of the East–West corridor of the city has accommodated a shared space for cyclists and motor vehicles on the side of its segregated bus line, where the street received traffic-calming attributes. In a year of operation, this new-shared infrastructure was able to increase the number of cyclists substantially (IPPUC 2014a, 2014b), presumably contributing to air quality and improving health in the city.

Not only is Curitiba a rainy city but also it is well known as the coldest state capital in Brazil. Therefore, thermal comfort is an important issue that is aggravated by the urban canyons of Curitiba. During winter when the sun is low, shadows minimize the sun's exposure to buildings along the corridors. The realization of this perverse effect along Curitiba's corridors led to new legal standards in 2000 which set a mandatory H/6 relationship for buildings, i.e. the space between one building and the next (new building) should respect the height of the former divided by six. Campos (2005) modeled the effect of H/6 on the axis of Curitiba and concluded that this would bring benefits in terms of sun exposure. It seems plausible that it may also have an effect on ventilation and consequently on air quality along the corridors – a positive co-benefit yet to be proven.

Furthermore, the concentration of SO_2, smoke and TSP declined continually over the previous decade due to state legislation that controls emissions from industries as well as technological improvements in motor vehicles and, importantly, the reduction of sulfur in fuel (IAP 2012).

Curitiba seems compelled to constant innovation. A variety of fuels (usually biofuels mixed with traditional fuels) has been tested in part of the bus fleet over the years. From 2009, the city began having part of its bus fleet running on 100 percent biofuel. This alone has reduced CO_2 emissions by 30 percent per bus compared to the same bus running on a mix of diesel and 4 percent biofuel. As for smoke, the reduction was over 60 percent. In 2014, there were 34 buses running on 100 percent biofuel. Together with these, in 2012 the city included ten hybrid buses (featuring Euro III engines[2]) running on electricity or diesel, reducing PM by 89 percent, CO_2 by 35 percent and NO_x by 80 percent (URBS 2016). Today there are 28 hybrid buses, with fully electric buses likely to be integrated into the fleet in the near future.

Unintended positive outcomes and urban innovation

During the 1960s, Brasília was the symbol of the best Brazilian urbanism and architecture. The high quality of its layout and architecture was praised worldwide. During this time, global media coverage about Curitiba was nonexistent. After the United Nations Conference on Environment and Development held in Rio de Janeiro in 1992, Curitiba came to the forefront of urban discussions due to several of its environmentally friendly policies, including the link between land use and public transport. In the 2000s, after the success of Transmilenio, a Bus Rapid Transit system implemented in Bogota, overtly inspired by Curitiba, consolidated the city's innovative image at the global level – showing that co-benefits sometimes take time to consolidate.

In 2009, Forbes ranked Curitiba as one of the top 'smart cities' (Kotkin 2009) for its environmentally friendly programs, public transport, economic development, urban planning and overall quality of life. In 2012, Traveller's Digest put Curitiba among the top ten livable cities in the world. Exame (2014), a well-known Brazilian business magazine, ranked Curitiba as the third best city in the country for investments. And Siemens (2012) ranked Curitiba at the top of the Latin American Green City Index, with a special mention to its public transport system.

Such indices and rankings are controversial. However, this media exposure brought attention to the city and created, within the country, a positive image of a city with a high quality of life. It helped to attract huge national and foreign industries and consultancy firms, as an alternative to better known but more crowded, expensive and polluted cities like Rio de Janeiro and São Paulo. With these companies, a series of other businesses boomed, bringing with it a more cosmopolitan profile to the city.

Volvo, which provides the buses to Curitiba's Bus Rapid Transit, has its national headquarters in the city, and exports its technology to other Latin American countries. In a clear co-benefits strategy, Curitiba profits from Volvo's technological developments to keep innovating in public transport – recent examples are the implementation of biofuel and electric buses on some of its main routes, whilst Volvo takes advantage of Curitiba's international exposure to promote its bus technology.

Conclusion

The 'multiple outcomes with a single policy' rubric of co-benefits can at times bring unexpected negative results, as well as unexpected positive results. Part of the success of Curitiba in making public transport and land-use zoning a key driver to quality of life and urban innovation has been, on one hand, to incorporate some unexpected positive results in its long-term plans and, on the other hand, fix those planning measures which were initially thought as good ideas but eventually produced negative outcomes.

Driven by an eagerness to innovate (as, for example, in the case of alternative fuels) as well as some self-criticism (e.g. in the case of the increased space between buildings), Curitiba attempts to remain a city strongly associated with urban sustainability. Curitiba shows that a mix of clear objectives and flexible planning tools is necessary in order to achieve co-benefits. It also shows that unintended positive outcomes can be incorporated along the way to reshape planning processes. Planning, like cities themselves, must understand this process and embrace an ever-changing environment in order to continually achieve better results.

Notes

1 At this time, new infrastructure along the bus corridors was built to allow, for the first time, bus overtaking (representing an increased risk for cyclists on the bus lines). This, together with resources available for infrastructure improvements due to the 2014 World Cup, provided the opportunity to implement the shared and calmed street infrastructure (Leal 2015).
2 Currently a vast majority of the city buses are Euro III, while since 2012 Euro V buses have been increasing. These standards play an important role in air quality control in the city.

References

Campos, RF 2005, 'Análise da influência da orientação da testada dos lotes na ocupação do setor estrutural de Curitiba', doctoral thesis, Universidade Federal do Paraná, Brazil.

Danni-Oliveira, IM 1999, 'A cidade de Curitiba/PR e a poluição do ar: Implicações de seus atributos urbanos e geoecológicos na dispersão de poluentes em período de inverno', Tese (Doutorado), Universidade de São Paulo, Brazil.

Danni-Oliveira, IM 2000, 'Considerações sobre a poluição do ar em Curitiba – PR face a seus aspectos de urbanização', *Raega – O Espaço Geográfico em Análise*, no. 4, pp. 101–110.

Exame 2014, 'As 100 melhores cidades do BR para investir em negócios', *Revista Exame*, vol. 48, no. 8.

Instituto Ambientaldo Paraná (IAP) 2012, *Relatório da Qualidade do Ar na Região Metropolitana de Curitiba – Ano 2012*, e-book, Instituto Ambientaldo Paraná, Brazil, viewed 9 May 2016, www.iap.pr.gov.br/arquivos/File/Monitoramento/Relatorio_Qualidade_do_Ar_Anual_IAP_2012.pdf.

Instituto de Pesquisa Econômica Aplicada (IPEA) and Associação Nacional dos Transportes Públicos (ANTP) 1998, *Redução das Deseconomias Urbanas com a Melhoria do Transporte Coletivo: Relatório Síntese*, e-book, Associação Nacional dos Transportes Públicos (ANTP), Brazil, viewed 9 May 2016, http://files-server.antp.org.br/_5dotSystem/download/dcmDocument/2013/01/10/057A84C9-76D1-4BEC-9837-7E0B0AEAF5CE.pdf.

Instituto de Pesquisa e Planejamento Urbano de Curitiba (IPPUC) 2014a, *Pesquisa com Usuários de Bicicleta na Sete de Setembro: Contagem de Tráfego de Bicicletas*, Instituto de Pesquisa e Planejamento Urbano de Curitiba, Brazil.

Instituto de Pesquisa e Planejamento Urbano de Curitiba (IPPUC) 2014b, *Pesquisa com Usuários de Bicicleta na Via Calma da Avenida Sete de Setembro*, Instituto de Pesquisa e Planejamento Urbano de Curitiba, Brazil.

Kotkin, J 2009, 'The world's smartest cities', *Forbes*, viewed 9 May 2016, www.forbes.com/2009/12/03/infrastructure-economy-urban-opinions-columnists-smart-cities-09-joel-kotkin.html.

Leal, MCCD 2015, *Via Calma de Curitiba: Análise das Variáveis, do Uso Compartilhado da Via e da Segurança do Ciclista*, Faculdades Instituto Nacional De Pos-Graduacao INPG, Brazil.

Lee, T and van de Meene, S 2013, 'Comparative studies of urban climate co-benefits in Asian cities: An analysis of relationships between CO_2 emissions and environmental indicators', *Journal of Cleaner Production*, vol. 58, no. 1, pp. 15–24.

Puppim de Oliveira, JA, Doll, CNH, Kurniawan, TA, Geng, Y, Kapshe, M and Huisingh, D 2013, 'Promoting win–win situations in climate change mitigation, local environmental quality and development in Asian cities through co-benefits', *Journal of Cleaner Production*, vol. 58, no. 1, pp. 1–6.

Rabinovitch, J and Leitmann, J 1993, *Environmental Innovation and Management in Curitiba, Brazil, Working Paper No. 1*, UNDP/UNCHS/The International Bank for Reconstruction and Development/WORLD BANK-UMP, USA.

Siemens 2012, *The Green City Index: A Summary of the Green City Index Research Series*, e-book, Siemens AG, Corporate Communications and Government Affairs Munich, Germany, viewed 10 May 2016, www.siemens.com/press/pool/de/events/2012/corporate/2012-06-rio20/gci-report-e.pdf.

Urban Development Authority of Curitiba (URBS) n.d, 'URBS URBANIZAÇÃO DE CURITIBA S.A.', presentation, Urban Development Authority of Curitiba (URBS), Brazil, viewed 10 May 2016, http://frotasefretesverdes.com.br/2014/palestras/5/Celso%20Ferreira%20-%20USO%20DE%20BIODIESEL%20E%20TECNOLOGIA%20UEN.URBS.pdf.

Urban Development Authority of Curitiba (URBS) 2016, 'Sustentabilidade, Transporte', *URBS*, viewed 10 May 2016, www.urbs.curitiba.pr.gov.br/transporte/sustentabilidade.

Xia, T, Zhang, Y, Crabb, S and Shah, P 2013, 'Cobenefits of replacing car trips with alternative transportation: A review of evidence and methodological issues', *Journal of Environmental and Public Health*, vol. 2013, pp. 1–14.

Zottis, L 2015, *How Transport Reform Is Helping Brazilian Cities Fight Climate Change. The City Fix*, blog, World Resources Institute, Washington, DC viewed 21 September 2016, http://thecityfix.com/blog/transport-reform-helping-brazilian-cities-fight-climate-change-luisa-zottis.

2.3 Yogyakarta, Indonesia
Technological change and institutional reform for sustainable urban transport

Puspita Dirgahayani

The transport sector is one of the major contributors to urban problems in Indonesia, including congestion, energy scarcity, and air pollution. Promoting the use of public transport is widely acknowledged to be one of the best solutions for efficient urban mobility. In order to achieve such a goal, Indonesian cities have to make concrete efforts in delivering reliable public transport services which can be effective enough to attract the increasing numbers of private mode users (see Chapter 2.1). Those efforts are not only related to providing appropriate technologies but also to reforming institutions. This is aligned with the fact that technological change and institutional reform (regulation and market organization) are the key success of revitalizing urban public transportation in many cities worldwide (Costa and Fernandes 2012).

This case provides a qualitative analysis of the implementation of these two approaches and the co-benefits that resulted. It focuses on the empirical practice made in Greater Yogyakarta, an urban agglomeration within the Special Region of Yogyakarta Province (YSR). A series of in-depth interviews with several stakeholders in Greater Yogyakarta, namely the Transportation Agency of YSR, public transportation operator companies (PT-JTT or Jogja Tugu Trans Ltd) and the Greater Yogyakarta Joint Secretariat (Sekber Kartamantul), were conducted between September 2013 and February 2014. Relevant report documents, regulations, and information from online resources were also collected to capture recent progresses up to 2016.

Greater Yogyakarta introduced a new bus system (Trans-Jogja) in 2008 as part of the nationwide urban public transportation revitalization pilot project following the footsteps of TransJakarta Busway system in Jakarta. Referring to the quality spectrum of public road transport (Wright and Hook 2007), the Trans-Jogja system can be categorized as a Bus Rapid Transit-lite system which runs without a segregated right-of-way.

Public transport improvement was the main driver of this intervention and reducing emissions connected to global warming was not on the agenda (Dirgahayani 2013). The main form of this improvement was to take place through a series of technological changes. More progressive approaches to attract a larger number of passengers and the promotion of mode shift from private vehicle users were not explicitly cited. This was reflected by the slow progress of route optimization and expansion. The route network was finally optimized by restructuring four one-way pair routes in 2015. However, it was still far from the ultimate plan to expand to 11 bus lines, consisting of 6 with one-way pair routes and 5 with two-way routes (Governor Decree Number 22, 2014).

Technological change

Despite these limitations, Trans-Jogja's existence has led to numerous transportation-related technological innovations, a timeline of which is shown in Figure 2.3. First, there was an improvement in vehicle technology involving the conversion of old buses to Euro-II compliant diesel, medium-sized buses from 2008. By 2016, Trans-Jogja comprised 34 buses owned by PT-JTT, which have been available since the beginning of Trans-Jogja's operation, and 40 more recent buses (2012) owned by PT Anindya Mitra International (AMI Ltd; local government-owned company) (20 buses) and PT-JTT (20 buses). Regulations promoting the conversion to more environmentally friendly vehicles have been in place in Yogyakarta since the enactment of Governor Decree Number 6.1 in 2011 and its amendment, Governor Decree Number 53, in 2013. The Governor Decree Number 22 in 2014 mandated the conversion ratio from other old transit vehicles to Trans-Jogja buses: three van-type transits to one Trans-Jogja bus and two old medium buses to one Trans-Jogja bus. The conversion programme will be carried out gradually.

Second, in 2009, permanent bus shelters equipped with e-ticket card readers and turnstiles for ticket validation have distinguished the Trans-Jogja system from similar bus systems in Indonesian cities. However, there are some segments of the bus corridors where sufficient land was not available to build such permanent shelters. Therefore, the authority introduced the first mobile shelter

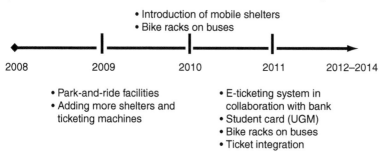

Figure 2.3 Technological changes of the Greater Yogyakarta bus system.
Source: analysis based on interview results, 2014.

in 2010 and continued to install several additional portable bus shelters in 2012. These mobile shelters were designed only for passengers who have e-tickets because the shelter is not equipped with manual ticketing booths and, thus, no cash transaction is allowed. Consequently, the authority installed on-board ticketing machines at the same time.

Third, multimodal integration was initiated in 2008 by the Transportation Agency of YSR. It was then followed up by PT KAI (Indonesian Railway Company) and PT Angkasa Pura 1 (the Airport Management Company for Eastern Indonesia). The multimodal integration was achieved by unifying access to the airport, railway station, and Trans-Jogja shelters in one location. It was enabled by the existence of a railway underpass to the airport. Therefore, airport users can directly access the railway station and Trans-Jogja shelter once they exit the airport terminal, without having to pass across the railway track. It took just two months of preparation before it was unveiled at the end of August 2008. In 2009, the authority built park-and-ride facilities at two termini located near popular tourist spots (Prambanan and Ngabean).

Fourth, bicycle racks have been provided on Trans-Jogja buses since 2010 and at the shelter since 2011. The use of bicycles as feeders to Trans-Jogja, however, has not yet been optimized due to lack of promotion and land availability. To support bicycle use, bicycle lanes which are integrated with Trans-Jogja routes have been provided by the Transportation Authority of the Municipal and Regency Governments within the YSR administrative area in coordination with the Transportation Authority of YSR.

Fifth, a bus tracking system and off-board electronic ticketing system has been developed in collaboration with Telkomsel Ltd (the largest Indonesian cellular phone provider company) since 2012. Utilizing free GPS, the management body of Trans-Jogja (UPTD Trans-Jogja) is able to receive transaction data from all bus shelters through a wireless system on a daily basis. The media for e-ticketing itself, known as e-money, was provided by four national banks (BCA, Mandiri Bank, BNI, and BRI). More recently, the University of Gadjah Mada, the largest university in Greater Yogyakarta, contributed to integrating student ID cards with Trans-Jogja's e-ticket system. This breakthrough was made in order to encourage more new students to use Trans-Jogja. Besides the physical integration in the form of an integrated transfer point for Trans-Jogja, the airport railway, the e-money provided by BNI has allowed passengers to travel easily using Trans-Jogja and Prameks railway since 2011.

In addition to GPS, the YSR Government has also worked with Telkomsel to introduce a bus tracking system by which the real-time position of each bus fleet can be tracked and informed to the waiting passengers through 30 LCD screens in Trans-Jogja's shelters. However, the system often encounters problems and has not worked properly. Telkomsel Ltd encounters difficulties due to the high bandwidth requirement for running both the e-ticketing application and the bus tracking system.

Sixth, as well as paper-based leaflets, since 2008, Trans-Jogja service information can also be accessed through an app (mTransportDIY). This Android-based application was developed in 2008 initiated by the Transportation Authority of YSR. The vendor of this application, Gamatechno, built a system that contains not only Trans-Jogja information but also the entire public transportation system in Yogyakarta, including the schedules and routes of buses, trains, and flights, as well as the information fed by the Trans-Jogja bus tracking system and traffic surveillance camera.

Finally, another technology still in progress is the traffic signal priority system for buses through the Area Traffic Control System (ATCS). This system has been established since December 2012. It was developed by the Provincial Transportation Agency of YSR and was inaugurated by the Vice Minister of the Transportation Ministry together with the inauguration of the bus tracking system and e-ticketing of Trans-Jogja. Although the technology was ready in 2012, implementation was delayed until 2014. There are institutional and technical constraints that need to be solved to smooth its implementation. Institutional constraints involve the preparedness of operators in estimating business scenarios as well as establishing communication between the central government and the operator for transmitting data at certain radio frequencies. Technical constraints are due to the fact that intersections in Yogyakarta are operated autonomously and, thus, cannot be centrally controlled. In the future, the authority is planning to establish one independent entity that will focus on managing ATCS. This is due to the plan being studied to add 100 more traffic lights allocated not only within Yogyakarta City but also in other areas in YSR. The authority also continues to build bus shelters in strategic places and promote the Trans-Jogja service through various media.

Institutional reform

The whole transit institutional reform process in Yogyakarta was first formally initiated in 2001 through local regulation of the maximum vehicle age in order to deliver safe, secure, rapid, orderly, organized, convenient, and efficient public transportation. Five years later, in 2006, a Governor Decree restricted the issuance of new bus route permits and enforced bus renewal. It was a year before the Governor stipulated three circular corridors of the Trans-Jogja. In 2009, the Trans-Jogja Management Unit (UPT Trans-Jogja) was established to help plan the Trans-Jogja network and to set up the contracting process with the operator. Afterwards, PT-JTT was selected to be the operator of Trans-Jogja. The company was a consortium consisting of major incumbent operators. Through the existence of these two new entities, Yogyakarta officially separated the role of government as a regulator and the role of the private sector as the operator.

However, the contract with PT-JTT did not allow more routes to be added. There was also little incentive for PT-JTT to boost Trans-Jogja's performance. Therefore, once the contract ended in 2015, the government temporarily handed over the Trans-Jogja operation to AMI Ltd. As of 2016, Trans-Jogja is in a transition phase. In this phase, the company is obliged to provide new buses, while the government has to renew Trans-Jogja's buses, especially those that are no longer road-worthy.

Concluding remarks

Technological change and institutional reform are the most essential contributors to achieving co-benefits of public transportation service improvement. This has been proven by the experience of the Trans-Jogja implementation process from 2008 to 2015. Having been implemented for seven years, the system has essentially returned to square one in 2016. From the perspective of technological change, all instruments that have been introduced were aimed at attracting higher demand. However, the route network and fleet size could not be further expanded from their initial state in 2010. The barriers to optimize the route network and fleet size can only be solved by reforming the market. Introducing regulated competition in the transit industry might offer promising options.

Dirgahayani (2013) revealed that the co-benefits of Trans-Jogja could have mainly resulted from the avoided motorized trips from motorcycles and conventional buses. The motorcycle is indeed the main competitor. Its advantage over public transportation in terms of faster and door-to-door travel should be taken into consideration. Accordingly, the success of Trans-Jogja will also rely on the degree of multimodal integration with feeder systems connecting the Trans-Jogja network with peripheral regions of Greater Yogyakarta. Further roll-out of bicycle routes and parking facilities near to Trans-Jogja's shelters could be among these indicators. The larger the shift from the aforementioned competing modes, the larger the impact of any technological changes taking place as part of Trans-Jogja.

Acknowledgements

This chapter is part of the co-benefits project at the United Nations University-Institute of Advanced Studies (UNU-IAS), which is supported by the Ministry of Environment Japan.

References

Costa, A and Fernandes, R 2012, 'Urban public transport in Europe: Technology diffusion and market organisation', *Transportation Research Part A: Policy and Practice*, vol. 46, no. 2, pp. 269–284.

Dirgahayani, P 2013, 'Environmental co-benefits of public transportation improvement initiative: The case of Trans-Jogja bus system in Yogyakarta, Indonesia', *Journal of Cleaner Production*, vol. 58, pp. 74–81.

Wright, L and Hook, W 2007, *Bus Rapid Transit: Planning Guide*, 3rd Edition, Institute for Transportation and Development Policy, New York, USA.

2.4 Rio de Janeiro, Brazil
The Bus Rapid System

*Flavia Carloni, Tomás Bredariol and
Emilio La Rovere*

Introduction

The Bus Rapid System (BRS) initiative[1] in the City of Rio de Janeiro started in 2011 with the objective of optimizing public transport by bus through preferential lanes and organized bus stops. The preferred corridors for buses and taxis with passengers aim to sort the bus lines and increase the comfort and efficiency of the system, reorganizing traffic and public transport, while reducing users' travel time. Currently, there are 11 corridors, resulting in 27 km of dedicated lanes between the South Zone and the Center. According to the city administration (Cidade Olimpica 2016), travel time has reduced by 25.6 per cent on average, with reductions as high as 45 per cent (in Botafogo). Estimates indicate that the present BRS corridors are responsible for a mean annual reduction of 35,200 tonnes CO_2e (La Rovere *et al.* 2013).

This case study analyzes the BRS through the lens of innovation capabilities to understand how the system has produced co-benefits to the city of Rio de Janeiro. The theoretical framework used defines co-benefits as positive impacts from projects that are not related to its prime objectives.

The methodology was based on a broad base of information, including: interviews with the stakeholders related to the BRS; documents and studies concerning this initiative; and direct observation. The analysis of the information collected provided an understanding on the following points:

- how the socio-technical transitions for co-benefits took place;
- what the level of necessary technological capability was;
- how the city was able to gain the technological capability to carry out the transition for generating co-benefits;
- what the factors were that enabled or disabled the final results in terms of co-benefits, in order to understand the links between technological capabilities and final co-benefits outcomes.

To address the above points, four dimensions of analysis were carried out about the BRS systems and its context of development:

1   Mapping the socio-technical system;

2   Assessment of the level of technological capability of the innovation system;
3   Understanding the learning mechanisms for building the technological capabilities;
4   Understanding the enabling institutions and interventions in the socio-technical system that facilitated the outcomes of the innovation.

The results are presented according to these four basic dimensions of analysis.

Dimension 1: the socio-technical system for on-road public transport in Rio de Janeiro

Figure 2.4 describes a fairly complex picture, with several interconnected elements: the infrastructure (roadways, signalization, control mechanisms, etc.); the maintenance requirements; the regulatory agencies (CET-Rio, Transport Bureau); the public on-road transport operators and their syndicates (bus companies, Rio Ônibus, Fetranspor); the public transport users; and the universities and consultants. The term institution is used here to mean the existing formal rules and informal constraints (North 1991), culture being a main element of the second type. It is interesting to note, for example, that without traffic institutions the whole public transport system would be jeopardized. Much of the innovation that enabled the BRS initiative was related to institutional change.

Restricting our analysis to the main actors that interacted in the implementation of the BRS, we reach a simpler picture. On one side, there is the regulating power: the city hall, with its planning agency – the Transport Bureau (Secretaria de Transporte) – and CET-Rio, a sub-unit responsible for traffic control and monitoring. On the other, the public transport operators that work in consortiums and are organized in a trade union, Rio Ônibus, which in turn is assisted by the state bus lines operators' federation (Fetranspor). Lastly, one should consider the civil society that uses the public transport system. Basically, these organizations interact as follows: the Transport Bureau defines the bus system's design and controls its implementation through the consortiums – while the civil society uses the service. Civil society is organized according to the regions of the city in neighborhood associations and participated in the process but not exactly in the implementation, giving their opinion in the first months of use through surveys conducted by the operators.

Dimension 2: assessment of the levels of operational and innovation capabilities

In terms of the levels of technological capabilities defined by the degree of complexity and novelty in the technological activities that the city is able to undertake, we made two distinctions. First, we differentiated between the types of resources, skills and knowledge bases which are static and involved in the non-creative use and operation of technologies, and those which are dynamic and

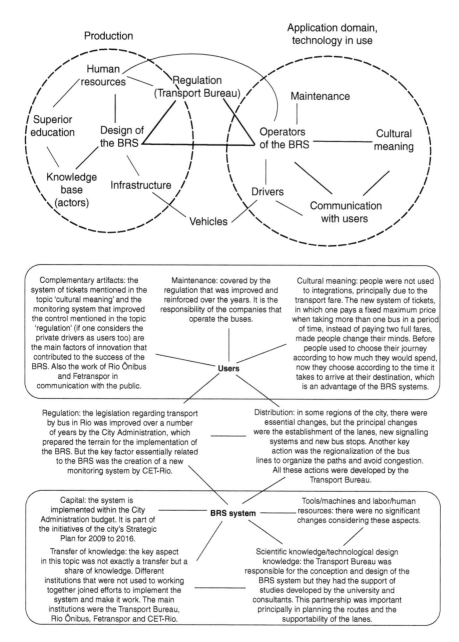

Figure 2.4 Elements of the BRS socio-technical system.

associated to the creative activities needed to change technologies (Bell 2006). We call the first set 'operational capabilities' and the second 'innovation capabilities'.

The city performed actions that indicated a good level of operational capabilities, since the operators are required to develop monitoring processes that assess: average speed of buses; number of passengers; situation on the bus stops; number of kilometers traveled; and similar data. Thus, the city is able to evaluate which are the most critical routes and understand how the demand for the public on-road transport system varies during the day. Environmental concerns are not critical, but since traffic has an obvious impact on the environmental quality, the operational improvement actions implemented bring co-benefits in terms of air pollution, noise and life quality. Indeed many of the data collected in the monitoring process are precisely what are needed to evaluate co-benefits (see the transport tool discussion in Chapter 9).

In terms of innovation capabilities, the evidence shows that the city of Rio de Janeiro may be moving from an intermediate to an advanced innovational capability. The main initiatives on course are mostly adaptations to existing technologies in other cities, as is the case of the BRS and the BRT. The existing monitoring systems enable the city to improve the road public transport system's performance and devise measures to reach greater efficiency.

Dimension 3: analytical description of the learning mechanisms

This technological change – an exclusive bus lane – was already in view in the 1990s, but only in 2010 was it truly developed. This advancement is due not only to old factors, such as the technical support (transport engineering) from the Federal University of Rio de Janeiro (UFRJ), but also to the emergence of simple but new technologies and demands from the stakeholders in the system. Next, we describe the main learning mechanisms that enabled capabilities related to the BRS project.

The main institutions of this socio-technical system have existed for more than a decade and have developed substantial capabilities. The presence of graduate and post-graduate programs that provide qualified personnel in the transport engineering field supported the staff formation of the Transport Bureau as well as the public transport operators. Nonetheless, these resources did not suffice to provide more than a good innovation capability. Attesting to this is the fact that the City of Rio de Janeiro had already tried to implement an exclusive bus lane in the 1990s, but the project did not bring the expected results and was abandoned. The key factor for the success of today's initiative compared with the one of the 1990s was the control: a system of cameras developed by CET-Rio monitors the vehicles through pictures. A private car is allowed to enter the exclusive lane only if it is going to turn right; if it goes straight and the system gets two pictures of the same car, the driver is penalized. In the 1990s, this control was done in person and was very ineffective.

The BRS therefore benefited from three chief learning mechanisms: former experience; monitoring efforts; and technological improvements; as well as crucial cooperation among its main implementing agents.

Dimension 4: analysis of the factors linking technological capability and results in terms of co-benefits

The Transport Bureau defined a structure based on axial routes which would receive BRTs and a complementary network of BRSs. Furthermore, the relationship between the regulatory power and the operators was reconstructed, establishing a clearer legal institution for the public on-road transport.

After this reorientation of the system, the envisioned projects were initiated. The first BRS corridor, with two lanes, was implemented in Nossa Senhora de Copacabana Avenue, one of the main arterial roads in the heart of the tourist district of Copacabana – where the prior attempt had been made. In order to overcome the past obstacles, such as the failure in making other vehicles comply with the exclusivity of the lanes for buses, the control system described above was set up along with an optimization of the fleet and bus stops. Therefore, the bus lines were separated in groups which had their own stops – permitting longer distances between stops. Moreover, some lines had the number of circulating vehicles reduced or were divided in order to allow some buses to return before the start of the exclusive lane. Hence, the fleet was diminished by about 15–20 per cent. These two key modifications resulting from monitoring efforts and technological improvements enabled an average reduction in travel time of almost 50 per cent (in rush hour). Meanwhile, private automobiles suffered a mere 10–15 per cent increase in travel time (personal communication, information obtained from interviews).

Nonetheless, the project's evolution is not without hindrances, and it was able to adapt to adjust some problematic issues. The neighborhoods of Ipanema and Leblon received BRS on two main avenues. However, in these streets only one lane was available and that posed the question of how to allow overtaking in the proximity of bus stops. The solution was to make bus bays where the sidewalks provided sufficient space and, elsewhere, permit the buses to leave the corridor in short stretches. These solutions were considered and discussed in technical meetings organized among the Transport Bureau, Fetranspor, Rio Ônibus and consultants invited to participate. The main tool to help them in those discussions was the feedback from drivers and passengers consulted in the streets. Furthermore, in some of the most important roads in Rio de Janeiro's center, a BRS corridor with two lanes was established. Here, another challenge appeared: the volume of passengers and vehicles. Even with operational improvements, bus stops distancing and fleet reduction, the tracks were still saturated. This observation, supported by monitoring efforts, allowed the Transport Bureau and Fetranspor to deal with the Rio de Janeiro State sphere, pursuing to divert part of the intermunicipal bus traffic to other roads. The proposition was partly accomplished, enabling acceptable vehicle loads on the BRS downtown.

Conclusions

Summing up, the BRS brought significant gains in terms of mobility and environmental quality through simple operational enhancements and low-cost physical and technical intervention. In a certain way, this altered the established view in the city that the transport system would only improve with costly and time-demanding projects, such as the enlargement of the subway network. Therefore, future expansion is planned as it is in the interest of every agent of this socio-technical system: the government, because it brings popularity without excessive costs; the bus companies, due to the economy of fuel and vehicles; and the population, since it allows for more mobility as well as less air pollution and noise. This alignment of interests was, and should remain, critical to ensuring cooperation between the main actors and, thus, enabling the solution to the arising problems.

The BRS is an innovation that was developed in the relatively complex socio-technical system of the public on-road transport system of Rio de Janeiro City. Clearly, an important factor driving the changes comes from the prospect of hosting major events, such as the 2016 Olympic Games. However, other factors are also influential in this context – for example, the political alignment of the federal, state and municipal governments, which facilitate the cooperation and coordination of actions.

The co-benefits approach reveals an aptitude to study such innovations, since in an urban context there is an intense relationship among the variables and agents of the system. In this particular case, a number of co-benefits are present, mostly concerning pollution reduction and increased life quality. But one could also note benefits in terms of commerce in the near areas or comfort during the bus trips. Lastly, it is interesting to note that the success of this project has brought the attention of other cities in Brazil and, thus, this practice could well develop in other regions and bring further positive impacts.

Note

1 A BRS (Bus Rapid System) uses preferred corridors with fixed bus stops for the ordinary buses. By contrast, a BRT (Bus Rapid Transit) system employs exclusive lanes for articulated special buses.

References

Bell, M 2006, 'Time and technological learning in industrialising countries: How long does it take? How fast is it moving (if at all)?' *International Journal of Technology Management*, vol. 36, nos 1–3, pp. 25–39.

Cidade Olimpica 2016, *Cidade Olimpica BRS*, Prefeitura do Rio de Janeiro, viewed 17 May 2016, www.cidadeolimpica.com.br/brs/.

La Rovere, EL, Carloni, FB, Nadaud, G, Malaguti, G, Turano de Carvalho, P, Aragão, R, Solari, R, Loureiro, S and Bredariol, T 2013, *Greenhouse Gas Emissions Inventory of the City of Rio de Janeiro in 2012 and Updating of the Municipal Plan of Action for Emissions Reductions, Technical Summary*, Universidade Federal do Rio de Janeiro, Brazil.

North, DC 1991, 'Institutions', *The Journal of Economic Perspectives*, vol. 5, no. 1, pp. 97–112.

3 Land use

Osman Balaban

The climate problem, cities and the co-benefits approach

Climate change, as a global environmental challenge, will have drastic impacts on human life and settlements. Some of these impacts, like changes in weather and precipitation patterns, and a rise in sea levels, are already being observed in various parts of the world. Cities are the most appropriate places for key measures addressing climate change to be developed and implemented. On the one hand, cities are major sources of energy consumption and greenhouse gas (GHG) emissions; and on the other hand, they are highly vulnerable to climate change impacts due to their location in risky areas like coasts and riversides. Despite their contribution to the climate problem, cities can also be an essential part of the climate solution (Balaban 2012a). City administrations can control and manage various processes which may affect GHG emissions and climate vulnerabilities as part of urban planning and management interventions (Bulkeley 2013).

Developing cities in Asia and Africa are of particular importance in this respect, as much future urban growth will take place in these regions. For instance, the urban population in the whole of Asia grows by over 45 million a year on average. By 2050, nearly 90 percent of the future urban population growth (2.5 billion people in total) will be concentrated in Asia and Africa (UN-DESA 2014). In addition, cities in Asia are the major driving force of economies, generating 80 percent of the region's GDP with only 42 percent of the region's total population (UN-HABITAT 2010). Urban and economic growth in the developing world will increase the environmental footprint of developing cities. According to UN-HABITAT (2010), more than 10 km² of (mainly productive) rural land is converted to urban uses every day in Asia. Therefore, developing cities will be compelled to achieve their developmental targets and tackle global and local environmental problems simultaneously in the near future.

Since the mid-1990s, cities have increasingly been involved in the climate change agenda. City networks, such as C40 Cities and ICLEI, have provided the world's cities with opportunities to learn from each other and transfer plausible solutions to their localities. However, despite the growing reliance on roles to be played by city administrations, there is still a considerable gap between the rhetoric and reality of urban policymaking for climate change (Bulkeley 2010). Involvement of cities in climate policymaking is still a major challenge for many nations, especially developing countries. The multiple problems that developing nations face in their development trajectory cause reluctance among decision-makers to take environmental actions. The priority given to socio-economic development targets usually delays the approval and achievement of environmental objectives. Therefore, new policymaking approaches may encourage cities to develop policies to tackle the climate problem simultaneously with other local problems. The co-benefits approach, as an emerging approach to environmental policymaking, could be an important option here.

In general, the co-benefits approach is an instrument to achieve more than one outcome with a single policy (Puppim de Oliveira *et al.* 2013). The approach principally aims at addressing climate change mitigation concerns, while also addressing specific local problems or helping achieve specific development targets at the same time. One of the multiple outcomes of the approach is reduction in GHG emissions, with others ranging from improved air quality or health conditions in cities to economic benefits and savings. The delivery of a local co-benefit along with the climate co-benefit can help to engage decision-makers to take action for climate change mitigation, which is not normally a top priority (Balaban and Puppim de Oliveira 2016).

As yet, most co-benefits policies have addressed urban environmental management in specific sectors or projects in isolation to each other, and the mutual impacts and interactions of various co-benefits policies have not been sufficiently considered (Puppim de Oliveira 2011). For instance, the land-use sector, which has the potential to coordinate a wide range of other urban sectors, has not been adequately involved in the co-benefits debate. The extent to which the co-benefits approach could be mainstreamed in land-use planning and management remains mostly understudied. This chapter sets out to address this gap by discussing the conceptual and practical links between the land-use sector and the co-benefits approach. Lessons learnt from particular case studies will help illustrate the conceptual discussion. Two cases follow this chapter, though due to a close relationship with the transport sector, the Curitiba case given in Chapter 2.2 is also relevant in this section.

Links between the co-benefits approach and urban land use

Land use, in general, refers to the human use of land. In the urban context, land use constitutes the physical basis on which major aspects of urban life and processes materialize. Therefore, land-use structure of a city can be defined as the organization of all key functions and activities that form and shape an urban system. Such an organization of various uses over urban land is usually not random but rather a result of specific public action, namely urban planning. In other words, land use is a key term and a particular focus of urban planning activity (Guttenberg 1959). Cities utilize land-use planning and management practices with the aim of regulating the use of land for various purposes in scientific and aesthetic ways so as to prevent conflicts and inefficiencies. Preventing conflicts and inefficiencies might also help the delivery of multiple benefits.

The structure of land-use organization in a city defines the form of that city. Urban form refers to the size of land area occupied by a city, and to the physical layout of the built-up area of a city. For instance, sprawl or compactness is a matter of size of land area occupied. On the other hand, terms, such as 'linear city' or 'radial city', refer to the physical layout or form of the built-up area of cities. A linear city, for example, has a long and narrow shape, mainly because major land-use elements are located along a transport route, a coastline or river; whereas radial cities, which are usually monocentric, grow in a circular shape around their core.

Land-use organization and urban forms differ substantially among the world's cities. Different socio-economic development patterns in different regional contexts may have varying impacts on urban forms. For instance, there is a fundamental difference between cities in the US and those in Europe, which are characterized by different socio-economic development patterns. The US cities were developed as urban agglomerations facilitated by mass car ownership, spanning large land areas and thus categorized by sprawled patterns of urban development. By contrast, historical European cities are relatively smaller in population size and land area than their counterparts in the US. Some cities in Europe are indicated as good examples of compact cities, including Barcelona, Copenhagen and Amsterdam. Figure 3.1, which was originally developed by

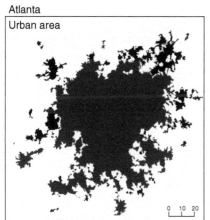
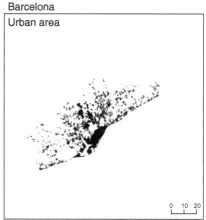

Population: 5.3 million   Urban area: 7,692 km²   Population: 5 million   Urban area: 648 km²
Transport carbon emissions p.c: 6.9 tonnes   Transport carbon emissions p.c: 1.16 tonnes

Figure 3.1 The built-up area of Atlanta (US) and Barcelona (Spain) compared on the same scale.

Sources: LSE Cities 2014a; Litman 2015.

Bertaud and Richardson (2004), is a well-known illustration of the difference between the US and European cities in land-use structure and urban form. Although both cities accommodate similar populations, Atlanta occupies a land area 12 times larger than that of Barcelona.

Another factor that causes differences between land-use structure and forms of cities is the legal and institutional framework for urban land-use management and planning. In contexts where there are strict density and zoning regulations that apply to inner cities, suburbanization and urban development along peripheries are likely to be seen. India is a good example, where density regulations that limit inner-city floor space indices to very low levels have served as an additional driver of sprawl (World Bank 2013). The master plan of Delhi (India) aimed to limit the growth of the core city by constructing a green belt around it, yet it paved the way for a multi-centric and sprawled pattern of urban development in the city (Ahmad et al. 2013). Likewise, strict zoning regulations may also have sprawl-like outcomes due to segregation of activities from each other. The 'Green Paper on the Urban Environment' (Commission of the European Communities 1990), released by the European Commission in 1990, criticizes the 'modern' urban planning approach, particularly taking aim at strict zoning policies. The report emphasizes that strict zoning policies of the past decades led to separation of land uses and subsequent development of extensive residential suburbs, which has in turn stimulated commuter traffic and associated environmental problems (Commission of the European Communities 1990). On the other hand, where there are loose controls over land-use development, urban sprawl can also take place owing to pressures and initiatives of the construction industry to develop peripheral lands into residential areas of middle- and high-income groups (Balaban 2012b). A plausible solution to this dilemma could be to promote infill development and urban regeneration projects in inner cities (Balaban and Puppim de Oliveira 2014), and apply strict land-use controls and zoning regulations on peripheral locations.

Urban forms may have substantial implications for climate policy. The energy and resource consumption as well as the expenditures for service provision in cities are highly determined by their form and land-use structure. Sprawled urbanization, for instance, results in higher per capita land development, dispersal of urban activities and thus longer travel distances. The practical outcomes of urban sprawl are observed in the form of higher infrastructure requirements and costs as well as increased demand for motorized travel (Litman 2015). Ribbon development in Metro Manila (Philippines), a precursor of urban sprawl, has increased average trip lengths from 5.3 to 6.4 km, and average commuting times from 36 to 51 minutes between 1980 and 1996 (Lebel et al. 2007). There is now a consensus to prevent sprawled patterns of urban development and develop cities in more compact forms so as to make people live close to work places and everyday services. Recent research shows that doubling densities within metropolitan regions in the US can reduce vehicle-kilometers-travelled (VKT) by up to 25 percent when also concentrating employment (Rode et al. 2014). In Portland (US), per capita vehicle trips were decreased 17 percent by promoting compact urban growth since 1990, and GHG emissions were kept at 1990 levels, despite a 16 percent growth in population (Condon *et al.* 2009). The difference between land areas of Atlanta and Barcelona manifests itself with the six-fold difference between their transport-related CO_2 emissions per capita (Figure 3.1).

Structurally, the land-use sector encompasses actions that shape spatial organization of key functions and activities in a city. In this respect, the land-use sector is a crosscutting one that directly or indirectly influences other key sectors in an urban system, such as transportation, infrastructure, buildings, etc. The effectiveness of any action or policy intervention in the latter mentioned sectors may or may not be deepened by the land-use pattern of that city. The land-use sector, thereby, promises substantial co-benefits through its linkages with other urban sectors. However, the emergence of co-benefits in the sector could also be realized via particular elements or components of urban land use.

Thus, appropriate strategies are required to achieve co-benefits in the land-use sector. The Avoid-Shift-Improve (A-S-I) framework provides an essential conceptual basis on which a variety of co-benefits strategies could be envisaged. The A-S-I framework was initially utilized in the urban transport sector to replace the traditional measures with new and innovative strategies that bring about sustainable solutions for transport problems. The framework aims to develop alternative mobility solutions and sustainable transport systems that deliver co-benefits in terms of GHG mitigation, energy savings, less congestion, etc. (Deutsche Gesellschaft für Internationale Zusammenarbeit [GIZ] 2011). In this respect, the framework can be employed in other urban sectors, including the land-use sector, where appropriate policies promise significant co-benefits.

The A-S-I framework provides three fundamental pathways for strategy development, which are *Avoid*, *Shift* and *Improve* (GIZ 2011). With the application of the A-S-I framework in the land-use sector, strategies for co-benefits can take the form of particular actions or policies that either *avoid* or *shift* urban development as well as *improve* the use of urban space accordingly to achieve better energy and resource efficiency and to mitigate adverse environmental impacts. Natural areas like forests and wetlands not only serve as carbon sinks but also help mitigate air pollution. Besides, such green spaces are useful to mitigate flood risks and the urban heat island effect (Handley *et al.* 2007). Therefore, as part of urban and land-use planning interventions, strategies could be developed to *avoid* urban development over critical natural reserves and green spaces. In case there are degraded natural areas in and around cities, land-use strategies should focus on *improving* both the already degraded areas and the entire land-use structure so as to ensure green space provision and connectivity. Furthermore, future urban development in cities should be *shifted* away from suburbs and towards places that are close to public transport systems. The 'Split-Zoning' strategy of the eThekwini Municipality in Durban (South Africa) is a good example to materialize the Avoid-Shift-Improve approach (see Chapter 3.1). In order to improve the conservation situation of environmentally sensitive areas, city government divides a zone into 'residential portion' and 'conservation portion', and *avoids* urban development in the 'conservation portion' by *shifting* the development rights from the 'conservation portion' to the 'residential portion'. Figure 3.2 conceptualizes the use of the A-S-I framework in the land-use sector and underlines the major strategic pathways and likely co-benefits of initiatives in the sector.

Consequently, there are two conceptual dimensions of the land-use and co-benefits debate, in each of which relevant land-use policies and strategies could bring substantial co-benefits. These dimensions can be classified as *land-use patterns* and *land-use elements*. The following sections elaborate on each of these dimensions as possible areas for co-benefits in the land-use sector and discuss the likely co-benefit strategies with regard to each dimension.

Land-use patterns

As a crosscutting sector of urban development, the land-use sector has strong ties with many other urban sectors. Among them is the urban transportation sector, which is one of the major sources of GHG emissions and local environmental problems. The transport sector is one of the key sectors in climate change mitigation. The sector is responsible for 21 percent of the world's energy-related CO_2 emissions and this share is expected to increase up to 23 percent by 2030 (Grazi and Van den Bergh 2008). Urban transport deserves particular attention, since more than 60 percent of all kilometers traveled globally take place in urban areas (Van Audenhove *et al.* 2014). Urban transportation is also responsible for local problems, including air and noise pollution, accidents, etc. For instance, vehicular pollution is the major contributor to worsening air quality in Delhi (India) with 70 percent contribution to the city's total pollution in 2000–2001 (Sidhartha 2003).

Urban transport, as the largest source of transport-related GHG emissions and urban air pollution, deserves to be a major focus of environmental policy-making. Innovative policies are required to minimize the contribution of urban transport to global and local environmental problems. However, this cannot be done easily without intervening in the physical structure of cities. In other words, policy options in the urban transport sector should consider urban forms and be supported with policy interventions in the land-use sector. The reason is that urban accessibility pathways and mobility patterns are created through the co-dependence of land-use and urban transport systems (Rode *et al.* 2014). Thus, one critical factor for effective co-benefits policies in the transport sector is integration of these policies with land-use strategies (Grazi and Van den Bergh 2008; Lebel *et al.* 2007; Dulal *et al.* 2011; Muniz and Galiando 2005).

Land-use structure shapes the spatial distribution of urban functions, and thus affects travel demand, travel distances, travel times and mode choices by increasing or decreasing the physical separation of urban functions, destinations and citizens (Santos *et al.* 2010; Grazi and Van den Bergh 2008). Sprawled urban development calls for increased use of private vehicles for urban transportation. In sprawled and dispersed cities, large areas of land which are

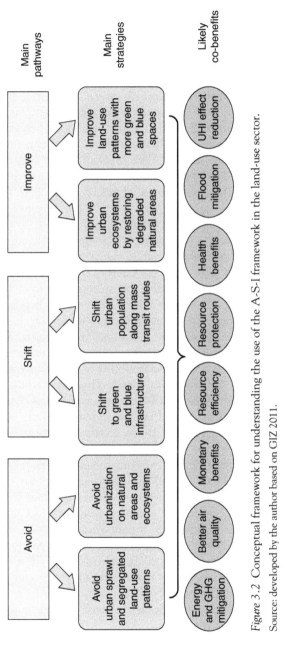

Figure 3.2 Conceptual framework for understanding the use of the A-S-I framework in the land-use sector.

Source: developed by the author based on GIZ 2011.

occupied by various urban uses are hard to access and require longer trips, leading to a dependence on private vehicles (Lebel *et al.* 2007). Alternatively, compact cities, where people, organizations and activities are in close proximity, can increase the number of possible destinations that can be reached within the same range of distance, and this in turn can promote a shift in travel mode choice from private to public transport (Grazi and Van den Bergh 2008). Figure 3.3 clearly illustrates that sprawled cities could be categorized as car-oriented agglomerations, whereas compact cities appear to be walkable and public transport-based urban environments (Rode *et al.* 2014).

Furthermore, the cost of provision of public transport infrastructure in sprawled cities is very high due to the need for longer routes to cover as many neighborhoods as possible and therefore more resources required to provide an acceptable standard of service. High costs of public transport infrastructure usually discourage city administrations of sprawled cities to invest in public transport systems. There are substantial differences in levels of access to public transportation between sprawled and compact cities (Figure 3.3).

Land-use strategies also affect travel habits through the spatial distribution of population, and more specifically, population density. Densely populated settlements may be more amenable to public transportation and non-motorized travel options (Muniz and Galiando 2005). US-based studies show that more intensive and denser land use can give a reduction of 10 percent in urban transport activity without reducing accessibility (Grazi and Van den Bergh 2008). In parts of cities where the population is concentrated more densely, it may be possible to have well-traveled corridors organized as mass transit routes. The overlapping of well-traveled corridors and mass transit routes may increase ridership levels and contribute to the effectiveness and feasibility of transit systems. This issue could also be dealt with the other way round. Through land-use strategies, urban population can be concentrated along mass transit routes to create corridors traveled by mass transit systems. In this regard, much can be learnt from the city of Curitiba in Brazil. Since the 1970s, Curitiba has been working to provide high-capacity and reliable bus services in segregated corridors to attract more users to the system, and for concentrating the growing population along the bus system via special land-use and zoning regulations (see the Curitiba case, Chapter 2.2). This policy is known to result in significant co-benefits in Curitiba. For instance, 45 percent of all commuting trips in Curitiba are made by buses, which is the highest rate of public transportation ridership in Brazil, whilst fuel usage in Curitiba is 30 percent lower than the fuel usage in Brazil's other major cities (Suzuki *et al.* 2010; Friberg 2000), though the middle- and high-income dwellers living next to the corridors tend to use cars as a means of urban transport (see Chapter 2.2). The high use of buses in urban transport as well as the fleet renovation that leads to the use of young buses has reduced pollution in the city markedly.

Consequently, urban land-use strategies and transport policies need to be well-coordinated and integrated in order to increase effectiveness of transport policies in bringing co-benefits. Different modes of the urban transport sector

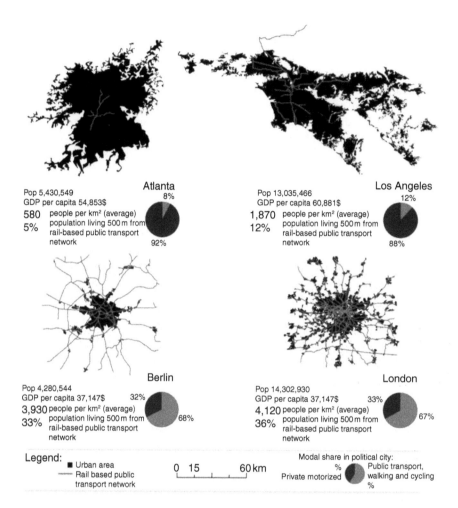

Figure 3.3 Urban form and modal share (black in pie chart is private motorized) of selected cities.

Sources: LSE Cities 2014b; Rode *et al.* 2014.

should also be integrated to achieve multi-modal connectivity. Urban planning can play a key role in coordinating and integrating transportation initiatives and land-use strategies through a number of instruments like zoning of urban functions, building density regulations and infrastructure provision. The core principle of integrated land-use and transport policies still persists in Curitiba, with the bus system having grown substantially over time, currently reaching almost 90 percent of the entire city area (Suzuki *et al.* 2010).

Other intersectoral (crosscutting) impacts of the land-use sector can be seen in the housing sector. Land-use structure and urban form also shape housing provision in cities in terms of housing types and densities. Sprawled cities are usually characterized by housing developments in peripheries and such housing developments consist of large and detached suburban houses, which provide its inhabitants with greater indoor spaces and large gardens. This type of housing provision brings with it significant environmental footprints due to higher energy and resource demands. Energy use in suburban houses is considerably higher than that of houses in central locations of compact cities, which are easier served via district heating and cooling systems. Estiri (2012) argues that, in the US, the biggest difference between cities and suburbs in energy consumption originates from building characteristics, underscoring that suburban houses are 19 percent more influential in increasing per-capita energy consumption. In a similar direction, Rode et al. (2014) found that compact and taller building types can improve energy efficiency at the neighborhood level by a factor of six compared to detached houses. Furthermore, water consumption is also higher in sprawled cities, where suburban residents enjoy their large lawns and gardens, which are regularly watered.

Another intersectoral (crosscutting) link could be drawn between land-use and infrastructure sectors. Infrastructure provision is a key component of economic costs and energy consumption in cities. In sprawled cities, as the built-up areas span larger areas, infrastructure-related costs increase. The cost increase comes in two forms; first, the additional costs of infrastructure provision to larger areas and, second, the additional energy costs used to operate larger infrastructure systems. Recent research has shown that external costs of urban sprawl in the US correspond to about US$400 billion per year, 65 percent of which is due to the increased cost of providing public services such as water and waste and to increased capital investment needs for infrastructure such as roads (Litman 2015). As per the suggestion made by the World Bank, China could manage to save up to US$1.4 trillion in infrastructure spending (15 percent of the country's 2013 GDP) with more compact city development (Rode et al. 2014). Appropriate strategies may help replace costly concrete structures and hard infrastructure measures with natural systems and green spaces, and decrease the total expenditure made by city governments, as in the example of Durban city (see the Durban case that follows). Likewise, in Curitiba, the flooding problem has been addressed by creating natural drainage systems and enhancing the green areas and recreational facilities rather than controlling water flow by means of concrete structures (Suzuki et al. 2010). The cost of building parks and relocating the informal settlements from flood-prone sites were found to be five times less than the cost of building concrete canals and structures (Suzuki et al. 2010).

The crosscutting links of the land-use sector with other sectors are potential fields where appropriate policy interventions could generate substantial co-benefits. Table 3.1 below presents an overview of potential co-benefits that could be delivered by means of land-use sector policies.

Land-use elements

Direct and indirect climate benefits could be generated via specific elements of urban land use. Among the most important of such land-use elements is a range of green and blue spaces. Vegetation, soils and water bodies provide multiple benefits at both local and global levels. For instance, green areas can contribute to reducing air pollution thus decreasing negative health effects on urban residents, while mitigating GHG emissions by absorbing CO_2. Literature on health co-benefits of climate mitigation in urban areas focuses mostly on the linkages between GHG mitigation policies and resulting reduction in $PM_{2.5}$ and ozone precursors (Darby and Kinney 2007). Likewise, land-use policies can be effective for creating compact urban forms that facilitate the preservation of nearby resources (water catchment areas, forests, agricultural lands, etc.) and mitigate carbon emissions mainly from reducing land appropriation for development and transportation of people and goods. On the other hand, co-benefits can also emerge the other way round. Policies targeting to improve the city ecosystem, often in collaboration with local communities, can have significant outcomes, such as GHG and air pollution reduction, while generating additional health benefits (i.e. improved food access) and achieving broader developmental goals (e.g. community inclusion).

Intersectoral or crosscutting linkages emerging from green and blue infrastructure provision can be especially relevant for developing cities, especially the Asian and African mega cities, where big shares of their residents are vulnerable to climate change, and suffer from pollution and derived health impacts. The following sections explore the co-benefits potential of specific green and blue infrastructure elements in terms of climate mitigation, air pollution control, and other social, economic and environmental benefits.

Urban soils

The importance of protecting or increasing the carbon storage capacity of cities by terrestrial carbon sequestration (biological sequestration or bio-sequestration) is highly acknowledged in the climate change debate. Terrestrial carbon sequestration not only refers to forest areas but also to degraded soils. Urban soils have the potential to sequester large amounts of carbon, despite regional variations and land-cover distributions (Pouyat *et al.* 2006). Yet, many urban soils lack adequate carbon storage capacity as a result of development and/or pollution impacts. In order to improve urban soils' capacity for carbon storage, new technologies are being developed. In Japan, for example, some experiences exist with soil remediation using innovative technology combining air spraying and water injection for soils damaged by benzene, cyanide and hydrocarbons, which can in turn eliminate the emission of pollutants from the soil and restore the soils' capacity to store carbon.

Urban greenery and trees

Appropriate management of urban trees can be a multifaceted co-benefit instrument by contributing positively to GHG and air pollution mitigation while providing other social, economic and ecological co-benefits. First of all, urban trees store carbon, and thus contribute to climate change mitigation. A Japanese cedar tree, for instance, can absorb 14 kg of CO_2 in a year (Suzuki et al. 2010). Trees in New York are known to store approximately 1.2 million tonnes of carbon, which corresponds to the amount emitted by residents of New York in about ten days (Nowak and Crane 2000). The city of Kanazawa on the northern coast of Japan is an example of how urban forests can play a role in contributing to mitigation and local pollution control efforts, while providing additional benefits ranging from increased recreational space and spiritual value, local sources of construction and public works materials and bio-energy, together with ecological corridors and urban biodiversity (UNU-IAS 2011).

Temperature regulation is a major benefit of urban greenery, and urban trees in particular. Transpiration and canopies are known to affect air temperature, radiation absorption and heat storage, wind speed, relative humidity, turbulence, surface albedo, surface roughness and thus the evolution of the mixing-layer height. These changes in local meteorology can alter pollution concentrations in urban areas (Nowak et al. 1998). Thus reduced air temperature via trees can improve urban air quality, as the concentration of many pollutants and/or ozone-forming chemicals are temperature dependent. In addition, decreased air temperatures can also provide cooling for urban buildings and reduce air conditioning demand up to 30 percent (Nowak et al. 1998).

Moreover, urban greenery is also known to provide regulating type ecosystem services such as flood mitigation. The green spaces absorb the excess rainfall and decrease surface runoff, which in turn reduces the risk of flash flooding. The use of green spaces, parks and recreational areas as flood prevention measures is becoming a common and a cost-effective solution among the world's cities. Curitiba has been working to expand the green cover in the city, turning the riverbeds into parks and constructing lakes to contain floodwaters and control flooding in a natural way (Suzuki et al. 2010). In a similar vein, Durban has prioritized Ecosystem-Based Adaptation (EBA) as a key climate protection strategy through provision and conservation of an open space system. Durban's Metropolitan Open Space System (D'MOSS) was designed as an interconnected green space system comprising ecological valuable areas in both private- and public-owned lands with the aim of achieving various ecosystem goods and services (see Chapter 3.1).

Green curtains and rooftops

There are numerous initiatives around the world regarding the use of green curtains and rooftops for cooling purposes. On rooftops, plants give off moisture and provide insulation, and lower temperatures both inside and outside buildings.

However, the benefits of rooftop greenery are not limited to cooling of buildings. In Singapore, a survey by the National Park Board showed that rooftop gardens, which are called 'skyrise greening' in the local context, can effectively bring multiple environmental benefits, including alleviation of heat islands by shading heat-absorbing surfaces, reduction of flash floods, air quality improvement and enhancement of biodiversity (Skyrise Greenery 2016). Even food production can be regarded as one of the co-benefits of green roofs, considering increasing use of green roofs for urban agriculture (Whittinghill and Rowe 2012). Recent research has shown that, if properly managed, an extensive green roof system can be productive in vegetable and herb production (Whittinghill *et al*. 2013).

In Japan, the use of green roofs in urban development has increased noticeably in recent years due in large part to some local policies and actions. In April 2001, the Tokyo Metropolitan Government enacted an ordinance that requires construction companies to install green roofs on 20 percent of all new flat roof surfaces on public buildings exceeding $250\,m^2$, and 10 percent of all flat roofs on private buildings exceeding $1,000\,m^2$. This policy is known to result in the construction of around $50,000\,m^2$ of green roofs annually (Harrison 2013). Moreover, most of the green buildings that were recently built in the Tokyo Metropolitan Area have either rooftop greenery or green curtains; in some cases, both strategies are applied in tandem (Balaban 2013).

Water bodies

The appropriate use of storm water is an essential way of achieving co-benefits through blue infrastructure management. Storm water runoff ponds are an increasingly common method to collect and store urban waters for several purposes, such as flood regulation and water recovery. In Curitiba (Brazil), flood control areas are principally used as parks and recreation areas. A former flood prone area that was occupied by slum dwellers has been converted into a 140-hectare urban park (Barigüi Park), which includes a 40-hectare lake that stores storm water. In addition, urban rainwater storage can provide co-benefits in terms of resource efficiency because stored water can be used locally for irrigation, and thus not only improves urban green spaces but also addresses water shortage. Table 3.1 summarizes some of the potential co-benefits that could be delivered by means of land-use sector policies.

Challenges and opportunities to enhance co-benefits

Although the land-use sector promises substantial co-benefits due to its linkages with other key sectors in an urban system, it is not straightforward to realize the multiple benefits that are rooted in urban land use. There are major and minor challenges that need to be eliminated for achieving wider co-benefits via policy interventions in the land-use sector. On the other hand, there are also emerging opportunities which may be useful to eliminate the major challenges that hinder the realization of potential co-benefits.

Table 3.1 Potential co-benefits of policy options in the land-use sector

Policy fields in the land-use sector		Types of likely co-benefits							
		Energy and GHG reduction	Better air quality	Monetary benefits[1]	Resource efficiency[2]	Resource protection[3]	Health benefits[4]	Flood mitigation	UHI effect reduction
Land-use patterns	Land-use-transport	✓	✓	✓			✓		
	Land-use-infrastructure	✓		✓	✓				
	Land-use-housing	✓	✓	✓	✓	✓	✓		
Land-use elements	Green spaces	✓	✓	✓	✓	✓	✓	✓	✓
	Blue spaces			✓	✓	✓	✓	✓	✓
	Urban soils	✓				✓		✓	

Notes
1 Monetary benefits originate from efficient use of energy and resources and also from use of local resources.
2 In terms of efficient use of natural resources, such as water, land, etc.
3 Protection of natural resources, such as agricultural lands, forests, biodiversity, etc.
4 In terms of reduction in traffic accidents, obesity, respiratory diseases and increase in local food production and improved food access.

Among the major challenges is the need for good coordination among key policy fields of an urban system. As discussed in previous sections, the land-use sector is a crosscutting sector with strong ties to other sectors, such as transport, housing, infrastructure, etc. Therefore, the success of any policy intervention in land-use planning and management is dependent on other key sectoral policies. In case of low or no coordination, adverse impacts that may offset co-benefits are very likely to emerge. For instance, in Curitiba, the zoning policy that promoted high-rise residential developments along bus routes was not well-coordinated with social policy concerns, and hence led to increase in real estate values. This turned the high-rise buildings along bus routes into gated communities of middle- and high-income groups, which predominantly opt for private cars as a means of urban transport (see the Curitiba case, Chapter 2.2).

Such good coordination among policies necessitates good communication among all relevant public bodies and policymakers. In most countries, governance systems are characterized by a departmental approach, in which there are specific departments to deal with different aspects of main policy fields. Under such a departmental approach, it may be difficult to ensure good coordination among various departments and thereby among different sectoral policies. Besides, in developing mega-cities, there may be different camps in the policy debate, working to influence government decisions on key urban planning and development issues. In such cases, the competition among different camps might lead to loss of opportunities and waste of resources. The Delhi Metro case is an example of such a situation. Delhi is known as a city where several institutions are working to improve the urban transport infrastructure by building BRT lines, monorail, light rail and metro systems, yet with limited coordination and cooperation (Thynell *et al.* 2010). One of the factors that limited the success of the Delhi Metro in terms of low ridership and the low level of shift to metro from car users is the lack of coordination between the metro project and land-use patterns as well as other transport modes in the city (Doll and Balaban 2013). Low ridership on the Delhi Metro and lower shift from private modes has been claimed to be caused by the unsuitable land-use structure of Delhi (Sahai and Bishop 2010; Mohan 2008). As a polycentric city with no clearly identifiable central business district (Sahai and Bishop 2010), economic activities and major employment areas are not concentrated but rather are dispersed throughout the city. Such land use structure in a city usually generates modest trip lengths for commuting, which are mostly less than 10 km in the case of Delhi (Sahai and Bishop 2010). Mass transit systems perform better in crowded and long commuting corridors, as alternative modes are either less convenient or costly in such corridors. On the other hand, shorter commuting trips may increase the attractiveness of private transport modes, discourage commuters to use mass transit systems or enable them to switch between public modes. In the Delhi case, the metro system has failed to attract many of the car and motorcycle users but has earned patronage from public buses. Recent research has shown that there is a mismatch between current urban development hotspots and metro corridors in Delhi (Ahmad *et al.* 2016).

Time is often overlooked as a barrier to achieve more co-benefits in the land-use sector. The benefits of policy responses in the land-use sector may only come in the long term, as most land-use policies are structural interventions in urban spatial organization. Such interventions usually require long lead times to be developed and implemented. Even if they are successfully implemented, time would still be required to obtain the outcomes. Nevertheless, city governments and politicians who are willing to stand out in the short term may not be patient enough to wait for such policies to bear fruit, since most benefits will come long after they have left office. Furthermore, it is not very easy to manifest and quantify the co-benefits of policy interventions in the land-use sector due to the timescale of policy implementation and the strong links to other sectors. The difficulty in manifestation of policy benefits may also serve as another factor that discourages politicians and decision-makers at the local level.

On the other hand, there are also opportunities which may help cities to develop policies for co-benefits in the land-use sector. The growing recognition of environmental problems and the cost of suburban living present a significant opportunity. In recent decades, urban residents in advanced developed countries, in particular the US, have started to move to cities rather than living in suburbs. As per the US Census Bureau data, in 2013, 2.3 million more people were found to live in cities rather than suburbs as opposed to the previous year (Westcott 2014). The trend in city living may encourage city governments to pursue policies for compact and mixed-use urban development.

Another opportunity is the rise of civil society initiatives in many cities and of city networks at regional and global levels. People are now highly aware of the fact that cities are responsible for environmental problems and also hold the key for a better and sustainable future. Urban activists urge city governments to take action towards making cities low-carbon, resilient and smart. In this sense, cities that are keen to develop strategies for low-carbon and resilient urban development now have the opportunity to learn from each other, thanks to the international city networks. In particular, cities with less capacity in the developing world could benefit from the guidelines developed and best practices documented by the city networks (see Chapter 9 on international cooperation).

Lifestyle change is a must to overcome the barriers towards more co-benefits in the land-use sector. Suburban living, occupation of large houses and use of private vehicles are matters of lifestyle choice. In many cases, people opt for such choices not because they have to due to the circumstances in cities but because they want to reach an affluent lifestyle and hence a higher social status. However, such lifestyle choices bring about high costs to the entire society, even to the global society. Policy and decision-makers should find ways to influence lifestyle choices of local people and convince them to opt for more sustainable consumption patterns. It is imperative to develop and implement policies for compact and mixed-use urban development, in which people live in smaller houses in high-rise developments and use public and non-motorized transportation.

Finally, the land-use sector is explicitly local. Most, if not all, of the policy interventions in the land-use sector can be developed, implemented and monitored at the local level. Therefore, it is mainly the local governments which should be given an active role in land-use planning and management. However, in many countries, governance systems are highly centralized and local authorities lack institutional capacities to properly deal with urban land-use problems and manage urban development. As their financial resources are mostly limited, local authorities refrain from involving themselves in structural policy fields. Another facet of low institutional capacity at the local level is lack of human resources. Structural policies that aim to alter land-use patterns involve complicated strategies. Therefore, a certain level of in-house expertise is required to develop integrated policies and strategies to deepen co-benefits in the land-use sector. Many cities are known to lack sufficient human resources even to deal with ordinary problems of urban development. In order to overcome the major barriers that limit land-use sector co-benefits, central governments should empower local authorities and provide them with necessary legal responsibilities as well as financial and human resources.

Conclusion

As a crosscutting sector, the land-use sector has strong links with other key sectors of urban development, including transport, housing and infrastructure. The strong links between the land-use sector and others make it a promising field for policymaking, where appropriate policy options could bring multiple benefits to address social, economic and environmental problems. The co-benefits of land-use sector policies could happen in two ways: first, by means of changes in land-use patterns and urban forms, and second, via specific land-use elements. The Avoid-Shift-Improve framework should be applied to land-use planning and management in order to create a conceptual basis, by which a range of co-benefits policies could be developed.

Accessibility patterns and travel habits in a city are shaped by the city's land-use structure. Urban form and the spatial distribution of functions and population in a given locality affect travel times, travel distances, number of trips and choice of transport modes. As opposed to sprawled urban agglomerations, compact cities with mixed-use quarters accommodate people and urban activities in close proximity, which, in turn, reduce travel distances and times, and promote shifts from private motorized modes to public and non-motorized modes. Land-use planning can play a key role in coordinating and integrating transport policies with land-use patterns through a number of instruments like different zoning and density regulations in inner cities and peripheries, development rights along mass transit routes, infrastructure provision, congestion charges, etc. In addition, land-use planning can also enhance multi-modal integration via, for instance, provision of an extensive network of pedestrian and cycling paths.

Specific land-use elements like urban soils, green spaces and water bodies (blue infrastructure) can address multiple social and environmental challenges simultaneously. Such land-use elements contribute to mitigation of GHGs and air pollutants, and deliver other additional social, economic and ecological benefits. Yet, current understanding of the role of green and blue infrastructure in the generation of co-benefits remains largely fragmented. This, in turn, jeopardizes the success of initiatives that aim to manage these land-use elements for obtaining environmental and human well-being goals at local and global scales. The mainstreaming of the concept of 'urban green and blue infrastructure management' into the land-use/co-benefits debate may promote the understanding of interconnected co-benefits that these two elements can provide. Besides, and even more importantly, we could make a stronger case for policy targeting urban ecosystem management in connection to broader global/local environmental and social benefits.

Good urban governance is key to achieving and supporting innovative initiatives in the land-use sector to promote delivery of co-benefits. The rise of civil society initiatives and city networks, and promotion of decentralization policies recently observed in some contexts are important opportunities towards achieving good urban governance. With the rise of civil society initiatives and city networks, not only do we have more public and private actors in policymaking and implementation, but we also have opportunities to learn from each other's experiences. Furthermore, promotion of decentralization is greatly required for making public decision-making closer to the local level and enabling local governments, which are at the most appropriate level of governance to implement policies, to achieve more co-benefits in the land-use sector.

References

Ahmad, S, Balaban, O, Doll, CNH and Dreyfus, M 2013, 'Delhi revisited', *Cities*, vol. 31, pp. 641–653.

Ahmad, S, Avtar, R, Sethi, M and Surjan, A 2016, 'Delhi's land cover change in post transit era', *Cities*, vol. 50, pp. 111–118.

Balaban, O 2012a, 'Climate change and cities: A review on the impacts and policy responses', *METU Journal of the Faculty of Architecture*, vol. 29, no. 1, pp. 21–44.

Balaban, O 2012b, 'The negative effects of construction boom on urban planning and environment in Turkey: Unraveling the role of the public sector', *Habitat International*, vol. 36, no. 1, pp. 26–35.

Balaban, O 2013, *Co-Benefits of Green Buildings and the Opportunities and Barriers Regarding their Promotion*, UNU-IAS Working Paper No. 171, United Nations University-Institute of Advanced Studies, Yokohama, Japan.

Balaban, O and Puppim de Oliveira, JA 2014, 'Understanding the links between urban regeneration and climate-friendly urban development: Lessons from two case studies in Japan', *Local Environment: The International Journal of Justice and Sustainability*, vol. 19, no. 8, pp. 868–890.

Balaban, O and Puppim de Oliveira, JA 2016, 'Sustainable buildings for healthier cities: Assessing the co-benefits of green buildings in Japan', *Journal of Cleaner Production*, in press, http://dx.doi.org/10.1016/j.jclepro.2016.01.086.

Bertaud, A and Richardson, HW 2004, *Transit and Density: Atlanta, the United States & Western Europe*, e-book, Ashgate Publishing Company, Burlington, Vermont, USA, viewed 3 May 2016, http://courses.washington.edu/gmforum/Readings/Bertaud_Transit_US_Europe.pdf.

Bulkeley, H 2010, 'Cities and the governing of climate change', *Annual Review of Environment and Resources*, vol. 35, pp. 229–253.

Bulkeley, H 2013, *Climate Change and the City*, Routledge, London.

Commission of the European Communities 1990, *Green Paper on the Urban Environment: Communication from the Commission to the Council and Parliament*, COM (1990) 218, European Commission, Brussels, Belgium, viewed 3 May 2016, http://aei.pitt.edu/1205/1/urban_environment_gp_COM_90_218.pdf.

Condon, PM, Cavens, D and Miller, N 2009, *Urban Planning Tools for Climate Change Mitigation*, *Policy Focus Report*, Lincoln Institute of Land Policy, Cambridge, MA, USA.

Darby, W and Kinney, PL 2007, 'Health co-benefits of climate mitigation in urban areas', *Current Opinion in Environmental Sustainability*, vol. 2, no. 3, pp. 172–177.

Deutsche Gesellschaft für Internationale Zusammenarbeit (GIZ) GmbH, 2011, *Sustainable Urban Transport: Avoid-Shift-Improve (A-S-I)*, e-book, Deutsche Gesellschaft für Internationale Zusammenarbeit (GIZ) GmbH, Eschborn, Germany, viewed 3 May 2016, www.transport2020.org/file/ASI-factsheet-eng.pdf.

Doll, CNH and Balaban, O 2013, 'A methodology for evaluating environmental co-benefits in the transport sector: Application to the Delhi Metro', *Journal of Cleaner Production*, vol. 58, pp. 61–73.

Dulal, HB, Brodnig, G and Onoriose, CG 2011, 'Climate change mitigation in the transport sector through urban planning: A review', *Habitat International*, vol. 35, no. 3, pp. 494–500.

Estiri, H 2012, *Residential Energy Use and the City-Suburb Dichotomy*, e-book, University of Washington, USA, viewed 3 May 2016, http://ssrn.com/abstract=2226806.

Friberg, L 2000, 'Innovative solutions for public transport: Curitiba, Brazil, 3rd edition', *Sustainable Development International*, pp. 153–156, viewed 3 May 2016, http://infohouse.p2ric.org/ref/40/39732.pdf.

Grazi, F and Van den Bergh, JCJM 2008, 'Spatial organization, transport, and climate change: Comparing instruments of spatial planning and policy', *Ecological Economics*, vol. 67, no. 4, pp. 630–639.

Guttenberg, AZ 1959, 'A multiple land-use classification system', *Journal of the American Planning Association*, vol. 25, no. 3, pp. 143–150.

Handley, J, Pauleit, S and Gill, S 2007, *Landscape, Sustainability and the City*, Landscape and Sustainability, 2nd Edition, Spon Press, London.

Harrison, B 2013, 'The use of greenery to combat urban warming in Tokyo', *Journal of Policy & Culture*, vol. 21, pp. 51–66.

Lebel, L, Garden, P, Banaticla, MRN, Lasco, RD, Contreras, A, Mitra, AP, Sharma, C, Nguyen, HT, Ooi, GL and Sari, A 2007, 'Integrating carbon management into the development strategies of urbanizing regions in Asia: Implications of urban function, form, and role', *Journal of Industrial Ecology*, vol. 11, no. 2, pp. 61–81.

Litman, T 2015, *The New Climate Economy*, NCE Cities – Sprawl Subsidy Report Analysis of Public Policies That Unintentionally Encourage and Subsidize Urban Sprawl, e-book, Victoria Transport Policy Institute, Canada, viewed 4 May 2016, https://files.lsecities.net/files/2015/03/NCE-Sprawl-Subsidy-Report-021.pdf.

London School of Economics and Political Science (LSE) Cities 2014a, *Better Growth, Better Climate: The New Climate Economy Report*, Cities, Chapter 2, e-book, London School of Economics and Political Science (LSE) Cities, UK, viewed 4 May 2016,

http://2014.newclimateeconomy.report/wp-content/uploads/2014/08/NCE-cities-web.
    pdf.
London School of Economics and Political Science (LSE) Cities 2014b. *Transport Related
    Carbon Emissions in Atlanta and Barcelona: Updated Comparative Calculations*, Working
    paper, London, LSE Cities.
Mohan, D 2008. *Metros, Mythologies and Future Urban Transport*. TRIPP Report, 08.01.
    Transportation Research and Injury Prevention Programme, Indian Institute of Tech-
    nology Delhi, New Delhi.
Muniz, I and Galindo, A 2005, 'Urban form and the ecological footprint of commuting:
    The case of Barcelona', *Ecological Economics*, vol. 55, no. 4, pp. 499–514.
Nowak, DJ and Crane, DE 2000, *Integrated Tools for Natural Resources Inventories in the
    21st Century, The Urban Forest Effects (UFORE) Model: Quantifying Urban Forest
    Structure and Functions*, e-book, United States Department of Agriculture, USA,
    viewed 4 May 2016, www.nrs.fs.fed.us/pubs/gtr/gtr_nc212/gtr_nc212_714.pdf.
Nowak, DJ, McHale, PJ, Ibarra, M, Crane, D, Stevens, J and Luley, C 1998, 'Modeling
    the effects of urban vegetation on air pollution', *Air Pollution Modeling and Its Applica-
    tion XII*, vol. 22, pp. 399–407.
Pouyat, RV, Yesilonis, ID and Nowak, DJ 2006, 'Carbon storage by urban soils in the
    United States', *Journal of Environmental Quality*, vol. 35, no. 4, pp. 1566–1575.
Puppim de Oliveira, JA 2011, *ASPA 11th International Congress, Planning for Sustainable
    Asian Cities, Urban Co-benefits Policies and Innovation Capacity in Cities: Planning for
    Tackling Local and Global Environmental Challenges in Asia*, Asian Planning Schools
    Association, Tokyo, Japan.
Puppim de Oliveira, JA, Doll, CNH, Kurniawan, TA, Geng, Y, Kapshe, M and Huisingh,
    D 2013, 'Promoting win–win situations in climate change mitigation, local environ-
    mental quality and development in Asian cities through co-benefits', *Journal of Cleaner
    Production*, vol. 58, no. 1, pp. 1–6.
Rode, P, Floater, G, Thomopoulos, N, Docherty, J, Schwinger, P, Mahendra, A and
    Fang, W 2014 *Accessibility in Cities: Transport and Urban Form, NCE Cities Paper 03,
    The New Climate Economy*, e-book, London School of Economics and Political Science
    (LSE) Cities, UK, viewed 4 May 2016, http://newclimateeconomy.report/2015/wp-
    content/uploads/2016/04/LSE-Cities-2014-Transport-and-Urban-Form-NCE-Cities-
    Paper-03.pdf.
Sahai, SN and Bishop, S 2010, 'Multi modal transport in a low carbon future', in *India
    Infrastructure Report 2010*, pp. 310–330, viewed 21 September 2016, www.idfc.com/
    pdf/report/Chapter-19.pdf.
Santos, G, Behrendt, H and Teytelboym, A 2010, 'Part II: Policy instruments for sustain-
    able road transport', *Research in Transportation Economics*, vol. 28, no. 1, pp. 46–91.
Sidhartha, PG 2003, 'Present scenario of air quality in Delhi: A case study of CNG
    implementation', *Atmospheric Environment*, vol. 37, no. 38, pp. 5423–5431.
Skyrise Greenery 2016, *Gardens in the Sky*, viewed 4 May 2016, www.skyrisegreenery.
    com/.
Suzuki, H, Dastur, A, Moffatt, S, Yabuki, N and Maruyama, H 2010, *Eco2 Cities: Ecolo-
    gical Cities as Economic Cities*, The World Bank, Washington DC.
Thynell, M, Mohan, D and Tiwari, G 2010, 'Sustainable transport and the moderniza-
    tion of urban transport in Delhi and Stockholm', *Cities*, vol. 27, no. 6, pp. 421–429.
United Nations, Department of Economic and Social Affairs (UN-DESA), Population
    Division 2014, *World Urbanization Prospects: The 2014 Revision, Highlights*, e-book,

United Nations, New York, USA, viewed 4 May 2016, http://esa.un.org/unpd/wup/Publications/Files/WUP2014-Highlights.pdf.

United Nations, Human Settlements Programme (UN-HABITAT) 2010, *The State of Asian Cities 2010/2011*, e-book, United Nations, Human Settlements Programme, Fukuoaka, Japan, viewed 4 May 2016, www.rrojasdatabank.info/citiesasia1011.pdf.

United Nations University Institute of Advanced Studies (UNU-IAS), Operating Unit Ishikawa/Kazanawa 2011, *Biodiversity in Kanazawa: Through the Four Seasons, Kanazawa City, Japan*, e-book, United Nations University Institute of Advanced Studies, Ishikawa, Japan, viewed 4 May 2016, http://archive.ias.unu.edu/resource_centre/Bio diversity%20in%20Kanazawa.pdf.

Van Audenhove, FJ, Korniichuk, O, Dauby, L and Pourbaix, J 2014 *The Future of Urban Mobility 2.0*, e-book, Arthur D. Little, headquarters worldwide and International Association of Public Transport UITP, Belgium, viewed 4 May 2016, www.uitp.org/sites/default/files/members/140124%20Arthur%20D.%20Little%20%26%20UITP_Future%20of%20Urban%20Mobility%202%200_Full%20study.pdf.

Westcott, L 2014, 'More Americans moving to cities, reversing the suburban exodus', *The Wire, News from the Atlantic*, viewed 4 May 2016, www.thewire.com/national/2014/03/more-americans-moving-to-cities-reversing-the-suburban-exodus/359714/.

Whittinghill, LJ and Rowe, DB 2012, 'The role of green roof technology in urban agri-culture', *Renewable Agriculture and Food Systems*, vol. 27, no. 4, pp. 314–322.

Whittinghill, LJ, Rowe, DB and Cregg, BM 2013, 'Evaluation of vegetable production on extensive green roofs', *Agroecology and Sustainable Food Systems*, vol. 37, no. 4, pp. 465–484.

World Bank 2013, *Urbanization beyond Municipal Boundaries: Nurturing Metropolitan Eco-nomies and Connecting Peri-Urban Areas in India*, e-book, World Bank, USA, viewed 4 May 2016, www-wds.worldbank.org/external/default/WDSContentServer/WDSP/IB/2013/03/04/000333037_20130304151629/Rendered/PDF/757340PUB0EPI0001300pub date02021013.pdf.

3.1 eThekwini Municipality (Durban), South Africa

Greenspace planning for climate co-benefits

Wan-yu Shih

Introduction

The impact of climate change is a pressing concern for developing countries. Despite the fact that these countries contributed to fewer GHG emissions, they are often more vulnerable to climate change impacts due to the lack of socio-economic development, political constraints and limited access to technology (IPCC 2014). The 2011 United Nations Framework Convention on Climate Change (UNFCCC) Seventeenth Conference of the Parties (COP 17) in Durban, South Africa, shed light on the need of advancing adaptation in climate change through the formation and implementation of National Adaptation Plans (UNFCCC 2011; Munang *et al.* 2013). It acknowledged that 'national adaptation planning can enable all developing and developed country parties to assess their vulnerabilities, to mainstream climate change risks and to address adaptation' (UNFCCC 2011).

In line with this decision, the Durban Local Government Convention: Adapting to a Changing Climate – Towards COP 17 and Beyond in 2011 further drew attention to adaptation planning at the local level, stating that:

> local governments play a strategic role in addressing climate change, because of their direct activities in delivering local government functions; their responsibility for laws and regulations that can influence adaptation and mitigation; and their ability to demonstrate leadership and innovative solutions in this area.
>
> (eThekwini Municipality 2011)

This gives city governments an unprecedented challenge in terms of attaining its mandates of socio-economic development, and at the same time mitigating GHG emissions and reducing negative climate impacts on societies. The Durban Adaptation Charter launched at the convention urges mainstreaming adaptation into all local development planning (eThekwini Municipality 2012). It noted the need of alignment between adaptation and mitigation strategies and prioritised the role of functioning ecosystems as a core municipal green infrastructure (eThekwini Municipality 2011). To some extent, this encourages the transformation of an open space system, which is often a part of urban planning, into an Ecosystem-based Adaptation (EBA) approach for meeting the dual missions of adaptation and mitigation of local governments.

EBA is the use of biodiversity and ecosystem services as part of an overall adaptation strategy to help people to adapt to the negative effect of climate change (SCBD 2009). Through the management, conservation and restoration of ecosystems, a wide range of environmental benefits, such as carbon sequestration, temperature regulation, flood control, erosion prevention and buffering natural hazards, will help cities to reduce the risk of climate disasters (Munang et al. 2013). This concept is aligned with the proposition of Green Infrastructure (GI). GI is a strategic greenspace planning method, which argues that various types of greenspaces can be linked in an interconnected network so as to provide multiple social, economic, environmental and ecological functions (Handley et al. 2007). As GI might be established by optimising existing open space systems in cities, it provides a critical framework and a feasible approach to mainstream climate change into spatial planning systems.

In Durban, the open space system has been regarded as an available, cost-effective and sustainable strategy to cope with climate change (Roberts et al. 2012; ASSAf 2011). It has evolved from a conservation-orientated network into a more multifunctional GI that is expected to deliver several co-benefits: namely, conserving biodiversity, reducing environmental hazards, improving carbon storage and eliminating poverty (eThekwini Municipality & ICLEI Africa Secretariat 2007; Roberts et al. 2012). This case introduces how the open space system in Durban has been transformed to explicitly consider the generation of climate co-benefits.

City context

Durban is the largest harbour city located on the east coast of South Africa, with approximately 3.5 million inhabitants in 2015 (eThekwini Municipality 2016). It extends over an area of 2,297 km² (Figure 3.4) and is planned and managed by the eThekwini Municipality (ibid.). The city of Durban is one of the most important growing economic hubs of South Africa, which (in 2009) contributed 64.1 per cent and 10.4 per cent to the provincial and national GDP respectively (ASSAf 2011). The growing economy over the past decades has resulted in an increase in energy use, leading to more greenhouse gas emissions (eThekwini Municipality 2013). In order to meet South Africa's obligations and commitments to global GHG reduction, the municipality has planned to transform Durban into a low-carbon city.

Meanwhile, rapid urban expansion has given rise to enormous socio-economic and environmental challenges to the city. This includes widespread poverty, a high level of unemployment, deficiency in basic infrastructure (e.g. housing, drains, roads) and destruction of natural areas (e.g. wetlands, grasslands, forests) (Cadman et al. 2010). The census in 2011 showed that over a quarter of households still lived in informal settlements (White et al. 2016) and a large population in the city still depends on ecosystem goods and services for

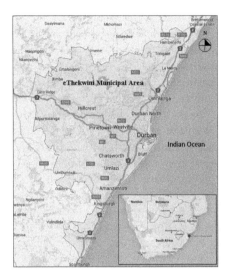

Figure 3.4 The location of the eThekwini municipal area.

Source: Google Maps 2016 (annotated by the author).

sustaining basic livelihoods. Under this condition of underdevelopment, the impact of climate change on existing infrastructure and ecosystems is a serious threat to vulnerable local communities. Hence, the municipal government regards climate change adaptation that helps local communities to reduce environmental and socio-economic vulnerability and to adapt to extreme weather conditions as an imperative mission (Roberts 2012).

Against this development context, Durban proposed the Municipal Climate Protection Programme (MCPP) in 2004 to synergistically respond to both adaptation and mitigation (Douwes *et al.* 2015). The MCPP programme consisted of four major phases. Phase 1 was conducted during 2004–2006 to assess the local impacts of climate change as well as carbon storage and sequestration (Roberts 2014). In Phase 2, extensive discussions were conducted amongst municipal departments to identify the sectors and the extent to which they are vulnerable to climate change impacts; and the ways they can and/or have engaged with climate adaptation (Carmin *et al.* 2009). This exercise produced appropriate adaptation and mitigation responses and strategies at the municipal and community level that takes into account ecosystem-based adaptation and urban management strategies (Roberts 2014). Phase 3, started in 2007, developed a toolkit for integrative assessment and will take cost–benefit analysis into account; finally Phase 4 focuses on mainstreaming climate protection into the areas of the Integrated Development Plan, institutions, key city events, international advocacy and Durban Climate Change Strategy (ibid.). During this process, the Durban Metropolitan Open Space System (D'MOSS) was regarded as a critical ecosystem-based adaptation strategy in the Municipal Adaptation Plans (ibid.), as well as a central element for low-carbon urban development by serving as a carbon storage system (Diab and Roberts 2012).

Durban's Metropolitan Open Space System (D'MOSS)

Durban is the first city in South Africa to formally include an open space system in its town planning schemes. This city-wide open space system was first developed in 1979 to protect important natural areas from urban development (eThekwini Municipality and ICLEI Africa Secretariat 2007). The system has been transformed over years due to the availability of data as well as changing attitudes to the environment and planning. Currently, D'MOSS is an interconnected green-space system comprising 95,000 ha of ecologically valuable areas in both private- and public-owned lands (eThekwini Municipality and ICLEI Africa Secretariat 2007), including thickets, woodlands, forests, grasslands, freshwater wetlands, estuarine areas and artificial waterbodies (Roberts and O'Donoghue 2013).

Unlike open space systems in many cities, which have a recreational emphasis, D'MOSS originally focused on the conservation of ecologically valuable areas, as globally significant biodiversity hotspots are located in the municipal region. As South Africa democratised from the 1990s, there has been the need to address social and economic sustainability in spatial planning (eThekwini Municipality and ICLEI Africa Secretariat 2007). Hence, understanding the societal benefits from environmental goods and services provided by the open space system became a planning priority. In the 2002 mapping, the concept of ecosystem services was integrated into D'MOSS and its economic values were systematically evaluated (Roberts *et al.* 2012). According to studies, the replacement value of various ecosystem goods and services is estimated at US$387.5 million annually (eThekwini Municipality and ICLEI Africa Secretariat 2007), with a long-term carbon storage potential of 6.2 to 6.8 MtC and a sequestration rate of 8,400 to 9,800 tC/y (ASSAf 2011).

The expansion of D'MOSS in 2002 considered a range of criteria to determine priority areas to be prohibited from urban development. These included a range of habitats, such as: critical (as determined by the role of ecological functions in the system and the importance of delivering ecosystem services); priority (large and intact areas particularly located in upper river catchment areas, around dams and in the coastal zones); and developable; as well as nature reserves, over-steep areas, floodlines (areas affected by once-in-100-year flood events), unstable land and landslide prone areas. It subsequently included areas with vital ecosystem functions into the system to help mitigate climate impacts (eThekwini Municipality and ICLEI Africa Secretariat 2007), such as the protection of wetlands to facilitate the absorption of surface runoff and thus reduce the risk of flooding. More recently, the updates of the system further considered the dynamic interaction between species and ecosystem processes (Roberts *et al.* 2012). This allows for projected climate change and possible impacts on the system to be addressed. For example, hydrological processes were understood and modelled, so the impact and associated economic loss due to climate impacts or inappropriate urban development could be predicted (Roberts *et al.* 2012).

Greenspace projects to improve climate co-benefits

Under the D'MOSS spatial planning framework, several projects have been developed and implemented to emphasise climate co-benefits through greenspace planning and management. Considering the high level of poverty in the municipality, a Community Ecosystem-based Adaptation (CEBA), which is a combination of community-based adaptation and ecosystem-based adaptation, has recently been developed to emphasise the local benefits gained from climate actions (Douwes *et al.* 2015). CEBA often involves poor communities in environmental stewardship schemes and provides jobs for improving local livelihoods and eradicating poverty.

The Buffelsdraai Landfill Site Community Reforestation Project

The Buffelsdraai Landfill Site Community Reforestation Project is one such CEBA project. It was initiated in November 2008, to offset a portion of CO_2 emissions (declared as 307,208 tCO_2e) associated with Durban's hosting of several matches during the 2010 FIFA World Cup™ (Douwes *et al.* 2015). The project is located in the buffer area of the Buffelsdraai Landfill Site, comprising sugarcane farmlands, woodlands and riverine forests. Considering limited productivity and the deterioration of ecosystems, the municipality decided to restore sugarcane lands to their original forest state. As of January 2015, a total of 660,523 indigenous trees had been planted in an area over 412 ha (eThekwini Municipality 2011). The carbon to be captured by the project was initially estimated at some 45,000 tCO_2, over 20 years of forest regeneration (Douwes *et al.* 2015). Whilst climate change mitigation was the primary objective, the reforestation has remarkably enhanced biodiversity since inception and simultaneously improved the ecosystem functions of catchment, such as water quality, flood control, sediment protection and river flow regulation (Douwes *et al.* 2015; eThekwini Municipality 2011). This project also directly improved the local livelihoods of surrounding poor communities. Through the 'tree-preneur' programme, unemployed people were assisted to collect indigenous seeds, establish tree nurseries in their homelands, plant trees in the project areas and maintain the forest. The tree seedlings grown by the tree-preneurs are designed to be paid for in credit notes, which can then be used to buy food and basic goods and to pay school fees at regular 'tree stores' held in each of the participating communities (eThekwini Municipality 2011).

Green Roof Pilot Project

In the urban environment, the Green Roof Pilot Project is designed as an urban management tool in the MCPP (eThekwini Municipality, n.d.). About 10 per cent of municipal buildings have implemented green roofs using indigenous plants or vegetables (ASSAf 2011). The key objective of the programme is to mitigate the urban heat island effect and to reduce stormwater runoff. However, it has also drawn several species to the rooftop habitats (EPCPD 2011). According to on-site measurements, the green roofs (Figure 3.5) have successfully retained stormwater and postponed peak time runoff during a rainfall event. The average temperature difference between a bare roof and a green roof was measured at 18°C from March to November in 2009. This cooling effect is expected to reduce energy demand for the use of air-conditioning inside buildings, and thus offset GHG emissions (EPCPD 2011).

Lessons learnt

The extent to which urban greenspaces may mitigate climate change, contribute to climate change adaptation and enhance city resilience will depend on the degree of integration of urban green infrastructure into the urban development process. Although every city has specific environmental problems and development status, the way that Durban developed its open space systems shows a systematic, comprehensive and evidence-based approach that can be integrated into the existing urban development framework. The awareness by the

Figure 3.5 Green roof on the municipal building.

municipality of ecosystem goods and services of urban greenspace other than its recreational function was an important driver to promote D'MOSS as a climate co-benefits strategy in Durban. This can be supported by a city-wide GI mapping that integrates various spatial information and reveals the significance of conservation. Together with substantial climate studies and projection models, different climate and development scenarios have been provided to inform decision-making. The estimation of multiple ecosystem functions of the D'MOSS and conversion into monetary values also provides a useful tool to communicate with different development sectors. Finally, the innovative effort to involve local communities in the implementation and management of this ecosystem-based climate approach provides a model for other cities, allowing for differences in their specific socio-economic and environmental context.

References

Academy of Science of South Africa (ASSAf) 2011, *Towards a Low Carbon City: Focus on Durban*, Report of the ASSAf Consensus Study on Low Carbon Cities, Pretoria, South Africa.

Cadman, M, Petersen, C, Driver, A, Sekhran, N, Maze, K and Munzhedzi, S 2010, *Biodiversity for Development: South Africa's Landscape Approach to Conserving Biodiversity and Promoting Ecosystem Resilience*, South African National Biodiversity Institute, Pretoria.

Carmin, J, Roberts, D and Anguelovski, I 2009, *Planning Climate Resilient Cities: Early Lessons from Early Adapters*, Presented at the World Bank Urban Research Symposium on Climate Change, Marseille, 28–30 June 2009.

Diab, R and Roberts, D 2012, 'Towards a low carbon city: the case of Durban', *Informationen zur Raumentwicklung*, vol. 5, no. 6, pp. 313–320.

Douwes, D, Rouget, M, Diederichs, N, O'Donoghue, S, Roy, K and Roberts, D 2015, *Buffelsdraai Landfill Site Community Reforestation Project*, XIV World Forestry Congress, 7 September, Durban, South Africa.

Environmental Planning & Climate Protection Department (EPCPD) 2011, *Creating Space for Biodiversity in Durban: Guideline for Designing Green Roof Habitats*, Durban, South Africa, pp. 15–17.

eThekwini Municipality n.d., *Green Roof Pilot Project*, Municipal Climate Protection Programme: Information Pamphlet, Durban, South Africa, pp. 1.

eThekwini Municipality 2011, *Buffelsdraai Community Reforestation Project*, viewed 27 April 2016, www.durban.gov.za/City_Services/development_planning_management/environmental_planning_climate_protection/Projects/Pages/Buffelsdraai-Community-Reforestation-Project.aspx.

eThekwini Municipality 2012, *Durban Adaptation Charter*, viewed 24 April 2016, www.durban.gov.za/City_Services/development_planning_management/environmental_planning_climate_protection/Projects/Documents/DAC_Pamphlet.pdf.

eThekwini Municipality 2013, *Final Summary Document: eThekwini Greenhouse Gas Emission Inventory 2013*, viewed 24 April 2016, www.durban.gov.za/City_Services/energyoffice/Pages/GHG-Inventory.aspx.

eThekwini Municipality 2016, *Draft Integrated Development Plan: Annual Review 2016/2017*, viewed 24 April 2016, www.durban.gov.za/City_Government/City_Vision/IDP/Pages/default.aspx.

eThekwini Municipality and ICLEI Africa Secretariat 2007, *Durban Biodiversity Report 2007*, Local Action for Biodiversity (LAB) Report, Durban, South Africa.

Handley, J, Pauleit, S and Gill, S 2007, 'Landscape, sustainability and the city', in J Benson and M Roe (eds), *Landscape and Sustainability*, 2nd edn, Routledge, London, pp. 167–195.

Intergovernmental Panel on Climate Change (IPCC) 2014, *Climate Change 2014: Impacts, Adaptation, and Vulnerability*. Cambridge University Press, Cambridge. [online] Available at: www.ipcc.ch/report/ar5/wg2/.

Munang, R, Thiaw, I, Alverson, K, Mumba, M, Liu, J and Rivington, M 2013, 'Climate change and ecosystem-based adaptation: A new pragmatic approach to buffering climate change impacts', *Current Opinion in Environmental Sustainability*, vol. 5, no. 1, pp. 67–71.

Roberts, D 2012, 'Thinking globally, acting locally: Institutionalizing climate change at the local government level in Durban, South Africa', in D Dodman, J Bicknell and D Satterthwaite (eds), *Adapting Cities to Climate Change: Understanding and Addressing the Development Challenges*, Routledge, London, pp. 253–269.

Roberts, D 2014, *Working Towards a 'Climate Smart' African City: From Blue Sky to Coal Face*, Conference of Climate Adaptation 2014: Future Challenges, 1 October, Gold Coast, Australia.

Roberts, D and O'Donoghue, S 2013, 'Urban environmental challenges and climate change action in Durban, South Africa', *Environment and Urbanization*, vol. 25, no. 2, pp. 299–319.

Roberts, D, Boon, R, Diederichs, N, Douwes, E, Govender, N, McInnes, A, McLean, C, O'Donoghue, S and Spires, M 2012, 'Exploring ecosystem-based adaptation in Durban, South Africa: "Learning-by-doing" at the local government coal face', *Environment and Urbanization*, vol. 24, no. 1, pp. 167–195.

Secretariat of the Convention on Biological Diversity (SCBD) 2009, *Connecting Biodiversity and Climate Change: Report of the Second Ad Hoc Technical Expert Group on Biodiversity and Climate Change*, CBD, UNEP, Montreal, Canada.

United Nations Framework Convention on Climate Change (UNFCCC) 2011, *National Adaptation Plans: Draft Decision – /CP.17*, Durban, South Africa, viewed 1 May 2016, https://unfccc.int/files/meetings/durban_nov_2011/decisions/application/pdf/cop17_nap.pdf.

White, R, Huang, C-Y, Oule, H, Onyach-Olaa, M, Bachmann, J, Dale, D, Goldberg, B, Pechin, M and Turpie, J 2016, *Promoting Green Urban Development in African Cities: eThekwini, South Africa – Urban Environmental Profile*, World Bank Group, Washington, DC.

3.2 Yogyakarta, Indonesia

Inter-governmental cooperation and land-use coordination by Joint-Secretariat Kartamantul

Norihisa Shima

Asian cities are experiencing a rapid urbanization that the world has never previously experienced. The role of urbanization as the driving force of the economic growth of Asian countries is tempered by that fact that uncontrolled urbanization would lead to environmental degradation at the local level as well as at the global level. In addition to the fact that cities themselves are the generator of GHG emissions at a global level, the process of urbanization can involve direct changes in land use, as formerly agricultural land becomes incorporated within built-up areas, reducing vegetation area that potentially absorbs CO_2. Indeed, land-use change contributes to 18.2 percent of global GHG emission (UN-HABITAT 2011). Thus, controlling urbanization through land-use planning and management is critical to prevent environmental degradation.

Achieving co-benefits should therefore be a potential option, and cities can utilize land-use planning and management practices in a way to control urbanization by preventing conflicts and inefficiencies, leading to delivery of multiple benefits through appropriate policy options, particularly given that the land-use sector has strong links with other key sectors of urban development, including transportation, housing and infrastructure. Among the challenges to promote the delivery of co-benefits, good urban governance is key to achieving and supporting appropriate policies. The rise of civil society and the promotion of decentralization, recently observed in Asian countries, can be opportunities toward achieving good urban governance (Shima *et al.* 2011).

Yogyakarta, a regional city of Indonesia with a population of 4,000 people, has also experienced rapid urbanization, especially since the 1980s. The actual urban area of Yogyakarta is split over the administrative area of Yogyakarta City, expanding into the neighboring Sleman Regency and Banul Regency, forming Greater Yogyakarta. Indeed, the population increase is higher in the peri-urban area. And the construction of universities, housing complexes, shopping centers and facilities supporting them has driven land conversion from agricultural uses, particularly in the Bantul and Sleman Regencies. Consequently, in addition to the environmental degradation, urban infrastructure and services in the peri-urban areas are poorly provided due to lack of coordination among the three local governments, where inter-governmental cooperation is required to address these problems under rapid urbanization (Sekber Kartamantul and GTZ Urban

Quality Yogyakarta 2006; Subanu 2008). In this regard, the case of the Joint-Secretariat Kartamantul, established by the three local governments of Yogyakarta City, Bantul Regency and Sleman Regency for inter-governmental cooperation, shows good lessons toward achieving good urban governance.

Establishment of Joint-Secretariat Kartamantul

The inter-governmental corporation among the provincial government and the three local governments of Yogyakarta dates back to the 1980s, when Indonesia's national program, Integrated Urban Infrastructure Development Programme (IUIDP), was launched. As a pilot project of IUIDP, the Yogyakarta Urban Development Project (YUDP) was launched in 1989, aiming to integrate various urban sectors, including water supply, sewage and sanitation, drainage, roads, solid waste management and other environmental matters, into urban infrastructure planning and thus strengthen local institutional and financial capacities. Part-time local government task forces, dedicated to urban planning, infrastructural, institutional and financial matters, were formed to strengthen interagency relations within and among the local governments. Finally, the 1993–1998 medium-term Infrastructure Investment Programme (PJM) was jointly accepted by Yogyakarta City, Bantul Regency and Sleman Regency in 1991.

The Piyungan Landfill project was started in 1992 as waste management was an urgent issue for the three local governments and none of them had a solid waste disposal facility fulfilling relevant technical and environmental criteria. The three local governments agreed to build a shared 12.5 ha solid waste disposal facility in Piyungan, Bantul Regency. At first, the facility was managed by the provincial government for five years, and then, by the Letter of the Governor of the province issued in 1999, management was handed over from the provincial government to the three local governments, planned to start in the fiscal year 2000/2001.

In this way, the experience of YUDP could help to create a shared understanding of Greater Yogyakarta as a single unified urban area and thus the importance of a systematic approach to the management of infrastructure. Indeed, development cooperation was officially agreed by the joint decree by the three local governments in 1996.

Initiated by the 1999 decentralization laws, the decentralization policy reform was started, involving a big shift of several government functions, tasks and responsibilities from the central government to the local government. In Greater Yogyakarta, the shared understanding and more practically the letter concerning the management of Piyungan Landfill made it relatively easy to continue the cooperation. In 2001, when the 1999 decentralization came into force, a joint decree by the three local governments was issued to establish a Joint-Secretariat Kartamantul, standing for Yogyakarta, Sleman and Bantul as a permanent organization, aiming at more efficient urban infrastructure management with inter-governmental coordination among the three local governments. Since the establishment, the institutional framework of Kartamantul had been

strengthened through several revisions of joint decrees by the three governments as well as several regulations by the central government. In addition, the
Urban Quality Project by GIZ (*Deutsche Gesellschaft für Internationale Zusammenarbeit*) in 2003–2005 technically as well as financially supported Kartamantul at the early stage of its establishment (Firman 2010; Frenkel 1995; Sekber
Kartamantul and GTZ Urban Quality Yogyakarta 2006; Shima *et al.* 2006).

Major achievements by Kartamantul

As stated in the joint decree defining the sectors of cooperation issued in 2001,
Kartamantul put the focus of cooperation on the six sectors of solid waste management, sewerage/waste water management, water resource management,
urban transportation management, urban road management and urban drainage
management, based on the three philosophies of cooperation: 'care (having the
same orientation to improve the public services, especially preparation and
management of the basic infrastructure)'; 'share (having the same commitment
to share the budget, share the risk [technical, social and environmental] and
share the experience)'; and 'fair (having the same commitment to solve the
problem with 'win–win solution' methods)'. Several projects are achieving the
results, further encouraging inter-governmental cooperation among the three
local governments.

Piyungan Landfill

The management of Piyungan Landfill was the first project after Kartamantul
was established, but the cost became the biggest challenge. Though the three
local governments had an agreement of cost sharing based on the amount of
garbage disposed by each government, the operating and management cost of
the landfill had gradually increased. The cost shared by the three local governments could cover only 25 percent, and the actual management had depended
on subsidy. The three local governments started discussions to revise the policy
and charge fees for waste management.

As the amount of garbage increased, leading to increasing management costs,
the three local governments agreed to involve the private sector, and a
cooperation agreement was made between Kartamantul and PT Global Waste
Solusi in 2005. In accordance with the agreement, PT Global Waste Solusi had
a role in managing the transformation of waste into energy to sell, while the
three local governments continued other operations and management of the
landfill (Chaidir 2011; Sekber Kartamantul and GTZ Urban Quality Yogyakarta
2006; Shima *et al.* 2006).

Sewon Waste Water Treatment Plant

The management of Sewon Waste Water Treatment Plant, located in Bantul
District, was also handed over to the three local governments in 2003. As in the

case of the Piyungan Landfill, the challenge was cost. The operation and management cost of the plant depended on the provincial subsidy as the three local governments covered less than 25 percent of the cost. One reason for this low-cost coverage was because the local governments' income from sewage service was very low. For example, Yogyakarta City was still using the fee set in 1991. Under the facilitation of Kartamantul, a revision of Yogyakarta City's local regulations for waste water management was discussed, which was expected to lead to the introduction of the similar local regulation in the other two local governments. Though the final level of fees depended on the people's social and economic circumstances, the three local governments agreed on a principle of full cost coverage by the fee[1] (Chaidir 2011; Sekber Kartamantul and GTZ Urban Quality Yogyakarta 2006; Shima *et al.* 2006).

Trans-Jogja

One of the recent achievements is the introduction of a new public bus service, Trans-Jogja (see Chapter 2.3), which provides bigger buses with comfortable seating and fixed bus stops, and which began operating in 2008. Based on the cooperation agreement by the three local governments issued in 2001, their role is the management of facilities and infrastructure in the transport system. Learning from the experience of TransJakarta, a Bus Rapid Transit (BRT) system operated in the capital, Jakarta, the operating company, PT Jogja Tugu Trans (PT-JTT), was established by several bus service operators, such as Koperasi Kopada, Koperasi Aspada and Koperasi Puskopkar. The provincial government provides 20–30 buses and some subsidy with PT-JTT. By sharing roles in this way, Trans-Jogja continues to operate (Chaidir 2011).[2]

Land-use coordination in Mirota Area

Spatial planning became a new sector of cooperation by Kartamantul, aiming to synchronize planning, budgeting and control related to spatial planning, to institutionalize zoning regulation, such as recharge, housing/settlements, green areas and public spaces, and to standardize building permits.

The border area of the three local governments, Mirota Area along Godean Street, under increasing land-use conversion from rural to urban use, was chosen for the pilot project. To collect the information about the area, a series of workshops was held, inviting community leaders from the three local governments. After discussing the physical, economic, social and institutional problems they face, the ideas from the community were documented, covering various issues such as road construction/rehabilitation, bridge construction/rehabilitation, traffic lights, sidewalks, parking, police inspection, water supply and vacant land. Finally, the alternative idea for the land use and infrastructure development of the area was summarized into a report, which is expected to be taken in the official spatial plan, based on Spatial Planning Law, which will be revised by the three local governments respectively and the following local regulation concerning building permits that will be coordinated among the three local governments (GTZ-GLG, n.d.).

As of May 2015, the three local governments had already prepared their general spatial plan, which will be followed by the detailed spatial plan and zoning regulations that have actual controlling power over the land use and building construction. Now the detailed spatial plan and zoning regulation of each local government is under discussion by the local parliament and is expected to reflect the workshop discussion of Mirota Area.

Although the final achievements of the land-use coordination at Mirota Area are still in progress and can only be evaluated following the detailed spatial plan and whether zoning regulations work effectively or not for Mirota Area, the experience of Joint-Secretariat Kartamantul provides several important lessons toward good urban governance. First of all, as seen in the case of Piyungan Landfill, it should be noted that they started cooperation in the face of a common challenge, which helped to reach a relatively easier consensus and naturally expanded their cooperative projects, such as Sewon Waste Water Treatment Plant, Trans-Jogja and sector spatial planning, by sharing their experience in cooperation. It is also important to highlight that, in this process of cooperation, they changed the governance structure from time to time and from project to project. These have included a gradual reform of institutional frameworks of cooperation from ad-hoc task forces of IUIDP, agreement on development cooperation in 1996 to the establishment of a permanent organization, Joint-Secretariat Kartamantul in 2001, and the strategic involvement of different sectors – the private sector in Sewon Waste Water Treatment Plant and Trans-Jogja and the community in Mirota Area. Naturally, but strategically, this would be key to achieving good urban governance.

Notes

1 In terms of the cost, there was an innovation, too. The effluent flow from the plant was used to generate electricity, which covered the lighting electricity of the plant and the area around it. With this electricity, they could cut some of the costs of the State Electricity Enterprise (PLN). Of the 25 million Rupiah in electricity monthly fees to PLN, the saved cost was four to five million Rupiah. Though the saved cost was small, the fact that they had the idea in itself is worth highlighting.

2 In terms of role sharing, the rehabilitation of Blambangan Bridge is also interesting. When the Blambangan Bridge over the Winongo River, located in Sleman Regency, and the pipeline under the bridge, owned by Local Water Supply Enterprise (PDAM) of Yogyakarta City, were damaged in 2005, the rehabilitation was carried out in less than three months by sharing the following roles:

- The provincial government: Building a new bridge because the bridge is over the river, which the provincial government manages.
- Yogyakarta City: Improving the pipeline and the broken asphalt road because they are the owner.
- Sleman Regency: Releasing or acquiring land for widening the bridge because it is located in Sleman Regency.

It is also worth highlighting that the rehabilitation was initiated by a letter from the community (Chaidir 2011).

References

Chaidir, S, with the support of APEKSI (Association of Indonesian Municipalities) 2011, 'Cooperation between local governments to address shared needs, Yogyakarta-Sleman-Bantul (Kartamantul), Indonesia', in Partnership for Democratic Local Governance in Southeast-Asia (DELGOSEA) (ed.), *Best Practices on Institutional Governance in Southeast-Asia (Volume 2)*, viewed 16 March 2016, www.delgosea.eu/cms/content/download/773/5712/file/DELGOSEA-Best_Practices-Institutional_Governance.pdf.

Firman, T 2010, 'Multi local government under Indonesia's decentralization reform: The case of Kartamantul (the Greater Yogyakarta)', *Habitat International*, vol. 34, no. 4, pp. 400–405.

Frenkel, R 1995, 'Yogyakarta case study: Test ground, pilot base and turning point', in H Suselo, JL Taylor and EA Wegelin (eds), *Indonesia's Urban Infrastructure Development Experience: Critical Lessons of Good Practice*, in cooperation with the United Nations Centre for Human Settlements (HABITAT).

GTZ-GLG n.d., *Model Kerjasama Penataan Ruang Kawasan Perbatasan: Kusus Kawasan Mirota Jl. Godean, Yogyakarta*, GTZ-GLG, Yogyakarta.

Sekretariat Bersama Kartamantul and GTZ Urban Quality Yogyakarta 2006, *Bersama Mengelola Perkotaan: Kerja Sama Antardaerah Kartamantul*, Sekretariat Bersama Kartamantul and GTZ Urban Quality Yogyakarta, Yogyakarta.

Shima, N, Balaban, O and Moreno-Panaranda, R 2011, 'Challenges and opportunities toward achieving environmental co-benefits through land use planning and management: Experiences from Asian metropolitan cities', *Proceedings of APSA Congress 2011*, pp. 1147–1157.

Shima, N, Kidokoro, T, Onishi, T, Subanu, LP and de Duque, SH 2006, 'Challenges and scopes toward inter-governmental coordination in decentralized Indonesia: Through a case of Joint-Secretariat Kartamantul', *Proceedings of 20th EAROPH World Congress & Mayor's Caucus*, CD-ROM.

Subanu, LP 2008, 'Governing urban development in dualistic societies: A case study of the urban region of Yogyakarta, Indonesia', in T Kidokoro, N Harata, LP Subanu, J Jessen, A Motte and EP Seltzer (eds), *Sustainable City Regions: Space, Place and Governance*, Springer, Tokyo.

United Nations Human Settlements Programme (UN-HABITAT) 2011, *Global Report on Human Settlements 2011: Cities and Climate Change*, Earthscan, London.

4 Buildings

Ping Jiang

Energy use, carbon and pollution emissions in buildings

Urbanisation is synonymous with the built environment. Over 90 per cent of urban growth is taking place in developing countries (United Nations Human Settlements Programme 2008). For instance, the urban population of South Asia is expected to double by 2030 (Atkins 2012) and more additional infrastructures and dwellings need to be built to match this urban expansion. Urbanisation in Asia has significantly enhanced economic and social development by creating an enormous amount of new jobs and increasing national wealth. As such, many Asian countries have put the policy focus on urban development and the economic growth associated with it. However, some negative effects have emerged with the rapid urban development in Asia. Namely, the unprecedented resources and energy needed to support this kind of urban growth at this scale, and emerging issues of environmental degradation associated with this development. The urbanisation process consumes huge amounts of fossil fuels, releasing billions of tonnes of greenhouse gases (GHGs) into the atmosphere every year. Air pollutants (e.g. SO_2 and NO_x) are also made by consuming fossil fuels and other pollutants produced by municipal wastes (including waste water and solid wastes – see Chapter 7). Furthermore, the fossil fuels which have thus far driven urban development are finite, and concentrated in relatively few countries and regions like the Middle East and Africa, where potentially unstable political and economic situations put the global energy supply at risk. Considering these elements, the energy supply for supporting this quick economic development becomes a serious issue: energy security.

Approximately 200 million people will be added to the global urban population every year between 2000 and 2030, with 90 per cent of this increased population coming from developing countries (Puppim de Oliveira *et al.* 2012), which means that there will be greater demand for urban dwellings. More than 70 per cent of primary energy is consumed in supporting sectors related to the rapid growth of urbanisation in developing countries (UN Population Division 2011). These sectors include energy, land use, transportation, building, etc.

Among these sectors, a significant proportion of energy consumption is from the building sector.

Besides energy use for maintaining normal operation in buildings and keeping occupants in comfortable living conditions, materials and services are used in constructing buildings, such as concrete, steel and plastics consuming energy in their manufacture and transport process, and water consumption, wastewater and waste treatment in the building sector also require energy to run (Reinhard and Yasin 2011). In the US, for example, the building sector uses 39 per cent of total energy, 12 per cent of total water and 68 per cent of total electricity, accounting for 38 per cent of total CO_2 emissions (US EPA 2015).

This chapter presents the co-benefit framework for the building sector and derives its Avoid-Shift-Improve (A-S-I) analogues. It draws heavily on the Chinese experience of promoting co-benefits in the building sector to understand how the interplay between legislation, technology and behaviour change can generate co-benefits. Two cases are presented in the supplementary sections following this chapter. The first compares two projects by looking at the co-benefits of energy conservation, carbon reduction and cost saving achieved in a commercial store and within a commercial and office development in China and Japan, respectively. The second case study looks at an innovative *Avoid* strategy of the first city-level cap and trade system in Tokyo, part of the largest urban agglomeration in the world.

The co-benefits approach to the building sector

Potential co-benefits achieved in sustainable buildings

There are millions of buildings in the world of different types, sizes and utilities. Broadly speaking, buildings can be categorised as either residential or non-residential based on their function. For instance, in China, this definition is usually described as public (i.e. non-residential) and residential buildings. Buildings may also be classed as old or new, and also can be treated as commercial buildings (e.g. hotel, restaurant, gym) and non-commercial buildings. Many countries have issued building regulations or codes with the aim of reducing energy use, CO_2 emissions, pollution and waste. Thus, a larger share of the building stock is taken up by sustainable buildings, which are not only more energy efficient but can also improve the well-being and efficiency of the people working in them. Green buildings are typical buildings that have also addressed many countries' sustainable development strategies. Several green building codes have developed, such as the Leadership in Energy Environment Design (LEED) scheme in the US, the Building Research Establishment Environmental Assessment Method (BREEAM) in the UK and the Comprehensive Assessment System for Building Environmental Efficiency (CASBEE) in Japan. These green building coding systems have significantly enhanced green building development not only in these three countries but also in other countries. Table 4.1 provides a general overview of the LEED, BREEAM and CASBEE systems.

The building sector has a vast impact on the natural environment, human health and the economy. By adopting green, low-carbon or eco-building strategies, we can maximise both economic and environmental performance. Sustainable methods can be integrated into buildings at any stage, from design and construction, to operation, renovation and deconstruction. However, the most significant benefits can be obtained if an integrated co-benefits approach from the earliest stages of a building project are carried out. Generally, three kinds of potential benefits – environmental benefits, economic benefits and social benefits – can be achieved with a co-benefits approach (Figure 4.1).

For instance, the effect of Indoor Environmental Quality (IEQ) in non-industrial buildings, such as offices, schools or residential, is an increasingly important topic in public health (World Green Building Council 2014; (Connecticut Department of Public Health 2016). It is clear that IEQ can significantly influence employees' satisfaction, productivity or absenteeism. Increasing ventilation, illumination and exposure to views is strongly related to an increased perceived level of comfort, reduced risk of short-term sick leave and an increase in productivity (EPA 2015). According to the World Health Organization (WHO), 'health is a state of complete physical, mental and social well-being and not merely the absence of disease or infirmity' (World Green Building Council 2014). The link between well-being and productivity is widely understood, but the market is not fully aware of the scope of factors that are

Table 4.1 Introduction and coverage of green building coding systems in the US, UK and Japan

Name	Country	Year of issue	Building types	Rating standards	Standards
LEED	US	1995	• Commercial buildings • Public buildings • New buildings	4 stars	Construction, water, energy and environment, materials and sources, indoor environment and innovation
BREEAM	UK	1990	• New buildings • Existing buildings	4 grades	Management, energy, traffic, pollution, materials, water resources, land use, ecological value, physical and mental health
CASBEE	Japan	2003	• New buildings • Existing buildings	5 grades	Energy consumption, resource reuse, the local environment, indoor environment

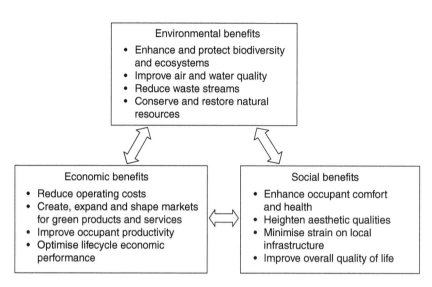

Figure 4.1 Potential co-benefits can be achieved in sustainable buildings.

considered in sustainable buildings. A lack of accessible sustainable building data further hampers this situation. Environmental conditions inside buildings have an impact on our health, which was the reason for setting basic regulations for different types of buildings, including offices.

These generalised co-benefits described above belong to a broader definition of co-benefits, which include environmental benefits, while at the same time maintaining the economic benefits and social benefits in the building sector.

A narrower sense of co-benefits refers to the synergies of energy conservation and pollution reduction (reducing GHG and pollutant emissions). The varying use of this term in 'climate co-benefits' and 'climate and air co-impacts' indicates that there is almost no agreement on assessing co-benefits with diverse methods and tools (State Council of the People's Republic of China 2005). Different institutions and organisations have a different understanding, definition and interpretation. For instance, there is the narrow sense of co-benefits defined by the Ministry of the Environment of Japan (MOEJ) and the Intergovernmental Panel on Climate Change (IPCC) that co-benefits is the process of controlling GHG emissions and reducing other local emissions (e.g. SO_2, NO_x, CO, and PM); on the other hand, local pollution control in the sustainable development process can also reduce or absorb CO_2 and other GHG emissions (State Council of the People's Republic of China 2010; National Development and Reform Commission of China 2010). This chapter puts the substantive focus on the co-benefits of reducing CO_2 emissions and air pollutants in buildings (i.e. the narrow sense of co-benefits).

Co-benefits of energy saving, CO₂ and air pollutant reduction in the lifecycle of a building

Generally, there are three phases in a building's lifecycle: (i) the production phase, (ii) the management/occupation phase and (iii) the destruction phase. This is a complex process involving other industries. The energy flow runs through every phase of the lifecycle and GHGs and other pollutants are emitted as by-products. Figure 4.2 shows the lifecycle of a building related to energy consumption (Davies 2006).

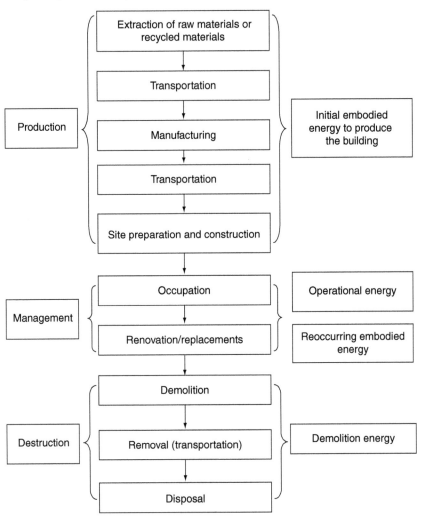

Figure 4.2 Lifecycle of a building related to energy consumption and GHG emissions.

Source: reprinted from the *Journal of Cleaner Production*, 58, Ping Jiang, Wenbo Dong, Yi Hsiu Kung and Yong Geng, 'Analysing co-benefits of the energy conservation and carbon reduction in China's large commercial buildings', 112–120, Copyright 2013, with permission from Elsevier.

Three main kinds of energy consumption in the lifecycle of a building can be defined:

- Embodied energy is the energy utilised during the production phase of the building, which includes energy content of all materials used, transportation to the site, manufacturing and construction/erection.
- Operational energy is consumed during the occupation/management period. It can be briefly described as the energy for heating, ventilation and air-conditioning (HVAC), running appliances and indoor hot water. This phase accounts for 80–90 per cent of total energy use in the building's life-cycle (Ramesh *et al.* 2010). This variation of energy consumption in the building sector is due to the variation between countries and even within a country with different climatic zones.
- Demolition energy is required to demolish the building and dispose of waste materials.

Most GHGs and air pollutants are emitted directly and indirectly by consuming energy in these three phases. The co-benefits approach which is formed in this chapter aims to achieve simultaneously a reduction in GHG emissions and other pollutants and also an economic benefit in the buildings sector.

Addressing co-benefits of energy saving, CO_2 and air pollutant reduction through the A-S-I framework

In order to work out a comprehensive co-benefits approach in the buildings sector, the Avoid-Shift-Improve Framework (A-S-I) can be adopted as a method for addressing all aspects of co-benefits. The A-S-I framework was initially used in the transport sector with the aim of providing sustainable strategies by inputting new and innovative solutions (GIZ 2011). The framework formed through A-S-I aims to address aspects of energy use, CO_2 emissions and pollution generation and develop an effective approach to achieve co-benefits. Thus the framework can also be employed in the building sector.

In principle, changing part or all aspects related to energy use in the life-cycle of a building could lead to more or fewer co-benefits in terms of carbon emissions and pollution. However, energy consumption and carbon emissions vary across different countries because of different living habits, levels of economic development and weather conditions. Thus, relevant strategies of co-benefits in the context of saving energy and cutting carbon emissions in buildings should focus on local realities. Therefore, how to form an effective co-benefits approach regarding the local conditions is becoming the core issue.

Based on the description of lifecycle energy use, carbon and pollution emissions in the previous section, a comprehensive framework of the co-benefits approach, which includes all aspects related to co-benefits and how they interact

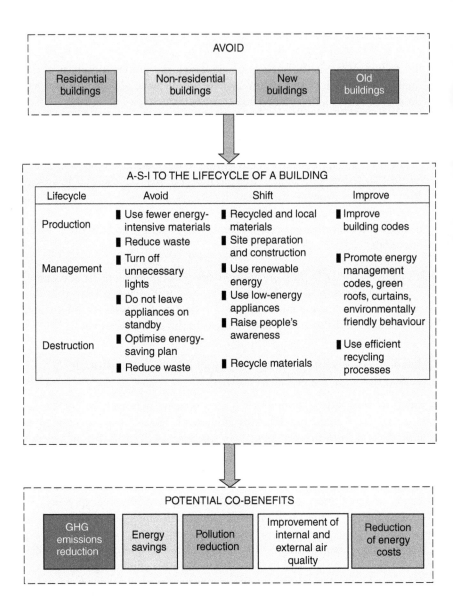

Figure 4.3 A-S-I framework of the co-benefits approach in the building sector.

with each other, is presented in Figure 4.3. Note that there are links here with both the previous land-use chapter (Chapter 3), through the mention of green elements such as green roofs and curtains, which offer benefits to the building itself as well as the surrounding environment, and the forthcoming energy chapter (Chapter 5), through the explicit shifting to low-carbon energy technologies and energy-efficient devices.

Barriers to achieving effective co-benefits – the Chinese experience

China is the biggest developing country with the highest growth in urbanisation; it is also the biggest GHG emitter in the world and faces severe effects of climate change and environmental pollution. China's building sector is used as the main case study in this chapter. The existing barriers to tackling the issues of climate change and local pollution, and the solutions to overcome these obstacles to deliver co-benefits and promote sustainability, are analysed in the subsequent section through the case study of China's building sector.

Energy performance and carbon emissions in China's building sector

With high economic growth and urbanisation in the past 30 years, China has been the largest energy consumer and CO_2 emitter in the world since 2010. China shared 22.4 per cent of global primary energy consumption and emitted 27.1 per cent of global CO_2 emissions in 2013 (BP 2014). Its coal-dominated energy system leads to much higher emissions of CO_2, SO_2, NO_x and PM for producing per unit of GDP than many developed countries (National Bureau of Statistics China 2014), whilst SO_2, CO, NO_x and PM emissions have led to serious local air pollution, which has a huge impact on the ecosystem and on human health. The climate in China has experienced many noticeable changes through the increase in GHG emissions over the last century (National Development and Reform Commission of China 2007). Approximately two billion square metres of new buildings (over 90 per cent of which are urban) appear each year, and approximately 21 billion square metres of floor area in new buildings are expected to be constructed by 2020 in China's pursuit of urban growth (World Bank 2008), which is equivalent to the current building area of the EU-15 countries (Ecofys 2006). With improved living conditions, an on-going increase in the energy consumption levels of China's buildings is projected up to 2050 (Qiu et al. 2007). Approximately 25 per cent of total energy is consumed in urban buildings (Qiu et al. 2007; National Bureau of Statistics of China 2010). This energy use is associated with over five billion tonnes of CO_2 equivalent (CO_2e) emissions in 2009. With 11 per cent of annual growth in energy consumption in buildings in recent years (Figure 4.4), it is predicted to continue into the coming decades along with rapid urban development (Jiang and Keith 2013). In many cities, such as Beijing and Shanghai, the average energy use in large public buildings (i.e. single public buildings with a floor area over

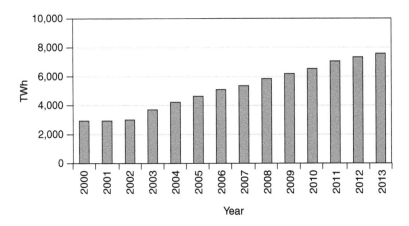

Figure 4.4 Energy consumption in the building sector in China between 2000 and 2013.

20,000 m²) is around 180 kWh/m² (Qiu *et al.* 2007; Jiang 2011), which is close or even higher than the level of energy use in similar buildings in western cities. Currently, energy consumption in urban buildings has retained an annual growth rate of 11 per cent in China since 2000 (National Bureau of Statistics of China 2010). The increasing urban population and growing demand for higher living conditions is a great challenge for long-term, low-carbon sustainable development in China's building sector.

In total, 95 per cent of the 43 billion m² of buildings in China consist of high-energy consumption buildings, and 80 per cent of all new buildings do not adopt (or adopt only a few) energy-saving measures (Jiang *et al.* 2013). One core objective of China's 'Twelfth Five-Year Plan' is to ensure long-term sustainable urban development. Promoting green building development is the main goal of this plan. According to the 'The National New Urban Planning 2014–2020' document, the proportion of green buildings in the set of all new buildings will increase from 2 per cent in 2012 to 50 per cent in 2020 (MOHURD 2014).

Current legislation on energy conservation in China's buildings

In recent years, China has pursued policies that focus on energy conservation or GHG emissions reduction and also lead to air pollution reduction. The most important national development strategy with respect to key policies for energy conservation and mitigating climate change is the national five-year plan. The first national plan to include the explicit objective to reduce energy use was 'The Eleventh Five-Year Plan (2005–2010)'. It required a reduction of energy consumption per unit of GDP by 20 per cent by 2010 compared to 2005 (State Council of the People's Republic of China 2005). The following national plan, 'The Twelfth Five-Year Plan (2011–2016)', had stricter and more specific objectives focused on GHG emissions reduction for reducing carbon emissions intensity per unit of GDP by 17 per cent by 2015 compared to 2010 levels (State Council of the People's Republic of China 2010). Another important national policy entitled 'China to Address Climate Change Policies and Actions' was issued in November 2010 with a more ambitious objective of cutting GHG emissions per unit of GDP by 40–45 per cent by 2020 (State Council of the People's Republic of China 2010). The National People's Congress also approved an important law, 'The Energy Conservation Law of China', in October 2007, which also includes specific rules on energy saving in the building sector, and local energy-saving regulations and design standards relevant to the building sector shall be compliant with this law (Standing Committee Meeting 2007).

The policies and laws presented above will fundamentally influence China's overall energy conservation and GHG emissions reduction plans in all sectors, including the building sector, at both the national and local level. More specific requirements relevant to energy efficiency in the building sector have been issued by China's central and local governments in a series of energy-saving and efficiency standards since 1986 (Table 4.2).

The mandated energy-saving objectives are also set out in these standards. For example, energy consumption in all new and refurbished public buildings (i.e. non-residential, though not factories) should be reduced by 50 per cent compared to the energy performance in public buildings in the 1980s under the GB50189–2005 standard (Chinese Construction Ministry 2005). Some local municipal governments have also issued their own building energy efficiency design standards associated with the national standards in Table 4.2. For instance, the Beijing government issued the 'Beijing Public Building Energy Saving Design Standards', which came into effect in June 2006. The Beijing standards are designed to achieve the energy-saving objective of a 65 per cent reduction in energy consumption compared to energy use in the same public building sector in the 1980s (Beijing Construction Bureau 2005).

Analysis of barriers to achieving effective co-benefits

Despite the array of building policies which could lead to achieving more or fewer co-benefits, some obstacles substantially prevent the co-benefits of energy conservation, GHG emissions and air pollution reduction from being achieved. First, some of the current national and local policies are not robust enough and need to be updated and improved for continued reduction of GHG emissions and pollution with the process of urban development.

The current policies presented above need to be updated and improved based on the real situation of urban development at local levels. Jiang (2011) makes a detailed assessment of the weaknesses in current energy-efficiency standards and recommends solutions. For instance, regarding the Public Buildings Energy Efficiency Design Standards (GB50189–2005) and local public building energy-efficiency design standards in Beijing and Shanghai, the choice of the 1980s

Table 4.2 Current standards/codes on energy conservation in the building sector in China

No.	Title	Status	A-S-I
1	Thermal Design Code for Civil Buildings (GB50176–93)	Implemented	Improve
2	Design Standard for Energy Efficiency of Civil Buildings – Heating in Residential Buildings (JGJ26–95)	Implemented	Improve
3	Technical Specification for Energy Efficiency Retrofit of Heating Residential Buildings (JGJ129–2000)	Implemented	Shift
4	Building Water Supply Drainage and Heating Engineering Code for Acceptance of Construction Quality (GB50242–2002)	Implemented	Improve
5	Code for Acceptance of Construction Quality of Ventilation and Air Conditioning Engineering (GB50243–2002)	Implemented	Improve
6	Code for Design of Heating, Ventilation and Air Conditioning (GB50019–2003)	Implemented	Improve
7	Technical Specification for Ground Radiation Heating (JGJ142–2004)	Implemented	Shift
8	Standard for Lighting Design of Buildings (GB50034–2004)	Implemented	Improve
9	Design Standard for Energy Efficiency of Public Buildings (GB50189–2005)	Implemented	Improve
10	Technical Specification for Solar Water Heating System of Civil Buildings (GB50364–2005)	Implemented	Shift
11	Standard Operation Management of Air Conditioning and Ventilation Systems (GB50365–2005)	Implemented	Improve
12	Code for Engineering Technology of Ground Source Heat Pumps (GB50366–2005)	Implemented	Improve
13	Energy Consumption Data Collection Standard Construction (JGJ/T154–2007)	Implemented	Improve
14	Code for Construction and Acceptance of Building Energy Saving Engineering (GB50411–2007)	Implemented	Improve
15	Cold Storage Air Conditioning Engineering Technology (JGJ158–2008)	Implemented	Shift
16	Standard for Energy Efficiency Inspection of Residential Buildings (JGJ/T 132–2009)	Implemented	Improve
17	Urban Heating System Evaluation Criteria (GB/T50627–2010)	Implemented	Shift
18	Design Standard for Energy Efficiency of Residential Buildings in Hot Summer and Cold Winter Area (JGJ134–2010)	Implemented	Improve
19	Technical Regulation Urban Geothermal Heating Project (CJJ 138–2010)	Implemented	Shift
20	Technical Specifications Sun Shading of Building Engineering (JGJ 237–2011)	Implemented	Shift
21	Civil Building Heating, Ventilation and Air Conditioning Design Specification (GB50736–2012)	Implemented	Shift
22	Tianjin City Residential Building Energy Saving Design of Technical Index	To be issued	Improve
23	Technical Specification for the Public Building Energy Saving Reconstruction	To be issued	Shift
24	The Thermal Environment of Residential Design Standards	To be issued	Improve
25	Technical Specification for Centralised Heating Systems at Room Temperature Control and Heat Metering	To be issued	Shift
26	Meteorological Parameter Standard for Energy Efficiency of Buildings	To be issued	Improve
27	Effect of Standard of Whole Life Cycle Building Sustainability Assessment	To be issued	All
28	Specification for Energy Saving in Heating Systems of Towns	To be issued	Shift

benchmark for energy consumption in public buildings is questionable and will lead to confusion and misinterpretation for achieving co-benefits in carbon and pollution reduction.

China's rapid development over the last two decades means that these standards have very little relevance to much of the new building stock. In particular, the provision of thermal comfort relied little on air conditioning and on many fewer appliances. Consequently, there is little if any data on which to base a useful benchmark. A better solution would be to select a baseline that is more relevant relating, say, to the year 2004, or the average carbon emissions level over a time period such as 2000–2004. Local standards can also make their benchmarks of GHG emissions using the same method based on the local realities. In particular, local policies, standards and regulations for energy conservation and environmental protection in the building sector should focus on both local environmental improvement and GHG emissions reduction.

Another issue to be addressed is that many local policies focus only on the elimination of air, water and waste pollution, but not the reduction of GHG emissions. For example, there were 218 projects designed to reduce pollution locally, implemented under the main policy entitled 'Three-Year Action Plan', on the environmental protection in Baoshan District, Shanghai, between 2009 and 2011 (Baoshan District Environmental Protection Bureau 2011). Although GHG emissions reduction was overlooked in the 'Three-Year Action Plan', most of these projects have reported co-benefits despite them not being specifically mandated (see Baoshan case in Chapter 5.3).

In 1998, the Chinese State Council promulgated 'The Notice on Accelerating the Urban Housing System Reform and Hosing Construction', which first established a market-oriented building and construction industry. This industry is a key contributor to urban economic development in China, and keeps growing by approximately 30 per cent every year (Zhang *et al.* 2007). However, energy efficiency and carbon reduction are always considered secondary issues or less important points in the building sector (Li *et al.* 2009).

In this regard, there can be considerable barriers for three inter-related reasons:

- investment barriers, which include weak investment incentives, financial risks and the lack of knowledge and information on costs and benefits in energy and carbon reduction;
- technology barriers, mainly caused by risks in the process of utilising, maintaining and operating technologies, and the lack of knowledge and experience;
- capacity barriers, deriving from the lack of effective management and professional knowledge and abilities; the lack of active engagement from stakeholders with different benefits also cause capacity barriers that need to be addressed.

A report from Tsinghua University shows that 80–90 per cent of buildings do not take any measures at all or just adopt the minimum level of energy

conservation, carbon reduction and pollution elimination because of technology barriers (Jiang *et al.* 2007). Normally, new technologies often need high
investment in R&D, and there are high costs in their purchase and operation.
The adoption of new and advanced energy-saving technologies is considered a
higher risk for investors and operators. Furthermore, integrating different new
technologies together in a system and making them operate effectively with
regard to energy performance in buildings will need higher levels of investment and cause higher risks. The familiarity with established and prevailing
technologies also prevents the uptake of new technologies in the building
sector. The lack of knowledge, experience and skills is another barrier to the
utilisation and operation of these new technologies and systems for creating
co-benefits in cutting GHG emissions, pollution and energy costs in buildings
in China.

The capacity barriers deriving from the lack of effective management and
professional knowledge and abilities also need to be addressed. Improved management of energy performance can be made not only through better operation
and implementation of technologies and systems, but also by carrying out comprehensive action plans to achieve the long-term co-benefits in buildings.
According to surveys by Jiang (2009), around 70–80 per cent of current urban
buildings (especially public buildings) in China have not taken any effective
energy management with a co-benefits objective. The lack of capacity is related
to good-quality energy management and professional staff. Otherwise, the lack
of active engagement between stakeholders (e.g. investors, developers, users of
buildings) who have received benefits in energy saving and carbon reduction
activities also contributes to capacity barriers. In particular, the principal–agent
problem, where the person paying for the improvements is not the prime benefi-
ciary, is a particular problem in the building sector, either through landlords
who cannot recoup costs through rent, or owners who do not see their investment reflected in the resale value.

Opportunities to achieve carbon emissions and pollutant reduction under the co-benefits approach in buildings

The analysis presented above on the barriers to achieving the co-benefits from
reducing GHG emissions, local pollution and energy costs is made based on the
realities of the building sector in China. These issues are common for many
other countries, especially developing countries with similar urban development
levels.

In order to overcome these barriers and achieve sustainable development in
the building sector under the co-benefits approach, all relevant aspects related
to energy consumption and carbon emissions must be addressed. First, despite
the aims of the latest Chinese building standards to promote energy conservation, these are still very inferior to standards in many other countries and are
barely comparable with standards in the UK from 25 years ago. Furthermore,
there is a lack of clarity leading to an ambiguous interpretation when the

standards often relate to savings (e.g. 50 per cent) on the standards of buildings built in the 1980s, when the aspirations for thermal comfort etc. were much lower than they are today.

Sound policies based on the real national and local situations of energy performance and carbon emissions are the key to overcoming barriers at policy level for achieving co-benefits in solving environmental and developmental problems in China and other countries. The findings and evidence from relevant research also show that only when developers, investors, managers and occupants of buildings have the incentive and capacity to take real action to reduce GHG emissions and pollution will these barriers be overcome effectively. An effective and comprehensive co-benefits strategy should therefore take a holistic approach to all aspects of building energy use, including:

1   awareness raising;
2   improvements in energy management;
3   implementation of technical measures for energy conservation;
4   deployment of renewable energy; and
5   offsetting methods.

It is important to recognise that many of the more cost-effective solutions can be achieved by adopting a strategy that tackles the above areas in approximately the order shown. For example, awareness raising with the aim of behaviour change is often overlooked as a means for cutting energy consumption. Effective campaigns and training promoted by 'Energy Champions' can provide the necessary encouragement and improvement, and this can be a particularly cost-effective approach to overall energy conservation. If awareness, management and integrated dialogue have been established among all the stakeholders in large commercial buildings, it may be possible to gain agreement to 'ring-fence' any monetary savings arising from actions taken, which can then be used to finance more costly technical measures.

The adoption of *Improve* strategies, such as energy-saving technologies and measures such as improved insulation, the installation of combined heat and power (CHP), heat pumps, absorption chillers, etc., can help to reduce energy use, but often there are financial issues which can affect their uptake. Utilising a 'ring-fence' approach provides a potential additional incentive when combined with a methodology such as the Clean Development Mechanism. Some financial mechanisms or economic incentives (e.g. carbon trading mechanism, subsidies, carbon tax and energy performance contract) are also effective ways to overcome investment barriers (see the Tokyo case of cap-and-trade in Chapter 4.2).

Conclusions

Urbanisation has significantly enhanced economic development and social change. With an increasing urban population, additional infrastructure and services are needed to meet this level of urban expansion. The unprecedented resources and energy needed to support the building sector is a fundamental threat to keeping environmental degradation and GHG emissions to a minimum. Energy is used both directly in maintaining the day-to-day operation of buildings and to keep occupants in comfort, and indirectly through the materials, transport, water and waste treatment used in constructing and demolishing buildings. Considering the huge carbon and air pollution emission potential in the building sector, the co-benefits approach has an important role to play in all of these aspects based on local realities.

Three kinds of barriers for achieving the co-benefits of reduction of carbon emissions and energy costs have been identified:

1   a weak investment incentive in the absence of legislation and/or financial return;
2   high costs and risks of installation as well as operation and maintenance;
3   a lack of awareness and capacity about energy-efficient technologies and practice.

In order to overcome the barriers to achieving co-benefits in buildings, measures need to be carried out such as adopting sound policies and advanced energy-saving technologies, improving energy management and providing economic incentives. The A-S-I method is utilised for working out a comprehensive co-benefits strategy approach for addressing all aspects related to energy saving, and carbon and pollution reduction. The A-S-I methodology in the building sector is critical because of the strong links to both the land-use and the energy sectors. Moreover, climate change and environmental degradation are global issues and international collaboration and efforts are needed. The Chinese experience with co-benefits in the building sector holds some important lessons for other developing countries like India, Indonesia and Brazil, especially with regard to legislation. Greater collaboration in technology and knowledge development and transfer between different cities and countries in both the developed and the developing world should be encouraged to solve these twin local and global challenges.

References

Atkins 2012, *Future Proofing Cities*, viewed 4 November 2016, http://futureproofingcities. com/downloads/FPC_Report_HiRes.pdf?dl=1.

Beijing Construction Bureau 2005, *Design Standard for Energy Efficiency of Public Buildings*, China Architecture and Building Press, Beijing.

Baoshan District Environmental Protection Bureau 2011, *The Environmental Protection in Baoshan Between 2009 and 2011 and the Three-year Action Plan*, viewed 23 September 2016, http://bshbj.baoshan.sh.cn/baoshanWeb/home/plan/disilun/4gongzuojianbao.aspx.

British Petroleum (BP) 2014, *Statistical Review of World Energy 2014*, British Petroleum, London, viewed 4 July 2014, www.bp.com/content/dam/bp-country/de_de/PDFs/ brochures/BP-statistical-review-of-world-energy-2014-full-report.pdf.

Chinese Construction Ministry 2005, *Design Standard for Energy Efficiency of Public Buildings (GB50189–2005)*, China Architecture and Building Press, Beijing.

Connecticut Department of Public Health 2016, 'Indoor air quality testing should not be the first move', viewed 12 May 2016, www.ct.gov/dph/lib/dph/environmental_health/eoha/pdf/ieq_testing_should_not_be_the_first_move_6-10.pdf.

Davies, T 2006, *Developing Fully-Integrated Approaches to Low Carbon Design, Practice and Management*, Report by University of East Anglia, p. 45.

Ecofys 2006, *Mitigation of CO2 – Emissions from the Building Stock in EU*, Amsterdam, viewed 23 September 2016, www.ecofys.com/en/publication/mitigation-of-co2-emissions-from-the-building-stock/.

GIZ 2011, *Sustainable Urban Transport: Avoid-Shift-Improve (ASI)*, Fact sheet, Deutsche Gesellschaft für Internationale Zusammenarbeit (GIZ) GmbH, viewed 29 September 2015, www.transport2020.org/file/asi-factsheet-eng.pdf.

Jiang, P 2009, *A Low Carbon Sustainable Strategy Using CDM Methodological Approach to Large Commercial Buildings in Beijing and Shanghai*, PhD Thesis, University of East Anglia.

Jiang, P 2011, 'Analysis of national and local energy-efficiency design standards in the public building sector in China', *Energy for Sustainable Development*, vol. 15, pp. 443–450.

Jiang, P and Keith, T 2013, 'Improving the energy performance of large commercial buildings in China using effective energy management', *International Journal of Green Energy*, vol. 10, pp. 387–401.

Jiang, P, Dong, WB, Kung, YC and Geng, Y 2013, 'Analysing co-benefits of the energy conservation and carbon reduction in China's large commercial buildings', *Journal of Cleaner Production*, vol. 58, pp. 112–120.

Jiang, Y, Li, Q, Li, Z, Gao, Y, Zhu, X, Wei, Q and Yan, D 2007, *Energy Saving in the Building Sector in China*, Building Energy Saving Workshop, Tsinghua University, Beijing.

Li, J, Colombier, M and Barbier, C 2009, *Shaping Climate Policy in Urban Infrastructure: An Insight into the Building Sector in China*, viewed 8 January 2012, www.iddri.org/Publications/Collections/Analyses/an_0903_JunLi_BuildingChina.pdf.

Ministry of Housing and Urban Rural Development (MOHURD) 2014, *The National New Urbanization Plan (2014–2020)*, viewed 3 December 2014, http://dilemma-x.net/2014/03/17/china-national-new-type-urbanization-plan-2014-2020/.

National Bureau of Statistics of China 2010, *China Statistical Yearbook 2010*. Chinese Central Government, viewed 8 January 2012, www.stats.gov.cn/tjsj/ndsj/2010/indexch.htm.

National Bureau of Statistics of China 2014, *China Statistical Yearbook 2013*, Chinese Central Government, viewed 8 January 2012, www.stats.gov.cn/tjsj/ndsj/2013/indexeh.htm.

National Development and Reform Commission of China 2007, *China's National Climate Change Programme*, viewed 21 January 2012, www.china.org.cn/english/environment/213624.htm.

National Development and Reform Commission of China 2010, *China to Address Climate Change Policies and Actions*, viewed 31 December 2011, www.ccchina.gov.cn/WebSite/CCChina/UpFile/File927.pdf.

Puppim de Oliveira, JA, Suwa, A, Balaban, O, Doll, CNH, Jiang, P, Dreyfus, M, Moreno-Peñarada, R, Dirgahayani, P and Kennedy, E 2012. 'Good governance in cities for promoting a greener economy', in *Green Economy and Good Governance for*

Sustainable Development: Opportunities, Promises and Concerns, UNU Press, Tokyo, pp. 286–305.

Qiu, B, Jiang, Y, Lin, H, Peng, X, Wu, Y and Cui, L 2007, *Annual Report on China Building Energy Efficiency*, China Architecture and Building Press, Beijing, pp. 58–77.

Ramesh, T, Ravi, P and Shukla, K.K 2010, 'Life cycle analysis of buildings: An overview', *Energy and Buildings*, vol. 42, pp. 1592–1600.

Reinhard, M and Yasin, S 2011, 'Impacts of urbanization on urban structures and energy demand: What can we learn for urban energy planning and urbanization management?', *Sustainable Cities and Society*, vol. 1, no. 1, pp. 45–53.

Standing Committee Meeting 2007, *Energy Conservation Law of China*, The 28th National People's Congress of China, viewed 23 September 2016, www.npc.gov.cn/englishnpc/Law/2009-02/20/content_1471608.htm.

State Council of the People's Republic of China 2005, *People's Republic of Economic and Social Development Eleventh Five-Year Plan*, Chinese Central Government, Beijing.

State Council of the People's Republic of China 2010, *People's Republic of Economic and Social Development Twelfth Five-Year Plan*, Chinese Central Government, Beijing.

United Nations Human Settlements Programme (UN-HABITAT) 2008, *The State of the World Cities 2008/2009: Harmonious Cities*, Earthscan Publications, London.

UN Population Division, 2011 *The National Accounts Main Aggregates Database*, viewed 20 October 2013, http://unstats.un.org/unsd/snaama/introduction.asp.

US EPA 2015, *EPA's Indoor Environments Program*, viewed 29 September 2015, http://archive.epa.gov/greenbuilding/web/html/components.html.

World Bank 2008, *State and Trends of the Carbon Market 2008*, Report, viewed 2 February 2013, http://siteresources.worldbank.org/NEWS/Resources/State&Trendsformatted06May10pm.pdf.

World Green Building Council 2014, *Health, Wellbeing & Productivity in Offices The Next Chapter for Green Building*, viewed 10 September 2014, www.worldgbc.org/activities/health-wellbeing-productivity-offices/.

Zhang, H, Weng, S and Zhou, X 2007, 'Housing price fluctuations across China: An equilibrium mechanism perspective', *Tsinghua Science and Technology*, vol. 12, no. 3, pp. 302–308.

4.1 Shanghai, China, and Yokohama, Japan

Energy efficiency at the building and district scale

Ping Jiang

Two cases from China and Japan are presented here which quantify the level of energy, cost and carbon reductions that can be achieved through the implementation of technology and management strategies.

IKEA Xuhui store, Shanghai

Non-residential buildings account for approximately 37 per cent of the total area of buildings but consume around 70 per cent of the total energy in Shanghai (Jiang and Tovey 2010). Among these non-residential buildings, the large commercial buildings (those greater than 20,000 m^2) have an average energy consumption of 180 kWh/m^2, which is four times higher than the average energy use of residential buildings in Shanghai. IKEA is the world's largest furniture and home products retailer and is controlled by the Dutch Stichting INGKA Foundation. They operate two stores in Shanghai, one of which is the Xuhui store, which is located in Xuhui District and contains one furniture and home products retail store and a Swedish food restaurant over a total floor area of 35,000 m^2. The total energy consumption of IKEA Xuhui store, including electricity and natural gas consumption between 2004 and 2011, is presented in Figure 4.5.

In 2009, energy use increased by 8 per cent from the previous year because the store added 2,000 m^2 of retail area. Six main energy-saving technological measures were taken from 2008 (Table 4.3), which reduced energy use by 3.2 per cent in 2011 and by 1.5 per cent between 2004 and 2011.

The contribution of the measures outlined in Table 4.3 enabled energy saving and carbon reductions as shown in Table 4.4. The biggest contribution comes from the set of lighting improvements in the three areas of the store. There was a total GHG emissions reduction of over 1.3 million tonnes of CO$_2$e every year.[1]

Before adopting each measure, the investment plan was carefully worked out based on the real conditions in the store. For instance, the investment to the energy efficiency improvement in the storage lighting system was RMB11,000 (US$1,736). After taking this measure, 32,000 kWh was saved per annum, equivalent to around RMB19,744 (US$3,118[2]) in reduced energy costs (Shanghai

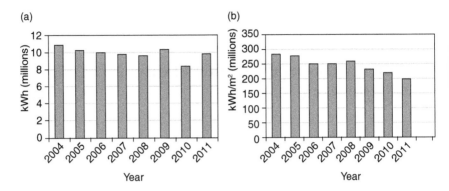

Figure 4.5 (a) Energy use, and (b) consumption per square metre at the IKEA Xuhui store, 2004–2011. Energy consumption per m² was reduced by 4.1 per cent from 2004 (i.e. increased energy efficiency per unit area) along with carbon emissions by association.

Source: reprinted from *Journal of Cleaner Production*, 58, Ping Jiang, Wenbo Dong, YiHsiu Kung and Yong Geng, 'Analysing co-benefits of the energy conservation and carbon reduction in China's large commercial buildings', 112–120, Copyright 2013, with permission from Elsevier.

Table 4.3 Energy-efficiency measures taken in the IKEA Xuhui store from 2008

No.	Item	Description	Year
1	Energy efficiency improvement in the lighting system	• 179 metal halide lamps replaced • 79 normal lighting lamps replaced • 2,900 Halogen lamps replaced	2008
2	Energy efficiency improvement in the basement lighting system	1,200 fluorescent lamps were replaced with 708 lamps which were more energy efficient. The automatic induction system was installed	2010
3	Energy efficiency improvement in the storage lighting system	The infrared induction lighting system was installed for 95 lamps, and 20 normal fluorescent lamps were replaced with low-energy lamps	2010
4	Energy efficiency improvement in air conditioning and ventilation systems	Installation of the heat recovering utility and natural ventilation system	2008
5	Energy efficiency improvement in the escalator system	Installation of the automatic frequency induction system for the escalators	2008
6	Central solar water heating system	Installation of the central solar water heating system for supplying hot water	2008

Source: reprinted from *Journal of Cleaner Production*, 58, Ping Jiang, Wenbo Dong, YiHsiu Kung and Yong Geng, 'Analysing co-benefits of the energy conservation and carbon reduction in China's large commercial buildings', 112–120, Copyright 2013, with permission from Elsevier.

Table 4.4 Energy saving and carbon reduction by taking technical measures in the IKEA Xuhui store between 2008 and 2011

No.	Item	Energy saving (kWh/year)	Carbon reduction (kg.CO₂e/year)
1	Energy efficiency improvement in the lighting system in the retail area	1,107,500	977,400
2	Energy efficiency improvement in the basement lighting system		
3	Energy efficiency improvement in the storage lighting system		
4	Energy efficiency improvement in air conditioning and ventilation systems	170,000	150,000
5	Energy efficiency improvement in the escalator system	20,000	17,650
6	Central solar water heating system	196,000	173,000
	Total	1,493,500	1,318,050

Source: reprinted from *Journal of Cleaner Production*, 58, Ping Jiang, Wenbo Dong, YiHsiu Kung and Yong Geng, 'Analysing co-benefits of the energy conservation and carbon reduction in China's large commercial buildings', 112–120, Copyright 2013, with permission from Elsevier.

Electricity Power Company 2012), easily paying back the investment within one year. By contrast, the central solar water heating system investment was RMB660,000 (US$104,216), yielding an energy cost saving of RMB120,932 (US$19,096) per year. So, the investment will be returned in five and half years.

The total investment for the six measures listed in Table 4.3 was RMB5,189,000 (US$819,359), and based on the total reduction of energy consumption (i.e. 1,493,500 kWh/year; see Table 4.4), the annual energy cost saving is RMB921,490 (US$145,506). Thus, the return on investment period is 5.63 years for the IKEA Xuhui store. Based on further information gathered from interviews and seminars with the store's energy managers, IKEA's efforts to the co-benefits are summarized as follows:

- Complying with national and local policies on energy conservation and environmental protection and closely collaborating with local government. The store works closely with the local government of Xuhui District and has applied for funding from the Bureau of Finance of Xuhui government for supporting further activities in saving energy and reducing carbon emissions.
- Besides utilizing technical measures in improving energy efficiency in lighting, air conditioning, ventilation and escalator systems, and using solar energy for supplying hot water, the store has its own energy management system which contains procedures and schemes for effectively managing energy performance in the store. A third-party auditor has been appointed

for this. All relevant investment plans have been formed carefully and implemented based on local realities with a reasonable and acceptable return period.

- Establishing an energy management team which is responsible for energy performance. The general manager of the store is also the leader of the energy management team. The annual energy saving objectives, feasibility studies and action plan are made by the team. Related awareness raising, information sharing and basic training are undertaken regularly among the whole staff. Special training programmes are also designed for the team members. All these measures have strengthened the capacity to implement the energy saving and carbon reduction activities.

- Actively engaging in efforts towards low-carbon sustainability in the local community. Some events have been made by IKEA for awareness raising in local schools, district centres and youth centres. Environmental protection and energy saving campaigns and advertisements have been undertaken in the store to encourage more public engagement with IKEA.

The IKEA Xuhui store is a useful case for analysing the implementation of a co-benefits approach for achieving the reduction of energy consumption, carbon emissions and energy costs in the building sector. As mentioned in Chapter 4, more than 80 per cent of urban buildings in China have adopted no, or only minimal, energy-saving measures (Jiang et al. 2007). In order to overcome these barriers and achieve long-term, low-carbon sustainable development in the building sector, the co-benefits approach must be addressed with comprehensive consideration of aspects related to overall energy performance and carbon emissions, and implemented based on the local conditions.

Case study in Japan

The Minato Mirai 21 District (MM21) was built in 1983 as a new urban centre in Yokohama, and is now established as one of the newest urban business districts with a good reputation for having an environmentally friendly living and working environment.

The Minato Mirai 21 District Heating and Cooling Co. Ltd. (MM21 DHC) was established in 1986 for supplying heating and cooling for 36 commercial and residential buildings in MM21. The district heating and cooling systems operated by MM21 DHC are made up of two local plants that produce cold water and steam for cooling and heating and also supply hot water and a network of supply pipes which service the buildings. According to the Heat Supply Business Act (Ministry of Economy of Japan 1972), as one of the public utilities in Japan, MM21 DHC must supply heating and cooling to MM21 in compliance with the relevant Japanese national and local energy conservation and climate change policies and building design codes.

The energy resources used by MM21 DHC include natural gas, industrial steam and electricity. Annual energy use increased by 8 per cent between 1996 and 2010 due to business expansion in the area. Meanwhile, the total floor area of residential and non-residential buildings in MM21, which is serviced by MM21 DHC, grew from 822,000 m² in 1996 to 2,697,000 m² in 2010; a growth rate of 15.2 per cent per annum (MM21 DHC 2012). The derived graph of energy consumption per m² (Figure 4.6) reveals that overall energy efficiency improved by 2.2 per cent per year. This also implies similar levels of cost savings and carbon emission reductions.

The co-benefits from the district heating and cooling systems in MM21, Yokohama can be generally categorized as follows:

- Energy saving and GHG emissions reduction benefits from improved efficiency of operating a system with centralized facilities and advanced technologies of thermal storage and effective energy management. With the continuous capacity building, compared to most conventional systems (e.g. urban buildings are heated and cooled individually) which are used widely in China, the district heating and cooling systems in Yokohama can reduce energy consumption and carbon emissions by 15 per cent.
- Reduction of local air pollution benefit. Since the city uses gas, which contains no sulphur, the system significantly reduces SO_2 emissions.
- Mitigation of the heat island phenomenon. The heat island phenomenon occurs when urban environments maintain temperatures higher than their surrounding environments. With the centralized boiler and chiller plants, and good management, the district heating and cooling systems in MM21 can significantly reduce the amount of exhaust heat when producing the heating and cooling.

With an increasing demand for energy conservation and environmental solutions in Japan, especially after the Great East Japan Earthquake of March 2011,

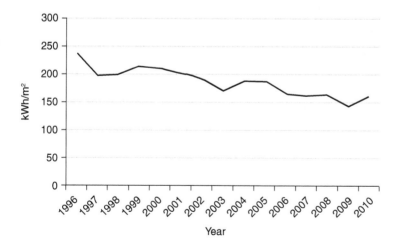

Figure 4.6 The energy consumption per m² in buildings serviced by MM21 DHC between 1996 and 2010.

Yokohama is promoting district heating and cooling and is actively pursuing widespread application of these systems. This raises the potential for further low-carbon technologies and state-of-the-art equipment to be utilized for a cleaner and more efficient energy service supply in Yokohama and other Japanese cities.

Notes

1 Taking a value of $0.88\,kg.CO_2e/kWh$ as the emission factor in Shanghai (National Development and Reform Commission of China 2008).
2 The price of electricity is $RMB0.617/m^3$ in Shanghai. The annual energy cost saving is: $32,000 \times 0.617 = RMB19,744$.

References

Jiang, Y, Li, Q, Li, Z, Gao, Y, Zhu, X, Wei, Q and Yan, D 2007, *Energy Saving in the Building Sector in China*. Building Energy Saving Workshop, Tsinghua University, Beijing.

Jiang, P and Tovey, K 2010, 'Overcoming barriers to implementation of carbon reduction strategies in large commercial buildings in China', *Building and Environment*, vol. 45, no. 4, pp. 856–864.

Ministry of Economy of Japan 1972, 'Heat Supply Business Act', viewed 10 January 2016, www.cas.go.jp/jp/seisaku/hourei/data/HSBA.pdf.

MM21 DHC 2012, 'Advantages of district heating and cooling', viewed 11 May 2016, www.mm21dhc.co.jp/english/merit/index.php.

National Development and Reform Commission of China 2008, 'Baseline emission factors for regional power grids in China', viewed 10 July 2015, www.sepacec.com/cecen/cdm1/Information/Domestic_Information/200807/P020080731475294834048.pdf.

Shanghai Electricity Power Company 2012, 'The price of electricity in Shanghai', viewed 10 July 2015 www.sh.sgcc.com.cn/html/main/col7/2016-06/21/20160621144920167955047_1.html.

4.2 Tokyo, Japan

Low-carbon policy for buildings

Hitomi Roppongi

Tokyo is one of the largest metropoles in the world, with an estimated day population of 15.6 million (Statistics Japan 2015). The capital is by far the biggest centre of economic activity in Japan, where nearly 20 per cent of the GDP is generated and prefectural income per capita is 150 per cent of the national average (TMG Bureau of Industry and Labor Affairs 2015). In the fiscal year 2013, annual energy consumption in Tokyo was about 832 PJ, of which more than 68 per cent is attributed to industrial and commercial sectors (METI 2015a).

Being the largest economic hub in the country with continuous influx of population, Tokyo faces urban development challenges that are shared with many other rapidly growing cities. Implementing climate change mitigation measures while providing socio-economic opportunities is one of them, and the Tokyo Metropolitan Government (TMG) has taken an innovative approach to tackle this challenge by introducing a mandatory cap-and-trade and emission reporting scheme. Cap-and-trade consists of the mandatory capping of CO_2 emissions on all large-scale buildings (termed large business facilities[1]), supplemented by an emission trading system (ETS) for the facilities that could not internally reduce their own emissions by themselves. The capped facilities are obliged to reduce CO_2 emissions within each compliance period and submit reduction plans annually. Large tenants of the building facilities are also mandated to submit emission reduction plans and cooperate with building owners to conserve energy. Reporting of CO_2 emissions is mandatory for large business facilities and is either mandatory or voluntary for small and medium-sized business facilities[2] depending on the total energy use (TMG Bureau of Environment 2015a).

How useful is the policy?

The TMG's low-carbon policy demonstrated benefits that are specific to the built environment and also played a role in information sharing. Report generation has helped facilities and tenants to visualize energy use patterns and identify their own areas for potential improvement. This would not have been possible without emission inventories of buildings and the existence of a dedicated technical manager on each facility as per the policy's obligations. Involving tenants in the low-carbon scheme also created an opportunity for building owners and tenants to collaborate in energy conservation. Fifty-six per cent of the tenants made energy-saving proposals to building owners according to the 2013 survey, which signifies willingness on the part of tenants' initiatives to cooperate with building owners'. Behavioural changes among tenants have also been observed, such as unplugging of appliances not in use, which increased from 26 per cent to nearly 50 per cent between 2010 and 2013 (TMG 2015c).

The policy also contributed to a change in the business sector's perception towards energy saving. Large business facilities have expressed that the TMG's policy was a catalyst to start business-wide energy conservation and accumulate knowledge in ways to reduce energy use. The TMG's schemes also raised awareness and allowed institutional learning amongst those involved, which is deemed useful when faced with energy conservation tasks. For instance, a new central monitoring system that allowed all employees to access centrally controlled energy consumption data raised awareness and participation of employees (TMG 2015c). According to the TMG's survey conducted in 2014, 72 per cent agreed or strongly agreed that business leaders have been increasingly aware of energy conservation and that employees have become more cooperative to reduce energy use after the implementation of the Tokyo's cap-and-trade programme in 2010 (TMG 2015a). Notably, reduction of energy consumption has become a regular part of business activities for many large business facilities due to the TMG's low-carbon scheme.

The usefulness of this policy was widely confirmed when Japan faced an energy crisis in 2011 following the Great East Japan Earthquake, as planned blackouts were carried out over the course of several months. The high-energy consuming business sector was challenged with a sudden cut in electricity supply and Tokyo was no exception in the midst of the nation-wide crisis. As a result, total domestic energy consumption was reduced by 2.8 per cent in 2011 compared to the previous year, of which Tokyo accounted for a reduction of 4.1 per cent (METI 2015a, 2015b). More notably for industrial and commercial sectors, energy consumption of Tokyo's regulated facilities reduced by nearly 10 per cent compared to around 3 per cent for equivalent buildings in the rest of the country. Although energy consumption increased in 2012 on average for the industrial and business operation sectors in Tokyo, energy use of regulated facilities have maintained their energy consumption at a level 20 per cent below that of 2005 (TMG 2015a).

What has been learnt so far?

Understanding how such a policy could be implemented in spite of common resistance from the industrial sector has attracted both scholarly and practical interest. Several works have been published to describe policy design, policy process and enabling factors of effective reduction (Niederhafner 2013; Nishida and Hua 2011; Roppongi et al 2016; Satou and Yamamoto 2012; Rudolph and

Kawakatsu 2012). Innovation is found in the definition of regulated actor, process of policy-making and institutional conditions that enabled the implementation and delivery; all of which provide lessons to any sub-national government. To this end, the TMG has been sharing its experience and knowledge at various forums to provide learning opportunities, both domestically and internationally.

At the domestic level, the neighbouring prefecture of Saitama approached the TMG directly to learn from their policy and adapted the design for their local needs,[3] implementing their own voluntary cap-and-trade scheme in 2011 granting national offset credits (J-VER), which are not tradable in Tokyo's scheme.[4] Mandating the reduction was discussed with stakeholders, but obligation was not deemed to be the best approach for a prefecture whose target facilities largely consist of factories.[5] The policy remains voluntary and focused on target-setting, so as to respect discussions with stakeholders and scholars. The two prefectures have also agreed on credit exchanges under their cap-and-trade schemes and have been proposing to the national government to implement a nation-wide cap-and-trade scheme that suits the existing local initiatives (Saitama Prefecture 2015; TMG 2015b). More recently, knowledge is shared in meetings (lead by the Ministry of Environment) of prefectures and domestic local networks, which implies there is wider interest in further domestic policy diffusion.

The TMG has also been active in sharing its experience and policy design with international networks. In 2014, the TMG presented its achievement at a UNFCCC technical meeting in Bonn and hosted C40 workshops and forums in Tokyo. The TMG also co-authored a report with the C40, which has been published as a case study in reports written by various organizations, including the International Emissions Trading Association, the International Carbon Action Partnership (ICAP) and the World Bank (TMG 2015c). Interested government entities have also approached the TMG directly, which includes one-to-one questions regarding the role of tenants in the scheme addressed by participants of seminars and meetings. Neighbouring East Asian countries are no exception to this, and have also visited the TMG to learn from their pioneering ETS.[6] South Korea started a nation-wide ETS from 2015 and China plans to develop a nation-wide ETS in coming years (ICAP 2015).

Challenges ahead

Tokyo's experience in developing the world's first city-level ETS shows that a local climate policy dedicated to buildings could induce both technological and behavioural changes, which ultimately generated various benefits in return to the society. The TMG's case also presented a conceptual evolution that the building-based approach enables an evidence-based planning and control of GHG emission using local inventories. Involvement of stakeholders from earlier stages of the policy process was a key to attaining stakeholder agreements and the sub-national autonomy in climate policy is now seen as a viable alternative approach to the gridlock at higher levels of government. Design and achievements of the TMG's policy has been widely shared, yet there remain challenges to disseminate the experience to other cities around the world since it requires adapting to the local need and institutional environment. Rather than studying the technical details of policy design alone, focus should rather be shifted to the concept, mechanism and visions of climate change mitigation presented by the TMG's low-carbon policy. Such an approach would be useful to the future development of sub-national climate policies elsewhere.

Notes

1 Business facilities that consume energy for more than 1,500 kl equivalent of oil are called large business facilities and there are 1,281 facilities as of June 2015 (TMG 2015a).
2 Business facilities that consume energy for less than 1,500 kl equivalent of oil are called small and medium-sized business facilities. Business owners whose total energy consumption exceeds 3,000 kl equivalent of oil are subject to mandatory emission reporting and for others reporting is voluntary. As of December 2014, there are 22,413 mandatory submissions and 11,829 voluntary submissions (TMG Bureau of Environment 2015b).
3 Interview with officials from the Saitama prefecture on 17 November 2015.
4 There are five types of credits issued in Tokyo: (i) exceeding credits; (ii) small and medium-sized installation credits within Tokyo area; (iii) renewable energy certificate; (iv) outside Tokyo credits; (v) Saitama credits (for Saitama, this is termed 'Tokyo credits').
5 As of 5 May 2015, there are 607 large facilities subject to the mandatory reporting and voluntary cap-and-trade scheme in the Saitama prefecture. Nearly 80 per cent of these are factories and the remaining are office buildings.
6 Interview with TMG officials on 16 November 2015.

References

International Carbon Action Partnership (ICAP) 2015, 'Emission trading worldwide', *ICAP Status Report 2015*, ICAP, viewed 22 March 2016, https://icapcarbonaction.com/images/StatusReport2015/ICAP_Report_2015_02_10_online_version.pdf.

METI 2015a, 'Todofuken betsu enerugi shohi tokei chosa (Statistical survey on energy consumption by prefectures)', Ministry of Economy, Trade and Industry, viewed 22 March 2016, www.enecho.meti.go.jp/statistics/energy_consumption/ec002/results.html #headline2.

METI 2015b, 'Sogo enerugi tokei (Comprehensive energy statistics)', Ministry of Economy, Trade and Industry, viewed 22 March 2016, www.enecho.meti.go.jp/statistics/total_energy/results.html.

Niederhafner, S 2013, 'The governance modes of the Tokyo Metropolitan Government emissions trading system', *Invited Fellow Discussion Paper No. 26*, Hitotsubashi University, viewed 22 March 2016, http://hdl.handle.net/10086/26005.

Nishida, Y and Hua, Y 2011, 'Motivating stakeholders to deliver change: Cap-and-trade program', *Building Research and Information*, vol. 39, no. 5, pp. 518–533, doi: 10.1080/09613218.2011.596419.

Roppongi, H, Suwa, A, and Puppim de Oliveira, JA 2016, 'Innovation in sub-national climate policy: The mandatory emissions reduction scheme in Tokyo', *Climate Policy* [Online], 8 March, doi: 10.1080/14693062.2015.1124749.

Rudolph, S and Kawakatsu, T 2012, 'Tokyo's greenhouse gas emissions trading scheme: A model for sustainable megacity carbon markets', in L Kreiser, JE Milne and H Ashiabor (eds), *Market Based Instruments: National Experiences in Environmental Sustainability'*, Edward Elgar Publishing, Cheltenham, pp. 77–93.

Saitama Prefecture 2015, *Kuni no seisaku* (National policies), viewed 22 March 2016, www.pref.saitama.lg.jp/kense/sesaku/index.html.

Satou, H and Yamamoto, K 2012, 'An evaluation of carbon dioxide emissions trading among enterprises: The Tokyo cap and trade program', *Journal of Communication and Computer*, vol. 9, no. 9, pp. 1008–1020, viewed 22 March 2016, www.davidpublishing.com/show.html?8001.

Statistics Japan 2015, *Jinko suikei: Heisei 26 nen 10 gatsu 1 nichi genzai* (Population estimate as of 1 October 2014), viewed 22 March 2016, www.stat.go.jp/data/jinsui/2014np/index.htm.

Tokyo Metropolitan Government (TMG) 2015a, *Cap & trade seido 4 nenme no sakugen jisseki hokoku* (Report on the reduction achievement in the 4th year of the cap-and-trade scheme), TMG, viewed 22 March 2016, www.metro.tokyo.jp/INET/OSHIRASE/2015/02/20p2j700.htm.

TMG 2015b, *Kuni no shisaku oyobi yosan ni taisuru teian yokyu* (Proposals and requests to national measures and budgets), TMG, viewed 22 March 2016, www.seisakukikaku.metro.tokyo.jp/kouiki/teianyoukyu.htm.

TMG 2015c, *Tokyo Green Biru Report* (Tokyo Green Building Report 2015), TMG, viewed 22 March 2016, www.kankyo.metro.tokyo.jp/climate/tokyogreenbuilding2015/docs/report2015.pdf.

TMG Bureau of Environment 2015a, 'Daikibo jigyosho heno onshitsu koka gasu haishutsu sakugen gimu to haishutsu ryo torihiki seido: Gaiyou (An overview of the mandatory reduction of total emission and ETS for large business facilities)', TMG Bureau of Environment, viewed 22 March 2016, www.kankyo.metro.tokyo.jp/climate/large_scale/attachement/seidogaiyou_201505.pdf.

TMG Bureau of Environment 2015b, 'Heisei 26 nendo chikyu ondanka taisaku hokokusho no deta shukei kekka (Aggregate results of reports on measures against global warming)', TMG Bureau of Environment, viewed 22 March 2016, www8.kankyo.metro.tokyo.jp/ondanka/news/20150312/pdf/20150312_dataprocessing.pdf.

TMG Bureau of Industrial and Labor Affairs 2015, 'Industry and employment in Tokyo: A graphic overview 2015', TMG Bureau of Industrial and Labor Affairs, viewed 22 March 2016, www.sangyo-rodo.metro.tokyo.jp/toukei/sangyo/graphic/2015/.

5 Energy

Hooman Farzaneh

Introduction

Urban density and spatial organization are key factors that influence energy consumption, especially in the transportation and building sectors. In developed countries, emissions in cities are driven less by industrial activities, and increasingly more by the energy services required for lighting, heating and cooling, electronics and transport. Growing urbanization and rapid economic growth in different regions will necessitate a shift in urban energy use from traditional energy sources such as biomass to more energy-dense (and by association more CO_2 intensive) sources. Figure 5.1 shows the different energy end-use distribution in cities according to their size and their stage of economic development.

In megacities such as Beijing and Shanghai, industries consume more than 50 percent of total energy use, reflecting the fast growth of the Chinese economy, while in large cities of countries whose economies are growing at a slower pace, it is the transportation sector which consumes more than half of the total energy (UN-HABITAT 2009). Industry and power generation are major contributors to the carbon footprint of Chinese cities (see China cases) in

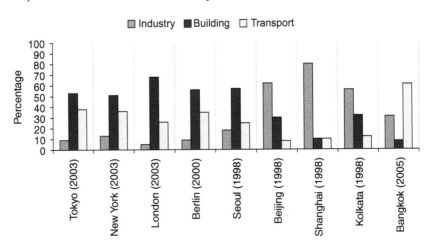

Figure 5.1 Share of different sectors in energy consumption in selected cities.

particular because the energy mix is dominated by coal (Figure 5.2). Meanwhile, residential and commercial buildings account for more than half of the energy consumed in cities such as London and Tokyo.

The concerns of policy makers dealing with energy in cities focus not only on issues related to availability or its use, but also on the implication of its use as many energy sources ultimately produce local air pollutants and greenhouse gases as waste, which exert serious local and global implications on human health due to their unacceptable concentrations (see Chapter 12). The link between the energy sector and climate change mitigation may be studied through understanding the effect of the main key factors that determine energy use in cities. These factors can be categorized as follows:

- *Urban form* is one of several critical factors influencing energy demand and greenhouse gas emission levels. The probability of high emissions *per capita* is indeed much higher in less densely populated areas (see Chapter 3) but urban form is not by itself a sufficient condition for attaining lower *per capita* emissions. Rather, it is a critical factor among several others, such as energy prices, the productive structure of urban areas or the public transportation network. As urban areas become denser and rely more on public transport, walking and cycling, carbon emissions tend to be reduced.
- The city's **geographic situation** influences the amount of energy required for heating, cooling and lighting. The climate characteristics of cities (cool, temperate, hot-arid and hot-humid) have greatly influenced energy use in

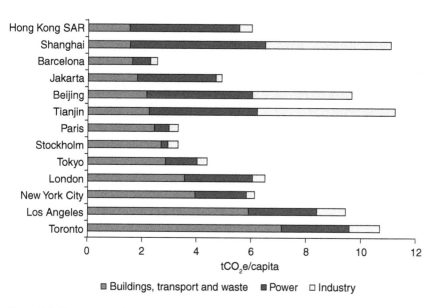

Figure 5.2 Per capita carbon emissions of selected cities in 2010.
Source: World Bank 2010.

its buildings as well. Hot and cold climate conditions directly affect energy use due to the greater demand for space conditioning.

- According to the summary for policy makers approved by the Intergovernmental Panel on Climate Change (IPCC) Working Group III (2007), changes in *lifestyles* and consumption patterns that emphasize resource conservation can contribute to developing a low-carbon economy that is both equitable and sustainable (Metz et al. 2007). Rather the way in which people move around the city, the sprawl that they produce and the way in which people use energy at home make cities the great consumers of energy and polluters that they are. A sprawl structure is probably the most consumptive housing pattern that cities could come up with which can affect the daily flow of energy and water used and waste generated to support the lifestyle of people in the buildings.

- The impact of energy consumption on greenhouse gases (GHG) emissions depends not just on the amount consumed, but also on the GHG emissions generated by the *energy source*, which in turn depends on the mode of energy production. Urban areas relying on inefficient or wasteful energy sources contribute more GHG emissions than those that consume the same amount from more efficient sources. There are many opportunities to shift energy supply from fossil fuels to low-carbon alternatives in cities. Key examples include electricity production for wind, nuclear or hydro power as well as equipping fossil fuel plants with carbon capture and storage (CCS) and replacing conventional transportation fuels with biofuels.

- Some of the key technologies relevant for cities are automobile fuel efficiency, appliance efficiency in the household and commercial sectors related to lighting, heating, cooling, cooking, electric appliances, etc. *Energy efficiency* improvements can significantly affect the energy use in cities. Building-related technologies such as air conditioners, district heating and cooling systems, insulation systems and other building energy management systems affect energy use significantly (see the building case for Shanghai and Yokohama, Chapter 4.1). These can be especially so when applied across industries in cities which are industrial hubs.

Studies seeking to understand the determinants of urban energy use are therefore increasingly important in order to identify where the most prospective points for public policy intervention exist. For local authorities seeking to craft a maximal effective energy or climate action plan, the co-benefits approach, which details local policy making competencies in an exhaustive way, appears to offer the greatest potential.

This chapter presents a conceptual framework for assessing climate co-benefits in the energy sector and discusses the classification of expected co-benefits in the urban energy system. The cases in this chapter follow two themes. The first two cases discuss modeling results from Japan's historical experience of pollution control (Chapter 5.1) and projected co-benefits from control policies applied to four large Chinese cities (Chapter 5.2). The second set of cases address in some detail the role of executive policy targets in supporting the reduction of energy use and pollution in Shanghai, China (Chapter 5.3) and Shenyang, China (Chapter 5.4).

Climate co-benefits in the energy sector

Climate change mitigation (i.e. reducing GHG emissions) generates both benefits and costs. The term 'co-benefits' is useful because it emphasizes an integrated approach, linking climate change mitigation to the achievement of sustainable development in the economic systems. The concept of considering GHG reduction strategies in the context of potential co-benefits is gaining attention. Reduction of GHG emissions, through the development of renewable energy, energy efficiency, reduction of transportation emissions and other initiatives can also reduce emissions or concentrations of criteria air pollutants, which can lead to improvements in air quality and public health. From a city-wide perspective, municipalities can address GHG reduction through their land-use planning practices (Chapter 3), regulatory tools, zoning, building and development permits, growth policies, by-laws, licenses, standards and through public education and outreach. Table 5.1 shows the potential areas of action for development needs-oriented efforts to address climate co-benefits in the energy sector.

While many of the energy conversion steps and processes (i.e. electricity generation, refining, storage, etc.) are not taking place in the cities, they should be considered in the overall system, particularly if they are being used to service urban energy demands. Moreover, even though cities might be seen as the net consumers of energy supplied from external resources, there are significant opportunities for local energy generation in cities (Farzaneh *et al.* 2016). Figure 5.3 presents these

Table 5.1 Needs-oriented efforts to address co-benefits in the energy sector

Development objectives/needs	Examples of assistance project	Concrete developmental benefits	Key actions	Climate change related benefits
Energy demand	Construction of power plants	Increased energy supply	EE, RE and turbine with higher capacity	GHG and AP reduction
Economic infrastructure	Mass transit development	Increased mobility of passengers	Modal shift (transport mode change)	GHG and AP reduction
Environmental protection	Upgrading waste process	Increased waste processing capacity, reduction of air and water pollution substances (e.g. SO_2)	Avoiding LFG, cleaner production	GHG and AP reduction
Advanced industrial production	Upgrading production facilities	Higher productivity and economic competitiveness	Demand-side EE	GHG and AP reduction

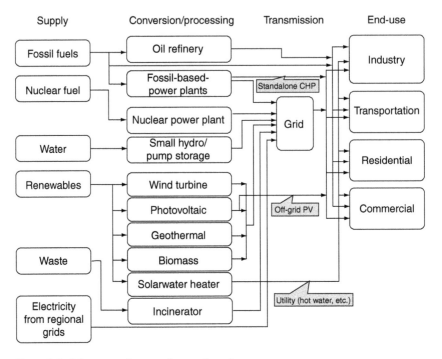

Figure 5.3 Schematic of energy flow in the urban energy system.

processes and their interactions, comprising energy supply, processing, conversion, transmission, allocation and utilization. Energy processing and conversion within the city comprises oil-refining processes and various power-conversion technologies. Specifically, crude oil can be refined locally into a number of oil products for end-users, while coal, liquefied natural gas (LNG), nuclear fuel and renewable energy resources are mainly used for electricity generation. Multiple conventional and renewable energy resources are available which can be selected for the energy processing and conversion for allocation to multiple end-users, while a range of pollution mitigation facilities are employed to control air-pollutant emissions.

Implementation of mitigation measures in the energy sector can play an important role in increasing the sufficiency of resources to meet energy demand at competitive and stable prices as well as improve the resilience of the energy supply system. Specifically, mitigation actions result in:

- strengthened power grid reliability through the enhancement of properly managed on-site generation and the reduction of the overall demand, which result in reduced power transmission and distribution losses and constraints;
- increased diversification of energy sources as well as the share of domestic energy sources used in a specific energy system.

GHG emissions reduction measures in the building, waste and transport sectors offer substantial urban climate mitigation potential through the implementation of efficiency measures.

In the transport and building sectors, upfront financing might be challenging, but costs reduce once investments have been made. These urban sectors, also known as the 'low hanging fruits', offer greenhouse gas abatement costs that yield long-term economic returns even without their participation in carbon markets (Figure 5.4). In several of the industrial sectors, average abatement costs are relatively high, whereas upfront investments are lower. Making the abatement happen in these sectors is more a question of compensating companies for the high costs, rather than financing of the investments themselves. Here, the implementation challenges are more practical rather than economic, namely, designing effective policies and effective ways of measuring and monitoring the abatement.

Four overarching sets of issues form the core of the co-benefit approach in the energy sector and are categorized as follows:

- **Definition and goals**: How can the co-benefit approach be defined in an urban energy system? Which potential scenarios can be identified, and among them, which ones generate the most desirable outcomes?
- **Policy best practices and policy coherence**: Which types of policy instruments and program activities tend to be most successful in developing a co-benefits approach in a city's energy sector? How can policy coherence at the city scale be ensured to allow synergies to occur?

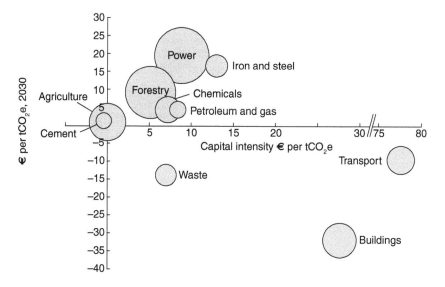

Figure 5.4 The 'low hanging fruits' of the urban energy sector GHG mitigation.

- **Measurement:** Which economic and environmental performance indicators indicate the presence of co-benefits and policy complementarities between environmental and economic objectives?
- **Obstacles to progress:** What institutional, regulatory and financing resource barriers inhibit the implementation of co-benefit strategies?

As shown in Figure 5.5, climate change concerns can be addressed by integrating relevant elements into development activities. Climate change-related activities may also cover development perspectives. In order to meet both needs (i.e. social/environmental development and climate protection) in a sustainable manner, it is useful to seek tangible benefits from both areas (co-benefits) through their respective processes, whereby further efforts by stakeholders are encouraged. There is great potential to introduce the co-benefits approach into ongoing development and climate-energy related activities, especially in developing countries. To do so, knowledge of means of implementation (e.g. finance, technology, etc.) is necessary, as is improved awareness and capacity on the part of policy makers, as it facilitates the ability to make integrated political decisions in favor of both development and climate protection.

In terms of the analytical approach to co-benefit evaluation in the energy sector, methodologies differ primarily based on how differently they represent the interactions between the energy system, emissions and the economy. Essentially, there are two major categories of methodologies: the top-down approach and the bottom-up approach (Johnstone 1994). Both approaches examine the relationship between the energy uses, which emit GHG emissions,

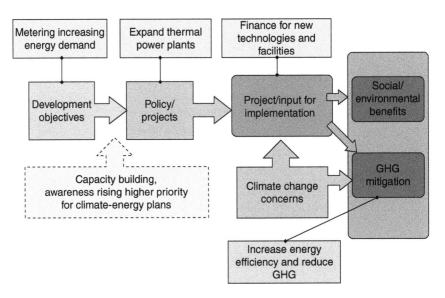

Figure 5.5 Overview of a co-benefits approach in the energy sector.

Source: Ministry of the Environment, Japan 2007.

and economic activities such as manufacturing, construction, mining, etc. The nature of each analytical approach, however, is quite distinct. The terms 'top-down' and 'bottom-up' themselves are shorthand for aggregated and disaggregated models. In the top-down approach, GHG emissions are assessed from the combustion of fossil fuels. The various fossil fuels, such as coal, oil and gas, are considered as energy inputs in a smooth aggregate production function (which include factors like capital, labor and other intermediate inputs). Hence, energy production (and the electricity sector in particular) deals more with discrete technology options and costs. In addition, technological change is sensitive to calibrated 'autonomous' technology improvement or exogenous parameter assumptions. By contrast, bottom-up models focus on either current or prospective technology options in detail, and are frequently used for optimal investment sectoral planning and instigating supply-side efficiency opportunities or demand-side energy conservation measures. The flowchart in Figure 5.6 illustrates how aggregated co-benefits in the energy sector can occur based on the bottom-up approach.

The A-S-I approach can be implemented through scenario planning in order to find available options for improving climate co-benefits in the urban energy system. Determining the right drivers helps to find the right ways to intervene

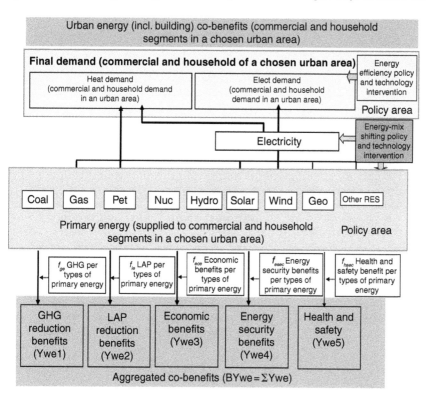

Figure 5.6 Flowchart of the aggregated co-benefits in the energy sector.

and create an action plan to achieve the sustainable goals in the urban energy system, as shown in Figure 5.7.

The A-S-I approach has the potential to contribute to emission reductions in the energy sector beyond current expectations. Energy security, better urban air quality and many other important co-benefits may be drivers that determine how to apply the A-S-I approach.

Avoid

The term *Avoid* refers to the need to improve the overall efficiency of the energy system (from resource to end-user) through the direct reduction of energy demand or its related emissions. A major co-benefit from GHG reductions in the energy sector is the simultaneous reduction in emissions of local air pollutants. The burning of fossil fuels, while a prime source of greenhouse gases, is also a major source of many key air pollutants, such as nitrogen oxides (NO_x), volatile organic compounds (VOC), carbon monoxide (CO) and particulate matter ($PM_{10/2.5}$). Figure 5.8 illustrates the connection between air pollutants and GHGs from the combustion of fossil fuels. These emissions are a precursor to smog, which plagues cities on an annual basis. By taking action to reduce energy use and the burning of fossil fuels, municipalities can reap the direct benefits of improved air quality.

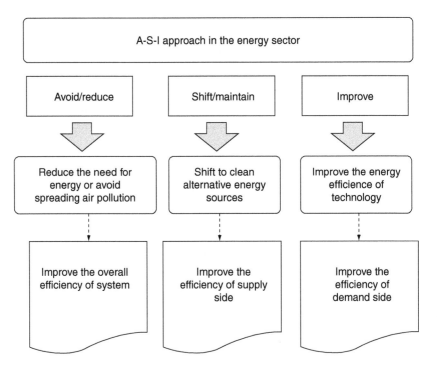

Figure 5.7 A-S-I approach in the energy sector.

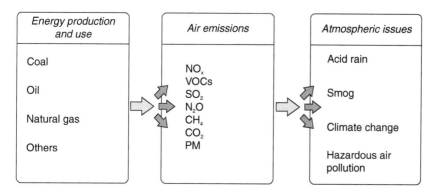

Figure 5.8 Anthropogenic GHG emissions and atmospheric issues in the energy sector.

Emissions not only occur from burning fossil fuels but also from their extraction and distribution. They currently contribute 5–10 percent of total fossil-fuel related GHG emissions. The move towards more energy-intensive production of oil and gas from unconventional sources such as shale and tight gas reserves would also cause this to increase. Furthermore, production requiring greater energy inputs at mature fields, mining of coal from deeper mines and longer transportation distances may also increase this contribution. Mitigation options include:

- capture and utilization of methane from coal mining;
- reduction of venting and flaring from oil and gas exploration, production and transportation.

CCS technologies are capable of significantly reducing CO_2 emissions of fossil fuel-fired power plants (Figure 5.9). Global warming is unlikely to be effectively addressed without the widespread adoption of CCS, and the cost of mitigation would be higher in the absence of CCS (Rubin *et al.* 2005). However, while all of the components of integrated CCS systems already exist, it has not yet been applied to a large, commercial fossil fuel-fired generation facility.

The Demand Response (DR) mechanism allows for a reduction in the need for energy in buildings and industries by encouraging customers to use less energy during peak hours, or by moving energy use to off-peak times, such as night-time and weekends. This gives customers more control over their energy usage and costs, while providing a valuable service to grid operators, namely load reduction during peak hours, when electricity is expensive or when grid reliability is compromised. Nowadays, DR technologies have become increasingly feasible due to the integration of information and communications technology within the power system, resulting in a new term: Smart Grid. A Smart Grid can improve traditional distribution grids through collecting information

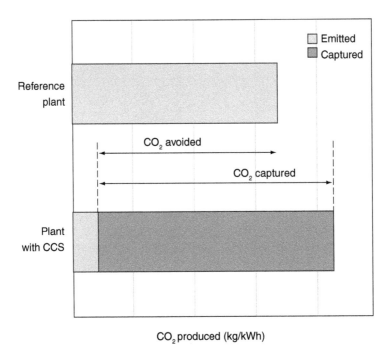

Figure 5.9 GHG reduction benefit from using CCS in power plants.
Source: Rubin *et al.* 2005.

on grid operating conditions, including electricity volumes, strengths and other characteristics, and transmit that information to utility computers. A Smart Grid can also perform continuous self-assessments to detect, analyze, respond to and restore grid components or network sections. It enables active participation by consumers and increased interaction with the grid brings tangible benefits to both the grid and the environment, while reducing the cost and amount of electricity delivered. Annual spending on global Smart Grid analytics is expected to grow from $700 million in 2012 to $3.8 billion by 2020 (Leeds 2012).

Sustainable urban design strategies can also have a profound effect on the health of citizens while decreasing the need for car use and its attendant GHG emissions. Strategies for reducing GHG emissions often involve getting people out of their cars. Not only does this result in improvements to local air quality, but it also encourages a more active lifestyle (Chapter 11). As a long-term co-benefit strategy, however, one cannot ignore the fundamental question of how much energy we actually need. Energy reduction strategies have become more and more attractive to decision-makers for interconnected security, environmental and economic reasons.

Shift

The impact of fuel switching from coal to gas can be compromised if fugitive methane release is not controlled. Replacing a higher-carbon fuel with a lower-carbon alternative can reduce overall emissions. For example, shifting from a current world-average coal-fired power plant to a modern natural gas combined cycle (NGCC) unit can halve emissions, provided that fugitive methane emissions are controlled.

Shifting from the conventional fossil fuels to renewable energy (RE) sources has significant potential for reducing GHG emissions. Hydropower is currently the largest single RE contributor, but solar, wind and bioenergy are expected to experience the biggest incremental growth. However, much will depend on regional specificities, with hydropower and geothermal continuing to be important in certain countries. RE is likely to penetrate most rapidly in electricity generation, at least in the near to medium term, followed by heating/cooling and transport. RE technologies still need direct support (e.g. feed-in tariffs, RE quota obligations and tendering/bidding) and/or indirect support (e.g. sufficiently high carbon prices for the internalization of other externalities), if their market shares are to increase. Expanding the use of RE in the electricity mix will bring increasing challenges associated with integrating generation facilities into the grid. Technical options exist for meeting these challenges, but may need additional policy support and may result in higher costs. RE can be integrated into all types of power systems, from large inter-connected continental-scale grids down to small stand-alone systems and individual buildings. Relevant system characteristics include the generation mix and its flexibility, network infrastructure, energy market designs and institutional rules, demand location, demand profiles, and control and communication capability. Wind, solar PV energy and concentrated solar power (CSP) without storage can be more difficult to integrate than dispatchable hydropower, bioenergy, CSP with storage and geothermal energy.

A large proportion of the city's energy consumption is for heating. Biomass is the single largest source of energy for buildings at the global scale, and it plays an important role for space heating, for production of hot water and for cooking in many developing countries. Compared to open fires, advanced biomass stoves provide fuel savings of 30–60 percent and reduce indoor air pollution levels by 80–90 percent for models with chimneys. Biomass heating can make a significant contribution, but with the constraints on biomass production, it is unlikely that this will meet all of the heating needs in cities, in particular given the opportunities for heat consumption reduction in existing buildings are limited. Therefore, for renewable heating it seems likely that some form of electric heating will be required – through heat pumps, for example.

As the penetration of variable RE sources increases, maintaining system reliability may become more challenging and costly. Having a portfolio of complementary RE technologies is one solution to reduce the risks and costs of RE integration. Environmental and economic benefits of adding renewable energy to a city's energy portfolio can include:

- generating energy that produces no greenhouse gas emissions from fossil fuels and reduces some types of air pollution;
- diversifying energy supply and reducing dependence on imported fuels;
- creating economic development and jobs in manufacturing, installation, and more.

Nuclear energy could make an increasing contribution to a low-carbon energy supply, but a variety of risks and barriers exist, with some countries such as Germany completely opting out of nuclear as part of its energy mix. Continued use and expansion of nuclear energy worldwide will require greater efforts to improve the safety, economics, uranium utilization, waste management and pro-liferation of materials. Research and development of next-generation nuclear energy systems, including new fuel cycles and reactor technologies, are currently underway.

Waste-to-energy systems reduce carbon emissions by offsetting the need for electricity from traditional generation sources while providing a reliable source of base load power. Municipal Solid Waste (MSW) plants emit half as much CO_2 per MWh as coal plants. MSW facilities recover energy from waste that would otherwise be buried in landfills, thereby reducing the methane emissions that would be released in decomposition (see Chapter 6 and Chapter 9, page 259). However, there are risks of dangerous air pollution if the technology is not managed properly, such as regular maintenance, waste quality and correct incin-eration temperature with respect to the type of waste burned.

Improve

Improving energy efficiency in power transmission, distribution and consump-tion could help reduce GHG emissions. Losses as a fraction of the energy gener-ated vary widely between countries, with some developing countries having losses of over 20 percent. Increased use of improved transformers and distributed power generation would reduce losses, while new technologies such as dynamic loading, gas-insulated transmission lines and high-voltage DC transmission (HVDC) could offer further reductions.

Energy efficiency can also be improved by retrofitting existing technologies in buildings and ensuring the efficiency of new ones; improving lighting and ventilation systems, cooking ovens and insulation materials. There are substan-tial differences in building energy use across the world, driven largely by behav-ior and culture. In developed countries where energy service levels are already high, lifestyle change can produce substantial energy use reductions. Similar reductions are not possible in developing countries where energy service demands need to grow to satisfy development needs. However, the rate of growth can be reduced by lower consumption lifestyles.

Lifestyle changes can reduce GHG emissions. Changes in lifestyles and con-sumption patterns that emphasize resource conservation can contribute to developing a low-carbon economy that is both equitable and sustainable. When the diversity of users' activities is taken into account, different technologies may be needed to satisfy the energy service demand. Therefore, cities and their energy infrastructure need to be designed, built and used to take into account culture, norms and occupant behavior. Behavior and local cultural factors can drive basic energy use practices, such as how people and organizations adjust their level of comfort in buildings during different times of the year. These settings are also influenced by cultural expectations and thus major energy savings and emission reductions can be achieved through changes in living standards. Many interventions to promote energy efficiency at city level do not succeed, at least to the extent expected, due to a failure to understand how people think about, and make decisions regarding, energy efficiency. One universal standard of 'high efficiency' based on certain cultural activities may increase the energy usage in cities with other cultural backgrounds, raising costs and emissions without actually improving living standards.

Heating and cooling networks facilitate mitigation where they allow the use of higher efficiency systems or the use of waste heat or lower carbon fuels (e.g. solar heat and biomass) than can be used cost effectively at the scale of the individual building. High-efficiency distributed energy systems, such as gas engines and solid oxide fuel cell co-generation, generate heat and electricity more efficiently than the conventional combination of centralized power plants and heating boilers, where heat can be used effectively. District heating and cooling, as well as district combined heat and power (CHP) plants, are excellent means of decreasing local energy costs, as they generally use local resources and waste less power. In regions with cold winters and hot summers, district energy systems can deliver both heating and cooling, usually at the city block scale, and primarily for commercial buildings. Larger benefits are possible by using waste heat from incineration plants and heat or cold from water source heat pumps. A growing number of EU cities – particularly those located in Northern, Central and Eastern Europe – are introducing, renovating and/or further expanding the district heating network in order to reduce fuel imports and diminish their residents' energy bills. An excellent example is that of Amsterdam (Netherlands), which has nearly completed a city-wide district energy belt (Covenant of Mayors n.d.).

With the industrial sector accounting for approximately one third of all energy used in cities, there is ample opportunity for Waste Energy Recovery (WER) to reduce energy usage. During industrial processes, 20 to 50 percent of the energy is ultimately lost. WER can improve efficiency of industrial processes by as much as 10–50 percent, depending on the process, while generating electricity that can be used onsite. WER both increases efficiency and displaces the need to purchase fuel and electricity, thus resulting in avoided emissions.

Thermal energy storage uses diurnal temperature variations to improve load factors, and therefore reduce heating and cooling system size, which will be particularly important if heating is electrified. Thermal storage technologies could also be important in regions with electricity systems using high levels of intermittent renewable energy. The use of storage in a building can smooth temperature fluctuations and can be implemented by sensible heat (e.g. changing the building envelope temperature) or by storing latent heat using ice or phase change materials in either passive or active systems. Several technologies can be used to store energy on the electricity transmission and distribution grid, including pumped storage hydro (PSH), compressed air energy storage (CAES), electrochemical batteries and flywheel systems. Energy storage systems can provide benefits to grid operations on three basic timescales: daily, hourly/sub-hourly and seconds-minutes. Each storage technology has strengths and weaknesses relative to these timescales. Daily applications include providing firm capacity reserves and system-wide peak shaving when demand is high. On the timescale of tens of minutes to a few hours, energy storage can help with load leveling (smoothing) and peak shaving, for example, to help smooth the output of variable renewable generation. Over timeframes of seconds to minutes, energy storage can help with frequency regulation, voltage support and reactive power. Batteries may be particularly good at these short-duration applications because they use power electronics and can respond quickly to changing grid conditions. In addition to these operational benefits, energy storage can help defer or avoid traditional investments in generation (peaking plants), transmission and distribution. And although energy storage itself can be a net consumer of energy, it enables air emission reductions that are expected to outweigh this energy use. The emission reductions benefits fall into three main categories: (1) increasing grid flexibility to allow for higher penetration of variable renewable generation; (2) offsetting emissions from older, dirtier plants for meeting peak demand; and (3) improving grid efficiency by relieving constraints when demand is high, since this is when transmission and distribution equipment losses are highest.

Table 5.2 shows examples of the key areas of the climate co-benefits in the energy sector. It is clear that the A-S-I approach will bring about different co-benefits, and these co-benefits may be different between developing and developed cities. Developing cities are dominated by large numbers of old high-polluting technologies on both demand and supply sides and the policies focusing on 'improve' will have relatively high co-benefits. With many cities in developing countries yet to develop a strong planning capacity, planning instruments can bring about higher co-benefits compared to cities in developed countries. Similarly, in developing cities, policy interventions targeting the end-user level can bring relatively large and immediate co-benefits compared to developed cities.

Opportunities for and barriers to achieving co-benefits in the energy sector

The co-benefits approach can become the leading paradigm in the energy sector over the next few years. Energy policies in the next decade may conceivably evolve in two ways: emphasizing a regulatory command-and-control approach such as mandatory energy consumption reductions; or utilizing more flexible and cost-effective programs. However, over the short term, both are encumbered by

Table 5.2 Examples of key areas of the climate co-benefits in the energy sector

Activity	Details of GHG reduction effect	Details of co-benefits	Type of co-benefit
• **Fuel switching** at thermal power plants or on-site power generators at a factory from heavy oil to natural gas with lower carbon content	Reduced CO_2 emissions due to fuel switching	Reduced SO_x emissions due to fuel switching	Air pollution prevention
• **Improve combustion efficiency** of the burners, furnaces, etc.	Reduced CO_2 emissions due to reduced fossil fuel consumption	Reduced SO_x emissions due to reduced fossil fuel consumption	
• **Install heat recovery systems** in power plants and factories to provide utilities (hot water, cooling, etc.) for the buildings	Reduced CO_2 emissions by using waste heat recovery and replacing fossil fuel use for power or heat generation	Reduced SO_x emissions by using waste heat recovery and replacing fossil fuel use for power or heat generation	
• **Improve end-use efficiency** by improving the lighting system, insulation and replacing the regular windows by double glazing windows in buildings	Reduced CO_2 emissions due to reduced fossil fuel consumption and improved electricity	Reduced SO_x emissions due to reduced fossil fuel consumption and electricity	
• **District heating system**	Reduced CO_2 emissions due to improved electricity	Reduced local pollutants (SO_x, NO_x, PM, etc.) due to improved electricity	
• **Reduction of power loss** by improving and upgrading, improving efficiency of electrical power transmission network	Reduced CO_2 emissions due to lower fossil fuel use for power generation, due to reduced power loss	Reduced local pollutants (SO_x, NO_x, PM, etc.) due to reduced use of fossil fuels	• Air pollution prevention • Lower power outage rate
• **Use of renewable energy** such as solar collector and ground source heat pump to provide heat and solar photovoltaic to generate electricity for the household sector	Reduced CO_2 emissions due to fuel shifting to the clean energy resources	Reduced local pollutants (SO_x, NO_x, PM, etc.) due to reduced fossil fuel consumption and electricity	• Air pollution prevention • Public health
• **Improvement of public transport** (LRT, BRT)	Reduced CO_2 emissions due to improved energy efficiency	Reduced local pollutants (SO_x, NO_x, PM, VOC, etc.) directly associated with public health	

strict monitoring and enforcement requirements and the need for accurate emission overviews and inventories. Thus, the co-benefits approach has the potential to become more relevant as the alternative that must be positioned complementarily to evolving policies in the energy sector. However, further conceptual clarification and consensus on an operational definition of co-benefits for the energy sector is required among the different researchers, governments, organizations and stakeholders who are actively interested. The applicable scope of the co-benefits paradigm spans a wide range of developments in the energy sector – for example, air quality, health, transport, land use planning, socio-economics and even disaster risk management.

Energy-related environmental policies should be integrated into overall urban development policies. This is necessary because it is perceived that the policies aimed at reducing the GHG emissions alone are difficult to put into operation if there are no accompanying local benefits, such as improvement in air pollution, the urban heat island effect, an increase in energy efficiency or other economic benefits. For example, increasing the energy efficiency in industries will bring a number of additional enhancements, such as lower maintenance costs, increased production yield, safer working conditions, amongst others, which in addition to reducing energy consumption will increase the productivity of the industrial sector. In addition, these improvements can significantly change the cost assessment of a technology and result in a more favorable evaluation.

Recently, international institutions have started to take an interest in the promotion of policies in industries and power plants which improve energy efficiency and promote new financial mechanisms, such as CDM was for the Kyoto Protocol. Such measures currently exist only on a limited, pilot-project basis. Although it is fairly accepted that co-benefit approaches are necessary, most international institutions have not operationalized explicit policies to promote such approaches. International institutions such as UN organizations, various intergovernmental panels, international research institutions and NGOs play a major role in directing international environmental debates and formulating action plans to support the co-benefits approach in the energy sectors of developing countries (Chapter 7).

Some barriers faced with the co-benefits approach in the energy sector occur when one party makes decisions affecting energy efficiency and pollution reductions in a given market, and a different party bears the consequences of those decisions. In fact, improvement of energy efficiency in a given market is an aggregate function of many small decisions. In many cases, the decision-maker in these small investments lacks the information or expertise to make a decision that would maximize both energy efficiency and economic efficiency. By contrast, energy supply investments, which typically occur in fewer and larger projects, are usually large enough to bear the cost of obtaining the expertise and information needed to make well-informed decisions. In this sense, the information costs attached to efficiency improvement decisions can lead to market failures.

It should be noted that all countermeasures optimizing air pollution benefits may not necessarily be the best ways to reduce GHG emissions in the energy sector. When there are several choices for controlling air pollutants, well-designed policies might yield benefits for GHG. For example, CNG has been introduced for air quality improvement in cities such as Delhi in India and Tehran in Iran, where CNG vehicles emit less NO_x and PM, and at the same time are more CO_2 friendly than conventional vehicles. While CNG reduces CO_2 emissions, it may also outweigh CO_2 benefits by increasing un-burnt methane (due to poor maintenance) in heavy-duty engines such as buses and trucks and, therefore, the city's inspection and maintenance systems have an important role in ensuring reduced GHG emissions. Another example, promoting mass transport and discouraging private cars can be considered to be an efficient policy to reduce CO_2 emissions, as it improves energy performance and reduces gasoline use. However, inefficient operation of mass transportation such as metro and bus systems tends to reduce their occupancy and promote private modes, which are usually more CO_2 intensive per passenger-km. In the waste sector, promoting landfill usage over incinerator usage can reduce CO_2 from incineration, but it may also increase methane, whose greenhouse warming potential is 21 times greater than that of CO_2 over the course of a century (UNFCCC 2014).

Conclusion

Climate change will affect the entire energy sector, through both impacts and policy. The scale of the low-carbon transition and the opportunities for investment are likely to be larger in the energy sector than in others. Scenarios project that a fundamental transformation will be necessary if governments are to meet the globally agreed 2°C target. Generally, these scenarios envisage three parallel processes: decarbonization of the electricity supply, expansion of the electricity supply into areas such as home heating and transport, and reduction in final energy demand. Much of the incremental investment will be in developing countries where demand is growing at a faster rate than in developed countries. The additional capital would be partly offset by the lower operating costs of many low-GHG energy supply sources. For government and regulators, a key challenge will be to ensure a price of carbon that incentivizes extra investment in low-carbon technologies, continued investment in research and development, and an attractive fiscal and regulatory framework.

It is clear that, with significant constraints on a sustainable energy supply, it is fundamental that attention is given to energy consumption reduction. Whilst much of this can be achieved through the reduction of unnecessary consumption without a notable impact on quality of life, it is likely that some sacrifices will need to be made and getting people to accept this will be a major challenge. It is therefore critical that the societal dimension of sustainability is understood and delivered upon.

References

Covenant of Mayors n.d., *Reducing Energy Dependence in European Cities*, viewed 24 March 2016, www.covenantofmayors.eu/IMG/pdf/CoM_Reducing_Energy_Dependence _for_web.pdf.

Farzaneh, H, Doll, CNH and Puppim de Oliveira, JA 2016, 'An integrated supply-demand model for the optimization of energy flow in the urban energy system', *Journal of Cleaner Production*, vol. 114, pp. 269–285.

Johnstone, N 1994, *The Integration of Bottom-Up and Top-Down Modeling of CO2 Emissions: Description of a Sectoral Analysis*, Energy-Environment-Economy Modeling Discussion Paper, no. 10, University of Cambridge, UK.

Leeds, D 2012, 'The Soft Grid 2013–2020: Big data and utility analytics for Smart Grid', *Green Tech Media Research*, viewed 8 November 2015, www.greentechmedia.com/ research/report/the-soft-grid-2013.

McKinsey & Company 2009, 'Pathway to a low-carbon economy: Version 2 of the global greenhouse gas abatement cost curve', Business Source Complete, viewed 1 January 2016, www.mckinsey.com/business-functions/sustainability-and-resource-productivity/ our-insights/pathways-to-a-low-carbon-economy.

Metz, B, Davidson, OR, Bosch, PR, Dave, R and Meyer, LA 2007, *Climate Change 2007: Mitigation of Climate Change*, Summary for Policymakers, Intergovernmental Panel on Climate Change (IPCC), Cambridge and New York.

Ministry of the Environment Japan (MOEJ) 2007, *Co-benefits Approach – Development Needs-oriented Efforts to Address Climate Change and CDM*, Overseas Environmental Cooperation Center (OECC), Japan.

Rubin, E, Meyer, L, de Coninck, H, Abanades, JC, Akai, M, Benson, S, Caldeira, K, Cook, P, Davidson, O, Doctor, R, Dooley, J, Freund, P, Gale, J, Heidug, W, Herzog, H, Keith, D, Mazzotti, M, Metz, B, Osman-Elasha, B, Palmer, A, Pipatti, R, Smekens, K, Soltanieh, M, Thambimuthu, K and van der Zwaan, B 2005, *IPCC Special Report: Carbon Dioxide Capture and Storage*, Technical Summary, viewed 17 January 2016, www. ipcc.ch/pdf/special-reports/srccs/srccs_technicalsummary.pdf.

UNFCCC 2014, *Global Warming Potentials*, viewed 17 January 2016, http://unfccc.int/ ghg_data/items/3825.php.

UN-HABITAT 2009, *State of the World's Cities 2008/2009*, 978-92-1-132010-7, London and Sterling, VA.

World Bank 2010, *Cities and Climate Change: An Urgent Agenda*, vol. 10, Urban Development Series Knowledge Papers, The International Bank for Reconstruction and Development/The World Bank, Washington DC.

5.1 Kawasaki, Japan

Revealing co-benefits of energy from environmental policies

Tsuyoshi Fujita, Huijuan Dong and Momoe Kanada

Introduction

It is well known that Japan experienced serious environmental problems during its period of vigorous economic development in the 1950s and 1960s (Ministry of the Environment Japan 1969). However, Japan has successfully overcome these challenges by developing high standards in environmental technologies and policy systems. The key to overcoming such air pollution issues has been the implementation of a comprehensive policy approach (Kanada *et al.* 2013). Moreover, most co-benefit research examines air pollutants and GHG emissions from a technological perspective (Geng *et al.* 2013; Yang *et al.* 2013) with only a few utilizing a broader policy perspective. This chapter introduces the Japanese case, which investigates the co-benefit effect of its environmental policies to enhance the effectiveness of policy design and implementation. This research can also expand and strengthen the co-benefit approach by revealing the linkages between policy and environmental change.

Background of case study area

Kawasaki City is the largest industrial centre in Japan, located between Tokyo and Yokohama (Figure 5.10), and is undergoing a drastic structural transformation from an industrial to a contemporary mixed-use city. Kawasaki City covers 144 km², and is home to 1.44 million inhabitants as of 2012. Kawasaki is well known not only for its industrial symbiosis, but also for actively initiating air pollution control policies as well as for successfully achieving environmental targets for SO_2 since 1979 (Dong *et al.* 2014). It was therefore selected as a case study for Japan's air pollutant co-benefit study.

Methodology

The Prais-Winsten estimation (1954) was applied to build a regression model. Three time periods (i.e. 1965–1985, 1965–1995, and 1965–2005) were defined and a regression analysis was performed for each period to assess how the significance of each variable changed over time. The two linear regression models are described in Equations (5.1 and 5.2).

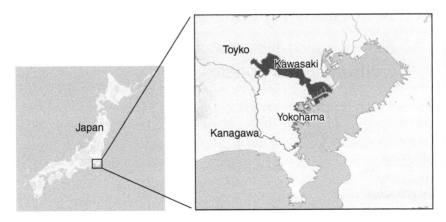

Figure 5.10 Geographic location of Kawasaki City in Japan.

Source: reprinted from *Energy*, 64, Huijuan Dong, Satoshi Ohnishi, Tsuyoshi Fujita, Yong Geng, Minoru Fujii and Liang Dong, 'Achieving carbon emission reduction through industrial and urban symbiosis: A case of Kawasaki', 277–286, Copyright 2014, with permission from Elsevier.

Five explanatory variables, namely: municipal environmental cost (ECT), number of facilities (FCT), oil price (OLP), two dummy variables for the agreement (DAGR) and the EIA ordinance (DEIA), were selected to build the regression model for atmospheric SO_2 level (ATML) and energy intensity (ENEGDP). ECT covered a wide range of costs related to municipal pollution activities, including funding, monitoring, research, education, and compensation. FCT was used to represent the influence of industrial structural change while OLP was included to represent an external factor that could have potentially impacted industrial activity. The two dummy variables were chosen to examine how those policies impacted both SO_x emissions and energy intensity.

$$ATMLi = \alpha_0 + \alpha_1 ECTi + \alpha_2 FCTi + \alpha_3 OLPi + \alpha_4 DAGRi + \alpha_5 DEIAi \quad (5.1)$$

$$ENEGDPi = \alpha_0 + \alpha_1 ECTi + \alpha_2 FCTi + \alpha_3 OLPi + \alpha_4 DAGRi + \alpha_5 DEIAi \quad (5.2)$$

Results and discussion

The estimated parameters for atmospheric SO_2 levels and energy intensity are shown in Table 5.3. While municipal environmental costs and the pollution agreement appeared to be significant factors for both atmospheric SO_2 levels and energy intensity, the environmental impact assessment law had a more significant impact on energy intensity than on atmospheric SO_2. This was an important finding in the context of co-benefits because the reduction in energy intensity was not one of the primary intentions of the environmental impact assessment law. Thus, the introduction of this law provided secondary environmental benefits.

Table 5.3 Results of multiple regression analysis for SO$_2$ emission and energy efficiency

Variables	1965–1985		1965–1995		1965–2005	
	Coefficient	t-statistics	Coefficient	t-statistics	Coefficient	t-statistics
Atmospheric SO$_2$ level (ATML)						
Constant	1.13E–01	8.66***	8.74E–02	9.12***	6.84E–02	15.92***
ECT	–1.36E–08	–2.59**	–1.90E–08	–5.26***	–1.78E–08	–5.30***
FCT	–1.53E–05	–3.03***	–5.62E–06	–1.52	1.81E–06	1.20
OLP	–2.43E–04	–2.37**	–9.51E–05	–1.24	–1.13E–04	–1.73
DAGR	–2.07E–02	–4.84***	–2.48E–02	–6.01	–3.02E–02	–8.91***
DEIA	–4.56E–03	–1.16	–6.21E–03	–1.47	–6.93E–03	–1.78*
R^2-adjusted	0.967		0.962		0.959	
F-statistics	170.7	(0.000)	159.2	(0.000)	196.8	(0.000)
DW	2.000		1.907		1.886	
Energy intensity (ENEGDP)						
Constant	419.46	6.35***	366.75	8.60***	311.08	14.42***
ECT	–8.25E–05	–2.91**	–1.00E–04	–6.10***	–9.24E–05	–6. 09***
FCT	–3.95E–02	–1.56	–1.98E–02	–1. 21	1.37E–03	0.18
OLP	–1.26	–2.04*	–0.55	–1.53	–0.51	–1.62
DAGR	–59.49	–2.64**	–67.77	–3.62***	–84.11	–5.22***
DEIA	–27.23	–1.18	–39.18	–2.02	–48.74	–2.74***
R^2-adjusted	0.956		0.964		0.963	
F-statistics	72.3	(0.000)	131.5	(0.000)	148.4	(0.000)
DW	2.021		1.961		1.956	

Source: reprinted from *Journal of Cleaner Production*, 58, Momoe Kanada, Tsuyoshi Fujita, Minoru Fujii and Satoshi Ohnishi, 'The long-term impacts of air pollution control policy: Historical links between municipal actions and industrial energy efficiency in Kawasaki City, Japan', 92–101, Copyright 2013, with permission from Elsevier.

Notes
* $p \leq 0.10$;
** $p \leq 0.50$;
*** $p \leq 0.01$ (indicated in bold).

Moreover, the significance of the impact was greater when averaged over a longer time period (1965–2005). This suggests that the EIA law could eventually offer benefits over a longer time period, which supports the idea that environmental policy can influence behavioural changes in industrial activities.

The number of facilities had a significantly negative impact on atmospheric SO$_2$ reduction for the period 1965–1985, indicating that the atmospheric SO$_2$ level decreased when the number of facilities increased (a result that was difficult to interpret). However, it may be that a break occurred in the linkages between atmospheric SO$_2$ level and the intensity of SO$_x$ emissions per facility in the late 1960s as a result of end-of-pipe treatments and low-sulphur fuels. The number of facilities slowly increased until 1970 and then remained stable until 1985. Conversely, both SO$_x$ emissions and the level of atmospheric SO$_2$ decreased slowly in the late 1960s and declined sharply during the 1970s and until 1985. Therefore, this could suggest a reduction in SO$_x$ emissions per facility.

Policy implications

Systems thinking and long-term strategic frameworks have direct implications for the development of sustainable innovation policies (Foxon and Pearson 2008). For that reason, we further described the co-benefits of air pollution reduction and energy intensity as well as their linkages to technological progress that may also lead to CO_2 mitigation and sustainable development (Figure 5.11). Our intention was to emphasize the importance of well-balanced policy measures that successfully reduce local pollution while simultaneously nurturing and stimulating industrial actions that lead to enhanced production processes and cleaner, lower resource-intense inputs. Such strategies can be created through an optimized combination of regulatory and voluntary measures and incentives. Here, we describe this concept as 'smart mix' policy design.

Conclusions

This study focused exclusively on identifying the linkages between policy and industrial energy intensity using an econometric approach. It proved that

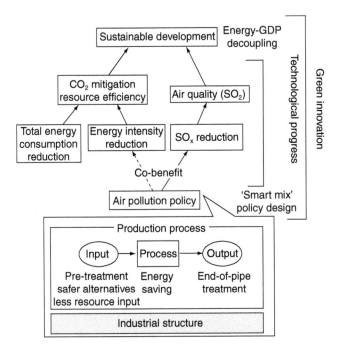

Figure 5.11 Conceptual illustration of the relationship between pollution policy, greenhouse gas (GHG) co-benefits, and green innovations towards sustainable development.

Source: reprinted from *Journal of Cleaner Production*, 58, Momoe Kanada, Tsuyoshi Fujita, Minoru Fujii and Satoshi Ohnishi, 'The long-term impacts of air pollution control policy: Historical links between municipal actions and industrial energy efficiency in Kawasaki City, Japan', 92–101, Copyright 2013, with permission from Elsevier.

considerable co-benefits of SO_2 reduction and a great reduction in energy intensity had been simultaneously achieved over a long time frame. Moreover, policy designs that nurture technological development require broader recognition and responsive actions to the causes of negative effects as well as a smart mix of policy measures. Japan has succeeded in establishing comprehensive environmental policies, which did not intend to control point source emissions directly but instead introduced a comprehensive framework for pollution prevention, involving public participation and increasing interventions. Such an approach to co-benefits is crucially important for other developing industrial cities, since the scope of policy designs influence both environmental behaviour and technological progress.

References

Dong, H, Ohnishi, S, Fujita, T, Geng, Y, Fujii, M and Dong, L 2014, 'Achieving carbon emission reduction through industrial and urban symbiosis: A case of Kawasaki', *Energy*, vol. 64, pp. 277–286.

Foxon, T and Pearson, P 2008, 'Overcoming barriers to innovation and diffusion of cleaner technologies: Some features of a sustainable innovation policy regime', *Journal of Cleaner Production*, vol. 16, supp. 1, pp. S148–S161.

Geng, Y, Ma, Z, Xue, B, Ren, W, Liu, Z and Fujita, T 2013, 'Co-benefit evaluation for urban public transportation sector: A case of Shenyang, China', *Journal of Cleaner Production*, vol. 58, pp. 82–91.

Kanada, M, Fujita, T, Fujii, M and Ohnishi, S 2013, 'The long-term impacts of air pollution control policy: Historical links between municipal actions and industrial energy efficiency in Kawasaki City, Japan', *Journal of Cleaner Production*, vol. 58, pp. 92–101.

Ministry of the Environment Japan 1969. *White Paper on Environmental Pollution in Japan [Showa 44 Nenhan Kougai Hakusho]*, viewed 12 May 2016, www.env.go.jp/policy/hakusyo/hakusyo.php3?kid=144.

Prais, SJ and Winsten, CB 1954, *Cowles Commission Discussion Paper No. 383: Trend Estimators and Serial Correlation*, Cowles Commission for Research in Economics, Chicago.

Yang, X, Teng, F and Wang, G 2013, 'Incorporating environmental co-benefits into climate policies: A regional study of the cement industry in China', *Applied Energy*, vol. 112, pp. 1446–1453.

5.2 Megaurban China

Air pollution co-benefits of carbon mitigation in four Chinese cities

Huijuan Dong and Tsuyoshi Fujita

Introduction

Facing rapid urbanization and industrialization, China is under great pressure to achieve both carbon emissions reduction and air pollutants control (Chan and Yao 2008; Dong et al. 2013; Dong et al. 2015a). Therefore, pursuing a co-benefits approach is an effective way to simultaneously respond to both issues (Ministry of the Environment Japan 2014). In contrast to the previous case in Kawasaki (Chapter 5.1), it is more important to forecast future situations than historical emissions so that effective measures can be taken going forward. Therefore, this research considers future forecasts of co-benefits of air pollution and low-carbon measures in Chinese mega-cities.

Chinese cities contribute around three quarters of national GDP and we consider the four largest cities, namely Beijing, Tianjin, Shanghai and Chongqing, as case areas to evaluate the co-benefit of air pollutants from low-carbon mitigation measures. The four cities are Chinese economic centres and their key characteristics are given in Table 5.4.

Methodology

The co-benefits evaluation framework is given in Figure 5.12 by combining the GAINS-China (Greenhouse Gas and Air Pollution Interactions and Synergies) model (Amann et al. 2011) with a CGE (Computational General Equilibrium) model (Wing 2004; Peace and Weyant 2008). Both models contain detailed information on 30 Chinese provinces for the period 2005–2030, which provides

Table 5.4 Comparison of four Chinese mega-cities in 2013 (National Bureau of Statistics China 2014)

City	Population (million)	GDP (billion Yuan)	Area (km²)	Urbanization level (%)	Industry ratio (%)
Beijing	21.2	1,950	16,807.8	86.3	22.3
Tianjin	14.7	1,437	11,305	78.3	50.6
Shanghai	24.2	2,160	6,340.5	88.0	37.2
Chongqing	29.7	1,266	82,400	58.3	50.5

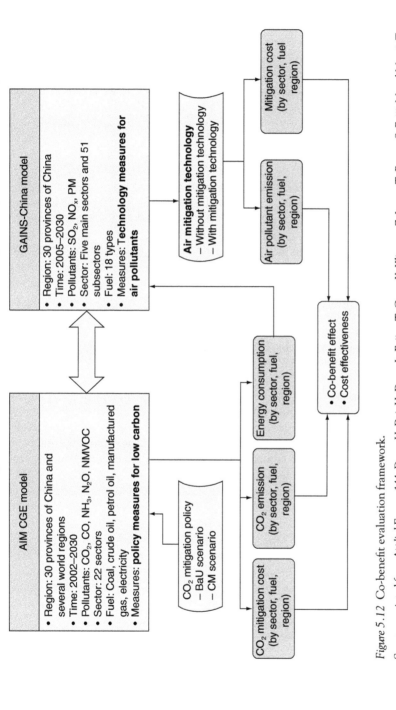

Figure 5.12 Co-benefit evaluation framework.

Source: reprinted from *Applied Energy*, 144, Dong, H, Dai, H, Dai, H, Dong, L, Fujita, T, Geng, Y, Klimont, Z, Inoue, T, Bunya, S, Fujii, M and Masui, T, 'Pursuing air pollutant co-benefits of CO₂ mitigation in China: A provincial level analysis', 165–174, Copyright 2015, with permission from Elsevier.

a solid foundation for evaluating future emissions and co-benefits of various Chinese provinces.

Four scenarios are set up by combining the two models (Table 5.5). The S1 scenario does not assume any mitigation measures, namely that neither CO_2 nor air pollution mitigation measures are adopted. S2 is the scenario without CO_2 mitigation (BaU) but with air pollution mitigation technologies (With-tech), whilst S3 considers CO_2 mitigation (CM) but assumes no air pollution mitigation technologies (No-tech). Finally, S4 includes both CO_2 and air pollution mitigation measures.

Results and discussion

Both the co-benefits of emissions reduction and cost reduction after implementing mitigation measures are studied in this case. The co-benefit of emissions reduction can be further classified into the traditional perspective of emission co-benefit (C_0) and real emission co-benefit (RC_0). The traditional perspective co-benefit (C_0) is defined as the difference between S1 emission and S3 emission, that is to say, the reduction of air pollutant emissions when only applying CO_2 mitigation measures. The real emission co-benefit (RC_0) is defined as the difference between S2 emission and S4 emission, namely, the reduction of air pollutant emissions when applying both CO_2 mitigation measures and air pollutant mitigation measures.

The co-benefit results for $PM_{2.5}$ for the year 2020 are illustrated in Figure 5.13. It shows that the traditional perspective emission co-benefit (C_0) is higher than the real co-benefit (RC_0), indicating that the real co-benefit is often overestimated by most traditional co-benefit studies. Moreover, although Shanghai and Chongqing have the highest $PM_{2.5}$ emissions, their co-benefits are not the highest, with real co-benefit values of about 2.0 kt and 1.3 kt, respectively. Tianjin has the highest co-benefit, with C_0 and RC_0 values of about 106 kt and 8.6 kt, respectively. As for Beijing, its co-benefit is negative, demonstrating that it cannot benefit from the low carbon policies.

The real co-benefit of three air pollutants for four Chinese mega-cities in 2020 are illustrated in Figure 5.14. It shows that the co-benefits do not have an absolute relationship with their GDP values. In contrast, the two cities Tianjin and Chongqing have the lowest GDP values but can achieve the highest co-benefit. By contrast, well-developed Beijing and Shanghai can only obtain marginal air pollutant co-benefits or even a negative co-benefit (Beijing). As for the three air pollutants, the co-benefit of SO_2 and NO_x is much higher than $PM_{2.5}$,

Table 5.5 Scenario setting after combining GAINS-China and CGE

Air policy/GHG policy	BaU	CM
No-tech	S1	S3
With-tech	S2	S4

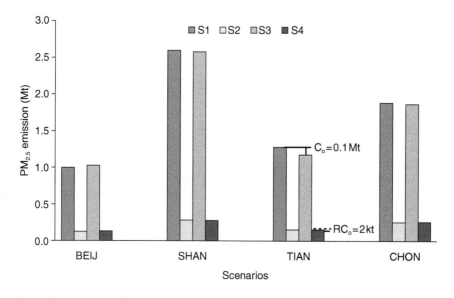

Figure 5.13 Co-benefits analysis of PM$_{2.5}$ in 2020.

Note
City codes are as follows: Chongqing – CHON; Shanghai – SHAN; Tianjin – TIAN; Beijing – BEIJ.

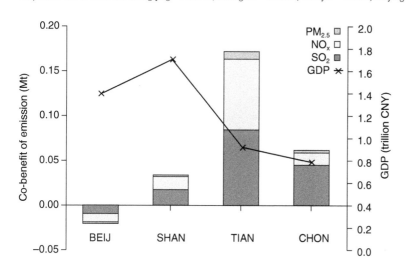

Figure 5.14 Real co-benefits of three air pollutants in 2020.

indicating that low carbon policies can effectively mitigate the SO_2 and NO_x emissions simultaneously, but cannot mitigate $PM_{2.5}$ that much. Such findings suggest that it is much easier to achieve co-benefits in less urbanized cities or more industrial cities.

Policy implications

Unit reduction costs can reveal the cost-effectiveness of different mitigation technologies, which is an important aspect for policymakers. Figure 5.15 shows the cost-effectiveness for the four Chinese mega-cities. The steeper the slope is, the higher the unit reduction cost and therefore the investment is less effective. It is apparent that the unit reduction cost of NO_x is the highest, ranging from 2,086 EUR/t to 5,445 EUR/t. Following this is SO_2, which ranges from 307 EUR/t to 945 EUR/t, whilst $PM_{2.5}$ has the lowest reduction cost, ranging from 126 EUR/t to 207 EUR/t.

As for the comparison of the four cities, it is found that Beijing is the least cost-effective city in mitigating the three air pollutants, while Chongqing is the most cost-effective city in mitigating SO_2 and $PM_{2.5}$. However, it is not effective for Chongqing to mitigate NO_x. Further considering that Beijing also achieves negative co-benefits, it is suggested that a larger proportion of environmental budgets should be invested in less developed and more industrial cities such as Chongqing and Tianjin.

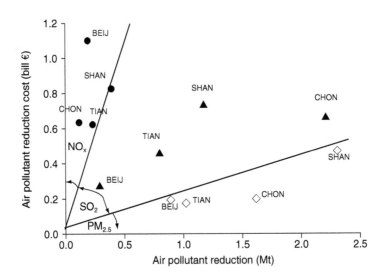

Figure 5.15 Unit reduction costs of three air pollutants.

Note
Air pollutants are shown thus: $\Diamond$ $PM_{2.5}$; $\blacktriangle$ SO_2; $\bullet$ NO_x.

Concluding remarks

This study forecasted the future co-benefit of air pollutants from low-carbon measures for four Chinese mega-cities by integrating the GAINS-China model and the AIM/CGE model. The results showed that measures implemented in the more urbanized cities of Beijing and Shanghai not only had minor or even negative co-benefits, but also exhibited lower cost-effectiveness. On the other hand, the less urbanized and industry-orientated cities of Chongqing and Tianjin, both exhibited higher co-benefits and greater cost-effectiveness. Such findings can be further extended to other Chinese cities, particularly less developed cities, to guide their air pollutants and CO_2 reductions.

Different stages of development should correspond with different policies in order to produce an adequate response to environmental problems. For less urbanized cities, pollution prevention action is typically the response to acute environmental and health impacts. At this stage, end-of-pipe treatments and mitigation of atmospheric substance levels by diffusing concentrations at emission sources are top priorities. It is also much easier for such cities to achieve co-benefits. For more urbanized cities, co-benefit opportunities from end-of-pipe mitigation technologies are limited. Therefore, multiple approaches that include end-of-pipe treatment, production process improvement, pre-treatment and industrial restructuring should be adopted. Moreover, comprehensive policy packages like Japan should be also focused on maximizing co-benefits.

References

Amann, M, Bertok, I, Borken-Kleefeld, J, Cofala, J, Heyes, C, Höglund-Isaksson, L, Klimont, Z, Nguyen, B, Posch, M and Rafaj, P 2011, 'Cost-effective control of air quality and greenhouse gases in Europe: Modeling and policy applications', *Environmental Modelling & Software*, vol. 26, no. 12, pp. 1489–1501.

Chan, CK and Yao, X 2008, 'Air pollution in mega cities in China', *Atmospheric Environment*, vol. 42, no. 1, pp. 1–42.

Dong, H, Geng, Y, Xi, F and Fujita, T 2013, 'Carbon footprint evaluation at industrial park level: A hybrid life cycle assessment approach', *Energy Policy*, vol. 57, pp. 298–307.

Dong, L, Dong, H, Fujita, T, Geng, Y and Fujii, M 2015a, 'Cost-effectiveness analysis of China's SO2 control strategy at the regional level: Regional disparity, inequity and future challenges', *Journal of Cleaner Production*, March, pp. 1–15.

Dong, H, Dai, H, Dong, L, Fujita, T, Geng, Y, Klimont, Z, Inoue, T, Bunya, S, Fujii, M and Masui, T 2015b, 'Pursuing air pollutant co-benefits of CO2 mitigation in China: A provincial level analysis', *Applied Energy*, vol. 144, pp. 165–174.

Ministry of the Environment Japan 2014. *Asian Co-benefits Partnership (ACP) White Paper 2014: Bringing Development and Climate Together in Asia*, viewed 12 May 2016, www.cobenefit.org/publications/images/ACPwhitepaper_FY2013.pdf.

National Bureau of Statistics of China (N.B.o.S.o.) 2014, *China Statistical Yearbook*, China Statistics Press, Beijing.

Peace, J and Weyant, J 2008, 'Insights not numbers: The appropriate use of economic models', *Pew Center on Global Climate Change*, viewed 12 May 2016, www.c2es.org/docUploads/insights-not-numbers.pdf.

Wing, I 2004, 'Computable general equilibrium models and their use in economy-wide policy analysis: Everything you ever wanted to know (but were afraid to ask)', *MIT Joint Program on the Science and Policy of Global Change*, viewed 12 May 2016, http://web.mit.edu/globalchange/www/MITJPSPGC_TechNote6.pdf.

5.3 Baoshan District (Shanghai), China

Co-benefits in the industry sector

Wenbo Dong

Introduction to Baoshan District

The Baoshan District (BSD), located in Shanghai, China, is one of the most important industrial centers for steel shipping containers and the export of items for the energy and port sectors in Shanghai. The intensive industrial activities in BSD, such as iron and steel production, rely on thermal power generation by burning fossil fuels, which account for most of the air pollution and GHG contributions (Baoshan District Environmental Protection Bureau 2011b). The industry sector of the BSD is a major sector that accounts for more than 60 percent of the district's revenue (Shanghai National Bureau of Statistics 2010). Important enterprises in this sector include the Baosteel Group Corporation, the Huaneng Power International Corporation and a large number of chemical industries. Not surprisingly, these industries generate over half the total GHGs and air pollution of Shanghai, which have resulted in complaints from residents (Baoshan District Environmental Protection Bureau 2011a). In the Eleventh Five-Year Plan (FYP), the industrial sector of the BSD has been identified as a priority area for intervention. The aim of this plan is to maintain stable growth of the industrial economy while simultaneously reducing the intensity of industrial energy use and the emission of pollutants through structural, technical and management approaches (Baoshan District Environmental Protection Bureau 2011b).

Many of the industries located in Baoshan are energy intensive, with a predominance of a coal-based energy source, which makes the consumption of per unit of energy in the BSD emit higher GHG emissions and other air pollutions (e.g. SO_2 and NO_x) than other energy sources. Figure 5.16 shows the relative amounts of the fuel types used (Shanghai National Bureau of Statistics 2010). Coal and coke are the main sources of consumption, with consumption rates of 81.2 percent and 6.7 percent, respectively. In 2010, industrial energy required 27 million tonnes of standard coal (tce), which is equivalent to 18 million tonnes of CO_2 emissions. In the present energy use categories, a total of 17 million tce were used as a direct energy source, accounting for 64.1 percent of total industrial energy consumption. The key industries in this region, such as iron and steel smelting, thermal power, non-ferrous metal smelting and gas

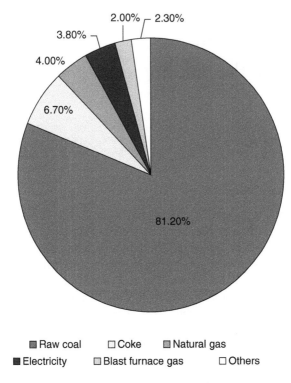

Figure 5.16 Types and shares of industrial energy consumption in BSD in 2010.

production, account for 78.0 percent, 14.6 percent, 0.3 percent and 0.3 percent of energy consumption, respectively (Baoshan Statistic Bureau 2011; Baoshan Development and Reform Commission 2010).

Legislation for energy saving and reducing air pollution in BSD

Three main measures have been carried out in BSD for energy conservation and air pollution control. These are:

- management measures of pollution control designed for energy conservation (e.g. regulations to improve monitoring and supervision, and promote capacity building);
- structural measures designed to reduce air pollution in local industries by the government through the relocation or foreclosure of enterprises with high-energy intensity;
- technical measures for utilizing and upgrading pollution control facilities and adopting energy saving and efficiency technologies.

Detailed interventions under these three measures are given in Table 5.6.

Table 5.6 Interventions of energy conservation in BSD

Item	Energy conservation/air pollution control
Management measures	• Audit and supervision; color grade management regulations • Management contract regulations • Increasing laboratory equipment plan • Recruiting top talent plan • Improving the level of information technology for research and monitoring
Structural measures	• Relocating high-energy and pollution-intensive enterprises • Closing high-energy and pollution-intensive enterprises
Technical measures	• Energy-saving technologies • Improving energy efficiency

Source: reprinted from *Journal of Cleaner Production*, 114, Ping Jiang, Bin Xu, Yong Geng, Wenbo Dong, Yihui Chen and Bing Xue, 'Assessing the environmental sustainability with a co-benefits approach: A study of industrial sector in Baoshan District in Shanghai', 114–123, Copyright 2016 with permission from Elsevier.

Energy conservation in the industry sector in BSD

In the period of the Eleventh FYP (2006–2010), energy intensity decreased by 26.7 percent compared to the level of 2001–2005 in the industry sector in BSD. For instance, the energy consumption by the Above Scale Enterprises (those with an annual revenue of over RMB5 million, approx. US$765,000) was 830,000 tce in 2006, which was reduced by 20.2 percent (210,000 tce) compared to 1,040,000 tce in 2005 (Baoshan Development and Reform Commission 2010). This means that the period of 2005 to 2006 saw a reduction of about 170,000 tonnes of CO_2 equivalent. Moreover, the policy resulted in a large reduction in air pollutants as well. We can see that significant co-benefits of carbon and air pollution reduction have been achieved in Baoshan.

Co-benefits achieved through structural and technical measures

Two hundred enterprises with the highest energy use and CO_2 emissions, such as electroplating factories and chemical plants, were forcibly closed and moved out of BSD between 2006 and 2010. Forty-five industrial manufacturing enterprises with low productive capacity and high energy consumption were upgraded with advanced energy-saving technologies. Energy savings of 110,000 tce were achieved through structural and technical measures, which is equivalent to the emission reduction of 71,632 tonnes CO_2 in the targeted enterprises between 2006 and 2010 in BSD. For example, a reduction of 4,015 tce consumption (i.e. the equivalent of reduction of 2,615 tonnes of CO_2) was achieved by closing Yuepu thermal power plant in 2009, which was located in the 'black grid' (i.e. the heavy-pollution area) in 2005.

According to the assessment made by the Baoshan Development and Reform Commission (2010), updated and deployed energy-saving technologies, and closing and relocating projects have substantially achieved the objective of energy conservation and GHG reduction in BSD (Baoshan Development and Reform Commission 2010). For instance, over 60 energy-saving technologies were utilized in 45 industrial enterprises with lower energy efficiency (including 54 new energy-saving technologies applied in industrial boilers and energy-saving lighting systems), with an annual reduction of around 500 tce in energy consumption between 2006–2010.

Co-benefits achieved through management measures

The Colored Management Index (CEMI) was adopted in BSD for presenting and comparing the levels of energy efficiency (i.e. energy consumption per unit value of CNY 10,000 of production) in enterprises. Enterprises rated as the best, good, medium, bad and the worst energy efficiency were respectively marked as green, yellow, orange, red and black enterprises. Five-hundred enterprises with annual energy consumption over 1,000 tce in BSD were chosen as research samples for making a qualified and quantified analysis of the energy efficiency changes in the study between 2007 and 2009.

Energy management requires strong monitoring and supervision, regulations and capacity building. An energy consumption statistical database was established for the improvement of energy management. All enterprises were required to provide monthly reports of energy consumption and energy saving to the district government, and all data and information from reports were input into the database. Thirty enterprises with an annual energy consumption of more than 5,000 tce were required to submit detailed reports on energy performance and energy-saving plans. Meanwhile, all new projects needed to provide the energy conservation and carbon reduction plans at the early design stage. For example, when a new steel plant was planned in the industrial park, the investor, Xin Yi (Chen Kai) Co. Ltd, was required to provide an energy saving plan in the design stage with the objective of 7,000 tce of energy use reduction.

During the implementation of the measure of improving energy management, CEMI is undertaken for assessing the energy management level of the 500 enterprises in BSD between 2007 and 2009. According to the results of CEMI presented in Figure 5.17, the number of black enterprises with the worst level of energy efficiency decreased by 12.3 percent and the red enterprises reduced by 26.9 percent. In the same period, the green enterprises with the best energy efficiency and yellow enterprises and good energy management increased by 4.5 percent and 29.8 percent, respectively. The number of orange enterprises also increased by 20.7 percent in the same period. It means that the enterprises with the medium level of energy efficiency have not taken energy management improvement measures within three years. The overall energy efficiency improved by 10.6 percent between 2007 and 2009 for the 500 enterprises.

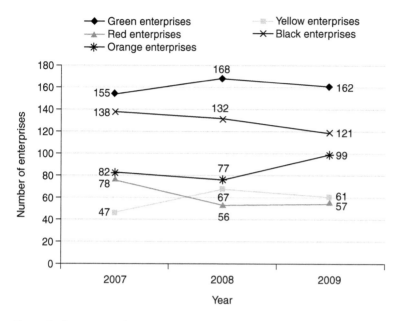

Figure 5.17 Energy performance in 500 enterprises between 2007 and 2009.

References

Baoshan Development and Reform Commission 2010. *The Achievements of Energy Saving and Carbon Reduction in Recent Years in Baoshan*, viewed 23 September 2016, http://jjw.baoshan.sh.cn/P005.aspx?catalogid=153.

Baoshan District Environmental Protection Bureau 2011a. *Database of Air Pollution in Baoshan District*, viewed 23 September 2016, http://bshbj.baoshan.sh.cn/baoshanWeb/home/plan/disilun/jianbao2011.aspx.

Baoshan District Environmental Protection Bureau 2011b, *The Environmental Protection in Baoshan Between 2009 and 2011 and the Three-year Action Plan*, viewed 23 September 2016, http://bshbj.baoshan.sh.cn/baoshanWeb/home/plan/disilun/4gongzuojianbao.aspx.

Baoshan Statistic Bureau 2011, *The Energy Consumption Industries in Baoshan*, viewed 8 January 2015, http://bstz.baoshan.sh.cn:8080/pub/bstj/tjsj/tjfx/tjfx2011/201110/t2011 1024_57708.html.

Shanghai National Bureau of Statistics 2010, *Shanghai Statistical Yearbook*, viewed 8 January 2015, www.stats-sh.gov.cn/data/toTjnj.xhtml?y=2010.

5.4 Tiexi District (Shenyang), China

Bing Xue, Yong Geng and Zhixiao Ma

Tiexi is a district located in the western part of Shenyang City of the Liaoning province in northeastern China. It is one of the largest industrial complexes in China and covers an area of $39.3\,km^2$ with approximately one million inhabitants. The industrialization process in Tiexi started from 1938 when it was occupied by Japan. The Tiexi District was planned to be a heavy industrial centre, long known as the 'elder brother' of industry for its central role in Mao's drive to industrialize China in the 1950s and 1960s. For instance, during China's first and second five-year plan period (1953–1962), one sixth of the state budget was invested in Tiexi to support its industrial development.

Since the start of the millennium, more than 130,000 workers in Tiexi have lost their jobs, and approximately 30 per cent of the factories were shut down as outdated technology and institutional factors made the area less competitive. In response to this situation and a desire to improve the environmental–economic–social characteristics of the area, the government decided to redevelop the Tiexi District by relocating enterprises from the old industrial bases to new industrial parks nearby in 2002 (Ren *et al.* 2014). The old industrial area of Tiexi was turned into a modern commercial and residential centre (Geng *et al.* 2014), playing a vital economic role in Shenyang city, contributing about two thirds of its total GDP (Jiang *et al.* 2013).

The redevelopment process of Tiexi's traditional industrial zone led to many co-benefits, such as the reduction in carbon emissions and local air pollutants, as well as an improvement in land-use efficiency. By employing a co-benefits analysis (Geng *et al.* 2013; Ma *et al.* 2013), the total amount of CO_2 emission from industry sectors in Tiexi District reduced from 3.52 million tonnes to 0.20 million tonnes between 2000 and 2014, while the emissions of air pollutants SO_2, NO_x and PM_{10} reduced from about 54,300 tonnes, 9,000 tonnes and 48,000 tonnes to about 1,000 tonnes, 230 tonnes and 2,000 tonnes in the same period, respectively.

Policy support, technology innovation and land redevelopment are the three main driving forces for bringing co-benefits from the Tiexi redevelopment.

At a national level, as early as in March 2003, the *Report on the Work of the State Council* proposed that the old northeast industrial bases needed to be revitalized for meeting long-term sustainable development. In October 2003, the

Central Committee of the Chinese Communist Party and the State Council jointly disseminated the official document entitled *Certain Opinions Regarding Implementing the Strategies of Reviving the Old Industrial Bases Including the Northeast*. The northeastern provinces, including Liaoning Province, were asked to better coordinate their economic development strategies to take into account environmental protection and social development. The support from central government provided a strong and solid basis for shifting the local developmental strategy from heavy pollution and high energy consumption to more environmentally friendly development. In 2005, the Chinese government initiated a comprehensive Energy Saving and Emission Reduction programme for sustainable production and consumption, and set up corresponding goals as part of the national five-year plan (Xue *et al.* 2014). As a result, Chinese manufacturers initiated their efforts to reduce total environmental pollution and energy consumption, particularly for the industrial areas such as Tiexi District. At the local level, the Shenyang municipal government decided to redevelop the Tiexi District, aiming to rebuild it as a liveable and more sustainable urban centre instead of a heavy polluted industrial zone. The key initiative was to relocate the factories from the centre (old industrial district) to the nearby new industrial park. Both the upper governments and the Tiexi District governments released a series of policy packages to ensure that the new development in Tiexi should be climate and environmentally friendly. For example, the government launched the new urban development plan and enhanced the green infrastructures.

Technology innovation made a direct impact on the achievement of the environmental and climate goals in Tiexi, generating co-benefits. Special funds from local governments were designed and planned for supporting the relocated enterprises to adopt new, cleaner technologies. For example, integrated wet dust-removal and desulfurization equipment are mandatory in the new factories, ensuring they meet national standards and targets, such as the goals set up in the Energy Saving and Emission Reduction programme. In order to improve their environmental performance, companies are encouraged to adopt international environmental standards and management systems, such as ISO14001. In order to reduce coal consumption, Tiexi altered the local energy structure by centralizing the heating system. This improved energy efficiency as well as effectively reduced CO_2 and air pollutant emissions because the small heating boilers, which were very popular in Tiexi, had low energy efficiency compared to the larger centralized heating system. This also improved public health and reduced household energy expenditure. However, there is potential for further improvement, such as building insulation. More sustainable buildings (Chapter 4) can reduce energy consumption by about 30 per cent compared to current buildings. Therefore, the local government could implement several additional measures. First, an organization could be set up to better manage the heating network. Second, the buildings should be installed with external wall insulation and measuring heating systems so that the buildings could save about 50 per cent of their energy consumption.

As the total amount of emissions in Tiexi continues to grow rapidly from electricity, heat production and industry, there are many opportunities to introduce new technologies on a large scale, such as geothermal energy. Geothermal heat pumps, or ground coupled heat pumps, are systems combining a heat pump with a ground heat exchanger (closed loop systems), or fed by ground water from a well (open loop systems). A geothermal heat pump reduces the use of coal for household heating. However, it also relies on electricity to operate. Thus, most power plants would need to burn additional quantities of coal to supply the same electricity. This would lead to an even greater reliance on coal consumption in Tiexi District. If Tiexi District cannot provide sufficient electricity for the geothermal heat pump projects, the electricity would be bought from other areas. In the end, CO_2 emissions and air pollution would move to another place, creating leakage.

Land redevelopment was key for creating the co-benefits, particular with regards to climate change, environmental protection and public health. For example, from 2002 to 2012, approximately 370 enterprises were shut down or moved out from the urban centre and relocated to a suburb where a new industrial park was established. This relocation created nearly 9 km^2 of brownfields in Tiexi. All of these sites, polluted by heavy metals, organic and other pollutants, have been redeveloped for residential, commercial and green spaces. The model of brownfield redevelopment in Tiexi has become a show-case for redeveloping other industrial bases in China (Xue *et al.* 2015).

In summary, the case study in the Tiexi District shows that the co-benefits can be created during a regional developmental process by integrating policy-driven technology innovation and land (brownfield) redevelopment.

References

Geng, Y, Liu, Z, Xue, B, Dong, H, Fujita, T and Chiu, A 2014, 'Energy-based assessment on industrial symbiosis: A case of Shenyang Economic and Technological Development Zone', *Environmental Science and Pollution Research*, vol. 21, no. 23, pp. 13572–13587.

Geng, Y, Ma, Z, Xue, B, Ren, W, Liu, Z and Fujita, T 2013, 'Co-benefit evaluation for urban public transportation sector: A case of Shenyang, China', *Journal of Cleaner Production*, vol. 58, pp. 82–91.

Jiang, P, Chen, Y, Geng, Y, Dong, W, Xue, B, Xu, B and Li, W 2013, 'Analysis of the co-benefits of climate change mitigation and air pollution reduction in China', *Journal of Cleaner Production*, vol. 58, pp. 130–137.

Ma, Z, Xue, B, Geng, Y, Ren, W, Fujita, T, Zhang, Z, de Oliveira, JP, Jacques, DA and Xi, F 2013, 'Co-benefits analysis on climate change and environmental effects of wind-power: A case study from Xinjiang, China', *Renewable Energy*, vol. 57, pp. 35–42.

Ren, W, Xue, B, Geng, Y, Sun, L, Ma, Z, Zhang, Y, Mitchell, B and Zhang, L 2014, 'Inventorying heavy metal pollution in redeveloped brownfield and its policy contribution: Case study from Tiexi District, China', *Land Use Policy*, vol. 38, pp. 138–146.

Xue, B, Mitchell, B, Geng, Y, Ren, W, Müller, K, Ma, Z, de Oliveira, JP, Fujita, T and Tobias, M 2014, 'A review on China's pollutant emissions reduction assessment', *Ecological Indicators*, vol. 38, pp. 272–278.

Xue, B, Zhang, L, Geng, Y, Mitchell, B and Ren, W 2015, 'Extended land use categories in urban brownfield redevelopment of China: Case of Tiexi District, Shenyang of China', *Journal of Urban Planning and Development*, 05015014.

6 Waste

Mehrnoosh Dashti

Introduction

One of the greatest challenges the world faces today is achieving the necessary reductions of greenhouse gas (GHG) emissions and environmental pollutants amidst the increasing quantities of waste we are expected to generate in the future. The world has experienced increasing solid waste generation due to the rapid growth of urbanization, accelerated socio-economic development, and changing of living patterns and standards in recent years. According to a 2012 World Bank report (Hoornweg and Bhada-Tata 2012) the amount of municipal solid waste (MSW) produced globally was 1.3 billion tonnes per year. That number is expected to reach 2.2 billion tonnes per year by 2025, representing an annual increase of 5 per cent and indicates a significant growth in per capita daily waste generation rates, from 1.2 to 1.42 kg by 2025. The challenging issue of sustainable waste management can be approached through consideration of environmentally efficient waste systems. Based on 2010 global GHG emissions data, for the total 50.1 $GtCO_2e$ which are emitted globally, 35 per cent of GHG emissions are predominantly associated with energy production and conversions (energy sector) and only 4 per cent of GHG emissions are from the waste and wastewater sector, as shown in Figure 6.1 (UNEP 2012).

Figure 6.2 illustrates the trends in global GHG emissions by sector in the world over the period 1990–2010. Global GHG emissions have increased by almost 11.8 GtCO2e (34.5 per cent of total emissions) over this period. Although the share generated by the waste sector has made a relatively small but constant contribution of roughly 4 per cent to global GHG emissions, the management of waste can be considered a potential priority to achieving the Sustainable Development Goals from the perspectives of resource recovery, climate change mitigation, and global health.

There is a basic relationship between economic activity and per capita CO_2 emissions. Figure 6.3 clearly illustrates that higher income countries are more likely to generate higher levels of GHGs relative to the lower income countries, which in turn is a reflection of wider factors, including the level of wealth, access to energy resources and technologies, energy market conditions, and so on.

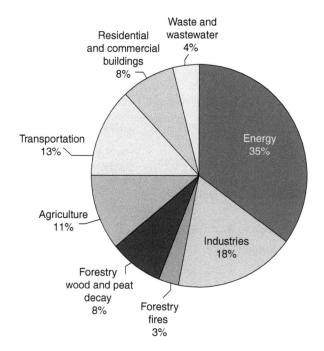

Figure 6.1 Global GHG emissions by sector.

Source: based from UNEP 2012.

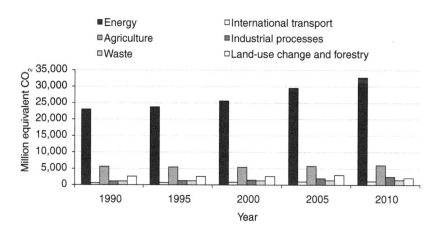

Figure 6.2 Trends in global GHG emissions by sector over 1990–2010.

Source: based on data from the US Environmental Protection Agency 2014.

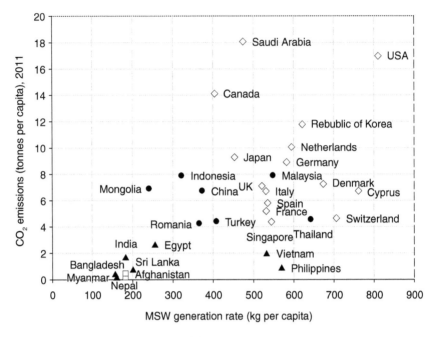

Figure 6.3 MSW generation rates and CO$_2$ emissions.

Sources: Hoornweg and Bhada-Tata 2012; World Bank 2013.

Note

◇: high income; ●: upper middle income; ▲: lower middle income; □: low income.

Various types of solid waste contain different amounts of degradable organic carbon (DOC) and fossil carbon. Therefore, one of the major factors which affect the environmental emissions generated by solid waste is its composition. The IPCC (2006) classification of MSW composition includes the following materials: food, paper and cardboard, wood, textiles, rubber and leather, plastics, metal, glass, garden and park wastes, nappies, and other refuse (e.g. ash, dirt, dust, soil, electronic waste). Country income level not only exerts an influence on the MSW generation rate, as seen in Figure 6.3, but also changes in waste composition, which are illustrated in Figure 6.4.

What is apparent in Figure 6.4 is that waste composition in high-level income countries tends to generate a greater proportion of recyclable (glass, plastics and papers) rather than organic waste. Considering the global distribution of waste generation in Table 6.1, and the population of these regions, we can deduce that the average rates of per capita waste generation are far lower for developing countries than for developed counties.

Considering now the status of waste management in developing countries (Dhokhikah and Trihadiningrum 2012; Hisashi and Kuala 1997), the main problems of solid waste management facing many developing countries are:

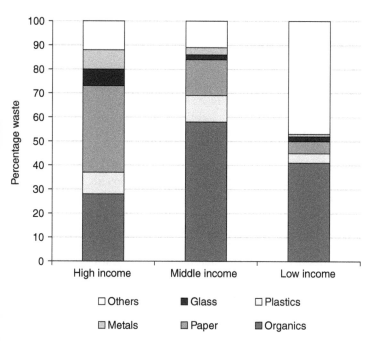

Figure 6.4 Waste composition by countries' income levels.
Source: based on Chandak 2010.

Table 6.1 Waste generation by region

Region/countries	Waste generation (%)
Africa region	5
South Asia region	5
Middle East and North Africa region	6
Europe and Central Asia region	7
Latin American countries	12
East Asia and Pacific region	21
OECD countries	44

Source: Hoornweg and Bhada-Tata (2012).

littering, the lack of separation at source, complicated collection processes, illegal waste dumping, openly dumped landfills, lack of control over gas emissions and leachate in landfills, harmful impacts on public health, the lack of overall plans for solid waste management at the local and national levels, and using traditional waste management systems in comparison to the modern, optimized facilities employed by industrialized countries. Comparing the waste management systems in developed and developing countries, various factors can be considered as main drivers for waste management system development at the local and national levels, such as: technical context, financial constraints, public health status, environmental issues, institutional issues, economic context, public awareness, socio-cultural context, political perspectives, and international support (Wilson 2007; Marshall and Farahbakhsh 2013). Understanding the past and current status of the drivers is a key point which will help to improve waste management systems and the movement towards sustainable cities, particularly in developing countries.

This chapter explores the waste system in its entirety, starting with the impacts on human health and the environment of improperly treated waste. Although commonly thought of as hazardous material, properly treated, waste can have huge benefits. The chapter then goes on to discuss the role of waste as a resource, not only in terms of material but also energy. With this in mind, the next section discusses the Avoid-Shift-Improve framework and how it relates to the waste sector and compares to other prevalent initiatives. The life cycle approach is then introduced as the key methodology, which will also be used in the tool discussed in Chapter 9 (pages 254–255). Finally, there is a brief discussion of some of the challenges with these techniques before summarizing with some concluding remarks.

The cases which follow this chapter connect to various aspects described in this chapter. The Yogyakarta case (Chapter 6.1) also uses the life cycle approach to examine the role of community-based solid waste management in promoting recycling and waste reduction. The Suzhou case (Chapter 6.2) takes a detailed look at the management of an urban complex and the revenue generated from collecting waste from a political economy perspective, whilst the Surat case (Chapter 6.3) discusses the urban management issues around the improvement of the sewerage system following an outbreak of pneumonic plague. The last two cases in particular focus on governance and leadership and complement the technical discussions in this chapter.

The impacts of waste

All three GHGs, carbon dioxide (CO_2), methane (CH_4), and nitrous oxide (N_2O), are produced during the process of waste disposal and storage. The largest contribution of GHG emissions by the waste sector comes from landfill methane, a greenhouse gas 21 times more effective than carbon dioxide. This is further compounded by the production of wastewater and nitrous oxide. The incineration of waste products derived from fossil fuels, such as plastics and synthetic textiles, also contributes minor emissions of CO_2. While the materials in municipal solid waste have different origins, such as households, commercial activities and industry, they must be properly managed to minimize their impact on the environment and human health.

Besides GHG emissions, pollutants present in waste traverse environmental boundaries and permeate the environmental conditions, affecting the air, soil, water, and food chains. They may contribute to adverse human health effects through various pathways, such as:

- inhalation of gas or particles;
- ingestion of contaminated food;
- drinking water from contaminated wells with leachate/wastewater;
- skin contact with contaminated soil;
- ingestion of contaminated soil.

Figure 6.5 shows a schematic of the potential exposure routes from dumped waste and waste processing that can create health hazards for human beings.

Different exposure pathways can lead to outbreaks of various types of infectious diseases, including air-borne, water-borne, food-borne, and vector-borne diseases, especially in susceptible populations, such as children or the elderly. Furthermore, the discharge of untreated wastewater can contaminate both surface and groundwater resources, and is one of the main sources of water pollution as well as water-borne bacterial diseases, particularly in developing countries. Decomposition of organic matter in wastewater leads to the emission of methane. Leaks of leachate from landfill sites can also serve to increase the growth of certain pathogens in water sources (Giusti 2009).

In addition to the pathways shown in Figure 6.5, household disposables as well as unmanaged or improperly managed waste disposal sites are breeding habitats for disease vectors. Insects, ticks, flies, and mosquitoes use standing

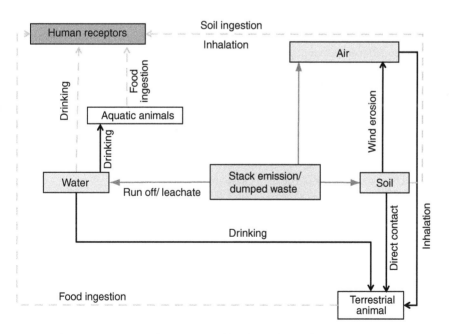

Figure 6.5 Exposure routes to hazards caused by dumped waste/waste processing.

water and openly dumped waste as breeding grounds. The infectious diseases, caused by various pathogens and parasites such as dengue fever, Lyme disease, salmonellosis, plague, malaria, amoebic and bacillary dysenteries, cholera, and yellow fever, can be transmitted by insects and rodents and spread between humans or from animals to humans as well (Giusti 2009). Studies have shown that people living in the vicinity of solid waste processing facilities and disposal sites are exposed to increased environmental health risks (Cointreau 2006). Workers and waste pickers handling solid waste are also susceptible to occupational health hazards, which include the risk of accidents related to emissions and content of the materials they are handling, and the equipment being used (Cointreau 2006). Assessments of the adverse health effects associated with different exposure routes on high-risk members of the population are generally difficult to ascertain, particularly for vector-borne diseases.

Accordingly, the waste sector not only becomes an important sector in terms of addressing environmental and public health, but also can deliver substantial economic benefits through material reprocessing. There is also an opportunity to promote the growth of green jobs through activities involving collection, transportation, sorting, and processing of waste.

Co-benefits approach: waste as a resource

Co-benefits are defined as an approach that provides a framework to simultaneously address local issues of environmental degradation of the type discussed thus far and global pollution related to climate change. Local co-benefits refer to positive externalities in the surrounding area derived from waste management actions such as benefits of air pollution control, public health improvement, energy security improving, etc. Accordingly, the co-benefit approach is predominantly used to estimate the environmental benefits of the different actions taken for reducing GHG emissions regarding climate change mitigation strategies. In addition, the treatment of the waste through different practices will also result in other environmental and economic benefits, including the reduction of air pollution and water pollution, the promotion of energy recovery, by-product (compost) production, and material recycling. Table 6.2 lists the common concerns in the waste sector and the related co-benefits which can be gained by management of the waste system as well.

The multiple benefits that can result from the co-benefits approach relate to the environment, energy and economics:

- *Benefits from GHG emissions mitigation:*
  Decomposition of organic matter in open-air dumped waste sites and improper waste disposal sites, including wastewater, leads to the emission of methane. The safe disposal of waste has become a prime concern from the point of view of climate change. In this regard, mitigation of methane coming from wastewater treatment facilities is one possible action area for many large cities in developing countries.

Table 6.2 Summary of issues and related co-benefits in the waste sector

Waste issue(s)	Source(s)	Co-benefit(s)
Methane emissions produced by decomposition of organic waste	• Open-air dumped waste • Unmanaged disposal sites • Wastewater	GHG emissions (climate change mitigation)
Gas and particles, mainly CO, NO_x, SO_x, $PM_{2.5}$, and PM_{10} produced by combustion of waste and fossil fuels	• Open-air burned waste • Waste transportation • Machinery used in waste treatment facilities	Air pollution reduction (cleaner environment)
Leachate and wastewater generated by waste disposal sites	• Open-air dumped waste sites • Unmanaged disposal sites • Landfills	Water pollution control (clean environment – Chapter 6.3)
Dissipation of organic waste latent heat	• Disposal of organic waste materials in landfills (rather than incineration) • Incinerators without energy recovery systems	Energy recovery (economic)
Disposal of recyclable materials	• Recycling materials through reprocessing or recycling waste materials into another usable form	Material recovery (economic – Chapter 6.2)
Loss of economic benefits by discarding organic waste materials	• Converting organic waste material to form a rich soil-like material, compost, through decomposition process	Material recovery (economic)
Loss of energy benefits	• LFG gas flaring • Disposal of organic waste materials in landfills (over biological treatment)	Energy recovery (economic)

• *Benefits from the air pollution reduction:*
Gas and particles which are produced by combustion of waste as well as fossil fuels contribute a substantial proportion of air pollution. One of the consequences of open-air dumped waste, improper waste disposal sites, and fossil fuel combustion is the emission of CO, NO_x, SO_x, $PM_{2.5}$, and PM_{10}. The socio-economic costs of air pollution remain extremely high due to the threat of airborne diseases and related costs of medical treatment.

• *Benefits from energy/material recovery:*
Two significant opportunities for energy conservation in existing waste management systems is the generation and utilization of heat energy (land-fill gas [LFG] combustion and waste incineration) and biogas, which can supplement the energy supply through combined electricity and heat (CHP) systems and biogas plants, respectively.

Heat energy can be used to reduce GHG emissions by providing an alternative to fossil fuels in transportation or energy production, producing the lowest carbon transportation fuels available, and avoiding methane emissions.

- *Economic benefits:*
  Using recycled materials reduces the production costs of materials as almost all recycling processes can achieve significant energy savings compared to virgin material production. For example, the recycling of aluminium cans saves 95 per cent of the energy required to make the same amount of aluminium from virgin sources.

Table 6.3 summarizes the various benefits of waste management practices in addition to the GHG emission reductions as the primary co-benefit.

In order to quantify the co-benefits of waste management system, it is necessary to calculate the entire potential of GHG emissions production at the source, and the potential of GHG emissions avoided for each particular waste management action. The net GHG emissions from each technology might further be aggregated based on the fraction of waste treated by that technology based on the integrated waste management system approach.

Accordingly, the net GHG emissions of each waste management action are quantified using the following equation:

$$\text{Net GHG emissions} = \text{amount of GHG emissions produced} - \text{amount of GHG emissions avoided} \tag{6.1}$$

Net GHG emissions can be positive or negative. A positive value for net GHG emissions indicates that GHGs are being produced by a course of action. In this case, a specific waste treatment strategy emits GHGs, which ultimately impact

Table 6.3 Waste management technologies and their co-benefits from recovery/recycling actions

WM technology	Recovery/recycle opportunities
Landfilling	Landfill gas recovered and used for electricity production Landfill gas recovered as heat and electricity (CHP) production Landfill gas recovered and used as diesel fuel
Incineration	Energy recovered as electricity Energy recovered as heat and electricity (CHP) production
Composting	Compost recovered for beneficial use in agriculture
Anaerobic digestion	Compost recovered for beneficial use in agriculture Biogas recovered and used as electricity in biogas power plants Biogas recovered and used as fuel replacing diesel
Recycling	Material recovered as metal, glass, plastics, paper and cardboard, wood, rubber and leather

on the climate. If the value of net GHG emissions is negative, it shows that the treatment strategy contributes to mitigation of GHG and serves as a carbon sink. One can also think of co-benefits in relative terms between different waste handling strategies to see which method produces fewer emissions. More detailed information about the main required input data is presented in Chapter 9 (page 256).

Waste management system: approach

Integrated solid waste management (ISWM) is the most promising approach to effectively deal with waste management problems and develop sustainable waste management through the climate co-benefits approach. Conceptually, ISWM can be defined as the integrated practices to address waste management, which deliver both environmental and economic benefits that respond to local conditions. The main drivers of ISWM are resource recovery (materials and energy) and reduction of environmental impacts, especially those associated with global warming, and should be based on the waste hierarchy. The waste treatment hierarchy prioritizes actions ranging from waste prevention to waste disposal in this regard and is shown in Figure 6.6. Different versions of solid waste treatment hierarchies often rank the options according to the following order:

1   Reduce: reduce/prevent the amount of waste generated in the first place.
2   Reuse: reuse waste materials instead of disposal.

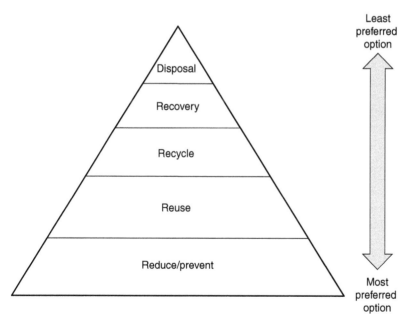

Figure 6.6 Waste treatment hierarchy.

3   Recycle: re-process waste materials to usable/new products.
4   Recovery: recover materials and/or energy from waste.
5   Disposal: safe and secure disposal of waste materials, especially for hazardous material.

The concept of 'Reduce, Reuse and Recycle' is usually referred to as the '3Rs' of the waste hierarchy. The preference of different waste management treatment technologies is often discussed to treat the remaining waste as efficiently as possible. The ranking order for incineration as thermal treatment technology and anaerobic digestion and composting as biological treatment options is often a challenge for policy and strategic decision-makers in the waste management sector.

The economic and environmental preferences of recycling over other waste treatment options might be set as the first priority in waste policy planning. Essentially, the main objectives of a waste management system based on the waste hierarchy are:

- less waste generation;
- GHG emissions mitigation;
- cleaner environment (air, water, and soil);
- more efficient resource recovery.

'Zero waste' is an emerging concept in sustainable waste management policy, which builds on the 3R approach but is more ambitious in its aim to achieve sustainable consumption and production, total recycling, and maximum resource recovery. A comprehensive review (Zaman 2015) carried out on the development of zero waste management analysing published studies between 1995 and 2014 found that there was a wide interpretation and application of the concept mainly in the areas of waste management (both municipal and industrial) as well as in regulatory policy. Accordingly, organizing zero waste initiatives has the potential to play a key role for achieving sustainable waste management goals. If taken in totality, the concept pushes the envelope in terms of thinking more fundamentally about closed loop systems, which also requires shifts in behaviour, consumption, product design, and production.

Generally, the components of the waste management system can be categorized into three stages: (a) waste handling; (b) waste processing or treatment; and (c) waste disposal. Waste handling includes collecting, picking up, storing, and also transporting of waste to the treatment facilities or disposal sites. Main waste processing/treatment methods can include recycling, biological treatments such as composting and anaerobic digestion, and thermal treatments such as incineration, while landfilling is the main method of disposal. The ISWM approach should be based on waste hierarchy at different levels, including transportation, processing, and disposal, to address possible actions in a waste management system. The effects of different waste management actions can be analysed in the framework of waste policy interventions. Waste policy interventions examine the effects of WMS strategies in supporting the promotion of the current waste management system through different pathways. Interventions should be fit for purpose to solve the challenges WMS looks to solve. Furthermore, policymakers are pursuing cost-effective interventions whereby the benefits of the intervention will exceed the costs, practically. Waste policy interventions can be classified according to the Avoid-Shift-Improve strategy and can be mapped onto the four main objectives of the waste hierarchy. Hence, the waste management system should explore how to link elements from the A-S-I strategy to those benefits in order to have the most effective interventions which respond to the local WM demands (Table 6.4).

Avoid

The 'Avoid' strategy components refer to reducing the amount of waste, especially in the first place, to avoid the generation of waste to be treated through recycling, energy recovery, or disposal. Implementation of 'Avoid' strategies result in the following outcomes:

- reduction of the GHG emissions and air pollution;
- decrease in the need for energy and natural resources to be used for the production, distribution, and consumption of products;
- reduction of recycling or disposal costs.

The implementation of the 'Avoid' pillar of the A-S-I strategy makes a direct connection to the first stage of the waste hierarchy (i.e. waste prevention and reduction) and is based mainly on policies and regulations. The 'Avoid' strategies cover two different levels: (a) upstream waste prevention/reduction at the

Table 6.4 The Avoid-Shift-Improve (A-S-I) strategy in the SWM system

Strategy	Avoid	Shift	Improve
Description	• Avoidance of the amount of waste generated	• Shifting waste disposal to the thermal, biological, or other safe disposal WM actions	• Improving different WM actions towards greater environmental efficiency
Main outcome(s)	• Reducing the amount of waste generated in the first place • Mitigation of GHG emissions	• Mitigation of GHG emissions from landfill/unmanaged disposal sites • Resource reuse, recycle, or recovery	• Mitigation of GHG emissions • Resource recovery or recycling
Waste hierarchy stage	Reduce	Reuse, Recycle, Recovery	Recycle, Recovery

manufacturing level, and (b) downstream waste prevention/reduction at the residential, commercial, and institutional level. At the upstream level, the producers/manufacturers are directly responsible for reducing waste while the downstream strategies will help drive the consumers at the residential and institutional level to generate less waste. In both these regards, legislation and programmes operated across all levels of government can be effective levers to this objective. Table 6.5 summarizes the strategies to achieve waste prevention and reduction as 'Avoid' strategies for upstream, downstream, and governmental levels.

Shift

To achieve reductions in the amount of material going to disposal sites, 'Shift' strategies and policies based on the waste management hierarchy need to be established. These strategies and policies act to shift waste away from landfills to the other waste reuse, recycling, and recovery options, which include recycling, thermal treatment, and biological treatment. Shifting from unmanaged waste dumping to managed landfill systems can also be categorized as a 'Shift' strategy. By shifting to other possible waste management practice(s), GHG emissions (mainly methane) produced during the degradation of organic waste at landfill sites can be removed. On the other hand, the recovered materials and energy which may be produced during shifting between treatments options have the potential to replace raw materials and energy sourced from power plants, which

Table 6.5 The 'Avoid' strategies in the SWM system

Avoid strategies	Level
• Reduce waste generation during production process by utilizing more efficient technologies • Produce more recyclable and durable products • Design goods with replaceable features, not disposable • Produce more durable products rather than once-through, disposable and limited-use products • Produce products with less excess packaging • Use recycled materials instead of raw materials during production process	Upstream
• Separate the waste at source • Limit one-way or disposable products (e.g. plastic and paper bags)	Downstream
• Establish National Zero Waste programmes • Support waste reduction projects through funding • Set quantitative targets to increase recycling (beverage containers, plastic bags, papers) • Set quantitative targets on annual per capita disposal upper limit • Set quantitative targets to reduce the use of one-way, single-use bags • Set legislation or regulations for generating less waste • Provide incentives for producers/manufacturers to incorporate environmental considerations	Government

are predominantly fossil fuel-based. This replacement results in reduction of GHG emissions as well as air pollutants. Accordingly, changing waste treatment options would help climate mitigation by contributing to reduce GHG emissions through both avoided organic waste landfilling and recovery of resources.

The following objectives can be achieved with a 'Shift' strategy:

- prevent waste of potentially useful materials;
- reduce consumption of raw materials;
- reduce energy consumption;
- reduce air pollution (from incineration) and water pollution (from landfilling) by reducing the need for waste disposal;
- reduce greenhouse gas emissions as compared to virgin production.

Improve

The 'Improve' pillar of A-S-I relates to the environmental efficiency of WM practices and technologies. It can contribute to the reduction of GHG emissions and improvement of air quality in the waste transportation vehicles, waste treatment facilities, and disposal sites. Furthermore, the technological improvement of waste treatment technologies can enhance material and energy recovery rates resulting in economic benefits. Technical improvement can be implemented through energy recovery of landfill gases, energy recovery of incinerators, promotion of biogas production, enhancement of the recyclables production rate, and renewal of waste treatment facilities and maintenance. Switching to the cleaner and more efficient fuels (e.g. gasoline to CNG) and using more efficient vehicles are other possible actions that can result in the reduction of GHG emissions and air pollution from waste transportation sector.

Table 6.6 lists some of the major interventions that can improve waste management systems, matching the interventions against the 'Shift' and 'Improve' strategies.

Table 6.6 Strategies for the 'Shift' and 'Improve' waste framework

Shift strategies	Improve strategies
• Shift from unmanaged waste dumping to managed landfilling • Shift from landfilling to thermal waste management actions (e.g. incineration) • Shift from landfilling to biological waste management strategies (e.g. composting or anaerobic digestion) • Shift from landfilling to recycling • Shift from thermal waste management practices (e.g. incineration) to recycling	• Collect LFG rather than flaring • Energy recovery from incinerators • Improve efficiency of recycling facilities • Focus on one technology and improve process efficiency by changing technology type, upgrading technology, renewing technology or maintenance • Change from traditional waste treatment technologies to modern technologies • Improve biogas rate production • Switch to cleaner and economic fuels for waste transportation

Mitigating GHG emissions, improving public health, and achieving social as well as economic benefits are the main drivers for the successful implementation of ISWM as a techno-political solution carried out through the climate co-benefits approach. In this context, potential waste policy interventions can be categorized as the A-S-I strategy components for understanding and selecting the most conducive way to move forward in developing potential sustainable waste management systems.

The Life Cycle Assessment method

Life Cycle Assessment (LCA) is an internationally standardized methodology for environmental assessment that can be applied as a methodological framework for tracking the environmental impacts of a system throughout the life cycle of a physical product from acquisition of the raw material to the final disposal stages. Considering life cycle stages for a waste management system, the LCA framework includes three levels: waste handling, waste processing or treatment, and waste disposal (Figure 6.7).

Each level as life cycle contributes in GHG emissions as well as air pollutants. According to the Standards ISO 14040 (2010), the LCA method covers four basic phases, according to Figure 6.8.

The LCA method can be used to evaluate the ranking order of different waste management technologies in the waste hierarchy. The LCA procedure and framework, definition of goal and scope, and the inventory analysis on the basis of any LCA study have been comprehensively introduced by Finnveden *et al.* (2005) and Rebitzer *et al.* (2004). They have outlined how to define and model a product's life cycle, and have investigated an overview of available methods and tools for tabulating and compiling associated emissions and resource consumption data in a life cycle inventory (LCI). Their work also discusses the potential applications of LCA in industry and policymaking.

The LCA can be used to address challenges and opportunities for improving the environmental performance of the waste sector, helping decision-makers by providing a selection of relevant indicators. In order to have a policy impact, a range of indicators and scenarios are required to understand where the interventions can be made. In this context, the waste indicators can be used to analyse and monitor sustainability towards climate change in terms of socio-economic and environmental performance of waste management strategies. It is expected that the waste indicators provide an integrated view on the links between environmental impacts and different levels of the waste system, including waste generation, transportation, processing, and disposal. The indicators defined by the LCA approach span the entire waste management chain and account for

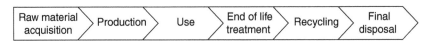

Raw material acquisition › Production › Use › End of life treatment › Recycling › Final disposal

Figure 6.7 The life cycle stages for a physical product.

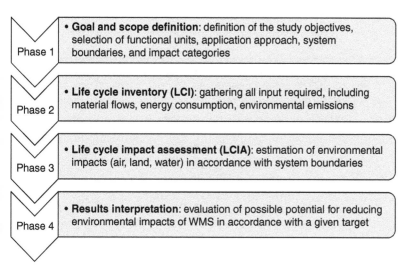

Figure 6.8 The LCA phases for analysis of environmental impact of waste management systems according to ISO 14010.

Source: International Standard ISO 14040. 1997.

associated benefits (material recycling, energy recovery, by-product production) as well. Furthermore, the indicators would prove valuable for evaluating and comparing the waste management practices through running different scenarios. The following data points provide a basis for defining performance indicators in the waste management sector (UNEP 2005):

- waste generation, such as the amount of waste generated;
- waste characteristics, such as waste composition;
- waste storage, such as container types;
- waste collection and transport, such as service coverage and frequency;
- resource recovery, such as an inventory of facilities and equipment, the amount of materials recycled, composted, and incinerated;
- landfill disposal, such as inventory facilities and equipment, capacity, and the volume of material under management;
- financial sustainability, including costs.

Accordingly, some common key indicators for measuring the progress made in achieving a standard or a goal in the sustainable waste management plan are presented in Table 6.7.

Table 6.7 Examples of common key indicators for monitoring sustainable waste management

Category	Indicator	Detail
Climate change	Global greenhouse gas (GHG) emissions (tonnes of carbon dioxide equivalent)	• GHG emissions of waste system
Air quality	Pollutant emissions	• Combustion products by CO, NO_x, SO_x, UHC, $PM_{2.5}$, PM_{10}, etc. • Noise and odour • Dioxin and furans, NH_3, VOCs
Water and soil quality	Leachate rate (from landfills) Ash (from incinerators)	• Heavy metals by As, Cd, Cr, Cu, Ni, Pb, Hg • Bottom ash
Waste generation	Quantities of daily waste generated per capita	• Waste types by households, commercial, industrial, and construction and demolition wastes (in kg/capita.day)
Waste generation	Waste characterization	• Waste compositions as percentage by paper, plastic, glass, metal, wood, food waste, yard waste, textiles, and other
Collection and transport	Service Performance Indicators	• Waste collection coverage by population, households, etc. • Waste collection frequency
Collection and transport	Resource Input Indicators	• Human resources involved in solid waste management (number of employees) • Physical resources (list of equipment)
Collection and transport	Efficiency Indicators	• Weight or volume collected daily per dollar of collection cost • Population served per worker • Population served per vehicle • Households served per worker
Resource recovery	Service Performance Indicators	• Processing plant capacity and throughput
Waste treatment and disposal	Waste Diversion	• Per cent energy recovery from waste • Per cent composting and/or anaerobic digestion of organic waste • Per cent recycling • Per cent incinerated • Per cent of waste landfilled
Resource recovery	Resource Input Indicators	• Human resources involved in solid waste management (number of employees) • Physical resources (list of equipment)

Table 6.7 Continued

Category	Indicator	Detail
Resource recovery	Efficiency Indicators	• Weight or volume processed • Processing cost per tonne • Quantity of materials recovered per worker
Final disposal	Service Performance Indicators	• Disposal capacity (total and remaining) • Waste acceptance rate
Final disposal	Resource Input Indicators	• Human resources involved in solid waste management (number of employees) • Physical resources (list of equipment)
Final disposal	Efficiency Indicators	• Cost for disposal (per tonne or cubic metre)
Resource recovery	Service Performance Indicators	• Processing plant capacity and throughput
Waste treatment and disposal	Waste Diversion	• Per cent energy recovery from waste • Per cent composting and/or anaerobic digestion of organic waste • Per cent recycling • Per cent incinerated • Per cent of waste landfilled
Resource recovery	Resource Input Indicators	• Human resources involved in solid waste management (number of employees) • Physical resources (list of equipment)
Resource recovery	Efficiency Indicators	• Weight or volume processed • Processing cost per tonne • Quantity of materials recovered per worker
Final disposal	Service Performance Indicators	• Disposal capacity (total and remaining) • Waste acceptance rate
Final disposal	Resource Input Indicators	• Human resources involved in solid waste management (number of employees) • Physical resources (list of equipment)
Final disposal	Efficiency Indicators	• Cost for disposal (per tonne or cubic metre)

Discussion and conclusion

The calculation of climate co-benefits in the waste sector is complicated by issues concerning data availability and accuracy. One of the potential limitations of quantifying co-benefits in the waste sector is the need to know the amount and composition of waste generated. Due to the common occurrence of informal activities in the waste sector, there are unaccounted amounts of waste that neither go to landfill nor are recycled but are nevertheless disposed of. Furthermore, the estimation of waste produced by component, waste treated or disposed by component, waste recycled by the formal and informal sectors are necessary parameters to calculate co-benefits and indicators as well.

There is a need for reliable waste generation and composition data in the development of waste management strategies. In this context, utilizing data collection sources at the international level may prove to be useful. Local authorities need guidelines to conduct evaluation and benchmarking of waste collection systems. A similar barrier relates to the appropriateness of emission factors upon which emission calculations depend. Although the life cycle inventory data such as emission factors differ across countries, regions, and cities, the inventory data generated by the IPCC and EPA can be used as almost most applicable references for estimating emission factors and technical assumptions required based on LCA method. On the other hand, these emissions and assumptions should be changed if the country or site-specific data are not available.

Estimating GHG emissions from recycling poses another challenge, as data collection at the local level will be necessary in order to evaluate climate co-benefits more accurately. In this regard, using inventory data to quantify GHG emissions from all the included countries is a large source of uncertainty in the estimated results. Therefore, local authorities have an important role to play in coordinating data collection to develop relevant evaluation and benchmarks of the waste system, starting with waste collection.

Although the share of the waste sector in global GHG emissions is only around 4 per cent, its distribution, like global GHG emissions, depends on a country's income level, lifestyle, geographical location, and energy marketing and resources. There is a tendency for a country to generate more recyclables (glass, plastics, and paper) rather than organic waste as the income level increases, which in turn changes the most suitable options.

Landfill sites are the largest source of methane, which additionally generate wastewater and nitrous oxide, whilst incinerators are a main source of combustion pollutants such as CO, NO_x, SO_x, and PM. In addition, pollutants, either present in waste or formed during waste processing, can traverse environmental boundaries via different media (air, soil, water, and food chain), resulting in the adverse effects on human health. People living and working in the vicinity of solid waste processing and disposal facilities are exposed to environmental health and accident risks.

Achieving sustainable waste management systems therefore presents an opportunity to create green jobs through collection, transportation, sorting, and processing of waste. In this regard, the management of waste should be considered as a potential priority towards achieving the Sustainable Development Goals. Meanwhile, emerging paradigms in waste management could also impact other SDGs on sustainable consumption and production, climate change, and health.

Integrated solid waste management (ISWM) is the most promising approach to effectively deal with the waste management problems sustainably. The main drivers of ISWM should be based on the waste hierarchy (reduce, reuse, recycle, recover, and disposal), which aims to achieve the following objectives:

- generate less waste;
- mitigate GHG emissions;
- foster a clean environment (air, water, and soil);
- increase levels of resource recovery.

The ranking order for incineration with energy recovery as a final disposal method, and anaerobic digestion and composting as biological treatment options often poses challenges for policy and strategic decision-makers in the waste management sector. However, the A-S-I framework can be useful in finding locally appropriate interventions, which support these four main objectives.

References

Chandak, SP 2010, *Trends in Solid Waste Management: Issues, Challenges, and Opportunities*, International consultative meeting on expanding waste management services in developing countries, Tokyo.

Cointreau, SJ 2006, *Occupational and Environmental Health Issues of Solid Waste Management: Special Emphasis on Middle and Lower-income Countries*, The World Bank, Washington, DC.

Dhokhikah, Y and Trihadiningrum Y 2012, 'Solid waste management in Asian developing countries: Challenges and opportunities', *Journal of Applied Environmental and Biological Sciences*, vol. 2, no. 7, pp. 329–335.

Finnveden, G, Johansson, J, Lind, P and Moberg, G 2005, 'Life cycle assessment of energy from solid waste – Part 1: General methodology and results', *Journal of Cleaner Production*, vol. 13, pp. 213–229.

Giusti L 2009, 'A review of waste management practices and their impact on human health', *Waste Management*, vol. 29, pp. 2227–2239.

Hisashi, O and Kuala, ML 1997, 'Sustainable solid waste management in developing countries', *The Global Development Research Center*, viewed 11 December 2015, www.gdrc.org/uem/waste/swm-fogawa1.htm.

Hoornweg, D and Bhada-Tata, P 2012, 'What a waste: A global review of solid waste management', *Urban Development Series; Knowledge Papers No. 15*, The World Bank, viewed 3 October 2016, http://siteresources.worldbank.org/INTURBANDEVELOPMENT/Resources/336387-1334852610766/What_a_Waste2012_Final.pdf.

IPCC 2006, *IPCC Guidelines for National Greenhouse Gas Inventories*, Volume 5, Chapter 2, 'National Greenhouse Gas Inventories Programme', HS Eggleston, L. Buendia,

K. Miwa, T. Ngara and K. Tanabe K. (eds), IGES, Kangawawa, Japan, viewed 27 November 2015, www.ipcc-nggip.iges.or.jp/public/2006gl/.

ISO/TC 207 Environmental Management Committee 2010, 'Life Cycle Assessment', *International Standard ISO 14040:2006*, International Organization for Standardization, viewed 27 November 2015, www.iso.org/iso.

Marshall RE and Farahbakhsh, K 2013, 'Systems approaches to integrated solid waste management in developing countries', *Waste Management*, vol. 33, pp. 988–1003.

Rebitzer, G, Ekvall, T, Frischknecht, R, Hunkeler, D, Norris, G, Rydberg, T, Schmidt, WP, Suh, S, Weidema, BP and Pennington, DW 2004, 'Life Cycle Assessment, Part 1: Framework, goal and scope definition, inventory analysis, and applications', *Environment International*, vol. 30, pp. 701–720.

United Nations Environment Programme (UNEP) 2005, *Integrated Waste Management Scoreboard: A Tool to Measure Performance in Municipal Solid Waste Management*, United Nations Environment Programme, Nairobi, Kenya.

United Nations Environment Programme (UNEP) 2012, *The Emissions Gap Report 2012*, United Nations Environment Programme, Nairobi, Kenya.

US Environmental Protection Agency (EPA) 2014, *Climate Change Indicators in the United States 2014*, viewed 3 October 2016, www3.epa.gov/climatechange/pdfs/climateindicators-full-2014.pdf.

Wilson, DC 2007, 'Development drivers for waste management', *Waste Management & Research*, vol. 25, no. 3, pp. 198–207.

World Bank 2013, *CO2 Emissions Per Capita*, viewed 14 January 2016, http://data.world bank.org/indicator/EN.ATM.CO2E.PC.

Zaman AU 2015, 'A comprehensive review of the development of zero waste management: Lessons learned and guidelines', *Journal of Cleaner Production*, vol. 91, pp. 12–25.

6.1 Yogyakarta, Indonesia

Potential co-benefits of community-based solid waste management

Retno W.D. Pramono and Leksono P. Subanu

This case presents co-benefits derived from the growing practice of community-based solid waste management (CBSWM) in Yogyakarta, Indonesia. Based on field surveys and technical simulations, this research argues that CBSWM, particularly those integrating the 3R (reduce, reuse, recycle) scheme, is a promising approach to effectively and efficiently reduce the amount of inputs to waste processing systems, thus contributing to reduce the impact of urban waste on global warming.

Some potential benefits of CBSWM are generally due to the lower use of non-renewable energy sources for transporting and processing waste, as well as the economic potential of reuse and recycle activities at the community level. When integrated with socio-cultural characteristics of communities and governmental policy, CBSWM can lead to wide environmental and economic benefits.

Potential co-benefits of solid waste management

Indonesia generates about 400,000 tonnes of waste per day. Indonesian cities contribute 38 percent, with the big cities in Java contributing 21 percent of total waste. According to the Ministry of Environment of the Republic of Indonesia (MOE 2008), the government can only manage 40 percent of waste in the cities and just 1 percent in rural areas.

The integrated practice of 3R is widely recognized as sustainable (Sinha and Amin 1995; Ackerman 2005; Kofoworola 2007). Recycling saves space for final dumping as well as energy. It may also save up to 95 percent of energy to produce aluminum from recycling rather than using raw material for production, which also reduces air pollution from incineration (Salvato 1992). Composting, another practice of 3R, has been observed to reduce up to 50 percent of degradable organic carbon (DOC), a parameter of methane (CH_4) emissions (IPCC 2008). Reductions in the volume of dumped waste may also reduce the risk to health within the community (Berry and Bove 1997).

Research framework

Although the practice of CBSWM in Indonesia is growing in popularity, there are currently gaps in the research about the ways and rates by which co-benefits are generated. There is a need to understand those processes by documenting, measuring and analyzing cases of communities which have various types of CBSWM by way of self-initiation, replication, programmed diffusion or other means.

This research compares cases of communities that practice CBSWM in the greater area of the city of Yogyakarta and tries to address the following questions:

1   What types of initiatives have emerged and spread from urban communities to cope with solid waste problems in their surrounding environment?
2   What benefits are generated by these initiatives?

Within the research, various benefits, variables and unit measurements are constructed based on inductive observations on the practice of CBSWM, which are selected as cases to represent CBSWM types existing in Yogyakarta, in particular those that have adopted CBSWM relatively rapidly through a diffusion[1] process. Life Cycle Analysis (LCA) (Yi et al. 2014; Pan and Kraines 2001) is used for calculation of benefits.

Life Cycle Analysis of Yogyakarta municipal solid waste

A LCA of Yogyakarta municipal solid waste is performed using secondary data and surveys of primary sources (Figure 6.9). The secondary data collected from municipality agencies include serial urban population data and its proportion that is serviced by municipal solid waste management, daily solid waste volume generated in the area and proportion that is transported to final disposal, its routes, gasoline consumed, and its related costs. Data collected from the primary survey include the number of CBSWM organizations in the area and their estimated community participation, the volume of solid waste and the treatment methods of those communities.

Figure 6.9 illustrates the process of waste management. Within this framework, there are two main sources of waste, household (90 percent) and non-household (10 percent). In terms of waste processing, household waste can be categorized as follows:

1   MS – HH = Municipality Serviced – Household.
    Waste from these households is transported by the government for final disposal.
2   OST – HH = On-site Serviced – Household.
    Each family manages their own waste in their houses by burning or burying it.

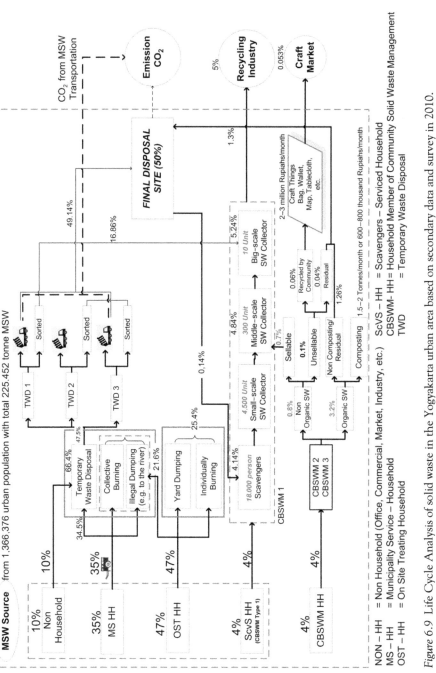

Figure 6.9 Life Cycle Analysis of solid waste in the Yogyakarta urban area based on secondary data and survey in 2010.

3   ScvS – HH (CBSWM type 1) = Scavenger – Household.
    The waste of this household is collected by scavengers. The scavengers sort
    the waste and sell recyclables to the recycling industry.
4   CBSWM – HH (CBSWM types 2 and 3) = Community-Based Solid Waste
    Management Serviced.
    The waste of this household is managed using a community-based system.
    The waste is sorted independently by the community to be processed
    further.

Research findings: co-benefits of CBSWM

The scheme illustrates a Life Cycle Analysis model for Yogyakarta municipal
solid waste in order to understand the benefits from CBSWM initiatives. The
benefits are computed by simulating three scenarios:

1   Scenario 1: situation without the existence of CBSWM;
2   Scenario 2: the existing situation with current growth of CBSWM;
3   Scenario 3: a situation in which significant growth of CBSWM is promoted
    by the government.

Those three scenarios were simulated to project the differences in CO_2 emissions from waste in Yogyakarta. This projection is based on statistics of city
development from 2003 to 2014, including the growth and the spread of the
city's population, the average waste production per capita, the growth of
CBSWM and the pattern of waste transportation and disposal by both the community and the government.

Based on a study of urban agglomeration (Bappeda 2014), the annual population growth from 2003 to 2030 is estimated at 2.4–3 percent. At that rate,
Yogyakarta's population, which was 1.37 million in 2010, would be 2.36 million
in 2030. Based on the survey, a person produces approximately 0.165 tonnes of
waste/year; the production of waste in 2030 would be up to 389,740 tonnes from
about 225,450 tons in 2010 (Figure 6.10). The characteristics and average solid
waste production by households are based on Abqary (2006), Sidik (2010),
Iswanto (2010), EAYP (2009), the Ministry of Public Work Act, No. 21/
PRT/M/2006 and Ministry of Public Work (2011).

The simulation of CO_2 emissions according to these three scenarios was used
to examine the significance of CBSWM in reducing the burden of waste treatment and the negative impacts of waste to greenhouse effects. Of the three,
scenario 2 is the closest to the current conditions of waste treatment in
Yogyakarta. Scenario 2 is the projection created based on the secondary data
from 2003–2010 and the primary survey in 2010. In scenario 2, the growth of
CBSWM is analyzed based on survey data up to 2010, as can be seen in
Figure 6.11.

For comparison, scenario 1 was created using the same data, but excluded the
contributions of scavengers, composting groups and recycling craft groups

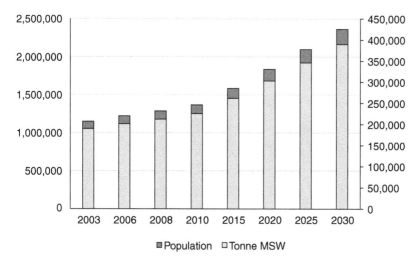

Figure 6.10 The projected growth of Yogyakarta's urban population (left axis) and solid waste generation in tonnes (right axis), 2003–2030.

(CBSWM types 1, 2 and 3); whereas scenario 3 was created using the assumptions that the government promotes the growth of CBSWM and other programs so that the growth of CBSWM would be higher than the current trend (scenario 2). Assuming the same population growth and the same waste production as shown in Figure 6.10, the difference of source of waste distribution can be seen in Figure 6.12.

Figure 6.13 shows that a greater volume of waste is managed by households serviced by scavengers (CBSWM type 1) than those participating in CBSWM type 2 and 3. This shift will result in a different urban waste treatment pattern, as can be seen in Figure 6.13 below.

There are two key points to note in Figure 6.13. First is the reduction of waste taken to final disposal sites, and the increase of waste volume sent to the recycling industry – approximately 36.4 tonnes per year in scenario 1 and 39.6 tonnes per year in scenario 3. The three scenarios also show the potential of CBSWM to alter the behavior of yard dumping, illegal dumping and collective burning, which in scenario 1 contributes CO_2 emissions of about 45.4 tonnes per year. In scenario 2, more people (9 percent) are involved in CBSWM and thereby reducing the volume of waste in yard dumping, illegal dumping and collective burning by 6.83 tonnes per year. The growth rate of CBSWM in scenario 2 is about 7 percent per year. If it is pushed to 13 percent per year as assumed in scenario 3, the proportion of the population involved in CBSWM will grow to 34 percent, allowing the average reduction of solid waste dumped to reach 22.1 tonnes per year.

CO_2 emissions reduction as a benefit of CBSWM was calculated using a model simulation. It is a function of methane and carbon dioxide emitted by

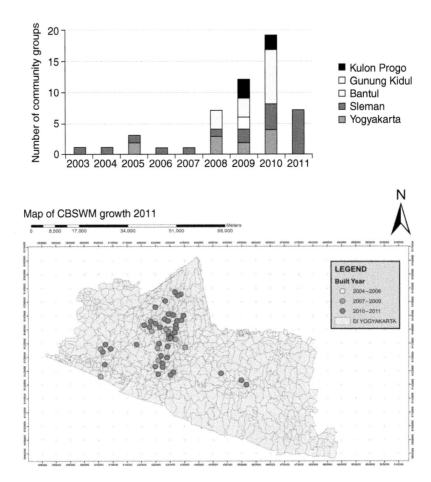

Figure 6.11 The establishment of CBSWM in Yogyakarta based on the model by Iswanto (2010) (top) and the spatial distribution of CBSWM in Yogyakarta Province based on the model by Sekber Kartomantul (2010) and the Environment Agency of Yogyakarta Province (2009) (bottom).

the solid waste volume dumped in open areas (including cities' final disposal sites), as well as burned solid waste and a function of energy consumed for waste transportation. To calculate CH_4 emissions, the IPCC formula (Sang-Arun et al. 2011) can be used (also see waste tool in Chapter 9, page 000). Fuel consumption emissions were obtained by assuming that one garbage truck can transport six tonnes of waste. In 2010, 18,823 trucks were needed to transport waste. The number of trucks was multiplied by the distance they travel in one day. Based on a mapping assessment, an average truck will travel 97.4 km for each trip, accounting for a total travel distance of 1,833,390 km per year and consuming 316,100 liters of diesel fuel. The emissions factors for CO_2

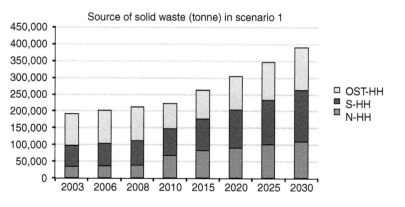

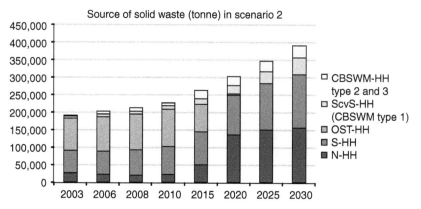

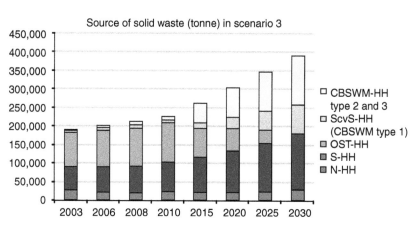

Figure 6.12 Source of MSW based on household typology in the three scenarios.

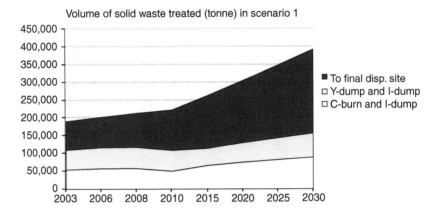

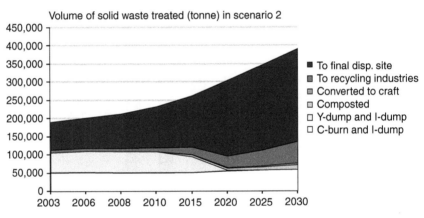

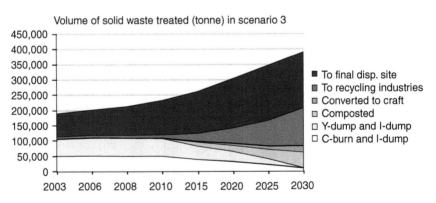

Figure 6.13 The pattern of MSW treatment based on household typology in the three scenarios.

were estimated using values published by DEFRA (2001).The projected data are based on the previous calculations, which were then used to project the effect of waste treatment patterns on CO_2 production in Yogyakarta (Figure 6.14).

Scenario 1 (without scavengers and CBSWM) shows that waste from the Serviced HH is the most dominant up to 2030, meaning that the residents of Yogyakarta will strongly depend on the government to manage their waste. CO_2 emissions will keep on increasing as a by-product of waste transportation. In scenario 2, assuming the current rate of growth for scavengers (households involved in CBSWM about 7 percent), a wider transportation service to final dumping sites will reduce illegal dumping as much as 11 percent per year, but it will still increase open dumping in final disposal sites as much as 20 percent per year. As in scenario 1, CO_2 emissions from garbage trucks will continue to increase. In scenario 3, policies that encourage the growth of scavenging and CBSWM will reduce the volume of waste sent for final disposal. With the growth of people involved in CBSWM at 13.3 percent per year, it is projected that, by 2030, the population of Yogyakarta will reach about 2.3 million and, if this scenario applies, approximately 34 percent of that population will be involved in implementing this concept.

In scenario 3, rates of CO_2 emissions can be significantly reduced, from 13 Mt in scenario 2 to 7 Mt per year in scenario 3. The impact of scenario 3 shows a downward trend in CO_2 emissions, which can be further reduced by implementing CBSWM at higher rates than in scenario 3.

However, people's awareness of the need to sort out their waste poses a significant challenge. Recycling is not commonly practiced for the upper and middle classes, while poorer sections of the community tend to be involved only when they see economic benefits. The time lag for recycling best practices to show benefits may discourage potential participants. Furthermore, CBSWM units do not easily profit from their reuse and recycling activities since their products are not well received by the market due to discrepancies with people's needs and the undeveloped branding of recycling products.

Other benefits of CBSWM

Besides reductions in CO_2 emissions, the existence of CBSWM can give rise to economic, health and social benefits, which can be enjoyed by local communities. The economic benefits of CBSWM come from several aspects of integration. First, reductions in the volume of solid waste can serve to reduce transport and management costs at the final disposal site, such as reducing land rent (see Table 6.8).

The second economic benefit of CBSWM is the practice of Reuse and Recycle in CBSWM. The economic value of reusing and recycling products was about IDR3.14 billion (US$340,000) in 2010 (from about 150 CBSWM units), which is generated mostly from handicraft production using plastic solid waste as raw materials.

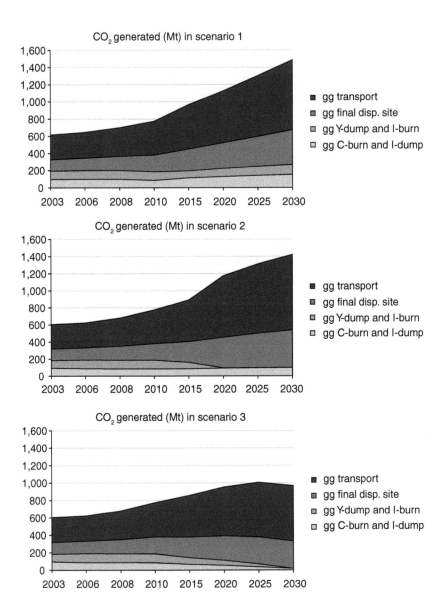

Figure 6.14 Estimated CO$_2$ emissions from the three scenarios.

Notes

The graphs show the greenhouse gas emissions produced by: (1) solid waste transport to final dumping ('gg transport'); (2) decomposition at final disposal site ('gg final disp. site') ; (3) household yard dumpsite and individual (household) burning ('gg Y-dump and I-burn'); and (4) collective burning and illegal (open) dumpsite (e.g. at riverside) ('gg C-burn and I-dump').

Table 6.8 Waste reduction unit conversion to transport (garbage truck), 2010

Description	Total	Unit
Amount of CBSWM	150	Group
Waste reduction from CBSWM	9,632	Tonne
Truck capacity	6	Tonne
Truck amount per year	1,605	Unit
Transport routes	97.4	Km
Diesel fuel consumption/truck/kilometres	5.88	km/liter
Diesel fuel consumption/truck/routes	33.13	Liter
Diesel fuel consumption (all)	53,185	Liter
Diesel fuel/liter	4,500	Rupiah
Transport cost reduction	**239,330,480**	**Rupiah**

Source: primary survey and interview with Yogyakarta Environmental Agency.

The growth of CBSWM represents the growth of clean communities. Through the practice of CBSWM, this community reduces exposure to the burning of solid waste and open dumping. Although there is no direct evidence of CBSWM's impact on the decreased incidence of dengue fever, in the research area, cases showed the tendency to decrease in line with the growth of CBSWM. CBSWM also promotes social benefits because it promotes social organization, which helps to forge stronger social bonds between individuals. The cases of Sukunan and Sidoakur villages demonstrate how CBSWM can translate into social activities through the work of the Environment Tourism Centers. The potential benefits of CBSWM growth in Yogyakarta are shown in Figure 6.15.

In summary, the growth of CBSWM within the community has the potential to provide social, environmental and economic co-benefits, for both the society and the government. Therefore, it is the duty of the government to promote the standard of 3R products produced by CBSWM and facilitate the growth of recycling industries cooperating with CBSWM.

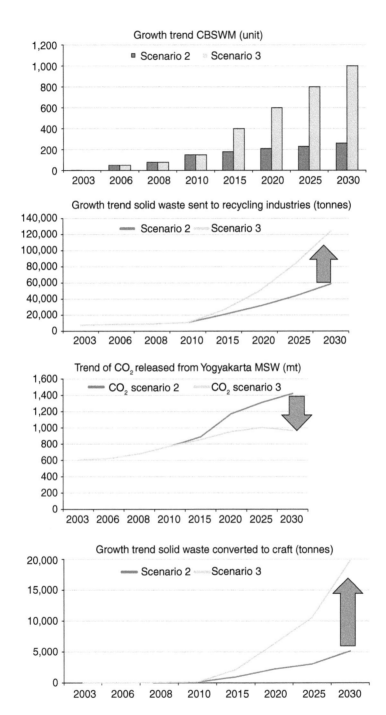

Figure 6.15 The important potential co-benefits of CBSWM in Yogyakarta.

Note

1 This research is the initial research done within the framework of the three-year research program under the auspices of UNU-IAS, during which further research into the diffusion of CBSWM is envisaged. Such diffusion research will provide important information on the comparative utility of programs to diffuse the practice of CBSWM to communities.

References

Abqary, Q 2006, 'Measuring of household consumption', *Balairung Journal*, 39th edition.
Ackerman, F 2005, 'Material flows for a sustainable city: Special feature on the environmentally sustainable city', *International Review for Environmental Strategies* vol. 5, no. 2, pp. 499–510.
Bappeda 2014, *Laporan Study Perencanaan Kebijakan Pengembangan Permukiman di Kawasan Perkotaan Yogyakarta* [*Study Report on Settlement Growth Policy in Yogyakarta*], Badan Perencanan Pmbangunan Daerah: Regional Development Agency, Unpublished.
Berry, M and Bove, F 1997, 'Birth weight reduction associated with residence near a hazardous waste landfill', *Environmental Health Perspectives*, vol. 105, no. 8, pp. 856–861.
DEFRA 2001, *National Scrapie Plan for Great Britain*, Schemes Brochure, pp. 1–28, Department for Environment, Food and Rural Affairs, London.
Environment Agency of Yogyakarta Province (EAYP) 2009, *Community Based Solid Waste Management*, EAYP, Yogyakarta.
IPCC 2008, *2006 IPCC Guidelines for National Greenhouse Gas Inventories – A Primer*, Institute for Global Environmental Strategies (IGES), Japan.
Iswanto, IS 2010, *Community Initiatives In Solid Waste Reduction, Sukunan Village, Sleman, Yogyakarta, Indonesia*, Green Cities International Conference, Putrajaya, Malaysia, March.
Kofoworola, OF 2007, 'Recovery and recycling practices in municipal solid waste management in Lagos, Nigeria', *Waste Management*, vol. 27, pp. 1139–1143.
Ministry of the Environment (MOE), 2008, *Statistics of Solid Waste in Indonesia*, Ministry of the Environment, Indonesia.
Ministry of Public Work, 2011, *Solid Waste for Dissemination and Socialization*, Ministry of Public Work, Indonesia.
Pan, X and Kraines, S 2001, 'Environmental input-output models for life-cycle analysis', *Environmental and Resource Economics*, vol. 20, no. 1, pp. 61–72.
Sang-Arun, J, Bengtsson, M and Mori, H 2011, *Practical Guide for Improved Organic Waste Management: Climate Benefits Through 3Rs in Developing Asian Country*, IGES, Japan.
Salvato, JA 1992, *Environmental Engineering and Sanitation* 4th edition, John Wiley and Sons, New York.
Sekber Kartamantul 2010, *Report of Networking Activities in Infrastructure and Facilities among Yogyakarta*, Joint Secretariat of Yogyakarta, Sleman and Bantul.
Sidik, US 2010, *Implementation of SMM in Indonesia Perspective*, MSW Management, Ministry of the Environment, Indonesia.
Sinha, M, and Amin, A, 1995, 'Dhaka's waste recycling economy: Focus on informal sector labor groups and industrial districts', *Regional Development Dialogue*, vol. 16, pp. 173–195.
Yi, S, Kurishu, KH and Hanaki, K 2014, 'Application of LCA by using midpoint and endpoint interpretations for urban solid waste management', *Journal of Environmental Protection*, vol. 5, p. 1091–1103. http://dx.doi.org/10.4236/jep.2014.512107.

6.2 Suzhou, China

Generation and distribution of waste management co-benefits

Wanxin Li, Eric Zusman, Jining Chen and Nirmala Menikpura

Introduction

Given the increase of 16.78 percent in the rate of municipal solid waste (MSW) collection and transport from 1979–2011 and the anticipated rapid urbanization in China, improved waste management presents the potential to deliver environmental, economic, and social co-benefits. The circular economy has become one of the priority policy areas set by the Chinese central government since the 11th Five-Year Plan (2006–2010). Suzhou, China is one of the two cities selected by the Ministry of Science and Technology for experimenting with the establishment of waste recycling systems in urban China, funded under the prestigious scheme *National Key Project for the 11th Five-Year Plan*. The authors participated in the project as investigators and were granted access to study the waste recycling system in the City Garden Estate, Suzhou. Interviews and participatory observations were adopted for data collection. A mixed method was adopted for data collection and analysis: documentary research for understanding the state control, and/or a lack thereof on the waste sector, and a case study on Suzhou's City Garden Estate for illustrating community self-governance on waste management and the effects of a top-down approach on the realization of co-benefits at a grass-roots level.

The case study found that state intervention broke the stable six-year bottom-up collaboration, which emerged between a migrant worker recycler, community residents, and the property management company in managing the waste in Suzhou's City Garden Estate. The erosion of the local partnership and social cohesion cost an estimated 2,700 to 3,400 tonnes of reduced CO_2e emissions per month and forwent an annual income of RMB42,000 (US$6,140) for migrant worker families and RMB20,000 (US$2,900) for the property management company. More generally, long studied political-economy questions such as 'who gets what, when and how' (Lasswell 1936) need to feature more prominently in research on environmental governance. By adopting this political-economy perspective, this case reveals the level of climate co-benefits often depends upon the magnitude and distribution of economic and social developmental co-benefits among stakeholders. The findings have implications for bridging research on waste management and state–society relationships as well as inclusive environmental governance.

Evolution of state involvement in waste management

China's central government started to regulate waste recycling in 1955. During the early stages of industrialization, the All-China Federation of Supply and Marketing Cooperatives and the State Commodities Bureau, together with local branches, were charged with collecting valuable waste and distributing recovered metals and other materials to different state-owned entities. By 1994, waste metals were classified as production and consumption waste and only the production category would be regulated. By 2002, the state-operated waste collection network had been completely phased out (Zhou 2008). The phase-out coincided with China's rapid industrialization and urbanization. China's fast-growing urban population with rising income (Figure 6.16) is forecast to generate 400 million tonnes of waste by 2020 – a volume equivalent to all of the waste generated by the world in 1997. At the same time, the informal recycling industry has grown to comprise about 5,000 enterprises, 160,000 waste collection centers, and a labor force of nearly ten million in China   (World Bank 2009). News reports as well as scholarly research described illegal workshops, poor working conditions, and serious pollution (Chi *et al.* 2011).

Suzhou is located in the Yangtze River Delta, about 106 kilometers away from Shanghai. It is one of China's most popular destinations for foreign direct investment with 138 of the World Fortune 500 companies operating branches in Suzhou. The waste challenges Suzhou faces are comparable to those in other fast-growing Chinese cities. For these reasons, it was chosen as a pilot site for the circular economy and offers an informative case study.

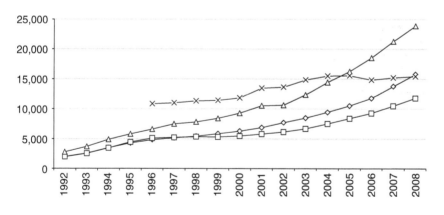

Figure 6.16 Increasing disposable income and municipal solid waste in China.

Sources: China Statistical Yearbooks 1993–2009; Suzhou Statistical Yearbooks 1993–2009.

Generation and distribution of waste management co-benefits in Suzhou

Community collaborative waste management emerged from the bottom-up

The City Garden Estate was located in the Suzhou Industrial Park, the result of a collaborative development project started in 1994 between the Singaporean and Chinese government. The Huaxin International Realty Co. Ltd is responsible for providing community services (street cleaning, garbage collection, gardening) to City Garden Estate residents. Starting in 2002, the manager of the Huaxin International Realty Co. Ltd., Mr. Huang Ke contracted out the City Garden Estate waste transfer station to a migrant worker, Mr. Zhong Bing. Mr. Zhong and his wife paid an annual fee of RMB20,000 (US$2,900) to the company for the exclusive right to collect recyclable waste from residents and to extract recyclables from the garbage sent to the waste transfer station; this exclusive right effectively forbade outside itinerant waste buyers from entering the neighborhood.[1]

By 2008, Mr. Zhong and his wife had been working in the neighborhood for six years. They were able to recycle approximately 300 kgs of paper, 600 kgs of cardboard, 1,050–1,700 kgs of plastics, 600 kgs of aluminum, 200 kgs of other metals, and some used electrical and electronic products each month. They earned RMB3,000 (US$437) per month by extracting recyclables from garbage and another RMB1,500 (US$219) from buying and reselling recyclables to dealers. This enabled Mr. Zhong to cover food, rent, and other necessities, as well as a RMB1,000 (US$145) per month remittance to relatives in his hometown. Prior to 2002, Mr. Zhong held less stable jobs in construction and restaurants, earning a monthly income ranging from RMB600–1,000 (US$88–145). Besides the increased income, Mr. Zhong built trusting relationships with residents. And with the exception of the occasional odor, Mr. Zhong and his family were satisfied with the arrangement.[2]

The Huaxin International Realty Co. Ltd also benefitted from the collaboration. The amount of garbage transported from the neighborhood by the Suzhou public utility bureau for final disposal was reduced by 750 tonnes per year. This reduction translated into an annual reduction of RMB50,000 (US$7,300) in payments made by the Huaxin International Realty Co. Ltd to the Suzhou public utility bureau.[3] It also reduced transaction costs for residents to sell their recyclables.[4] Furthermore, the recycling of paper, plastic, and metal also served to reduce GHG emissions. The diversion of organic waste such as paper and cardboard being sent to landfill cut down methane (CH_4) emissions, while avoiding production of virgin materials such as plastic and metal reduced energy use and CO_2 emissions.

Effects of state intervention on the distribution of economic and social co-benefits

In 2008, the Suzhou municipal government formed a task-force to consider establishing a recyclable waste collection network in Suzhou. The task-force leading group was headed by the deputy party secretary and executive deputy mayor; the Suzhou Federation of Supply and Marketing Cooperatives (SFSMC) – the agency once charged with waste management – was tasked with policy formulation and execution (SFSMC 2011). Mr. He Hong headed the newly created recyclable waste division under the SFSMC and he envisioned the state-owned recyclable waste collection network (Figure 6.17).

To create the waste collection network, the Suzhou municipal government invested RMB65 million (US$9.5million) to form the Suzhou Resource Recycling Investment and Development Co. Ltd, a state-owned enterprise (SOE) in May 2009. The SOE was charged with establishing 160 recyclable waste collection centers in communities; building an industrial park specialized in processing recyclable waste; and carrying out public education on waste separation and other relevant topics. In 2009 the Suzhou municipal government allocated a further eight million RMB (US$1.2million) to the SOE for operating costs. At the same time, the Suzhou municipal government outlawed private waste buyers for ensuring supply to the SOE. In 2010, 6,677 waste buyers lacking permits and 965 itinerant waste buyers were closed and fined (SFSMC 2011).

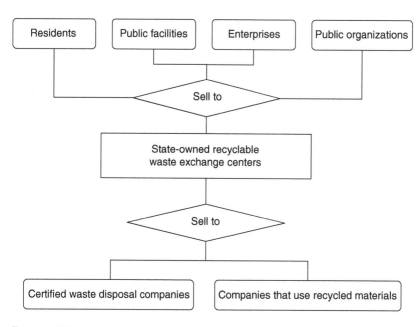

Figure 6.17 Envisioned state-owned recyclable waste collection network in Suzhou.

Effects of state intervention on climate benefits

Based on the primary data collected from collected from interviews with the waste recycler in the City Garden Estate, we estimated monthly avoided emissions of CO_2 and CH_4 (see Table 6.9 for data and calculations). Initial emission factors for paper, plastic, wood, aluminum, and steel are based on a study by Menikpura *et al.* (2012). The first step in estimating climate co-benefits is to determine how much CO_2 or CH_4 is avoided/generated for each tonne of recycled wastes. Arriving at these emission factors involves taking the sum of three variables: (1) the increase in GHGs from recycling materials; (2) the reduction in GHGs from recycled materials to replace creating new virgin materials; and (3) the reduction in GHGs from avoiding the anaerobic digestion of recycled materials (assuming that there is no CH_4 recovery). The sum of these variables is presented in column E in Table 6.9.

The next step is to determine the composition of the waste stream. The figures in columns F1 and F2 are based upon interviews within Mr. Zhong Bin's recycling center. F1 and F2 are labeled high and low respectively, reflecting the range of recycled plastics.

The third step is to determine the total amount of avoided GHGs. This involves multiplying the emission factors (in column F) by the volumes of different wastes (in columns G1 and G2). The amount of avoided GHG for each type of waste is presented in columns F1 and F2. To reach the net total of avoided GHGs, the figures running down columns G1 and G2 are summed. The total amount of estimated avoided GHGs for the City Garden Estate ranges from 2,676 to 3,368 tonnes of CO_2e.

Discussion and conclusions

More generally, the case illustrates that urban households, property management companies, and waste recyclers can identify cooperative waste management solutions. The benefits from working together include difficult-to-measure employment opportunities and sustainable livelihoods for often stigmatized migrant workers. The benefits also include quantifiable reductions in waste, energy, and avoided GHGs. Particularly, the socio-economic co-benefits flowing to Mr. Zhong's family, the Huaxin International Realty Co. Ltd., and community residents arguably exceeded the co-benefits associated with top-down state intervention. Thus, for the City Garden Estate, the conventional top-down approach in waste management forwent an estimated 2,700 to 3,400 tonnes of reduced CO_2e emissions per month and an annual income of RMB42,000 (US$6,140) for the migrant worker family and RMB20,000 (US$2,900) for the property management company.

This study clearly demonstrates that the interface between government policy and civil society needs to be reconfigured in China. A top-down approach necessarily disadvantages individuals and groups who do not have access to the policy-making processes. However, local knowledge and public participation are

Table 6.9 Avoided GHG emissions per month from recycling in the City Garden Estate, Suzhou

Material	(A)* GHG emissions from recycling (kg of CO_2 eq/tonne of waste recycled)	(B)* GHG emissions from virgin processes (kg of CO_2 eq/tonne of waste recycled)	(C) Net emissions from recycling (kg of CO_2 eq/tonne of waste recycled) C=A−B	(D)* Avoided emissions from sanitary landfill without methane recovery	(E) Net GHG emissions from paper recycling and avoidance of landfill E=C−D	(F1) Amount of waste (kg) (high)	(F2) Amount of waste (kg) (low)	(G1) % of waste (high) G1=F1/(F1)SUM	(G2) % of waste (low) G2=F2/(F2)SUM	(H1) GHG emissions avoided (high) (kg of CO_2 eq) E*G1	(H2) GHG emissions avoided (low) (kg of CO_2 eq) E*G2
Paper/cardboard	1,266	971	295	2,404	−2,109	900	900	0.33	0.26	−690.22	−558.26
Plastics	2,148	1,899	249	0	249	1,050	1,700	0.38	0.50	95.07	124.50
Aluminium	393	12,486	−12,093	0	−12,093	600	600	0.22	0.18	−2,638.47	−2,134.06
Metal (steel)	1,102	2,949	−1,847	0	−1,847	200	200	0.07	0.06	−134.33	−108.65
					(F)SUM	2,750	3,400		(H)SUM	−3,367.95	−2,676.47

Note
The parameters used in the calculation are adopted from Menikpura *et al.* (2012).

needed for optimizing both the generation and the distribution of co-benefits. It may be possible for the state to learn and to enable society to craft its own solutions to waste management problems. This realization eventually came to Mr. He of the SFSMC when he gradually changed his mind:

> I don't want to carry out the campaigns any more … I am now putting more emphasis on the role that could be played by the Recyclable Waste Industrial Association. For example, they can train the private recyclable waste buyers and help regulate the industry.[5]

This study also has implications for forming synergies between the environment and development under the realm of inclusive green growth (Davies 2007; Fay and World Bank 2012). China has announced the ambitious targets for carbon reduction and air pollution control. The Chinese government needs to adopt a bottom-up approach stimulating locally suitable measures that can both achieve those objectives and ensure not damaging marginalized and disadvantaged individuals and groups. The authors hope to see more studies on the political economy of waste management as well as other development issues in other contexts to allow inferences to be drawn on the quality of government, institutional innovation, and paths towards an inclusive green growth.

Notes

1 Interview 20080926–01 with Mr. Huang Ke, the manager of the Huaxin International Realty Co. Ltd, on 26 September 2008.
2 Interview 20080926–02 with Mr. Zhong Bing, on 26 September 2008.
3 Interview 20080926–01.
4 Interview 20080926–03 with Mr. Yao Maohu, the chairperson of the owners association of the City Garden Estate.
5 Telephone interview 20110504 with Mr. He Hong, head of the recyclable waste division of the SFSMC.

References

Chi, X, Streicher-Porte, M, Wang, MYL and Reuter, MA 2011, 'Informal electronic waste recycling: A sector review with special focus on China', *Waste Management*, vol. 4, no. 31, pp. 731–742.
Davies, A 2007, 'A wasted opportunity? Civil society and waste management in Ireland', *Environmental Politics*, vol. 1, no. 16, pp. 52–72.
Fay, M and World Bank 2012, *Inclusive Green Growth: The Pathway to Sustainable Development*, World Bank, Washington, DC.
Lasswell, HD 1936, *Politics: Who Gets What, When, How*, Whittlesey House McGraw-Hill book company, New York, London.
Menikpura, S, Nirmala M, Gheewala, S and Chiemchaisri, C 2012, 'Evaluation of the effect of recycling on sustainability of municipal solid waste management in Thailand', *Waste Biomass Valor*, vol. 4, no. 2, pp. 237–257

Suzhou Federation of Supply and Marketing Cooperatives (SFSMC) 2011, *Progress Report on Establishing Recyclable Waste Collection Network in Suzhou* (苏州市再生资源回收利用体系建设情况介绍及下一步工作目标), edited by Hong He, Suzhou Federation of Supply and Marketing Cooperatives, Suzhou.

World Bank 2009, 'Developing a circular economy in China: Highlights and recommendations.' *World Bank Policy Note*, No. 48917.

Zhou, H 2008, *Turn Waste into the Precious: A Study on Waste Recycling Industry and Policies in China*, edited by Chongqing Guo, *National Science Foundation Emergency Projects Series*, Science Publishing House, Beijing.

6.3 Surat, India

Urban innovation and climate co-benefits in municipal sewage management

Amit Chatterjee, Manmohan Kapshe and Paulose N. Kuriakose

Introduction

Rapid urbanization in India has put a lot of stress on the existing infrastructure in cities and, as a result, sewage[1] generated from urban areas has also increased. Urban India accommodated 377 million people (31.2 percent of total population) as per the 2011 census, the second largest urban population in the world (after China), spread across 7,935 urban centers, including 53 Urban Agglomerations (UAs), which are defined as cities with over a million population (Census of India 2011). Surat (population 4.4 million, 2011) is a rapidly growing city in India. The city was known to be one of the dirtiest cities in India and in 1994 suffered an outbreak of the pneumonic plague. Surat pursued a broad intersectoral approach to environmental management in the post-plague era to improve the urban environment, including transformation of the water management system. The Surat Municipal Corporation (SMC) is the first municipal corporation in India that is maintaining its sewage treatment plants (STPs) with biogas energy (methane recovery). Taking a co-benefits approach, in addition to the reduction of greenhouse gas emissions, a wide range of associated benefits of the project are also quantified. The main objective of this research is to analyze climate co-benefits, understand the socio-technological system, technological and innovation capabilities that lead to these co-benefits and analyze the factors that enabled Surat to achieve those capabilities in the waste sector and sewage management in particular.

Methane recovery and assessing climate co-benefits

The primary goal of this action is to recover methane for power generation. Carbon dioxide equivalent (CO_2e) emissions were analyzed from the four STPs in Surat and compared to the previous scenario without the project intervention. CO_2e emissions are estimated according to the United Nations Framework Convention on Climate Change (UNFCCC) guidelines (2012a, 2012b). A direct benefit of the project is that each plant is able to save between 15,000 and 22,000 tonnes of CO_2e, amounting to a total of 80,000 tonnes of emissions in Surat every year (Kapshe *et al.* 2013). Total CO_2e emission savings from the four STPs are shown in Figure 6.18.

A wide range of other co-benefits associated with the project includes increased employment, reductions in water pollution and reduction in water-borne disease and generation of organic solids for fertilizer, amongst others. As informed by officials of SMC, a total of 32 new jobs are created for the four plants. Waste products from dried sludge removed from the biogas digester are converted to organic manure and sold to farmers in the vicinity, contributing to the revenue of SMC. The total revenue generated by all the four STPs was around INR2.5 million (US$55,000) per year. It can be observed that when the raw sewage passes through the treatment process, there is an improvement in all parameters except the Total Dissolved Solids (Kapshe *et al.* 2013).

The intersectoral approach to environmental management also had significant impacts on health. Health-related problems such as amoebiasis, cholera and typhoid fever have also reduced in the city due to the concerted efforts of various stakeholders and the SMC in maintaining overall cleanliness in the city (Urban and Social Health Advocacy and Alliance [USHAA] 2011). More recent surveys have also shown continuing reductions in the incidence of some vector-borne diseases (SMC 2015). It took about 15 years to transform Surat into one of the fastest growing and cleanest cities after the spread of plague in 1994, and it has now become a role model for other cities of India (USHAA 2011; Taru *et al.* 2011). Through the embrace of a co-benefits framework, along with sewerage management, an improvement in a wider set of environmental outcomes was observed in Surat.

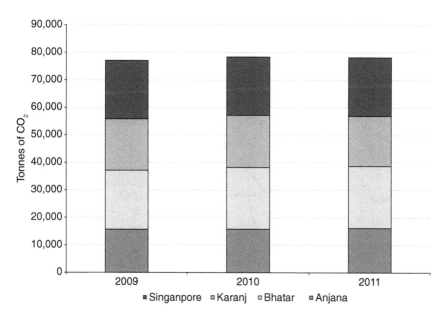

Figure 6.18 Total CO_2e emission savings from the four STPs.

Co-benefits: innovation capabilities and learning

It is interesting to know how a city (including the system of both governmental and non-governmental organizations), or specifically the waste sector in Surat city, learnt and built technological and innovation capabilities to generate co-benefits. A socio-technical system consists of a cluster of elements, including technology, regulation, user practices and markets, cultural meaning, infrastructure, maintenance networks and supply networks (Geels 2004). Understanding the socio-technical system of Surat is fairly complex, with several interrelated elements – the production domain (source of technology, transfer of technology, scientific and design knowledge, human resources, etc.); the application domain (repair and maintenance of STPs, communication and awareness, human resources, etc.) and governance and regulations (SMC, norms, devolutions, etc.) – that can play an important role in interlinking demand and supply side. Elements of the socio-technical system for STP cum captive power plant at Surat, Gujarat are mentioned in Figure 6.19.

Prior to the mid-1990s, Surat was notoriously filthy, even being described as a city 'floating on sewage water' (Swamy *et al.* 2010). The city government was facing several provision and management problems due to rapid population growth, thereby resulting in low quality of life in the city. Indian sources and the media organizations from abroad confirmed the outbreak of plague in India on 20 September 1994, and on 23 September 1994, pneumonic plague deaths were reported in Surat. The Journal of the American Medical Association (JAMA) reported that there were 5,150 suspected pneumonic and bubonic plague cases in India during the period 26 August to 5 October 1994 (Dutt *et al.* 2006). The panic was widespread; every person with swollen lymph nodes was thought to have plague.

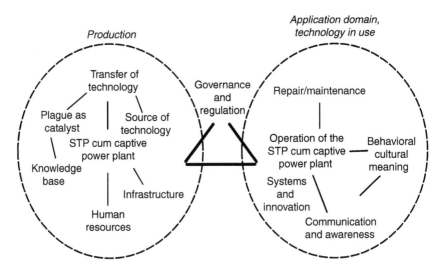

Figure 6.19 Elements of the socio-technical system for STP cum captive power plant at Surat.

The ideas for the initiative (STP cum captive power plant) originally came from the project by the United Nations Development Programme (UNDP). The UNDP commissioned a project in 1994 to initiate a few pilot case studies called 'Developing high-rate biomethanation processes as means to reduce greenhouse gas emission' to assess the possibility of biomethanization from anthropogenic waste (Akker and Deodhar 2005). Five municipal corporations were selected for the pilot project. SMC was chosen to start a STP biogas plant-based electricity generation.

Through its drainage wing, the SMC acts as the nodal agency for initiating and further management of ten operational STPs. There is an additional City Engineer under the Municipal Commissioner. The additional City Engineer is assisted by an Executive Engineer who takes help from eight Deputy Engineers. There are 37 Junior Engineers available to complete various tasks under the Deputy Engineers. Field Supervisors are employed to check progress of the implementation of any project under the drainage department. The SMC has given operation and maintenance contracts to private organizations for a specific period, after which the same can be renewed or a fresh contract can be initiated. The SMC acquired knowledge of the technology with the help of Sardar Vallabhbhai National Institute of Technology (SVNIT), Surat. The Indian Institute of Science (IISC), Bangalore helped the SMC install the gas generator and H_2S scrubber, which have been handed over to a private agency for managing. The generator was imported from Italy due to lack of good gas-based electricity generators in India.[2] Various key partners involved in attaining the success of Surat city's sewage management include national and international agencies like UNDP, central government, national level technical/scientific institutions and consultancies.

Visionary people have played a major role in bringing change to the SMC. This includes elected politicians and bureaucratic representatives. Using the 1994 plague panic as a launch pad to turn over a new leaf, two Indian Administrative Service officers, S.R. Rao and S. Jagadeesan, who served as Surat's Municipal Commissioners in quick succession in the mid- and late-1990s, turned Surat from one of the dirtiest cities in India into one of the cleanest cities. Mr. Rao led from the front; he coined a slogan: 'AC to DC'. AC stood for Air-conditioned Cabins and DC stood for Daily Chores. It basically meant that senior executives of the city government were expected to spend less time in the office and more time in the field. Mr. Rao himself led by example (Swamy *et al.* 2010). Mr. Rao developed the systems through strict monitoring and inculcating self-pride, changing the local civic culture, whilst Mr. Jagadeesan strengthened these systems, fortified the SMC's revenue stream and evolved long-term plans. Successive Commissioners, Messrs. Mohapatra, Aloria and Joshi, and Ms. Aparna, have continued the good work.[3] Over a period, the scope of activities has significantly enlarged. Business is back and booming. Surat pre-1994 was a dirty city with a rich city government. Today it is a clean, livable city with the city corporation occupying a well-deserved centrality (Swamy *et al.* 2010).

Political will combined with the fiscal strength of the municipal corporation are considered to be the major agents in bringing the change. Various changes brought under the sewage management in Surat had linked with the overall change in the city's perspective in improving the quality of life. Central, state and municipal administration worked together to achieve this success. Central programs for huge infrastructure funding under the Jawaharlal Nehru Urban Renewal Mission and programs for supporting non-conventional energy sources gave a major fillip to the SMC's initiatives. In order to recover energy from waste, the Gujarat Energy Development Agency has carried out studies in the state. A master plan prepared by the Surat Urban Development Authority and the vision to make a climate resilient city gives a clear direction for intensifying the decision to improve the sewage management sector by respective city governments (SMC 2008; Taru *et al.* 2011).

Conclusion

The STP cum captive power plant developed in Surat is an urban innovation with intensified function that was developed in a relatively complex socio-technical system of sewage management. By the end of the first decade of the 2000s, Surat was considered one of the cleanest cities in India. Visionary people have played a major role in bringing the change in SMC. This includes bureaucracy, elected and political representatives. Assistance from renowned technical and scientific institutes, SVNIT in Surat and IISC in Bangalore, supported SMC in the field of waste management. In Surat, the establishment of the Anjana Sewage Treatment and biogas-based electricity generation has taken good lessons from the first project (in 2003) and started three more projects in 2009. At present, three further projects are under commission and methane flaring from plants is practiced. One of the new sewage treatment plants at Bamroli is ready to be commissioned and has started the process of sewage treatment with the tertiary treatment process. In terms of technological functions, we can conclude that the SMC is currently at the stage of 'intensifying' the sewage management activity. Existing management of the current system with continuous research and development in collaboration with external agencies and enhanced number of plants with tertiary treatment processes (promoting good initiatives that happen in one part of the city to other parts) can be a learning example for many other municipal corporations in India. The success of this project has received the attention of other cities in India and this can be replicated by other cities for bringing positive impacts through a co-benefit approach.

Acknowledgments

The work presented here is a contribution towards a larger study, on 'Urban Development with Co-Benefits Approach', carried out in collaboration with the United Nations University – Institute of Advanced Studies (UNU-IAS),

Tokyo, Japan, submitted to the Ministry of Environment Japan (MoEJ). The authors gratefully acknowledge the technical and financial support received from UNU-IAS and MoEJ. From the larger study, a research paper has already been published, namely 'Analysing the co-benefits: Case of municipal sewage management at Surat, India', *Journal of Cleaner Production* (2013).

Notes

1 In India, 'sewage' and 'wastewater' is usually carried together. Further, the pipes that are used to carry sewage are termed 'sewer' and the system of sewers is called 'sewerage'.
2 Interview with Dy. Commissioner, Planning and Development, Surat Municipal Corporation.
3 Interview with Executive Engineer, Drainage Department, Surat Municipal Corporation.

References

Akker, J and Deodhar, V 2005, *Final Review of the UNDP/GEF Project IND/92/G32: Development of High-rate Biomethanation Processes as Means of Reducing Greenhouse Gas Emission*, viewed 1 January 2015, www.climate-eval.org/sites/default/files/evaluations/48%20Development%20of%20High%20Rate%20Biomethanation%20Processes%20as%20Means%20of%20Reducing%20GHG%20Emissions%20India.pdf.

Census of India 2011, *Provisional Population Totals, Paper 2 of 2011, India Series 1*, Office of the Registrar General and Census Commissioner, India.

Dutt, A, Rais, A and Melinda, M 2006, 'Review: Surat plague of 1994 re-examined', *South Asian Journal of Tropical Medicine and Public Health*, vol. 9, no. 4, pp. 755–760, viewed 30 January 2014, www.tm.mahidol.ac.th/seameo/2006_37_4/21-3658.pdf.

Geels, FW 2004, 'From sectoral systems of innovation to socio-technical systems: Insights about dynamics and change from sociology and institutional theory', *Research Policy*, vol. 33, no. 6–7, pp. 897–920, viewed 30 January 2015, www.sciencedirect.com/science/article/pii/S0048733304000496.

Kapshe, M, Kuriakose, PN, Srivastava, G and Surjan A 2013, 'Analysing the co-benefits: Case of municipal sewage management at Surat, India', *Journal of Cleaner Production*, vol. 58, pp. 51–60, viewed 30 January 2014, http://dx.doi.org/10.1016/j.jclepro.2013.07.035.

Surat Municipal Corporation (SMC) 2008, *Revised City Development Plan 2008–2013*, viewed 21 August 2013, www.suratmunicipal.gov.in/Downloads/CityDevelopment.

Surat Municipal Corporation (SMC) 2015, *Annual Report*, Vector Borne Diseases Control Department, viewed 23 September 2016, www.suratmunicipal.gov.in/Content/Documents/Departments/VectorBorneDiseasesControl/VBDC_Annual_Report.pdf

Swamy, HMS, Vyas, A and Narang S 2010, *Urban Innovations – Transformation of Surat from Plague to Second Cleanest City in India*, viewed 1 January 2015, www.indiawaterportal.org/sites/indiawaterportal.org/files/UI_1-Surat.pdf.

Taru, Surat Municipal Corporation (SMC), City Advisory Committee (CAC) and Institute for Social and Environmental Transition (ISET) 2011, *Surat City Resilience Strategy*, Taru Leading Edge, Surat Municipal Corporation, City Advisory Committee and Institute for Social and Environmental Transition, viewed 30 August 2014, www.indiaurbanportal.in/Publications/Publications181/Publications181755.PDF.

United Nations Framework Convention on Climate Change (UNFCCC) 2012a, *Clean Development Mechanism (CDM) Methodology Booklet*, Fourth Edition, viewed 20 March 2015, http://cdm.unfccc.int/methodologies/documentation/meth_booklet.pdf.

United Nations Framework Convention on Climate Change (UNFCCC) 2012b, *Indicative Simplified Baseline and Monitoring Methodologies for Selected Small-scale Clean Development Mechanism (CDM) Project Activity Categories*, AMS-III.H, viewed 20 March 2015, https://cdm.unfccc.int/methodologies/SSCmethodologies/approved.

Urban and Social Health Advocacy and Alliance (USHAA) 2011, *Health Impact and Adaptation, Surat India*, Asian Cities Climate Change Resilience Network (ACCCRN), viewed 21 August 2014, www.yumpu.com/en/document/view/49990642/surat-health-sector-study-india-acccrn.

Part II
Co-benefits by design

7 Recognizing and rewarding urban co-benefits

A survey of international climate mechanisms and informal networks

Eric Zusman, So-Young Lee, Kaoru Akahoshi and Andreas Jaeger

Introduction

Cities are major contributors to global climate change, accounting for up to 70 per cent of the world's greenhouse gas (GHG) emissions (UN-Habitat 2011). At the same time, many cities confront mounting near-term threats to their sustainability, including expanding waste streams, escalating pollution levels and diminishing green spaces (UN/DESA 2013). These global climate change and local sustainability challenges frequently stem from common causes; they are also often joined by shared solutions. The results of strategies that mitigate global climate change, whilst at the same time address local sustainability concerns, are known as co-benefits. International climate change mechanisms could potentially deliver the financial, technological and capacity-building support needed to help achieve these multiple benefits. The purpose of this chapter is to survey how formal climate finance and informal city and sectoral networks have evolved to help cities recognize and realize climate and other sustainability objectives.

The chapter shows there is an emerging ecosystem of formal climate and informal cooperation schemes potentially assisting cities to achieve joint climate and developmental ends. Formal mechanisms are equipping policymakers with the knowledge and tools to recognize an expanding range of co-benefits while encouraging policymakers to take the bottom-up actions needed to realize those benefits. Informal city and sectoral networks are also helping urban policymakers identify climate and other benefits while acquiring financing and technical assistance for achieving them. It nonetheless remains an elusive quest to craft multilateral climate change mechanisms that formally index financial and other forms of support to the pursuit of context-dependent sustainable development objectives. The chapter therefore argues that informal city and sectoral networks should not only aim to build capacities for planning and acquiring external support but also lobby for reforms that help to link that support to the dynamic needs of cities above and beyond mitigating climate change. The aim, therefore, should be for gradual convergence as opposed to full-fledged integration between formal climate finance mechanisms and informal city and sectoral networks.

Urban co-benefits

In the 1990s, the costs of acting – or failing to act – on climate change were generating a growing amount of interest. Spurred by this emerging awareness, researchers arrived at widely varying estimates of GHGs mitigation costs (Pearce 2000). The variation reflected the difficulties of estimating inherently global, long-term and relatively uncertain climate benefits (Krupnick et al. 2000). The nature of the climate benefits also made it challenging to persuade policymakers to invest resources in climate-only solutions. At around the same juncture, researchers began to demonstrate that investing in some policies and technologies that mitigate climate change could significantly reduce air pollution, improve public health, and save money and lives (Markandya and Rübbelke 2004). Numerous other local environmental as well as socio-economic benefits could also often offset the costs of well-designed climate policies and projects. Explicitly accounting for both the GHG mitigation and other development benefits could make climate actions more appealing to cost-conscious policymakers (Pearce 2000; Nemet et al. 2010; Mayrhofer and Gupta 2016).

It was also recognized that these benefits might also bring climate finance to a range of emerging development needs (Zusman 2012; Winkler et al. 2008). The potential for attracting carbon finance was particularly great in cities. More than half the world's population currently resides in cities. Recent surges in urban population have brought unprecedented demands for energy, transport and housing. Cities could meet these demands with low-carbon, sustainable energy, building and transportation systems; or they could become locked into unsustainable paths (Unruh 2002). Taking the more sustainable path would be helped by injections of new capital and technological flows. Tapping these flows would be eased with changes to the global climate change architecture that adapts to the needs of fast-growing cities. It would be particularly useful if climate finance mechanisms were able to recognize and reward cities for pursuing and achieving actions with multiple benefits (Zusman 2012).

It nonetheless merits noting that, even without global incentives for recognizing and rewarding co-benefits, many cities are already adopting innovative reforms capable of achieving multiple objectives. Some researchers have perceptively observed that, as national governments moved at a comparatively languid pace in UNFCCC negotiations, subnational governments proved relatively more adept at initiating and scaling transformational low-carbon actions (Bulkeley and Betsill 2005; Betsill and Bulkeley 2006) Further, city-to-city or other sector-specific networks were frequently playing an important role in cutting across formal governance structures and providing the tools and knowledge needed to drive innovative reforms (Markard et al. 2012; Betsill and Bulkeley 2006). The next two sections focus on the evolution of formal climate mechanisms and informal networks, respectively. The final section of this chapter reflects on possible interactions, convergence and integration between formal climate and informal city and sectoral networks.

Formal climate change institutions and mechanisms

The Clean Development Mechanism (CDM)

The links between climate change and sustainable development trace back to the 1992 United Nations Conference on the Environment and Development (UNCED). However, delivering climate finance to achieve broader development objectives did not capture significant attention until the 1997 negotiations over the Kyoto Protocol (UNFCCC 1997). A critical compromise between Brazil and the United States in those negotiations led to the creation of the Clean Development Mechanism (CDM) as one of three market-based flexibility mechanisms. The CDM was designed with two evenly weighted goals: the first was helping reduce the costs of climate change mitigation in developed countries; the second was helping developing countries achieve other sustainable development goals, including improvements in environmental quality, new jobs and clean technologies. In other words, CDM projects were supposed to deliver co-benefits (UNFCCC 1997).

The CDM's sustainable development requirement involved requesting host country Designated National Authorities (DNA) to devise context-appropriate criteria against which projects were to be assessed (UNFCCC 2001). The initial assessments of the CDM's performance in this regard were nonetheless relatively unfavourable (Olsen 2007; Schneider 2009) – though these have been balanced by more positive reviews lately (UNFCCC 2012). Several efforts to modify the CDM to make it more supportive of development-friendly projects have followed these critiques. Some of these efforts have focused on programmes of activities (PoAs), allowing a collection of similar, small-scale interventions to be grouped, registered and verified as a single project. This would facilitate the rewarding of smaller projects with a generally greater impact on development, though these have often been looked down upon by investors and developers due to higher transaction costs (Climate Focus 2011).

Several of the reforms concentrated on changing the rules governing the CDM. These include suggestions to scale up the CDM from the project to the policy or sectoral level, potentially supporting citywide nationally appropriate mitigation actions (NAMAs) and reducing the transaction costs from measuring GHG reductions (Li 2013; and discussed in greater detail in the next section). In yet another attempt to preferentially support projects with sustainable development impacts, the CDM Executive Board created a tool to provide a voluntary assessment of sustainable development '[and] highlight the co-benefits brought about by CDM project activities while maintaining the prerogative of the Parties to define their sustainable development criteria' (CDM Executive Board 2014). While some welcome the sustainable development tool, others argue its voluntary nature, absence of monitoring protocols and lack of incentives for use render it less meaningful (Arens *et al.* 2014).

Additional efforts have focused on creating a separate certification scheme for high-quality projects that sell credits on the CDM compliance or voluntary market. The most recognizable of these schemes is the Gold Standard. Gold Standard projects are required to demonstrate that they will have clear sustainable development benefits through a detailed impact assessment. This requirement is above and beyond fulfilling host country environmental and social requirements; a declaration must also be submitted by the project representatives verifying that the project complies with local environmental and social regulations (WWF 2015). Gold Standard projects therefore provide an incentive or financial reward for incorporating co-benefits into design and implementation; though the credits from these projects are purchased by a small group of investors often for corporate social responsibility (CSR) reasons.

A concern with the CDM and other market mechanisms is that additional screening for co-benefits increases the transaction costs of moving the project (or even a large-scale programme) through the approval process. This concern is particularly salient given drops in Certified Emission Reductions (CER) prices and related carbon market uncertainties that accompanied the global economic downturn from 2010 to 2013. These concerns notwithstanding, some evidence suggests eligibility and screening criteria can reduce the costs of recognizing co-benefits under the CDM and voluntary offset mechanisms. There have also been efforts to transition to mechanisms that are broader in scope or to move away from market mechanisms altogether. Many of these efforts are focused on a shift in the path of climate change mechanisms to Nationally Appropriate Mitigation Actions (NAMAs) and Intended Nationally Determined Contributions (INDCs).

NAMAs and INDCs

An important milestone in this regard was the Bali Action Plan – the work programme agreed to at the 13th Conference of the Parties (COP 13) to the UNFCCC outlining key elements of a future climate regime. Part of those key elements were NAMAs. NAMAs is a catchall term that applies to projects, programmes and policies 'in the context of sustainable development' that developing countries pledged to the UNFCCC to mitigate GHGs. The reference to these actions being both 'nationally appropriate' and linked to 'sustainable development' suggests that they should achieve not merely reductions in GHGs but other developmental benefits (UNFCCC 2008). Some of the so-called 'supported NAMAs' are supposed to qualify for financial, technological or capacity-building support. At present, out of the 192 NAMAs and related feasibility studies, approximately 81 have an urban dimension (Ecofys 2016). It is still too early to assess their on-the-ground impacts, but NAMAs helped put in motion a shift towards a more bottom-up architecture. This transition continues through the emergence of intended nationally determined contributions (INDCs). The difference between NAMAs and INDCs is shown in Table 7.1.

The notion of INDCs originated from a 2013 decision at COP 19 that Parties communicate to the UNFCCC secretariat climate actions in a manner that facilitates clarity, transparency and understanding (UNFCCC 2015b). While INDCs continued a bottom-up trend familiar to NAMAs, INDCs were distinct

Table 7.1 The difference between NAMAs and INDCs

Timeline	1992–1997	1997–2010	2010–2020	Post-2020
Annex 1	Limit GHG emissions	Economy-wide reduction targets		INDCs
Non-Annex 1	Take measures to mitigate GHGs		NAMAs	INDCs

Source: Boos *et al.* (2014).

in that they covered mitigation and other climate actions for both developed and developing countries during the post-2020 period. The varying domestic circumstances, including different emissions profiles, emissions-reduction opportunities, climate risks and resource needs, led to diverse INDCs. Though the performance of the INDCs will rest heavily on implementation, many of the INDCs make the link between GHG mitigation and city or subnational actions (UNFCCC 2015c). This will also depend on how future flow of carbon finance mechanisms are allocated and governed.

The Green Climate Fund and post-2020 carbon finance

Some have looked to the Green Climate Fund (GCF) to get a better sense of future directions in climate finance. Initially mentioned in the Copenhagen Accord (COP 15) and then further detailed in the Cancun Agreements (COP 16), the GCF was created to help promote a paradigm shift towards low-emission and climate-resilient development pathways. This was particularly important because the GCF is supposed to finance a portion of US$100 billion of annual climate finance by and beyond 2020 (UNFCCC 2009). The GCF is not a market mechanism and thus it may allocate finance based on other criteria such as improvements in local environment, the creation of jobs or the transfer of cleaner technologies.

In early 2015, the GCF developed a proposal template based on its six main investment criteria, including sustainable development potential. As Box 7.1 illustrates, the GCF emphasizes that environmental, social, economic co-benefits and gender impacts should be delivered by the proposed project/programme for this criteria. The GCF proposals also should be consistent with environmental and social safeguards (ESS) as the GCF is to be 'accessed against the GCF's fiduciary principles and standards, ESS and gender policy' (GCF 2016).

While the GCF is still in the early stages of operation and has only recently begun to finance projects, there are some reasons for hope that it will be able to help align climate and sustainable development objectives. One such indication can be found in the US$168 million allocated for the first eight GCF projects. The funded projects cover a various range of activities with economic, social and environmental co-benefits (i.e. job creation, energy security, health improvements, local participation, gender equality, education opportunity, poverty reduction, water availability, biodiversity, air quality improvement and so on). There is nonetheless the chance that the GCF encounters familiar

---

Box 7.1 Green Climate Fund funding proposal outline

A. Summary
B. Detailed description
C. Rationale for GCF involvement
D. Expected performance against investment criteria

   D.1. Impact potential
   D.2. Paradigm shift potential
   D.3. Sustainable development potential. Wider benefits and priorities.

Describe environmental, social and economic co-benefits, including the gender-sensitive development impact.

   D.4. Needs of the recipient
   D.5. Country ownership
   D.6. Efficiency and effectiveness

E. Appraisal summary
F. Implementation details
G. Risk assessment and management
H. Results monitoring and reporting
I. Timeline

Source: author's simplification of the GCF (2015).

---

challenges, such as lack of standardized methodologies to evaluate and then monetize co-benefits.

Another potentially relevant addition to the post-2020 climate landscape is the Sustainable Development Mechanism (SDM). The SDM is likely to be the next UNFCCC-governed market mechanism. As such, it may substitute for the CDM and other Kyoto flexibility mechanisms when the recently negotiated outcome of COP 21, the Paris Agreement, enters into force. It is expected that binding rules and international oversight might become comparable to that of the CDM. However, the SDM is intended to cover a wider scope of activities than the CDM. At this point, it is known that the SDM needs to facilitate additional mitigation efforts supplementing the host country's nationally determined contribution so as to increase the ambition from that host country. More defined rules, modalities and procedures, including those related to co-benefits, are likely to follow at subsequent COP meeetings (German Chambers of Commerce Worldwide Network [AHK] 2015).

The Paris agreement also makes reference to non-market approaches. These non-market approaches will allow parties to work together in a manner that 'is integrated, holistic, and balanced' (AHK 2015; UNFCCC 2015a). In this respect, they could be similar to supported NAMAs or bilateral mechanisms, such as the Joint Crediting Mechanism (JCM or Japan's bilateral crediting mechanism). The JCM has set up a platform for city–city exchanges that may be a precursor to future cooperative arrangements (Uematsu 2014). In principle, more complex climate activities could fall under the UNFCCC cooperative arrangement, including a cross-sectoral city dimension and potential for valuation of co-benefits. As with the SDM, there are still many details to be negotiated on the rules and modalities governing the operation of cooperative approaches.

Informal networks and partnerships

While the multilateral nature of climate negotiations suggest more resources could flow to cities generally, the past decade has witnessed the proliferation of informal climate change networks and other informal partnerships that are supporting cities specifically. Networks often concentrate on furnishing more fit-for-purpose tools and data that help city policymakers recognize climate and other co-benefits. In some cases, the networks are helping cities and other stakeholders apply for financial and technical support from climate finance mechanisms that could reward the achievement of multiple benefits. Networks are also playing a growing advocacy role, either inspiring an expanding web of cities to take climate action or calling for the inclusion of priority issues in UNFCCC processes. This section provides profiles of some networks, but it is not an exhaustive list. In so doing, it highlights (1) the tools they offer to recognize climate and other benefits; (2) the potential reward for making linkage between this recognition and finance or other forms of support; and (3) the advocacy for greater financing for cities from climate change and other formal policymaking processes.

City networks

With more than 10,000 cities, the International Council for Local Environmental Initiatives (ICLEI) is the world's largest city network with an explicit focus on sustainable urban development. Over the course of its two-decade history, ICLEI has developed numerous tools to support cities in improving performance in climate change and other sustainability issues. It has further become one of the highest profile organizers of international events as well as capacity-building seminars on sustainable urban development. This is done through both general as well as sector-specific programmes. In terms of more sector-specific activities, the EcoMobility programme concentrates on sustainable and inclusive transportation. In terms of broader based programmes, ICLEI supports training and dissemination of the Carbonn Climate Registry, a framework for standardizing the measurement, reporting and verification (MRV) of GHG emissions (Carbonn Climate Registry 2015). Perhaps most interestingly, ICLEI's recently launched Transformative Actions Programme (TAP) is an initiative designed to improve access to capital flows that could increase resources and incentivize implementation of multi-benefit actions such as NAMAs or INDCs, which could then qualify for support from international funders (ICLEI 2015).

The C40 initiative was founded in 2006 to help major cities with low carbon and climate resilient actions. As with ICLEI, C40 employs a combination of research and capacity-building activities that focus on several climate and related areas of concern (solid waste management, transportation, energy, sustainable communities). Since its creation, C40 has helped to document numerous actions in cities that mitigate GHGs; it has further recently placed a greater emphasis on not merely climate but co-benefits in cities. The third edition of the Climate Action in Megacities (CAM 3.0), for instance, is a report documenting the scope and content of the more than 10,000 climate actions taken by megacities from 2010 to 2015 (C40 Cities 2015b). The publication of a recent report on urban co-benefits is arguably even more pertinent to this chapter (C40 Cities 2015c). Sharing this kind of information and experiences is illustrative of how C40 encourages the replication of successful approaches. Moving forward, C40 has also joined with partners to form the C40 Cities Finance Facility, which will provide technical assistance to help secure investment for sustainable infrastructure projects. Like ICLEI TAP, this could help cities solidify the link between recognizing the benefits of sustainable investments and acquiring the new flows of finance needed to achieve them (C40 Cities 2015a).

The World Mayors Council on Climate Change (WMCCC) was established in 2005 to help unite city leaders and officials around the goals of strengthening climate resilience and reducing GHG emissions. The Mayor's council tends to draw upon resources of other networks like ICLEI for technical assistance and information sharing. Many of the Compact of Mayor's activities instead aim at helping existing city networks and their members advocate for innovative climate solutions from other cities as well as greater attention to urban issues in international policymaking processes. For instance, the Mayors Council on Climate Change helped to develop a voluntary initiative known as the Mexico City Pact through which local authorities commit to ten climate mitigation and adaptation action points (WMCCC 2010). These types of efforts can help ratchet up ambition across cities whilst at the same time pushing for changes to the climate finance architecture tailored to supporting cities.

Other networks and partnerships

In addition to the city networks, there are also several informal arrangements that focus on sectors relevant to cities. Established in 2009, the Partnership on Sustainable Low Carbon Transport (SLoCaT) is a clear example of such a partnership. SLoCAT currently brings together over 90 organizations to assist developing countries construct and maintain low emissions and sustainable transport systems. SLoCAT's key activities for 2015–2016 are organized around five work streams: (1) rural transport; (2) transport and climate change; (3) financing framework for sustainable, low-carbon transport; (4) SLoCaT results framework on sustainable transport; and (5) poverty and transport. SLoCAT also offers access to tools, data and knowledge that could help recognize the climate and other co-benefits of transport actions. SLoCAT further aims to influence not only the UNFCCC but also the 2030 Development Agenda and its Sustainable Development Goals (SDGs) by advocating for greater inclusion of sustainable transport in these process as well as greater access to financial and other means of implementation (MOI) for transport systems and services (SLoCaT Partnership 2015).

The United Nations Environment Programme's Sustainable Building and Climate Initiative (UNEP-SBCI) is a partnership that operates in a similar fashion to SLoCAT, albeit with an emphasis on buildings and infrastructure rather than transport. Formed in 2006, UNEP-SBCI aims to give building stakeholders a single voice and provide a global platform for participating in international policymaking processes. An objective of UNEP-SBCI that is particularly pertinent to this chapter is establishing globally recognized baselines based on a lifecycle approach for GHGs as well as other socio-economic and environmental benefits (water, materials consumption, waste generation, biodiversity, etc.). UNEP-SBCI similarly aims to assist countries in analysing their emissions related to building operations with the provision of these tools (see, for instance, UNEP-SBCI 2009; see also Chapter 4 and Chapter 9, pages 264–274).

The final relevant partnership reviewed in this chapter is the Climate and Clean Air Coalition (CCAC). The CCAC focuses on co-benefits from mitigating pollutants that degrade air quality and warm the climate in the near term, known as short-lived climate pollutants (SLCPs), such as black carbon, tropospheric ozone, methane (CH_4) and hydrofluorocarbons (HFCs). The CCAC is a voluntary multilateral initiative launched in February 2012 to catalyse the uptake and scaling of activities that mitigate SLCPs. The CCAC organizes its work in 11 sector-specific or cross-cutting initiatives. Among the sectoral initiatives, the diesel and waste management initiatives are particularly relevant to cities. The recently launched urban health initiative, one of the CCAC cross-cutting initiatives, aims for broader change within and then beyond the city. The CCAC's recently approved five-year implementation underlines it will aim: (1) to catalyze ambitious action through developing and sharing knowledge, resources, and technical and institutional capacity; (2) mobilize robust support through participation in key forums and awareness raising; (3) leverage finance at scale; and (4) enhance science and knowledge (CCAC 2015).

Table 7.2 provides a succinct description of the background, chief clients, operational scope and relevant programmes. It demonstrates that there has been the emergence of an increasingly dense network of programmes and activities related to co-benefits for cities generally and sectors specifically. These networks are increasingly tailoring their programming and activities to the varying needs of cities. Importantly, while there is some overlap, there appears to be considerable complementarity and cooperation across the networks with specialization based on the size of cities or the attention to advocacy. Furthermore, several of the networks are moving beyond just supporting cities in recognizing multiple benefits to acquiring external support to realize them. The growing

Table 7.2 Overview of city and sectoral networks

Name (Date of establishment) Participants	Scope • Relevant activities and programmes
ICLEI (1990) Over 1,000 cities	Ten urban agendas (including low-carbon, ecomobile and smart infrastructure) • Carbonn Climate Registry: to standardize measurement, reporting and verification of greenhouse gas emissions • Transformative Actions Programme: to improve access to existing and new capital flows to help cities raise ambitions and accelerate the implementation of climate actions
C40 cities (2005) 83 cities[1]	Low-carbon, resilient urban development • Climate Action in Megacities (CAM 3.0): definitive assessment of how the world's leading mayors have taken on the urgent challenge of climate change • The C40 Cities Finance Facility: to provide technical assistance to cities within the C40 network to prepare sustainable infrastructure projects for investment
WMCCC (2005) Approximately 80 city leaders/officials	Political leadership on low-carbon, resilient urban development • Mayors Pact: commits cities to a list of mitigation and adaptation actions
SLoCAT (2009) 94 organizations and institutions	Sustainable, low-carbon transport in developing countries • Provides resources to help measure impacts of sustainable, low-carbon transport • Lobbying for means of implementation (MOI) to flow to the transport sector
UNEP-SBCI (2006) Unspecified number of building stakeholders	Low-carbon, resilient buildings • Provides tools and experiences to help building stakeholders analyse lifecycle GHG emissions
CCAC (2012) Over 100 state and non-state partners	Technologies/activities that mitigate SLCPs • Provides tools and resources to help partners introduce and scale SLCP mitigation technologies (especially for diesel and waste management) • Newly launched urban health initiative might support citywide activities

Source: authors.

Note
1 This includes steering committee cities, innovator cities, megacities and observer cities.

emphasis on accessing resources from the climate regime is further supported by the expanding lobby efforts to factor urban issues into climate negotiations and ensure finance and other MOI flow to city policymakers. The increased interaction between formal climate mechanisms and informal networks raises a critical question: whether and to what extent should the links between these formal mechanisms and informal mechanisms be strengthened? The final section reflects on this question.

Future directions

The past two decades have witnessed the evolution of a climate change regime based on top-down targets and timetables with market mechanisms to one employing bottom-up pledges and reviews of climate actions and supportive non-market financing architecture. This shift has been driven by the emergence of NAMAs and INDCs and the creation of a GCF that could be complemented by a post-2020 SDM and cooperative approaches. To a significant extent, the changes in the formal climate mechanisms mirror the growing needs of cities for finance for sustainable, low-carbon services and infrastructure. It nonetheless merits underlining that some of the original challenges to allocating those resources based on not only climate mitigation but also broader development needs remain salient. Namely, it is very difficult to arrive at a mutually agreeable approach for measuring and monetizing non-climate benefits under a multilateral climate change regime. Even with the advent of a new 2030 Development Agenda and 17 SDGs, previous history suggests that the recognition and rewarding of co-benefits under a climate regime is likely to move slowly at best. This slow progress suggests that it may be imprudent to consider too much integration between formal climate mechanisms and informal networks. Said integration could lead to some of the same stumbling blocks that impeded progress in multilateral climate change mechanisms reappearing in informal networks.

At the same time, there may be growing opportunities for convergence without integration. To some degree, this is happening organically. The aforementioned changes to the climate change architecture and the thickening and strengthening of informal networks have found natural synergies with each other. Informal networks, for instance, are equipping each other with the knowledge and experiences to pursue co-benefits. Having said that, there does appear to be some scope for greater horizontal collaboration across networks. This could take the form, for instance, of integrating a widely recognized set of co-benefits (air quality) into ongoing carbon measurement tools and frameworks. In so doing, there should be an emphasis on harmonizing estimation methods and data-gathering protocols. Some tailoring will be needed to customize these methods and protocols to particular contexts and sectors. Similarly, as emphasized in the discussion of networks and partnerships, there is also growing opportunities for leveraging networks to advocate for greater recognition and rewarding of co-benefits across cities and, potentially, within formal climate change mechanisms. Some of the cross-city commitments to particular actions could be enhanced with parallel commitments to achieving other development goals (such as those offered in the SDGs).

This leads to a final comment on the city-related goals under the SDGs. The SDGs are not covered extensively in this chapter but they could play an important role in setting a relatively objective framework that cities and development agencies could use to shape future development trajectories. The brief review of climate mechanisms and informal networks suggest that there is a great deal of potential to examine how this framework can be tailored to the needs of different cities. One promising avenue of fruitful research might begin to look at subnational readiness conditions for implementing the SDGs and the new Paris agreement. A clearer understanding of those readiness conditions could strengthen the pursuit of joint climate and development goals.

References

Arens, C, Mersmann, F, Beuermann, C, Rudolph, F, Olsen, K, Bakhtiari, F, Hinostroza, M and Fenhann, J 2014, 'Reforming the CDM SD tool-recommendations for improvement, Copenhagen', *Carbon Mechanisms*, viewed 16 May 2016, www.carbon-mechanisms.de/en/publications/details/?jiko%5Bpubuid%5D=430.

Betsill, MM and Bulkeley, H 2006, 'Cities and the multilevel governance of global climate change', *Global Governance*, vol. 12, no. 2, pp. 141–159.

Boos, D, Fang, J, Vennemo, H, Oye, K and Sharma, S 2014, *How are INDCs and NAMAs Linked?*, GIZ, Eschborn, viewed 25 November 2016, www.igep.in/live/hrdpmp/hrdpmaster/igep/content/e54413/e54441/e61720/NAMAINDCPublication.pdf.

Bulkeley, H and Betsill, M 2005, 'Rethinking sustainable cities: Multilevel governance and the "urban" politics of climate change', *Environmental Politics*, vol. 14, no. 1, pp. 42–63.

C40 Cities 2015a, 'Germany and IADB achieve major breakthrough for developing cities – $1 billion in green infrastructure unlocked within four years', *Media, C40 Cities*, viewed 16 May 2016, www.c40.org/press_releases/press-release-c40-germany-iadb-achieve-major-breakthrough-for-developing-cities-1-billion-in-green-infrastructure-unlocked-within-four-years.

C40 Cities 2015b, 'Climate action in megacities 3.0', *ARUP C40 Cities*, viewed 16 May 2016, http://cam3.c40.org/#/main/home.

C40 Cities 2015c, *The Co-Benefits of Sustainable City Projects*, e-book, C40 Cities Climate Leadership Group, UK, viewed 16 May 2016, https://international.kk.dk/sites/international.kk.dk/files/uploaded-files/Co-Benefits of Sustainable final lowres.pdf.

Carbonn Climate Registry 2015, *Carbonn Climate Registry, 5 Year Overview Report (2010–2015)*, e-book, Bonn Centre for Local Climate Action and Reporting, ICLEI, Local Governments for Sustainability, Germany, viewed 16 May 2016, http://carbonn.org/.

CDM Executive Board 2014, *Reporting on SD Co-benefits Using the New CDFM SD Tool and Opportunities for Monitoring to Enhance the Profile of CDM projects and CER Price: What the Buyers Want!*, presentation, United Nations Framework Convention on Climate Change, Germany, viewed 16 May 2016, http://tinyurl.com/gwmtvzf.

Climate Change and Clean Air Coalition (CCAC) 2015, *5-Year Strategic Plan*, Climate Change and Clean Air Coalition (CCAC), Paris, France.

Climate Focus 2011, *The Handbook for Programme of Activities Practical Guidance to Successful Implementation*, e-book, Climate Focus, The Netherlands, viewed 16 May 2016, http://cd4cdm.org/Publications/Handbook_Implementation_PoA.pdf.

Ecofys 2016, *NAMA Database Pipeline*, Ecofys Sustainable Energy for Everyone, UK.

German Chambers of Commerce Worldwide Network (AHK) 2015, 'Paris COP21 – a historical step against global warming', viewed 3 October 2016, http://china.ahk.de/de/dienstleistungen/carbon-market/articles/politics/single-article/artikel/paris-cop21-a-historical-step-against-global-warming/?cHash=a94b318de8da69e14c93b76b41b039fd.

Green Climate Fund (GCF) 2015, 'GCF concept note template', viewed 6 May 2016, www.greenclimate.fund/funding/proposal-approval.

Green Climate Fund (GCF) 2016, *Accreditation to the GCF*, Green Climate Fund (GCF), Republic of Korea, viewed 4 October 2016, www.greenclimate.fund/documents/ 20182/319135/1.3_-_Introduction_to_Accreditation_Framework.pdf/4d44997c-6ae9- 4b0e-be5d-32da82e62725.

International Council for Local Environmental Initiatives (ICLEI) 2015, *Transformative Action Program (TAP)*, e-book, ICLEI, Local Governments for Sustainability, Germany, viewed 6 May 2016, http://newsroom.unfccc.int/media/358840/transformative-actions-programm.pdf.

Krupnick, A, Burtraw, D and Markandya, A 2000, 'The ancillary benefits and costs of climate change mitigation: A conceptual framework', Paper presented to the Expert Workshop on Assessing the Ancillary Benefits and Costs of Greenhouse Gas Mitigation Strategies, 27–29 March 2000, Washington, DC.

Li, J 2013, 'Governing urban infrastructure in developing cities: The role of carbon finance', in JB Saulnier and MD Varella (eds), *Global Change, Energy Issues and Regulation Policies*, vol. 2, Springer, The Netherlands.

Markandya, A and Rübbelke, DTG 2004, 'Ancillary benefits of climate policy', *Journal of Economics and Statistics*, vol. 224, no. 4, pp. 488–503.

Markard, J, Raven, R and Truffer, B 2012, 'Sustainability transitions: An emerging field of research and its prospects', *Research Policy*, vol. 41, no. 6, pp. 955–967.

Mayrhofer, JP and Gupta, J 2016, 'The science and politics of co-benefits in climate policy', *Environmental Science & Policy*, vol. 57, pp. 22–30.

Nemet, GF, Holloway, T and Meier, P 2010, 'Implications of incorporating air-quality co-benefits into climate change policymaking', *Environmental Research Letters*, vol. 5, no. 1, pp. 1–9.

Olsen, KH 2007, 'The clean development mechanism's contribution to sustainable development: A review of the literature', *Climatic Change*, vol. 84, no. 1, pp. 59–73.

Pearce, D 2000, *Policy Frameworks for the Ancillary Benefits of Climate Change Policies*, Centre for Social and Economic Research on the Global Environment.

Schneider, L 2009, *Is the CDM Fulfilling Its Environmental and Sustainable Development Objectives?*, Öko-Institut, Germany.

Sustainable Low Carbon Transport (SLoCaT) Partnership 2015, *Work Program 2015–2016*, e-book, Sustainable Low Carbon Transport (SLoCaT), viewed 16 May 2016, www. slocat.net/sites/default/files/u13/slocat_work_program_2015-2016_-_final.pdf.

Uematsu, T 2014, *City to City Collaboration and Its Case Studies under the JCM*, e-book, Institute for Global Environmental Strategies (IGES), Japan, viewed 16 May 2016, www.iges.or.jp/files/research/business/PDF/20150706/7_session5_Uematsu.pdf.

United Nations/Department of Economic and Social Affairs (UN/DESA) 2013, *The World Economic and Social Survey 2013: Sustainable Development Challenges*, e-book, United Nations, New York, USA, viewed 16 May 2016, www.un.org/en/development/ desa/policy/wess/wess_current/wess2013/WESS2013.pdf.

United Nations Environment Programme Sustainable Buildings and Climate Initiative (UNEP-SBCI) 2009, *Buildings and Climate Change: Summary for Decision Makers*, United Nations Environnment Programme (UNEP), Nairobi, Kenya, viewed 16 May 2016, www.unep.org/sbci/pdfs/SBCI-BCCSummary.pdf.

United Nations Framework Convention on Climate Change (UNFCCC) 1997, *Kyoto Protocol to the United Nations Framework Convention on Climate Change*, e-book, United

Nations Framework Convention on Climate Change (UNFCCC), Germany, viewed 16 May 2016, http://unfccc.int/resource/docs/convkp/kpeng.pdf.

United Nations Framework Convention on Climate Change (UNFCCC) 2001, *The Marrakesh Accords*, e-book, United Nations Framework Convention on Climate Change (UNFCCC), Germany, viewed 16 May 2016, http://unfccc.int/cop7/documents/accords_draft.pdf.

United Nations Framework Convention on Climate Change (UNFCCC) 2008, *Bali Action Plan, Decision1/CP.13*, Report of the Conference of the Parties on its thirteenth session, held in Bali from 3 to 15 December 2007, e-book, United Nations Framework Convention on Climate Change (UNFCCC), Germany, viewed 16 May 2016, http://unfccc.int/resource/docs/2007/cop13/eng/06a01.pdf.

United Nations Framework Convention on Climate Change (UNFCCC) 2009, *Copenhagen Accord, Decision 2/CP.15*, United Nations Framework Convention on Climate Change (UNFCCC), Germany.

United Nations Framework Convention on Climate Change (UNFCCC) 2012, *Benefits of the Clean Development Mechanism*, UNFCC, Bonn, viewed 4 October 2016 https://cdm.unfccc.int/about/dev_ben/ABC_2012.pdf

United Nations Framework Convention on Climate Change (UNFCCC) 2015a, *Adoption of the Paris Agreement*, e-book, United Nations Framework Convention on Climate Change (UNFCCC), Germany, viewed 16 May 2016, https://unfccc.int/resource/docs/2015/cop21/eng/l09r01.pdf.

United Nations Framework Convention on Climate Change (UNFCCC) 2015b, *Submitted Intended Nationally Determined Contributions (INDC)*, e-book, United Nations Framework Convention on Climate Change (UNFCCC), Germany, viewed 16 May 2016, www4.unfccc.int/submissions/indc/Submission Pages/submissions.aspx.

United Nations Framework Convention on Climate Change (UNFCCC) 2015c, *Synthesis Report on the Aggregate Effect of the Intended Nationally Determined Contributions/FCCC/CP/2015/7*, e-book, United Nations Framework Convention on Climate Change (UNFCCC), Germany, viewed 16 May 2016, http://unfccc.int/resource/docs/2015/cop21/eng/07.pdf.

United Nations-Habitat (UN-Habitat) 2011, *Cities and Climate Change: Global Report on Human Settlements 2011*, Earthscan, London, UK and Washington DC.

Unruh, GC 2002, 'Escaping carbon lock-in', *Energy Policy*, vol. 30, no. 4, pp. 317–325.

Winkler, H, Höhne, N and Den Elzen, M 2008, 'Methods for quantifying the benefits of sustainable development policies and measures (SD-PAMs)', *Climate Policy*, vol. 8, no. 2, pp. 119–134.

World Mayors Council on Climate Change (WMCCC) 2010, *Global Cities Covenant on Climate – Mexico City Pact*, viewed 16 May 2016, www.worldmayorscouncil.org/the-mexico-city-pact.html.

World Wildlife Fund (WWF) 2015, 'The Gold Standard: Optimal carbon offsets', viewed 16 May 2016, http://wwf.panda.org/what_we_do/how_we_work/businesses/climate/offsetting/gold_standard/.

Zusman, E 2012, *Recognising and Rewarding Co-benefits in the Post-2012 Climate Regime: Implications for Developing Asia*, Institute for Global Environmental Strategies (IGES), Japan.

8   Law for climate co-benefits

Magali Dreyfus

Introduction

The concept of 'co-benefits' is now well acknowledged in climate change studies to describe win–win interventions. Yet it has often been tackled through a technological lens or in work aiming to quantifying them. These approaches assume that the institutional frameworks are compatible with the realisation of co-benefits. However governance scholars are questioning this assumption. In particular, legal contexts appear to be a potential success or failure factor (Puppim de Oliveira 2013), thus it can be a hurdle or a driver for the definition and implementation of a co-benefits approach. This implies that each intervention will need a careful assessment of its institutional setting and that there is a wide variety of situations, which makes any policy recommendation and best practice hard to follow. Indeed legal contexts are multi-dimensional. They need to be examined in terms of competent authority that is considering which level of government has the power to take action and define the rules to apply. The difficulty here lies in the fact that often several authorities have jurisdiction and therefore their action has to be coordinated. Moreover, the legal basis for their action might not lay in the general legislation about division and delegations of powers but in sector-specific legislation, which makes it even more complicated to know for certain who the legitimate actor is in a specific area. This chapter aims to contribute to the understanding of the legal context within which a co-benefits approach can be efficiently developed.

Several nested dimensions of law are relevant for this chapter. First, a governance dimension defines the general legal framework at the national level (constitution and legislation) and the rights and duties of public as well as private actors. They fix the powers of the different stakeholders, especially in the decision-making process. Second, a policy dimension whereby pieces of legislation (laws, regulations, ordinances…) are adopted at different scales: national or federal, regional or state, and local, often in sector-specific areas. They are more action oriented and focus on the activities' design and realisation, and who is involved in it. Third, law can also refer to the implementing legal context. This 'project dimension' is to be found in legal instruments, such as regulations, contracts, permits, authorisations and other documents often connecting the local or competent public authority and private stakeholders. The co-benefits approach can be embedded in each of these dimensions.

The rest of this chapter is organised as follows: the next section highlights the link between the co-benefits approach and law, with the subsequent section providing a classification of laws. Then some opportunities laid in sectoral laws are presented, followed by the issues of their implementation. Finally, the chapter considers to whom co-benefits are addressed, a basic step in law-making, before a short conclusion.

Law and the co-benefits approach

First, law can be a hurdle. At the policy level, a law may have negative side effects. Ministries, at the national level, or municipal departments, at the local level, have specific competences and as a result often work in isolation. The risk is that they do not measure the impacts of their decisions, in different sectors. For instance, a law reducing oil prices, to support economic development, could also promote fuel-intensive technologies and curb the efforts of other agencies to promote renewable energies. Also tax incentives set to boost domestic production of fossil fuels in order to ensure energy security will indirectly cause an increasing amount of GHG emissions. Two areas of law may even conflict. For example, in France, Competition Law allows private companies to keep secret part of their environmental performance data when it is considered to be strategic information. This may impede local public authorities to make accurate GHG emissions assessments on their territory, although these are mandatory by law. At the project level, the law can obstruct the achievement of co-benefits activities. Legal uncertainty and weak legal institutions are a first general limit as this might deter private investors. Another example is law establishing monopolies over the distribution of energy; this might impede new entrants to penetrate the markets and introduce potential innovative technologies and products such as renewable energy generation systems.

The law can also create an enabling environment for the development of a co-benefits approach. If a legislator seeks to improve energy security, it may create market distortions to favour the use of renewable energies and thus mitigate GHG. This is widely acknowledged in the transport sector where measures aimed at reducing air pollution often simultaneously reduce GHG emissions (Chapter 2). At the project level, there is a wide variety of regulatory instruments which can be tailored to promote one or other goals. Taxes and subsides, environment impact assessments, building permits and codes lie among them. For instance, the Government of China has established a differentiated system of taxation for Clean Development Mechanism (CDM) projects depending on the benefits they provide. Thus public authorities can create incentives to support specific objectives (Curnow and Hodes 2009).

Analysing the laws

Given the variable role of the law, it is essential for the implementation of any win–win project to study carefully the institutional context.

In order to assess the legal context and the current rules in force as well as to screen future laws and regulations, classifications are a useful methodological tool (Dreyfus 2015). It has been used in particular to check the additionality condition of mitigation projects under the Kyoto Protocol (1997) regime. The classification helps to define the baseline scenario and prospects for future benefits. It also can be helpful to avoid adopting overlapping or contradictory decisions. Table 8.1 presents a legislation classification according to its goal. It is relevant for national legislation but also for lower level of governments' decisions as it should ease coordination and simplify the policy-making process.

For instance, in Delhi, India, measures for the development of the metro, a CDM project, could be classified as L + 1, as their aims include reducing GHGs. Measures for setting up a bus rapid transit (at present abandoned), which aim to improve public transport, would be L + 2. However, national subsidies for diesel would be classified as L – 1.

To fill in such a table, a lot of information may be required. Some relevant information on sources and specific fields to consider are presented in Table 8.2.

First, the context in which the legislation was adopted must be examined to understand the various drivers of action for the legislator and decision-makers. Among them lie the international obligations set in treaties such as the Kyoto Protocol targets for industrialised countries. National programmes of actions and political agendas are also incentives for the legislator to adopt a law. Finally, the legal mandate and division of powers between the national public authorities is

Table 8.1 Classification of opportunity and barrier functions of policy objectives in a domestic context

Opportunities	
Type L + 1	Laws that actually promote several goals, one being the reduction of GHG emissions
Type L + 2	Laws that incidentally produce co-benefits; these are regulations which pursue one particular goal but have side effects and thus generate climate co-benefits
Barriers	
Type L – 1	Laws that produce negative side effects, which affect mitigation initiatives
Type L – 2	Laws that impede the realisation of a project

Source: the author, based on CDM Executive Board.[1]

Note
1 The CDM Executive Board has also drafted a classification system to determine the baseline scenarios. See 'Clarifications in assessing the policies in determining a baseline scenario for CDM projects', *United Nations Framework Convention on Climate Change (UNFCCC)*, 2004, Annex 3, Clarifications on the treatment of national and/or sectoral policies and regulations (paragraph 45 (e) of the CDM Modalities and Procedures) in determining a baseline scenario.

Table 8.2 Legislation assessment method

Pre-law stage and context
International obligations (UNFCCC and Kyoto Protocol) or national voluntary
   commitments
National policies/programmes of action (ex. NAMAs, NAPAs)/political agendas
Relevant institutions/ministries/departments/sectors and division of powers between
   them
Content: legal provisions
Sector
Ministry/department responsible for the draft
Scope and jurisdiction (time, territory, addressees)
Objectives (preamble or first articles)
Content
Implementation
Date of entry into force
Authority responsible for the enforcement (autonomy and resources)
Direct or indirect (need of further legislation/decrees) enforcement
Complementary norms
Judicial enforcement (relevant decisions and pending actions)

also relevant as it determines the political agenda (e.g. the existence of a Ministry of Environment, the importance of such a Ministry, etc.).

Second, the actual content of the law adopted must be analysed to understand which consensus has been reached in the context observed previously, and to grasp which rights and obligations the policy-makers intend to create. The final stage of analysis deals with the implementation of the law to measure the actual effects produced by the adoption of the law. The law itself specifies the date of entry into force of the document. But then it is for executive authorities to ensure its application. In case of non-compliance, stakeholders may ask for the judicial enforcement of the measures.

Existing opportunities for co-benefits in sector-specific laws

Most of the measures addressing climate change, whether in mitigation or adaptation, are to be found in sector-specific legislation. Laws targeting GHG mitigation are not always labelled as 'climate change', nor do they always fall within the jurisdiction of an environmental ministry or department. Observing whether laws embed a co-benefits approach therefore require examination of sector-specific legislation. In our research, we found three key sectors for co-benefits policies.

Energy sector

Through energy conservation or the use of renewable energy resources, industries or households actually reduce their GHG emissions and contribute to climate change mitigation. However, the main and primary goal of the energy legislation is, in many cases, energy security. This is true for Japan (*Japanese Basic Act on Energy Policy 2002*), an industrialised country, as well as for other developing countries (e.g. *Indian Energy Conservation Act 2001*). These pieces of legislation would therefore be classified L + 2. The *Chinese Energy Conservation Law 2007, No. 77*, explicitly insists on the contribution of energy conservation to economic and social development (article 1).

Transport sector

Many air pollutants and GHGs have common sources (Metz *et al.* 2007). Vehicular pollution is one of them. In India and Indonesia, transport laws aim at the control and reduction of air pollutants as well as the facilitation of economic development and the reduction of congestion (*Indian Motor Vehicles Act 1988, Indian Central Motor Vehicles Rules 1989, Indonesian Law on Land Transportation 2009*) (here again Type L + 2 laws). Yet at the same time, these measures, which consist mostly of binding emissions standards for motor vehicles, often reduce GHG emissions provided that they do not result in an additional use of other energy sources (in that case they would be L – 1 type). Planning is key to overcoming these challenges.

Waste management sector

The waste sector also provides opportunities to integrate a co-benefits approach. In Japan, the Ministry of the Environment drafts waste legislation. Thus the primary goal of the *Japanese Basic Act on Establishing a Sound Material-Cycle Society 2000* is to ensure a healthy environment to present to future generations, through the development of a sound-material-cycle society. It aims at developing a sound economy with a minimised environmental load by promoting resources conservation. However, the reuse and recycle strategies (see Chapter 6.1) allow a reduction of GHG emissions produced by waste disposal. Thus environmental measures inspired by sustainable development concerns match GHG emissions objectives linked to climate change policies.

In the energy sector as well as in the transport or waste management sectors, the opportunities for innovation in GHG emissions reduction are important. Although GHG reduction is not the primary goal and climate change mitigation is not explicitly mentioned in most of the legislation, synergies with other environmental or social goals may be found. Moreover, green technologies can largely be used and benefit from new market opportunities, which could then help finance further research and investments.

Climate laws

Norms may also be primarily dedicated to climate change and aim at mitigation of GHG emissions or adaptation. These fall under the L + 1 category in Table 8.1.

Within the *Brazilian Law Establishing the National Policy on Climate Change* *(NPCC) 2009, Law n.12187*, article 1, its 'principles, objectives, directives and instruments' are defined. A national voluntary target of between 36.1 and 38.9 per cent GHG emissions reduction by 2020 is fixed. The Act essentially outlines the governance framework of the climate change policy in Brazil. Co-benefits are part of it, although not explicitly mentioned. In fact, article 4 states the aims of the NPCC and provides that climate change mitigation and adaptation should be combined with social-economic development, sustainable development and 'with the purpose of seeking economic growth, eradication of poverty and reduction of social inequalities' (*Brazilian Law Establishing the National Policy on Climate Change*, article 4). There are no concrete measures and, although it is binding, the law consists mostly of recommendations. However, important points of entry for co-benefits projects can be identified. In particular, the act foresees the establishment of an emissions trading system. It also requires the drafting of sectoral plans (energy generation and distribution; urban public transport and modal interstate cargo and passenger transportation systems; manufacturing industry and durable consumer goods industry; fine chemicals industry and basic chemicals industry; paper and cellulose industry; mining; civil construction industry; healthcare services; and agriculture and ranching (*Brazilian Law Establishing the National Policy on Climate Change*, article 11), pointing to where opportunities can be found in the future.

Going beyond the legal instruments analysis: the implementation issue

Implementation remains a major issue. Although legislation promoting co-benefits is now widespread, the question of the enforcement of the measures adopted is not solved and is a common problem in developed and developing countries. The implementation gap contributes to legal uncertainty and may be perceived as a high risk for private stakeholders involved in co-benefits projects.

Coordination between public actors and overlapping norms

National authorities through the parliament and government define the policies and laws applicable on the national territory. They also manage foreign affairs and negotiate international agreements, such as the United Nations Framework Convention on Climate Change or the Kyoto Protocol.

In the field of climate change, their role is particularly important given the global nature of the issue. In fact, climate change often emerged in the national context as a foreign policy issue. This is true in the industrialised countries like Japan (Pajon 2010) as well as in the developing countries like India (Dubash 2011). Hence, they are key actors, as they point out in the domestic policy context which objectives are important and shall be considered when drafting co-benefits projects.

For instance, the *Indian National Action Plan on Climate Change*, has integrated the climate change issue in the domestic context. It expressly refers to the concept of co-benefits. It provides that: 'The National Action Plan on Climate Change identifies measures that promote our development objectives while also yielding co-benefits for addressing climate change effectively.' It is to be noted though that the priority lies in the development goals and that climate change measures come second (Dubash 2011; Doll *et al.* 2013). Before the adoption of the *Indian National Action Plan on Climate Change*, policies were moved by domestic concern, such as energy security. The adoption of a national plan has therefore highlighted the relevance of climate issue in the domestic policy-making process.

To that extent, discussions at the national level are an important step. They show the commitment and potential support that all the actors will be able to find at the central level. It is also a promise of investments in technologies, human resources and research and development. Studies show that in central-ised states this commitment is essential to engage local authorities in climate change action (Qi *et al.* 2008).

Local authorities, and in particular cities, are another key stakeholder of the co-benefits debate. Urban areas are responsible for an important share of GHG emissions. They concentrate people, economic activities and transport. Con-sequently, this is also where opportunities are located (Corfee-Morlot *et al.* 2009).

City governments often have human and capital resources that allow them to take action. Coupled with an aspiration to exercise some leadership or to gain a presence on the international stage, some local authorities have proved to be enterprising and innovative. Finally, city governments are often responsible for the management of services (waste management, transport, buildings, land use), which are target activities to take action to mitigate climate change. It is important, therefore, to identify the opportunities and constraints that lie in local regulations.

Some local regulations may impose more stringent standards than the national ones. For instance, the *Indonesian Government Regulation on Air Pollu-tion Control, No. 41/1999* allows provincial governments to adopt more strin-gent limits. Thus, in Jakarta, the level of CO emission standards is lower than the national target (Council on Clean Transportation 2014). Article 13 of the *Chinese Energy Conservation Law* also provides for the possibility of more strin-gent standards to be defined by local authorities or even by private entities.

Consequently, knowledge of the national legal framework is not sufficient to have a complete picture of the legal requirements on a given territory. The level of decentralisation must also be taken into account. It highlights how much autonomy local governments afford, to develop proper policies and to define innovative solutions.

In Tokyo, Japan, the Metropolitan Government established in 2010 its own cap-and-trade system to mitigate GHG emissions. It covers large facilities such as office buildings and factories. Each facility is awarded an allowance for its GHG emissions. In case it does not manage to curb its emissions and needs more credits, it can buy allowances to facilities that have an excess number of them. This opportunity of trading allowances should act as an incentive to reduce emissions. The system is regulated in detail and needs careful examination of local ordinances (see the Tokyo case, Chapter 4.2, for more details).

However, the coordination between the various public authorities is a key element for effective implementation of norms facilitating co-benefits projects. Local initiatives can be contradictory to the general legal framework. This may affect efficiency on both sides.

In Sao Paulo, Brazil, the local government has adopted the *Sao Paulo State Policy on Climate Change 2009, ACT No. 13.798*, a municipal law that defines the city's adaptation and mitigation strategy. Among its measures, it sets a 30 per cent GHG reduction target by 2012 with respect to a 2005 baseline. To do so, actions are undertaken in public transport, energy efficiency, green building, land use and solid waste management (D'Almeida Martins and da Costa Ferreira 2011). It also creates an obligation for private partners, as it requires big-emitting businesses to draft a mitigation plan. In spite of this exemplary commitment, the municipal law has been criticised. Some commentators denounced the apparent contradictory character of the municipal law with the federal government's official position towards climate change (BMA 2009). In fact, the Ministry of Foreign Affairs and the Ministry of Science and Technology have declared that a developing country like Brazil should not be bound by targets such as those laid out in the first commitment period of the Kyoto Protocol. The government felt that good implementation of the Principle of Common but Differentiated Responsibilities could be affected by ambitious local initiatives.

Finally, in the CDM framework, ambitious local regulations may be seen as an obstacle to the implementation of projects. In fact, the additionality condition, required by article 12 of the Kyoto Protocol, demands that 'c) Reductions in emissions that are additional to any that would occur in the absence of the certified project activity'. So any domestic law that reduces GHG emissions makes it more difficult to reach additional benefits. The *Sao Paulo State Policy on Climate Change* is an example of this. The Brazilian central government has adopted several programmes to facilitate the implementation of CDM projects. Financial and credit mechanisms were created for that purpose (such as the Support Programme for CDM projects or the Clean Development Programme). But the reduction resulting from the municipal law may thwart the use of the national incentives mechanisms (Curnow and Hodes 2009).

Local regulations must therefore be studied as they may add particular constraints to the design of projects. But they need to be assessed also in the wider legal context in order to be sure that another authority will not repeal them, or take the matter to court.

Implementation through judicial review

Courts are key actors in ensuring that parties to a contract have their rights protected. They also guarantee that public authorities perform their duties in compliance with the laws enacted. Their activity is therefore key to build up confidence and trust in the law.

In that regard, India is a striking example of how significant judicial oversight can be. In Delhi, decisions from the courts have had important institutional, policy and technological impacts (Dreyfus 2013). They led to the creation of the Environment Pollution (Prevention and Control) Authority for Delhi, with wide powers to control pollution in the capital. They ordered the central and state governments to intervene and define action plans. The judiciary also made important technological choices, such as the phasing out from diesel to compressed natural gas for all public vehicles and taxis. Courts contribute to the 'design of innovative solutions, direct policy changes, catalyse law-making, reprimand officials and enforce orders' (Rajamani 2007). These decisions have shaped environmental policy in Delhi and other Indian cities.

In Brazil, the judiciary also proved to be active. For instance, the state of Sao Paulo started a lawsuit, later taken over by the federal prosecutor, against Petrobras, the national oil company. They sued the company for not complying with the national directives regarding the quality of the fuel. Some vehicle manufacturers were also tried for not developing new models able to fulfil the legal requirements (Lucon and Goldemberg 2010). So public as well as private actors are directly concerned by the activity of the judiciary.

It is difficult to peruse the case law of a country. However, a glance at some decisions may be enough to give an idea of how much protection can be found in the courts and the rule of law. More generally, the development of projects demands a good knowledge of the applicable legislation and how this is implemented.

From a governance perspective, the courts' decisions reveal local conflicts of interests and allow mapping stakeholders. They also highlight potential barriers for action. An important number of decisions point to deadlocks and the inaction of executive actors, in a particular city or sector. The screening of local case law may therefore be relevant to assess implementation issues to a given piece of legislation or a project.

Finally, litigation shows that several kinds of actors have claims over the benefits of public policies. It is therefore important to think about whom the co-benefits approach is really addressing.

Co-benefits for whom? Fostering participation for a better implementation

The analysis made in the previous section on legal institutions shows that institutions are a key aspect of the success of co-benefits projects. This is not only important at the level of implementation but also beforehand, in their definition. Benefits should be anticipated and considered in the decision-making process. In order to make the most robust identification of them, participation is essential. The question of 'co-benefits for whom?' is therefore central to any reflection upon the co-benefits approach and, consequently, a fundamental element to consider as it is a factor of success or failure.

In 'co-benefits' activities, the stakeholders may be foreign actors (international organisations, development agencies, private companies), the domestic public authorities (national, regional or mostly local governments), business actors and, of course, the local communities and the citizens.

Co-benefits make sense if they come from the bottom but currently they seem to be promoted from the top. International organisations (OECD, UNEP, World Bank), transnational networks of public authorities (ICLEI, C40 Cities) and national governments are dedicating important resources to the setting up of programmes tackling climate change in developing countries. Yet there are important discrepancies between foreign actors from the industrialised world, which provide assistance, and local stakeholders. The risk is to have all ready-made projects implemented regardless of the local context. The difficulty is then to get domestic actors in action when they have other priorities on their political agendas.

Indeed the direct addressees of any co-benefits projects are local policy-makers (Uchida and Zusman 2008). They are in charge of the general interest of their communities but also they have the powers to define land use, resources and other services that are necessary for the implementation of activities generating co-benefits.

A concern is that projects led by external actors who bring particular knowledge and technologies will reorient local policies. Some areas with a high technological dimension will be promoted, such as waste management or transportation, maybe at the expense of other pressing social issues, such as the eradication of poverty or education development. In fact, there are important bargaining powers of the external actors over the local stakeholders.

Involving local actors would therefore enhance effectiveness and ease the implementation of projects. Action is likely to be more effective if it is demand-driven (Cannon and Muller-Mahn 2010). Both sides of co-benefits, climate change and development, should therefore be equally valued. The challenge is to define the methodology and quantification to convince local policy-makers to undertake that kind of activity. To assume that one method fits all is not feasible as benefits differ from one context to another (Uchida and Zusman 2008).

So in addition to the definition of methodologies and quantification, there are also important governance structures to set up in order to allow for different actors to meet and discuss their respective priorities. Participatory processes allow for hearing local needs as well as highlighting potential deadlocks. Yet so far, since cooperation between international actors and domestic stakeholders mostly takes place at the national level, central authorities are defining their own policy goals without always consulting targeted local communities.

In addition to policy goals, legislative and policy frameworks aiming at achieving co-benefits should therefore include provisions on governance and participatory processes as a means to adjust their strategies to the local context and thus facilitate implementation.

Conclusion

This chapter has examined the concept of climate co-benefits from a legal and institutional perspective. We showed that the study of the legal context of a city or a country, or any relevant decentralised level, is fundamental to assess opportunities and risks in undertaking co-benefit projects. To fully develop a co-benefits approach, it is necessary to raise awareness of how legal measures can achieve different kinds of benefits while reducing GHG emissions. A screening of the applicable laws can contribute to that goal. Also, the study of legislation and regulations allows for targeting of co-benefits projects according to national and local political agendas right from the beginning of the decision-making process. To do so, participatory processes should be favoured in order to help identify local needs and priorities. The search for co-benefits should therefore be both policy and project based, which means combining institutional, local, scientific and technological knowledge and stakeholders.

References

Barbosa, Müssnich & Aragão (BMA) 2009, *Informativo Ambiental*, e-book, BM&A publications, Brasilia, viewed 3 May 2016, www.bmalaw.com.br/arquivos/Informativo_Ambiental_-_Julho_2009_Ing.pdf.

Cannon, T and Muller-Mahn, D 2010, 'Vulnerability, resilience and development discourses in context of climate change', *Natural Hazards*, vol. 55, no. 3, pp. 621–635.

Corfee-Morlot, J, Kamal-Chaoui, L, Donovan, MG, Cochran, I, Robert, A and Teasdale, PJ 2009, 'Cities, climate change and multilevel governance', *OECD Environmental Working Papers*, no. 14, pp. 1–126.

Council on Clean Transportation (ICCT) 2014, *Opportunities to Reduce Vehicle Emissions in Jakarta Briefing*, The International Council on Clean Transportation, USA, Germany, viewed 2 May 2016, www.theicct.org/sites/default/files/publications/ICCT_Jakarta-briefing_20141210.pdf.

Curnow, P and Hodes, G 2009, *Implementing CDM Projects: Guidebook to Host Country Legal Issues*, UNEP Risoe Center, Roskilde, Denmark.

D'Almeida Martins, R and da Costa Ferreira, L 2011, 'Climate change action at the city level: Tales from two megacities in Brazil', *Management of Environmental Quality: An International Journal*, vol. 22, no. 3, pp. 344–357.

Doll, CNH, Dreyfus, M, Ahmad, S and Balaban, O 2013, 'Institutional framework for urban development with co-benefits: The Indian experience', *Journal of Cleaner Production*, vol. 58, pp. 121–129.

Dreyfus, M 2013, 'The judiciary's role in environmental governance – the case of Delhi', *Environmental Policy and Law*, vol. 43, no. 3, pp. 162–174.

Dreyfus, M 2015, *The Co-benefits Approach at the Local Level: Legal Perspectives*, UNU-IAS Policy Brief, e-book, UNU-IAS, Tokyo, Japan, viewed 2 May 2016, http://i.unu.edu/media/ias.unu.edu-en/news/11145/UNU-IAS-Policy-Brief-No.-3-2015.pdf.

Dubash, NK 2011, 'From norm taker to norm maker? Indian energy governance in global context', *Global Policy*, vol. 2, no. s1, pp. 66–79.

Lucon, O and Goldemberg, J 2010, 'Sao Paulo – the "other" Brazil: Different pathways on climate change for state and federal governments', *Journal of Environment and Development*, vol. 19, no. 3, pp. 335–357.

Metz, B, Davidson, OR, Bosch, PR, Dave, R and Meyer, LA 2007, *Contribution of Working Group III to the IVth Assessment Report of the IPCC*, Cambridge University Press, Cambridge, UK and New York, USA.

Pajon, C 2010, *Japan's Ambivalent Diplomacy on Climate Change, Health and Environment Reports, no. 5*, e-book, Institut Français des Relations Internationales (IFRI), Paris, France, viewed 2 May 2016, www.ifri.org/sites/default/files/atoms/files/japanambivalent diplomacyonclimatechange_1.pdf.

Puppim de Oliveira, JA 2013, 'Learning how to align climate, environmental and development objectives in cities: Lessons from the implementation of climate co-benefits in urban Asia', *Journal of Cleaner Production*, vol. 58, pp. 7–14.

Qi, Y, Ma, L, Zang, H and Li, H 2008, 'Translating a global issue into local priority: China's local government response to climate change', *Journal of Environment and Development*, vol. 17, no. 4, pp. 379–400.

Rajamani, L 2007, 'Public interest environmental litigation in India: Exploring issues of access, participation, equity, effectiveness and sustainability', *Journal of Environmental Law*, vol. 19, no. 3, pp. 293–321.

Uchida, T and Zusman, E 2008, 'Reconciling local sustainable development benefits and global greenhouse gas mitigation in Asia: Research trends and needs', *Chiiki Seisaku Kenkyu*, vol. 11, no. 1, pp. 57–73.

Legislation

Brazilian Law Establishing the National Policy on Climate Change (NPCC) 2009, Law n.12187.

Chinese Energy Conservation Law 2007, Law No. 77.

Indian Central Motor Vehicles Rules 1989.

Indian Energy Conservation Act 2001, Law No. 52.

Indian National Action Plan on Climate Change 2008.

Indian Motor Vehicles Act 1988, Law No. 59.

Indonesian Government Regulation on Air Pollution Control, Regulation No. 41/1999.

Indonesian Law on Land Transportation 2009, Law No. 22.

Japanese Basic Act on Energy Policy 2002, Law No. 71.

Japanese Basic Act on Establishing a Sound Material-Cycle Society 2000, Law No. 110.

Kyoto Protocol to the United Nations Framework Convention on Climate Change 1998.

Sao Paulo State Policy on Climate Change 2009, ACT N° 13.798.

United Nations Framework Convention on Climate Change (UNFCCC) 2004, Annex 3, Clarifications on the treatment of national and/or sectoral policies and regulations (paragraph 45 (e) of the CDM Modalities and Procedures) in determining a baseline scenario.

9 Quantitative tools for assessing co-benefits

Christopher N.H. Doll, Hooman Farzaneh and Mehrnoosh Dashti

Introduction

Whilst the concept of co-benefits may be intuitively simple to grasp, trying to work out which policies and interventions provide which kinds of co-benefits is less straightforward given the myriad of options available. Simple tools are useful in order to first understand the level of emissions in the urban system and how they can be reduced.

As they are policy tools rather than engineering simulations, the data required for the tools are intended to be simple and robust, following a well-established set of methodologies of calculating emissions reductions. The tools aim to provide an accessible way of assessing a series of interventions within a sector to see their impact with regard to local and global emissions reduction. The general flexibility of the tools and their simplicity to use mean they can be used in conjunction with the qualitative decision-making tools (Chapter 10) in order to inform and improve decision-making at the city level.

This chapter describes a series of quantitative tools that were developed to assess co-benefits in three different sectors (transport, energy/buildings and waste) which are covered in this book.[1] It provides an overview of the tool structure, data inputs and options available in the tools but omits the details of the full range of equations here for sake of space and general comprehension. The chapter concludes with a discussion on how the tools can fit together in a broader urban context and offers a series of 'wise-use' guidelines on practical ways in which the tools may be utilised by local governments.

General form of the tools and their application to the A-S-I framework

The tools are a simulation model designed to evaluate the short-term climate co-benefits in different urban sectors. The methodology which has been applied through developing the tool is based on the scenario approach. In our approach, a 'scenario' is viewed as a consistent description of a possible short-term development pattern in any given sector, characterised mainly in terms of direction of local governmental policy (the so-called 'policy intervention'). Following this approach, the planner can make assumptions about the possible evolution of the social, economic and technological development patterns of a sector that can be anticipated from current trends and governmental objectives.

A certain amount of basic data needs to be collected in order to produce a baseline by which to compare proposed policies. The Avoid-Shift-Improve (A-S-I) framework, which provides the conceptual framework for classifying co-benefit policies, was initially developed in the transport sector by Dalkmann and Brannigan (2007), amongst others. This approach has been extended to two further sectors and also incorporates air pollution and, where relevant, other environmental pollutants. Calculations of component emissions for many of the elements in the tool follow a common format:

$$E = A \times F \qquad (9.1)$$

Where:
E is emissions in grams (g)
A is a volume of activity in some kind of unit (e.g. tonnes, litres)
F is the emission factor (g/unit)

The key therefore to evaluating component emissions is the accurate determination of the impacts of policy interventions on the relevant (activity units A) in the tools. Each tool also requires a library of emission factors. These refer to the amount of emissions produced per unit activity. In this sense, an activity could be waste produced, kilometres driven, or kWh of energy consumption. In general, both components have local variations; however, through the standardisation of technology, emission factors may be aggregated at the national level, whilst local activities have to be evaluated on a city-by-city basis.

As such, the tools calculate how activity reductions, shift in modes of production and the efficiency improvements of those modes change volumes and, in turn, emissions. Co-benefits are therefore defined as the difference (reduction) in the sum of these emissions between two policies.

The transport tool

Data for the tool

The transport tool is, in principle, a policy tool, rather than a transport model. It uses the ASIF model from Schipper *et al.* (2000). As with all models, the quality of the input data will largely dictate the quality of the output. Therefore, finding data for the tool is the most critical activity. The tool requires a series of input parameters to calculate emissions, some of which are calculated internally by the tool and some need to be externally specified. The structure of these data fields are shown in Table 9.1. Most data can be found in public records and registrations or through surveys.

Table 9.1 Structure of the data fields used in the transport tool

Data/value	Source	Units/definition
Number of vehicles (V)	User input	Units
Utilisation rate (UR)	User input	Fraction (%)
Fuel share of vehicle fleet (S)	User input	Fraction (%)
Average annual distance travelled (D)	User input	Kilometres (km)
Vehicle kilometres	Calculated	vkm – the number of kilometres travelled by any given mode (e.g. cars, buses)
Vehicle occupancy (Occ)	User input	Persons (may be a fraction)
Passenger kilometres	Calculated	Travel demand by mode
Mode share (MS)	Calculated	Fraction (%) – share of pkm in each mode
Fuel efficiency (FE)	User input/Default value	km/litre
Intensity	Calculated	$1/(FE \times VOcc)$
Emission factors (F)	User input/Default value	grams/litre
Emissions	Calculated	grams

In general, vehicle fleet data are not very difficult to obtain, as vehicles have to be registered and licensed in almost every city. Therefore, transport divisions of city governments are the primary address to obtain the data on vehicle numbers. This data could also be obtained from secondary sources, such as academic research or other publications. In some research, primary data are collected through transport surveys to make estimations on parameters such as travel demand. Such research could be useful to find the data on vehicle numbers. Public transport data are also usually available through the companies that operate the service.

The utilisation rate is introduced here as an extra factor to reflect that a fleet may not be in complete operation (e.g. a bus fleet may number 10,000 but only 9,000 are in routine operation, giving a utilisation rate). It is included because the commonly available figure is often the total fleet size, or registered vehicles, which may not be accurate. Estimating the utilisation rate can be difficult and may require consultation with experts.

The average distance travelled is the annualised run (in km) of different modes that prevail in the transport sector of a given city. Another way to obtain this data is to generate it through surveys. The average daily run of private modes such as cars, motorcycles, taxis and also three-wheelers could be gathered by making questionnaire surveys with users of private modes. In this case, sampling should be carefully determined. The daily run of public transport modes is easier to obtain as opposed to that of private modes. In cities where public transportation is run by the local government, such data could be taken from the relevant division of the local government. In cases where the private sector is responsible for running the public transport systems, the data could be collected by contacting the companies in the sector.

The average occupancy refers to the average number of riders per trip in different modes. This is usually obtained through surveys. Data for public transport can usually be obtained through their fare collection data and revenue generation.

Although mode share is calculated within the model (Eqn 9.4), trip data are collected and presented in this format as travel surveys sometimes ask for this mode of transport along with the number of trips. The tool understands mode share to be the share in terms of passenger kilometres rather than share of trips, which is another commonly understood interpretation of the term. The two are only the same if each trip is of equal length (which is rarely if ever the case) as motorised trips tend to be longer than non-motorised ones. If average trip length is available it may be possible to reverse engineer the data to work out parameters for the tool, alternatively it may be used to corroborate data collected.

Fuel efficiency refers to the fuel economy of a vehicle as a ratio of km/energy unit. Average values are available from manufacturers' data (although have recently been shown to be less reliable than previously assumed). The tool also contains a set of functions to determine fuel efficiency based on average speed and classes of vehicles. As average urban speed (an often quoted figure in relation to congestion) is lower than highway conditions, the fuel efficiency of vehicles in the urban environment is far lower. Emission factors are standard values based on the type of fuel that is used. Common types are petrol (gasoline), diesel and CNG but may also include ultra-low sulphur diesel and electricity generation for electric vehicles.

Doll and Balaban (2013) discuss the sources of data for their investigation of the Delhi Metro, noting that multiple datasets can be useful to corroborate and test assumptions about various data values in the dataset.

Calculating emissions

The tool works by assessing the emissions from each of the specified modes. It is up to the user to define these modes but they commonly include cars, buses, taxis, motorcycles and so on. In order to understand the level of emissions from each mode i, the level of activity is calculated according to Equation 9.2.

$$A_i = \prod VURDOcc \tag{9.2}$$

Where:
V is the number of vehicles (aka fleet size)
UR is the utilisation rate
D is the average distance travelled
Occ is the average occupancy

The total travel demand (Eqn 9.3) is therefore the sum of these over all modes i and the fraction of this for a mode is defined as the mode share (Eqn 9.4).

$$A_{Total} = \sum_{i=1}^{n} A_i \qquad (9.3)$$

$$MS_i = \frac{A_i}{A_{total}} \qquad (9.4)$$

The other factor used to calculate emissions is the intensity of the mode, which is a function of the fuel efficiency and vehicle occupancy, as shown in Equation 9.5:

$$I_{ij} = \frac{1}{(Occ_i \times FE_{ij})} \qquad (9.5)$$

Where
FE is the fuel efficiency for mode i with fuel j.

From this formulation, it is clear that increasing either the vehicle occupancy or the fuel efficiency of a vehicle will decrease the (pollution) intensity of a mode. The final factor is the emission factor for each pollutant (j) specified in grams/litre. It should be noted that this tool decomposes the emission factor into parts relevant to the quality of fuel (g/l) and the fuel efficiency (km/l), though these are often reported in a combined value (g/km). A unit analysis will show that, when multiplied together, all terms cancel out to leave the grams of emission.

The ASIF decomposition calculates emissions for a given pollutant (E) by summing the product of these factors by activity in each share of fuel (j) in each mode (i) as shown in Equation 9.6. An alternative formulation would take the total activity and multiply by mode share and fuel shares within each mode, hence there may be ambiguity as to whether S refers to mode share or fuel shares.

$$E(g) = \sum_{i,j=1}^{n} A_i S_{ij} I_{ij} F_j \qquad (9.6)$$

Where:
A is the activity in mode i
S is the share of fuel j in mode i
I is intensity of a mode i with fuel j
F is the emission factor for fuel j

Whilst most obviously applicable to road transport, electric transport can also be accommodated here by finding the appropriate efficiency and emission factors for the electricity generation (per kWh).

Changing options

The tool allows for variations in four different policy areas to assess the magnitude of changes in both GHG emissions and air pollution. This is done through an interactive datasheet (Figure 9.1). Changes are made via direct input or use of slide bars in the sheet. Doing so automatically generates a graph (top left), which dynamically changes with the inputs given. The table in the top right displays the

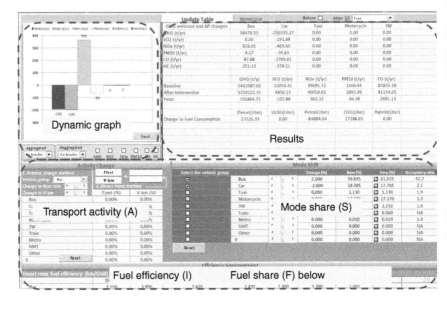

Figure 9.1 Analysis sheet of the tool, highlighting ASIF change areas (dotted line) and dynamic results graph and table.

emissions baseline and updates in accordance with the changes made in the four policy option areas. More detailed tabular reports are also reported in a separate sheet. Although not an automatic feature of the tool, the sequential use of the tabular reports in a separate spreadsheet can also be used to organise results and generate graphs on a range of scenarios (such as those presented by Doll and Balaban 2013), as shown in Figure 2.2 of this book (page 37).

Based on the formulation in Equation 9.2, activity (Travel Demand Management) options can be expressed as either a change in vehicle numbers or a change in travel distance (a change in vehicle occupancy is not provided as an option). This can be changed by sliders or entered numerically as a reduction in a specified number of vehicles or kilometres travelled.

Changing the activity will necessarily alter the total travel demand. If no activity change is made, the tool takes the initial baseline total travel demand as a constant that is to be reassigned through shifting the mode. Although mode share is endogenously calculated in the tool, it may be altered in the scenario sheet by adjusting the sliders for any given mode. As mode shift is essentially a zero-sum operation, adjusting the mode share will mean that other modes will be affected. This is handled by being able to select which modes are affected. If no selection is made, all other modes will proportionally allocate the change in mode of interest. Fuel efficiency and fuel shares are adjusted directly by editing the cells with the new value. In the case of fuel share, there is a check to ensure the new shares sum to 100 per cent.

Practical considerations

One thing that should become apparent is that the same policies can be represented in different ways in the tool. Modes are initially completely unspecified in the tool, which allows flexibility to specify a varying level of detail subject to data availability and the type of analysis of interest. For instance, analysing the co-benefits of phasing out old cars could be represented by an increase in the average fuel efficiency of the car fleet; alternatively, it could be represented by a mode shift away from old cars into new cars if configured as a separate mode. By increasing average efficiency, it is assumed the users of old cars will just upgrade to more efficient cars, which could be reflective of a buy-back policy for more efficient vehicles, for example. By the same token, the tool is flexible to the boundary of analysis – that is to say, it may be the city or a smaller subset (e.g. a fleet of buses), in which case there can be a more detailed analysis of different types within the fleet. With this in mind, the co-benefits only relate to those modes in the analysis.

Non-motorised modes may be considered in the tool. Although activities specified in the tool refer to motorised forms of transport and not walking or cycling (non-motorised or active transport). In this respect, shifts to non-motorised modes can either be represented as a direct reduction in activity (i.e. motorised passenger kilometres) or alternatively be explicitly included as a mode in the tool (with an emission factor of zero) so as to produce zero emissions. The 'occupancy' of the mode is therefore 1 and so pkm is analogous to the total kilometres walked or cycled.

Discussion

The tool has limitations, both in the structure of the model and in the requirements for good-quality data. In this respect, there are uncertainties over fleet data (i.e. fraction of active cars in the fleet) and how far they drive. Furthermore, given that cars are mobile, there is also the issue of how to account for cars that enter the city from outside the registration area. This has been characterised by Bongardt *et al.* (n.d.) as the inhabitant approach (used in the tool), which covers the activity of inhabitants in a given area versus the territorial approach, which would consider *all* the activity in a given spatial entity and require a different monitoring approach. Essentially, the tool is a linear representation of the transport system, with no feedbacks between the ASIF elements. With the focus on environmental co-benefits, costs are not represented and nor is a detailed representation of the travel demand in terms of where trips are being made. As it has no spatial element in it, it is not possible to talk about the differential impacts within the city or locality or plan where such policies should be implemented; rather this relies on the skill of the users. Emerging data sources could greatly aid the provision of data at finer resolutions (including spatial) than previously possible. The near ubiquitous proliferation of geolocation on mobile phones has the potential to provide large amounts of individual trip data, including distance and time of day.

Nonetheless, these insights and such experimentation with the different systemic levers in the tool rapidly build an understanding of how the different components of the transport system interact with each other as well as a feeling for developing target indicators for various policy goals.

The waste tool

The waste tool was developed as an assessment tool predominantly targeted at quantifying global and local co-benefits from a range of actions taken in management of municipal solid waste (Chapter 6). It uses the integrated solid waste management (ISWM) approach to analyse the waste management system in terms of estimation of GHG emissions, air pollution and the available potential for energy recovery from the waste. This computational model can be applied to help understand the current status of a regional/local waste management system and analyse the possible solutions to improve the system regarding environmental performance and energy recovery potential as well.

Considering the ISWM approach, the waste management practices are selected and integrated to cover main activities including waste generation, sorting and separation, transfer, recovery, processing and disposal, with a main emphasis on protecting the environment, public health and local conditions and needs. Basically, the main steps which are attributed in the waste management process are: (1) waste handling, including collection and transportation of waste from the point of generation to the point of treatment or disposal; (2) processing of the waste, through recycling, composting or anaerobic digestion; and (3) final disposal of the waste, including incineration or landfilling. Figure 9.2 shows how the waste management practices and system boundaries have been used in the waste tool regarding ISWM. Furthermore, the life cycle assessment (LCA) method has used for tracking environmental impacts of the system shown in Figure 9.1. Every step, including transportation, processing and disposal as 'life cycle', contributes to GHG emissions. In the current model, the LCA assessment has also considered the four basic standard steps for formulating the analysing framework (Chapter 6, Figure 6.8).

The net GHG emissions and climate co-benefits are quantified by calculating the difference between the amount of produced GHG emissions (sources) and the amount of avoided GHG emissions (sinks) for all waste management actions in the system. These include efficiencies in waste transport (both of the vehicles and in the collection) and offsetting emissions in the process of waste disposal with recovered energy generated by the waste. In the case of recycling, this can be offset against virgin production of new materials. Considering each waste management practice, different types of input data are required for calculating climate co-benefits, as summarised in Table 9.2.

For analysing the effects of different pathways on managing waste systems and evaluating their environmental performance, a policy intervention section

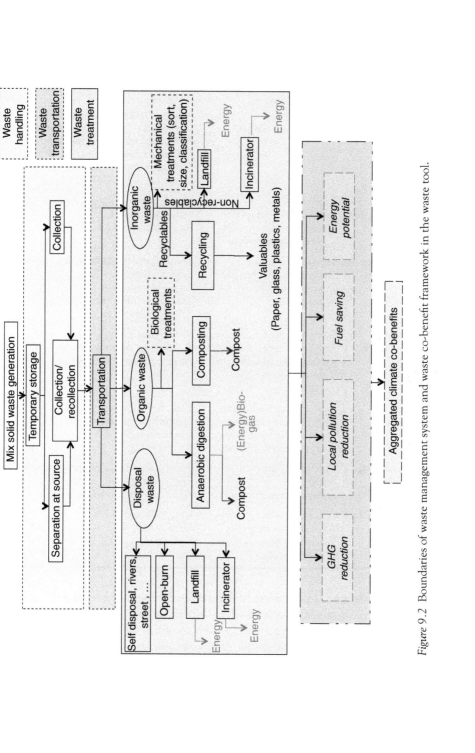

Figure 9.2 Boundaries of waste management system and waste co-benefit framework in the waste tool.

Table 9.2 Main required data for calculating climate co-benefits by each waste management practice

Type of data	Details	Metric
Waste data	Waste type Waste composition Waste volume Waste characteristics	Household, commercial, industrial, hazardous… Material fraction (food, paper, cardboard, wood, textiles, plastics, metal, glass…) Amount of waste (e.g. per capita) Dry matter content, fraction of carbon content, fraction of fossil carbon content…
Waste transportation	Type of fuel Type of transportation Transported distance or energy consumption	Diesel, gasoline (litres) or CNG (m^3) Number of trucks As kilometre or litre per tonne waste
Technology parameters	Type of technology Share of each technology Characteristics of technology	Thermal treatment, biological treatment waste disposal As percentage Type of incinerator, landfilling, biological treatment…
Recovery parameters	Composition of recyclables Amount of recyclable waste Recovery process efficiency for each recyclable material	Metal, glass, plastics, paper, wood… As kilogram per tonne waste As percentage (loss rates)
Energy recovery	Type of recovered energy Type of energy recovery device Energy recovery efficiency	Heat, fuel substitution, electricity Gas turbine, boiler, engine, CHP system… As percentage
Operational activities	Type of activity Energy type Energy consumption	Sorting, loading, conveying, cleaning… Electricity or fossil fuel (diesel…) As kW or litre per tonne waste
Inventory data	GHG emissions factors Air emissions factors Leachate composition and emission factors	CH_4, CO_2 and N_2O Such as CO, NO_x, SO_x, $PM_{2.5}$, PM_{10}… Such as Hg, Cd, Ni, As, Zn…

has been designed in the waste tool. Interventions should prioritise the minimisation of environmental impacts when deciding how to support and develop the current waste management system. Given the three different types of intervention in the A-S-I strategy, the following scenarios are considered in the waste tool:

- Scenario 1: Changing the waste volume and composition (Avoid strategy);
- Scenario 2: Shifting waste processing (Shift strategy);
- Scenario 3: Changing technology specifications (Improve strategy).

Specification

The tool considers six different municipal solid waste (MSW) technologies, namely, open burning, composting, anaerobic digestion, landfilling and recycling. The general specification and assumptions made during the development of the waste tool are as follows:

- In every technology, estimated emissions were calculated in units of mass emitted per mass of input waste rather than unit mass of final product. For example, for anaerobic digestion technology, the GHG emissions are expressed as 'CO_2eq/tonne waste' instead of 'CO_2eq/tonne compost'.
- Where appropriate, the input waste data are considered based on weight of wet waste.[2]
- The sequence of each MSW management strategy starts when the waste is transported to the technology and then leaves the system as materials, disposals, environmental impacts and/or energy carriers (electricity and/or heat).
- Estimation of emissions from landfills depends on the year for which emissions are of interest.
- When the fossil fuels are used for the technology, consumption of this fuel is included in GHG estimation, air pollutants and energy calculations.
- Recovered energy is considered as electricity and/or heat production. In the case of heat production, the heat potential is the estimated heat production (MJoule heat/year) from diesel combustion.
- Different types of energy recovery systems are considered where the energy can be recovered from the process as electricity and/or heat. These systems, which include gas turbines, steam turbines, internal combustion engines (ICE) and combined heat and power (CHP) systems, can be chosen by the user in the tool.
- The default concentration for specific GHG emissions and air pollutants compounds has been gathered by survey of different references. But there is the possibility in the tool to change the emissions factor to the actual site-specific test data by the user.
- Because specific air pollutant concentrations in the combustion products of an incinerator vary between different types, there is the possibility for the user to choose different types of incinerator in the tool.
- This study does not include carbon sequestration for calculating the GHG emissions.

Emission inventory

For calculating the GHG emissions and air pollutants, the following environmental emissions are accounted for in this study and therefore the appropriate emission factors are required:

- GHG emissions from the transport of solid waste to the technologies due to combustion of fossil fuels (gasoline, diesel and CNG);

- GHG emissions from operational activities;
- GHG emissions from waste management processes;
- avoided GHG emissions from fertiliser production in compost and anaerobic digestion technologies;
- avoided GHG emissions from reduced production of original materials when the original materials are replaced by recycling;
- avoided GHG emissions from electricity and/or heat production (energy recovery); these emissions are calculated when electricity and heat are provided by fossil power plants and diesel fuel combustion, respectively;
- avoided GHG emissions from 100 per cent landfilling in incineration, composting, anaerobic digestion and open burning techniques;
- air pollutants from the transport of solid waste to the technologies as typical combustion products like CO, SO_x, NO_x, PM_{10}, $PM_{2.5}$, VOCs and UHC;
- air pollutants released from incineration and open burning, which include typical combustion products and heavy metals;
- air pollutants released from landfill disposal site;
- heavy metals released from incineration;
- leachate production from landfilled disposal site;
- wastewater generation from landfilled disposal site.

Key equations

Recalling Equation 9.1, for different waste management activities/practices, including waste transportation, operational activities, incineration, open burning, composting, anaerobic digestion, leachate generation, energy recovery and compost production, the calculations of emissions (GHG, air pollutants, heavy metals and leachate) generated by combustion of fossil fuels/waste, utilisation of electricity and also waste landfilling estimate in accordance with the following common format:

$$Emission\left(\frac{Tonne\ Pollutants}{Year}\right) = A_{MSW}\left(\frac{Tonne\ Waste}{Year}\right)$$
$$\times F\left(\frac{g\ Pollutants}{Tonne\ Waste}\right) \tag{9.7}$$

Accordingly, building a robust emission inventory plays a key role in accurate estimation of climate co-benefits. The values of emission factors of selected atmospheric pollutants which are used in the tool are in accordance with IPCC (2006) and EPA (2008) emissions inventories. In the waste tool, there is also a possibility to change the emissions factor to the actual site-specific test data, which can be entered as user-defined emission inventories.

In the case of landfilling, the first-order biological delay model, which is adapted from the IPCC (2006) and the EPA (AP-42 series 2008), is used for calculation of CH_4 generation as follows:

$$CH_4 Emission\left(\frac{Tonne}{Year}\right) = \sum_{x=S}^{T-1} LW_x L_x' \left(e^{-k(T-x-1)} - e^{-k(T-x)}\right) \tag{9.8}$$

Where:
x = year in which waste was disposed
k = decay rate constant (1/Year)
S = start year of inventory calculation
T = inventory year for which emissions are calculated
LW_x = the quantity of waste disposed at the landfill site (tonne/year)
L'_x = CH_4 generation potential (tonne CH_4/tonne waste)

$$= MCF \times DOC \times DOCF \times F \times 16/12$$

Where:
MCF = methane correction factor (fraction)
DOC = degradable organic carbon (fraction [tonne C in waste/tonne waste])
DOCF = fraction of DOC which decomposes (fraction), generally assumed to be 0.5
F = fraction by volume of CH_4 in landfill gas, generally assumed to be 0.5

The MCF is classified according to the type of landfill site as given in IPCC (2006). Also, the following equations estimate DOC and k:

$$DOC = \sum_i WL_i \times DOC_i \tag{9.9}$$

$$k = \sum_i WL_i \times k_i \tag{9.10}$$

Where: DOC_i and k_i indicate the fraction of degradable organic carbon and the decay rate constant of component i in waste, respectively. The default parameters for DOC and k with respect to waste component are reported in Table 1 of the 'Technical Data' Excel sheet in the tool. The values of k_i are dependent on climate type, classified as dry, wet, dry tropical, and wet and most tropical climates. CO_2 emissions can be estimated by the following equation:

$$CO_2 Emission(kg/Year) =$$

$$Q_{CO_2} \times \frac{MW_{CO_2} \times 1\, atm}{8.205 \times 10^{-5} \left(m^2 \cdot atm/gmole \cdot K\right) \times 1000 \left(g/kg\right) \times (273 + T)} \tag{9.11}$$

Where:
MW_{CO2} = molecular weight of CO_2, which is 44 g/mol
Q_{CO2} = emission rate of CO_2, m³/year
T = temperature of landfill gas (LFG), °C

Equation 9.11 assumes that the operating pressure of the system is approximately 1 atmosphere. If the temperature of the LFG is not known, a temperature of 25°C is recommended.

To estimate Q_{CO2}, the following equation has been used:

$$Q_{CO_2} = \frac{Q_{CH_4} \times \dfrac{C_{CO_2}}{C_{CO_2} + C_{CH_4}}}{0.5} \tag{9.12}^3$$

Where:
Q_{CH4} = CH_4 generation rate, m³/year (calculated from Eqn 9.8)
C_{CO2} = concentration of CO_2 in LFG, ppmv
C_{CH4} = concentration of CH_4 in the LFG, ppmv

The GHG emissions from the recycling process are calculated by estimating the difference between: (1) the GHG emissions from manufacturing of materials and products from 100 per cent recycled materials, and (2) the GHG emissions from manufacturing of the materials and products from 100 per cent virgin materials. As GHG emissions of making materials from recycled inputs are typically less than virgin inputs, the net GHG emissions of the recycling process is negative. As less than one tonne of recyclable material is made from one tonne of recovered material (material loss in Figure 9.3), recycling can be evaluated in terms of tonnes of recyclable materials or tonnes of recovered materials.

By considering the GHG emission factors and the tonnes of material recycled reported by EPA (2008), the total GHG emissions of recycling can be estimated regarding GHG emissions of each material as follows:

Total GHG Emissions (Tonne CO₂ₑ/Year) = Σ$_i$GHG Emissions Factor$_i$ (Tonne CO₂ₑ/Tonne of Recycled Materials) × RW$_i$(Tonne of Recycled Materials/Year) (9.13)

where index *i* represents components of recycled material and *RW* indicates the recycled waste.

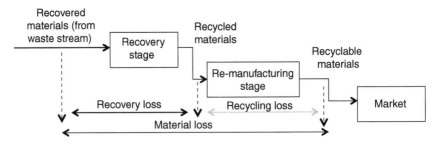

Figure 9.3 The loss rates concept in the recycling process.

How to use the tool

Users interact with the tool through Excel sheets and Excel VBA userforms to enter the input data and view the analysis and results.

Baseline scenario

The steps to develop the baseline scenario are as follows:

1 In the general input data userform, the user is first required to enter the required data for waste generation, total waste composition and distribution of waste generation.
2 In the next step, the technical specification of each waste management action (incineration, composting, anaerobic digestion, recycling, open burning and landfilling) should be entered by the user. Generally, the required data consist of waste transportation, waste composition and technology specifications for each action.
3 After saving and updating general and detailed required input data for each waste management (WM) action, the user can observe a summary and detailed results of GHG emissions, air pollutants and energy recovery potentials for the baseline scenario as userform.

Policy interventions

Considering the Avoid-Shift-Improve strategies, three different scenarios are considered in the waste tool, as shown in Table 9.3.

SCENARIO 1: AVOID STRATEGY

For avoid strategies, the total waste composition and the amount of waste may be changed. As the scenario 1 userform opens, the values of waste composition and waste volume of the baseline scenario are displayed for the user's reference. Values may be changed by entering a percentage change of waste volume for each waste type (food, paper and cardboard, wood...), which can be positive, negative or zero values for indicating increase, decrease or no change in the share of each component. For example, regarding implementation of source reduction policies and regulations for reducing the initial amount of waste generated, the inhabitants of these cities should separate the recyclables at source. For analysing the effect of 5 per cent and 8 per cent reductions in terms of plastics and paper waste generation, respectively, on climate co-benefits, for example, the user should enter the values of –5 and –8 per cent as the changing percentage of waste volume of plastics and paper. After entering the required data, the new tonnage of each waste element is calculated accordingly.

Table 9.3 Summary of different scenarios in the waste tool

Scenario	Description	Target	Directive(s)
Scenario 1 (Avoid)	Changing total waste generation and composition	Waste prevention and reduction, particularly in the first place	• Analysing possible WM actions to reduce waste generation • Seeking WM actions to reduce organic waste and generate more recyclables
Scenario 2 (Shift)	Changing the waste composition for each waste processing method	Shifting from unmanaged waste dumping and/or landfill disposal to other waste management practices	• Replacing recycling, energy recovery and biological treatments with landfilling and/or unmanaged waste dumping • Comparing different coordination of WM actions in terms of climate co-benefits
Scenario 3 (Improve)	Changing the technology specifications	Improving technologies of waste facility/ processing method in terms of environmental performance	• Introducing alternatives for transportation vehicles and waste treatment facilities • Energy recovery

SCENARIO 2: SHIFT STRATEGY

The new waste compositions of each WM action are required as input data for scenario 2. The user can shift the proportion of waste going to the six different WM processing methods by entering the new values of waste composition in the 'New' field. For example, regarding improvement of WMS, one possible solution is to shift from waste landfilling to waste recycling. In this context, user should reduce recyclable wastes (paper, can, metal, etc.) composition in landfilling and increase them in recycling. In scenario 2, the amount of total waste and diversity of waste management actions in the last run are displayed as 'Old' to provide the user with a comparison of the new values with the last ones. In this regard, the 'Old' values cannot be changed by the user in this userform.

SCENARIO 3: IMPROVE STRATEGY

Finally, the effects of technology specifications on GHG emissions and air pollutants as well as energy recovery potentials can be analysed. The parameters which can be changed include: type and amount of fuel used for waste transporting, required energy for operational activities and type of technology in each waste processing method and energy recovery options. As the scenario 3 userform opens, the last technology specifications for different technologies are displayed in the fields as user's reference to compare the new values with the last run.

Results

After entering input data, the results of the model can be seen as Excel sheets in three formats:

- **Baseline results:** this page shows the results for the baseline scenario.
- **Summary results:** this page shows the final results summary of the last run after considering all interventions (scenarios).
- **Detailed results:** this page shows the results for each scenario separately, including baseline scenario, scenario 1, scenario 2 and scenario 3.

All Excel sheets which show the results (baseline results, results summary or results details) include the following items:

RESULTS IN THE TABLE FORMAT

- Annual waste volume;
- Annual total GHG emissions;
- Overall waste composition;
- Annual shares of sub-divisions in GHG emissions production (transportation, WM actions, energy recovery and GHG avoided potentials).

RESULTS IN THE GRAPHICAL FORMAT

- Annual total GHG emissions by technology;
- Annual air pollutants by technologies, including CO, SO_2, NO_x, PM_{10} and $PM_{2.5}$;
- Annual electricity production by technologies;
- Annual heat production by technologies.

Furthermore, the tool is capable of estimating other pollutants, including heavy metals composition in incineration, leachate composition in landfilling and other corresponding air pollutants from different actions. The concentration of all air pollutants are available in the results userform designed for each WM action.

Discussion

The Excel VBA structure of the simulation in this tool provides simple and user-friendly results to understand the impacts of different waste management technologies. This tool can estimate the GHG emissions, air pollutants and energy recovery potentials as well as a cost–benefit analysis for these technologies. Moreover, the environmental impact of a range of ISWM approaches can be evaluated again a baseline scenario. Region/country-specific data can also be incorporated into the tool to provide more representative data (e.g. emission factors and other data from local authorities).

However, there are some limitations to the tool, which could be addressed in future developments:

- The ability to change default values, whilst a strength, also means that an extensive database of emission factors should be developed to reflect country/region-specific variation. At present the user must do this, which requires a degree of expert knowledge on their part.
- More region-specific data on recycling technology are required to estimate GHG emissions at the local authority level.

As mentioned in Chapter 6, calculation of climate co-benefits by this tool is subject to difficulties due to data availability and accuracy. In most cases, the default input data in terms of emissions factor and technical data have been derived according to the IPCC and EPA database. However, it is not just the emission factors that need to be accurately determined. The other component of Equation 9.7 is the determination of local waste parameters in terms of volume and composition. Using such a tool can also help waste managers collect and organise their data for mainstreaming environmental considerations into their activities.

The urban energy tool

The urban energy tool is perhaps the most complicated of the three tools as it requires more background data, which are harder to match to the definition of the urban boundary, as well as incorporating a wider array of policy interventions.

The tool assesses the structural changes in the energy system of a city. This is done by means of a detailed analysis of the social, economic and technological characteristics of the given city's energy system. This approach takes into account the energy service needs of the population, such as the demand for space heating, lighting and air conditioning, as a function of the distribution of population into different dwelling ranges, the city's policies concerning housing etc., as well as technological development. Based on this, the co-benefits resulting from the structural changes in the energy system are calculated. In order to do this, the methodology comprises the following sequence of operations, as arranged in Figure 9.4:

1 disaggregation of the total energy demand of the city into a large number of end-use categories in a coherent manner;
2 identification of the social, economic and technological parameters which affect each end-use category of the energy demand;

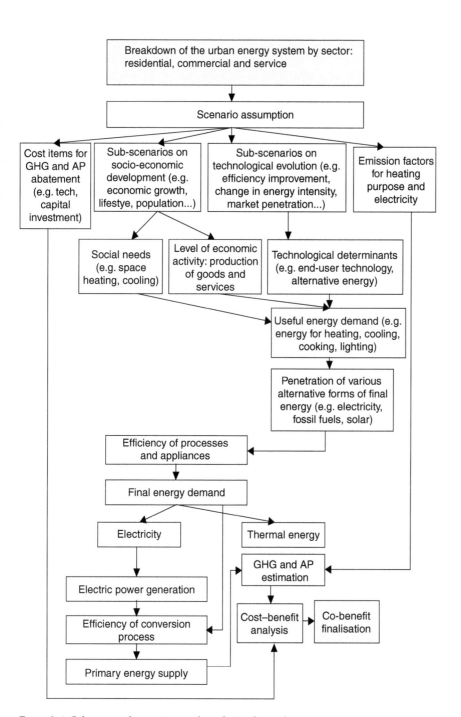

Figure 9.4 Scheme used to project co-benefits in the tool.

3   establishment in mathematical terms of the relationships which relate energy demand and factors affecting this demand;
4   establishment of the energy supply–demand balance in the city;
5   estimation of the energy-related GHG emissions and air pollution from different sub-sectors;
6   development of (consistent) scenarios (policy intervention) of social, economic and technological development for the given city's energy system;
7   evaluation of the climate co-benefits resulting from each scenario;
8   selection among all possible scenarios proposed of the 'most probable' patterns of development for the city through cost–benefit analysis (CBA) and system sustainability.

The tool, therefore, consists of four main parts, as listed in Table 9.4, and as explained in the rest of this section.

Table 9.4 Main elements of the tool

	Property	
1 – Baseline scenario		
Basic data	Input data	Regional demographic related data (population…)
Residential sector	Input data	Initial input data for the residential sector
Commercial sector	Input data	Initial input data for the commercial sector
Service sector	Input data	Initial input data for the service sector
Energy supply system	Input data	Initial input data for the city power supply system
2 – Policy intervention		
Lifestyle change	Action	Change in size and share of dwelling types and commercial sub-sectors
Alternative energy	Action	Use of different alternative energy technologies as DG heat and electricity
End-user technology	Action	Use of new technology to improve energy efficiency in each end-user group
Smart Grid	Action	Connect city to smart grid protocol
3 – Results		
Final report	Show	Final report in three categories: summary, baseline and after intervention
Energy balance	Show	Energy balances of the urban energy system in city
CBA	Show	Cost–benefit analysis of scenarios
MAC	Show	Marginal abatement cost curve for different scenarios
Sustainability analysis	Show	Sustainability indices for different scenarios
Sankey diagram	Show	Energy flow diagram of the urban energy system in city
4 – Database		
Energy factors	Default data	Energy efficiency and intensity factors
Emission factors	Default data	Emission factors per fuel/technology types

Setting up the tool; calculating energy demand

The tool calculates the total energy demand for each end-use category by aggregating the urban energy system into three main 'energy consumer' sectors: residential, commercial and service. According to this procedure, the demand for each end-use category of energy is driven by one or several socio-economic and technological parameters, whose values are given as part of the scenario.

Residential sector

The calculations for the residential sector are performed taking into account the living conditions of the population – that is, the place of residence (city local climate conditions) and type of residence (dwelling mode and size). This permits a better representation of the proper needs of the individuals and of their living style, as well as a more appropriate definition of the potential markets for the alternative forms of final energy and new technologies. The energy consumption for secondary appliances is calculated separately for electrified dwellings, for which the use of electric appliances is assumed, and for the non-electrified dwellings, for which alternative appliances using fossil fuels are considered (kerosene lighting, refrigerators on natural gas, etc.).

Commercial sector

Although the energy demand for commercial and for residential sectors have very similar calculations, they are executed separately due to the fact that the scenario parameters and related equations which characterise their energy consumption are not the same: in the residential sector, the determining factors are of a demographic nature (population, number of dwellings, etc.), whereas in the commercial sector they are related to the business level of activity of the sector. The categories of energy use considered in the residential sector are: space heating, water heating, cooking, ventilation, lighting, cooking refrigeration, office equipment, computers, etc.

Service sector

The service sector consists of the 'soft' parts of the economy – that is, activities where people offer their knowledge and time to improve productivity, performance, potential and sustainability, what is termed effective labour. The basic characteristic of this sector is the production of services instead of end products. It is sometimes hard to define whether a given company in the city is part of the commercial or service sector. For purposes of finance and market research, market-based classification systems such as the Global Industry Classification Standard and the Industry Classification Benchmark are used to classify businesses that participate in the service sector. In the tool, the service sector is considered as a separate sector, including those parts of the city's companies and firms which have a direct effect on the city's economic development. Therefore, the scenario parameters and related equations which characterise energy consumption in the service sector are related to the level of economic activity in the sector (sub-sectorial value added and labour force in the sector). The energy consumption for space heating and air conditioning is calculated on the basis of the specific space heating and cooling requirements (kWh/sqm/yr), while that for other thermal uses, specific uses of electricity and motor fuels is calculated as a function of the value added and energy intensity at the sub-sector level within the service sector.

Final energy calculation

When the demand of the given end user can be provided by various energy forms (space heating, water heating, cooking, air conditioning, etc.), this is calculated in terms of useful energy and not in terms of final energy. The final energy demand is then calculated from the penetration into the potential market and the efficiency of each energy form (network loss, heat loss, coefficient of performance [COP]), as specified in the baseline scenario. Table 9.5 shows a sample of the energy forms' penetration which has been distinguished in the final energy calculation in the tool.

City power supply system (energy conversion level)

This level of the urban energy system consists of the group of public and private companies, activities and installations used for the generation of electricity to meet the electricity demand in the city. The tool estimates the total electricity required to meet the energy demand for each end-use category, segregating the whole urban power supply system into different electricity generation technologies through considering two connection modes: on-grid (from the network) and off-grid (district generation). Different power supply technologies which have been considered in the tool include renewables, energy production from waste and co-generation, nuclear and conventional fossil fuels.

Table 9.5 Penetration of different energy forms through calculating final energy in the tool

Energy forms	Space heating	A/C	Appliances	Other thermal uses
Traditional	X			X
Biomass	X			X
Fossil fuels (town gas, LPG, kerosene…)	X			X
Electricity	X	X	X	
Renewable (solar, wind…)	X		X	X

Initial input data categories distinguished in the city power supply sector are:

- installed capacity;
- conversion efficiency;
- annual operation (h/yr);
- load factor;
- network loss (%).

Primary energy supply

The primary energy sources (fossil and non-fossil) must be available to the city to enable the production of energy carriers. The amount of primary energy sources can be estimated on the basis of the energy demand (electricity and heat) estimated in the city.

GHG emissions and air pollution estimation

There are strong linkages between global climate change and energy consumption in cities, and emissions from the combustion of fossil fuels contribute significantly to GHG emissions and air pollution (AP). Quantifying the co-benefits and the incentive power of participating in a global climate change strategy can be analysed with tool simulations using the extended range of emission factors in its library. There are also several abstractions in this analysis:

- The focus is on emissions from fossil fuel combustion in the electricity and non-electricity sectors, and process emissions for all substances as these impact exposure to particulate matter (PM) but are also the main source of GHG emissions, and thus the principal driver of both GHG and local air pollution (CO, $NMHC$, NO_x and SO_2).
- The focus is on fine PMs with a diameter of less than 2.5 μm (referred to as $PM_{2.5}$), which are responsible for deaths from particulates in the ambient air. The tool estimates the amount of GHG and AP for the city based on the life cycle analysis method, considering the operation, transportation and processing levels for each contributing technology.

Cost–benefit analysis (CBA)

CBA is considered in the tool as a systematic process for calculating and comparing benefits and costs of different policy interventions (scenarios) by pursuing the following two purposes:

1 to determine if it is a sound investment/decision (justification/feasibility);
2 to provide a basis for comparing scenarios.

It involves comparing the total expected cost of each option against the total expected benefits, to see whether the benefits outweigh the costs, and by how much. CBA is related to cost-effectiveness analysis. In this case, benefits and costs are expressed in monetary terms, and adjust for the time value of money, so that all flows of benefits and flows of scenario costs over time (which tend to occur at different points in time) are expressed on a common basis in terms of their 'net present value (NPV)'. Finally, benefit–cost ratio (BCR) and payback period (PBP) are used in the CBA to summarise the overall value for money of each scenario.

Policy intervention actions

The potential of GHG and AP reduction in this context is defined as the difference between emissions in the baseline scenario and emissions in the policy intervention scenarios. The details of the scenario definition procedures are stated below.

Lifestyle change

In this tool, change in urban lifestyle comprises any changes in dwelling size and share. The user can adjust new settings for the share distribution using the slide bars similar to those in the transport tool (Figure 9.1). There are also two push buttons that the user can press to activate the reset mechanism. It is notable that the sum of these shares must be 100 per cent. Otherwise, an alert 'Range is not allocated' will be announced, which shows that the user needs to ensure increases in share of one dwelling group are reflected by decreases in other groups. A handy data entry mechanism is provided to adjust the new size for different dwellings in this worksheet. A dynamic graph automatically reflects changes in term of GHG and AP reduction potential. A similar mechanism is provided for the commercial sector in the worksheet.

Alternative energy

The alternative energy policy intervention is a mechanism which enables the large-scale introduction of renewable energy in order to reduce GHG emissions and AP in cities. This worksheet contains several fields, which may be changed by the user to define the specific environment of a particular intervention scenario. The following categories of input data are specified in this worksheet:

- new added capacity for each alternative energy category (PV, wind, mini hydro, ground heat pump, waste to electricity, biomass and solar water heater);
- typical unit size of each technology (i.e. 2.8 kW for inclined roof PV, etc.);
- technology distribution in the new added capacity (i.e. 50 per cent for inclined roof PV, etc.);

- lifetime support for each technology (i.e. 25 years for inclined roof PV, etc.);
- conversion efficiency of each technology (i.e. 27 per cent for converting solar heat to electricity, etc.);
- annual operation or utilisation rate of each technology (i.e. 2,000 h/yr for inclined roof PV, etc.).

Having determined the above data, the potential for GHG and AP reduction can then be estimated by the tool.

End-user technology

Accelerating progress to make energy use in the residential, commercial and service sectors more efficient is indispensable. There is significant scope for adopting more efficient technologies in these sectors. This scenario can be defined as the introduction of end-user technologies which are effective in GHG emissions reduction through the provision of the following techniques:

- Wall-mounted occupancy sensors for lighting: occupancy sensors detect movements of people and automatically turn lights on and off. Electricity saving is estimated at about 45 kWh/yr based on available data from Schneider Electric for passive infrared (Schneider Electric 2010).
- White LED: light emitting diode (LED) technology for producing white lamps, which consume 25 per cent less energy than fluorescent light bulbs (which are already efficient) and last ten times as long as fluorescents.
- Compact fluorescent lighting.
- High-performance windows: a U-value of less than 0.25, which reduces gas space heating costs by roughly 0.8 MMBtu per window (ACEEE 2003).
- COP improvement in air conditioning.

Smart Grid

A Smart Grid is a modernised electrical grid that uses information and communications technology to gather and act on information, such as information about the behaviours of suppliers and consumers, in an automated fashion, to improve the efficiency, reliability, economics and sustainability of the production and distribution of electricity (Table 9.6).

The tool considers Smart Grid technologies that comprise the following applicable mechanisms in both customer and supplier sides:

Customers (end-user level):
- data monitoring, Advanced Impedance Monitoring (AIM) and system performance diagnostics.

Supplier (city's power supply system):
• load management
• voltage reduction and advanced voltage control
• support penetration of renewable energy generation.

The reductions in electric utility electricity and CO_2 emissions attributable to the above-mentioned mechanisms by direct and indirect effect are shown in Table 9.6, which has been addressed by the Department of Energy (Pratt *et al.* 2010). Evaluation of the co-benefits of Smart Grid is possible through having enough detailed data about the city's energy system. However, the only data that the user needs to enter in the Smart Grid worksheet contain:

1   a city's monthly average electricity consumption profile for the base year, or
2   average yearly electrical load factor.

With the above data, the user can tick the check box 'Smart Grid is connected' to see the results.

Table 9.6 Potential reductions in electricity and CO_2 emissions attributable to Smart Grid technologies

Mechanism	Reductions in electricity sector energy and CO_2 emissions[1]	
	Direct	Indirect
Conservation effect of consumer information and feedback systems	3	–
Joint marketing of energy efficiency and demand response programmes	–	0
Deployment of diagnostics in residential and small/medium commercial buildings	3	5
Measurement and verification (M&V) for energy efficiency programmes	1	0.5
Shifting load to more efficient generation	<0.1	0
Support additional electric vehicles and plug-in hybrid electric vehicles	3	0
Conservation voltage reduction and advanced voltage control	2	0
Support penetration of renewable wind and solar generation (25 per cent renewable portfolio standard [RPS])	<0.2	5
Total reduction	12	6

Note
1 Assumes 100 per cent penetration of the Smart Grid technologies.

Reporting results

The tool produces three types of final report: the summary report, baseline report and after intervention report. The summary collates the results of the baseline and intervention scenarios in the following sections:

1 Primary energy supply to the city:
   Primary energy is directly calculated from converting secondary energy carriers such as electricity and heat into primary energy carriers. It includes traditional fuels, fossil fuels, nuclear, solar, wind, biomass, geothermal, hydro, waste material and heat recovery for outside of the city.
2 Electricity demand/supply match:
   In some cases, a city may be faced with an increasing deficit in power supply, both in meeting its normal electricity requirements as well as its peak load demand. It means that the total installed power capacity is not sufficient to meet the city's electricity demand over a certain time period.
3 Electricity generation mix:
   The generation mix shows the contribution of different power generation technologies in the city's total electricity supply.
4 Total useful and final energy demand in different end users.
5 Urban energy system total emissions (GHG and LAP).
6 Urban energy system efficiency.

The overall functionality of the urban energy system can be evaluated through introducing different indicators. In this tool, fossil fuel intensity and heat island index are considered to represent the efficiency of the city's energy system (through a sustainability analysis). The baseline and after intervention reports contain more detailed data on the energy demand and GHG emissions based on the different technologies (heating, cooling, air conditioning, cooking, etc.) and sub-sectors (dwelling groups, commercial and service sub-divisions). These reports are supported by the production of city-level energy balance sheets, a cost–benefit analysis of the options under consideration, a Sankey diagram, marginal abatement cost and sustainability analyses. The sustainability analysis is a normalised rose diagram incorporating four factors: fossil fuel intensity; diversification of renewable energy (Herfindahl-Hirschman Index); urban heat indicator (based on waste heat production against ambient background temperature) and GHG emissions indicator.

Discussion

In the calculation framework, the substitution between alternative energy forms is not calculated automatically from the evolution of the price for each energy form and its corresponding coefficient of elasticity, but rather from an analysis made through formulating the possible scenarios of development by using the

CBA approach. This could be considered as a drawback of the tool; however, one should bear in mind that in the actual economic context, characterised by continual changes of energy prices, economists do not dispose of any proven technique, which would allow them to quantify the effect of changes in energy prices on energy demand. Besides, the considerable divergence of results in many studies on price elasticity demonstrates that the traditional manner of conceiving elasticities of demand is no longer satisfactory. Due to these reasons, the tool does not calculate energy demand directly from energy prices. For example, the demand for electricity is not calculated from a hypothetical price; this price is simply taken into account implicitly when developing the scenarios and serves as a reference for setting the parameters. In this case, the tool simply calculates the demand for electricity as a function of the local demographic and socio-economic parameters specified by the scenario of development: local climate change, population, dwellings by type and size, etc.

General considerations and wise-use guidelines

Whilst the tools are essentially stand-alone assessments of a given sector, taken together there are overlaps between the three tools. Transport is also included as a component of the waste tool and the waste tool has options that include energy recovery, which can inform the energy tool. Each tool relies on the accuracy of translating an intervention into a factor that can be input into the tool. The nature of the different sectors means that there are different levels of uncertainties around the various measures. Policies concerning behavioural change, be they sorting waste or changing mode of transport, tend to have greater uncertainties than higher level fuel switches or efficiency changes. This is because, in general, there are higher uncertainties dealing with thousands if not millions of individual actors rather than a limited set of power plants or waste disposal sites.

Beyond the general data limitations that such an approach entails, the tools are a linear representation of the various sectors (public transport, energy and waste systems) in a city, from which the implementation of policies in four areas can be evaluated in terms of its carbon and local air pollution emissions.

As such, one limitation is that the *Avoid*, *Shift* and *Improve* options are assessed independently of each other with no feedbacks. This may be less of an issue for some sectors and is perhaps easiest to understand in the transport sector. Increasing fuel efficiency, for example, can be calculated to provide a certain amount of co-benefits based on the fleet as specified in the initial set-up of the tool. However, in reality, such an efficiency improvement may have effects in other parts of the transport fleet. Increasing the efficiency of private cars may make car use more desirable in itself, which would in turn increase the vehicle.km of cars. Such feedbacks are not accounted for in the tool due to the variability in assessing what those effects may be across different fleet configurations and localities. It was mentioned in the introduction that these are essentially short-term assessments of co-benefits. Although the transport tool also contains a module to assess the long-term emissions in the sector, co-benefits are reported as essentially instantaneous when in fact they may take significant amounts of time to take effect; therefore, the results need to be read in the context of co-benefits upon full implementation.

From this discussion, it is apparent that the tools are intended to provide a first-order screening of possible options that can be further investigated using more sophisticated techniques, which have a more detailed representation of the policy in question. In this sense, the tools can be regarded as the preliminary process allowing planners and policy makers to evaluate how a sector may be developed before deciding on targeted interventions.

The utility of the models lies less in the precise determination of co-benefits but rather as a discovery tool that helps users to get a feel for the sensitivity of various actions to reduce emissions. The tools therefore can serve a useful purpose in the following domains:

- as a means of organising data that are collected in a sector (database building and storage);
- as a learning aid to discover the source and magnitude of emissions;
- to understand the relative sensitivity of various parameters on emissions reduction;
- for rapid generation of comparing first-order estimates from multiple scenarios;
- as a guide to setting policy targets;
- as a tracking tool to measure the progress in implementing policies;
- for presentation of options and discussion within and across city government as well as to the general public.

Once set up, the tools are a user-friendly way of discussing policy options and can be paired with the corresponding decision-making tools described in Chapter 10, to form a dialogue between discussing policies and understanding the potential impacts of those policies.

Acknowledgement

This chapter is based in part on material reproduced from three guidebooks which accompany the tools, Doll and Farzaneh (2014) for transport, Dashti and Doll (2014) for waste, and Farzaneh and Doll (2014) for energy, published online by the United Nations University Institute for the Advanced Study of Sustainability (UNU-IAS), Tokyo.

Notes

1 The tools use the commonly available Microsoft Excel® spreadsheets (Ver. 2007 and 2010) operating in a Windows environment that can be accessed through the UNU-IAS co-benefits tool page (http://tools.ias.unu.edu/). Guidebooks on each tool are available in handbooks produced by each tool, which provide greater details on calculations and practical steps in using the tool.

2 Waste is often classified as wet/dry. Dry waste includes items such as wood, glass and plastics, whilst wet waste is the term used for food waste and includes the moisture content therein.

3 In Equation 9.12, the value of 0.5 in the denominator represents the volume concentration of methane in LFG. The concentration of CO_2 and CH_4 can be obtained by considering 50 per cent methane and 50 per cent carbon dioxide in LFG. (Typically, LFG also contains non-methane organic compounds [NMOC] and volatile organic compounds [VOC], but in a very low concentration rather than methane and carbon monoxide.)

References

American Council for Energy Efficient Economy (ACEEE) 2003, *Consumer Guide to Home Energy Savings 8th edition*, American Council for Energy Efficient Economy, Washington DC, USA.

Bongardt, D, Eichhorst, U, Dünnebeil, F and Reinhard, C n.d., *Monitoring Greenhouse Gas Emissions of Transport Activities in Chinese Cities: A Step-by-Step Guide to Data Collection*, Deutsche Gesellschaft für Internationale Zusammenarbeit (GIZ) GmbH. Eschborn, Germany.

Dalkmann, H and Brannigan, C 2007, *Transport and Climate Change: Module 5a, Sustainable Transport: A Sourcebook for Policy-makers in Developing Cities*, Deutsche Gesellschaft für Technische Zusammenarbeit (GTZ), Eschborn, Germany.

Dashti, M and Doll, C 2014, *Guidebook to the Co-benefits Evaluation Tool for Municipal Solid Waste*, e-book, UNU-IAS, Japan, viewed 16 May 2016, http://tools.ias.unu.edu/sites/default/files/manual/Waste_Evaluation_Tool_Guidebook.pdf.

Doll, CNH and Balaban, O 2013, 'A methodology for evaluating environmental co-benefits in the transport sector: Application to the Delhi Metro', *Journal of Cleaner Production*, vol. 58, pp. 61–73.

Doll, C and Farzaneh, H 2014, *Guidebook to the Co-benefits Evaluation Tool for the Urban Transport Sector*, e-book, UNU-IAS, Japan, viewed 16 May 2016, http://tools.ias.unu.edu/sites/default/files/manual/Transport_Evaluation_Tool_Guidebook.pdf.

Farzaneh, H and Doll, C 2014, *Guidebook to the Co-benefits Evaluation Tool for the Urban Energy System*, e-book, UNU-IAS, Japan, viewed 16 May 2016 http://tools.ias.unu.edu/sites/default/files/manual/Energy_Evaluation_Tool_Guidebook.pdf.

Integrated Panel on Climate Change (IPCC) 2006, *IPCC Guidelines for National Greenhouse Gas Inventories, Volume 5, Task Force on National Greenhouse Gas Inventories Programme*, Institute for Global Environmental Strategies (IGES), Japan.

Pratt, RG, Balducci, PJ, Gerkensmeyer, C, Katipamula, S, Kintner-Meyer, MCW, Sanquist, TF, Schneider, KP and Secrest, TJ 2010, *The Smart Grid: An Estimation of the Energy and CO2 Benefits DOE- PNNL-19112, Revision 1*, e-book, U.S Department of Energy, USA, viewed 16 May 2016, http://energyenvironment.pnnl.gov/news/pdf/PNNL-19112_Revision_1_Final.pdf.

Schipper, L, Marie-Liliu, C and Gorham, R 2000, *Flexing the Link Between Transport and Greenhouse Gas Emissions: A Path for the World Bank*, e-book, International Energy Agency, Paris, France, viewed 16 May 2016, www.ocs.polito.it/biblioteca/mobilita/FlexingLink1.pdf.

Schneider Electric 2010, *Wall-Mounted Ultrasonic Occupancy Sensor*, viewed 9 June 2016 http://static.schneider-electric.us/docs/Power%20Management/Lighting%20Control/Square%20D%20Occupancy%20Sensor%20Products/Wall-Mounted%20Occupancy%20Sensors/1200HO0804.pdf.

United States Environmental Protection Agency (EPA) 2008, *AP-42, Fifth Edition, Volume I*, Chapter 2: 'Solid waste disposal. Compilation of air pollutant emission factors', viewed 16 May 2016, www3.epa.gov/ttnchie1/ap42/.

10 Decision-support tools for climate co-benefits governance

Csaba Pusztai and Aki Suwa

Introduction

Addressing local environmental challenges typically requires steering a range of actors who manage the relevant resources in a coordinated fashion for improved environmental outcomes. The concept of sustainability calls for problem definitions that recognise the complex interdependencies in socio-ecological systems and adequate interventions embracing this complexity via coordinated action. The transition from simple disjointed solutions to integrated long-term ones is not solely a technical matter as much as an organisational, institutional and political challenge that includes the careful consideration of opportunities, burdens and the trade-offs between them. There is an increasing attention to the role of various decision-support tools to assist steering the transition towards sustainability by providing insights into the nature of these complex policy challenges. Since the late 1990s, a number of theoretical studies have been carried out to actively steer governance processes at different levels of administration, including the international, national and sub-national/local levels. In particular, the local level of governance is recognised as a potentially influential intervention point to generate tangible changes necessary for achieving not just local but higher level environmental goals. The underlying assumption is that in many countries, local governments tend to have direct control over many of the resources and systems that have environmental implications. These include land use, building decisions, local transport planning, energy management and solid waste management (Bulkeley and Betsill 2003). Accordingly, building capacity and understanding in local government may be a critical success factor in transforming towards sustainability.

Relatively little is known about the potential of tools specifically designed to support the integration of environmental aspects into decision-making and development processes at the local level of governance. Recently, attempts have been made to explore quantitative tools aiming to assess certain environmental attributes. There is a broad range of quantitative sustainability tools available to address local environmental features (Bhagavatula *et al.* 2013; GIZ-ICLEI 2014). As presented in the previous chapter, the tools for transport, energy and waste sectors[1] are also obvious examples of tools focusing on quantification of co-benefits. At present, however, there is an absence of published tools that help with the often overlooked, more qualitative or hard-to-capture aspects of adopting potential interventions in practice. Certain solutions may be desirable from a stylised outcome point of view, but very challenging to implement due to local financial, organisational and political limitations. The limited number of tools to capture the non-technical aspects of local development probably reflects the relative interest that the co-benefits and local governance literature has spent on synthesising our understanding of institutional capacity requirements of various local co-benefit policies. Building on such a synthesis, qualitative analytical tools would ideally help identify how different local institutions can and should develop the transitional path to manage the organisational and institutional changes required to deliver the local environmental co-benefits.

A comprehensive institutional analysis would have a particular value in diagnosing capacity gaps and navigating the local governance to properly implement co-benefits policies and achieve desired outcomes. Against this backdrop, this chapter proposes an approach to assess the capacity and readiness of institutions to adopt co-benefits-oriented measures into their policy processes. This chapter takes the viewpoint that to achieve environmental co-benefits, it is worth recognising the levels of human factors and potential that would accumulatively support vital organisational change for better local environmental governance. A grading instrument, using a fundamental mathematical concept, the Analytic Hierarchy Process (AHP), is demonstrated to guide data collection and populate the tool. Thereafter, the importance and role of systematic tools to support co-benefits governance are discussed.

Addressing co-benefits at city level

The co-benefits approach here refers to the development and implementation of policies and strategies that simultaneously contribute to tackling climate change and solving local environmental and developmental problems. With respect to climate change, co-benefits can emerge in two major forms. On the one hand, there are local environmental and development co-benefits of climate change-related actions, like pollution control, improved health conditions, poverty reduction, etc. On the other hand, there are global climate change co-benefits like reduction in greenhouse gas (GHG) emissions and an increase in adaptation capacities.

The co-benefits approach thus explicitly connects the global and local scopes. As the academic and political discourse on the unsustainable nature of current economies and their global environmental impacts has unfolded during the past decades, micro-level perspectives have been strengthened, relative to national and international perspectives. The role of cities, in particular, has been highly emphasised in both creating many of the pressures leading to climate change as well as offering opportunities for laying down the foundations of an economy that may reduce climate change impacts.

One reason why cities are especially suitable entry points in tackling environmental issues is because the scope of cities as administrative units neatly coincides with the spatially concentrated human activities we know as cities. Despite variations from country to country, cities can typically enjoy a reasonable level of control over critical urban systems such as transport, energy, buildings and waste (Bulkeley and Betsill 2003). They have the ability and the experience to directly influence these systems, which makes them powerful actors to shape how patterns of human activity in cities emerge. For this reason, city-level investments, regulations and policy decisions regarding transport, energy, waste and other systems are often considered to have high potential in reshaping local development paths, also yielding benefits beyond individual cities (IPCC 2014).

Although cities may be recognised for their potential contribution to creating more sustainable societies, in practice, such goals may not necessarily be a top priority or even a relevant aspect in some local-level decision-making processes. In running critical urban systems, decision-makers typically face a range of simultaneous objectives often derived from private benefits, such as economic efficiency, affordability or accessibility. When considering venues for improvement, options are often evaluated and compared on the basis of their respective costs and benefits. Such comparison, however, is highly dependent on the scope of analysis (what costs and benefits are included) and valuation approach (how costs and benefits are measured in monetary or other hard terms that facilitate comparison). These two aspects are in close interplay.

By disregarding co-benefits, cities may miss many intervention options that could offer win–win solutions to the community as a whole. Moreover, as suggested by OECD (2010, p. 82), city-level policies are also the least-cost CO_2 mitigation strategies to pursue macro (national) level reduction targets, arguing that trade-offs between economic growth and environmental priorities are lower at the urban level due to complementarities of policies only observable at the local scale. Co-benefits, however, are challenging to integrate into decision-making processes because they are often societal and/or non-monetary benefits that are more difficult to measure compared to other benefits and cost. They may look too elusive and difficult to defend in political debates. Despite these challenges, there is some evidence that suggests that cities are becoming more willing to take the political risk and venture into new policies (and spending) with potential co-benefits even in the absence of exact valuations. Kousky and Schneider (2003) found that, in addition to rational economic choice (e.g. evident cost savings), perceived co-benefits were named as an important factor of implementing urban climate policies. This suggests that often the idea of co-benefits itself can sensitise local decision-making to environmental and climate change concerns. Of course, systematic indicators and tools to capture and plan for these societal and often non-monetary co-benefits will earn even more credibility and make it easier for such aspects to be seriously considered in decision-making.

Tools to support co-benefits governance

A number of efforts have been made to develop quantitative and qualitative indicators and tools to assist the evaluation of plans, projects, programmes or policies in terms of their environmental, societal and economic impacts. In recent decades, sustainability indicators have been widely applied to monitor sustainable development in a given area, assess progress against a set of goals and objectives set in terms of desired environmental outcomes as well as socio-political aspects, such as desired political and behaviour changes, public participation and communication (Moreno Pires *et al.* 2014).

Sustainability indicators (SIs) sometimes face the criticism of trying to capture natural and social complexities by applying a static quantitative measurement approach, while incapable of triggering change in strategic processes or building governance capacity that would enable the development and implementation of effective policies (Holden 2013). In the SI community, there is a growing number of examples of SIs being applied at the city (urban) level. These initiatives range from international rating of cities, the compilation of best practices, to city self-evaluations through indicators (Moreno Pires *et al.* 2014). There is, however, still a niche for indicators to benchmark specifically the capacity of a city to develop and implement effective policies, and to identify the potential to generate such capacity at the local government level to achieve co-benefits.

Recognising this gap, the urban administration literature has been investigating institutional enablers and barriers to climate action, and the importance of climate change governance on the municipal decision-making process (Leck and Roberts 2015). Governance in the context of climate change should be a system of dynamic and interactive institutional processes resting on the awareness that 'the complexity of cities as dynamic, open systems often means there are linkages and interactions between different components of the urban system' (Bai *et al.* 2010). It is important to better understand governance potentials that can steer the co-evolutionary process of urban environmental problems and urban policy.

Holden (2013) argued that the existing SIs are 'currently hitting the limits in terms of promoting the social and political change, necessary for a sustainable shift'. The use of indicators has been generally restricted to linear methodology to monitor and evaluate progress towards the specific goals and targets. The instrumental indicators are seen to be of little value to incubate policy changes, as they overlook the governance dynamics that actually enable any progress ever to be measured. A next generation of tools that would manage to more successfully address the interplay between the *softer* aspects of the policy context and the *harder* aspects of urban systems could potentially lead to more effective local governance for co-benefits.

Many of the decisions related to climate co-benefits may require the restructuring of city-wide systems, which often have substantial technological and infrastructural components. Such decisions are strategic in the sense that both their implementation and their anticipated benefits (and co-benefits) will typically occur in the longer run. They also often need larger scale investment in terms of resources (human capital, capital goods, etc.), which requires long-term commitment in the form of path dependency. Also, such decisions are often rendered more complex by the underlying relationship between policy alternatives, such as mutual exclusivity, complementarity and preconditions.

A degree of uncertainty in expert or scientific knowledge can be coupled with competing interests (political uncertainty), which makes these decisions related to climate or health co-benefits quite *wicked* as policy problems. Decision support tools can be helpful in structuring the process of co-benefits-oriented policy formulation by highlighting potential advantages, disadvantages, burdens and opportunities. Formal decision-making models and tools have long been used in production and service providing industries providing managers (decision-makers) attitudinal, management and technical support in solving business-related problems (Gonzalez et al. 2015). Similarly, urban decision-makers need models, solution approaches and tools to make decisions on a strategic level, not just on a tactical and operational level, and also to ensure that economic, environmental, societal and ethical aspects are balanced early on in the policy process.

Indicators may play a conducive role when applied in the assessment and building of institutional capacity. They would support:

> learning, understanding and structuring the definition of policy problems and interpretation of trends and solutions in fostering change readiness through learning to think about policy problems and sustainable trends from different perspectives suggested by interpretations and relations offered within the indicator system.
>
> (Holden 2013)

These indicators may play the valuable role of creating a dynamic platform to benchmark the capacity of different actors within an administrative system, and to steer collective efforts that produce conditions for change by matching goals with the engagement of policy makers, administrative structures, enforcement activities and human and financial resources.

Developing a qualitative tool for local energy governance

To illustrate how governance aspects could be included in the design and development of decision-support tools for city-level decision-making, we will now use local energy governance as an example. First, we briefly provide some context to local energy issues and then we discuss the conceptual underpinnings of a specific set of evaluation tools created for local energy climate co-benefits with a special emphasis on the qualitative or *governance* aspects of co-benefits-oriented interventions.

Background to local energy governance

Historically, energy networks have been largely owned and operated by utility companies (typically electricity and gas) in most of the industrial and industrialising countries. The utilities may be state-owned or private, and different in their scales depending on the national context. Most of them, however, have been highly influential over energy decisions. In contrast, local authorities have been fairly weak to let their preferences be reflected in the utilities' choices.

The global imperative for the low-carbon transition and the recognition of the significance of renewables in the local energy supply portfolio have made the global energy context become quite different from what it used to be. Moreover, the surge of the energy decentralisation and liberalisation movement created awareness of the importance of local energy governance. Over time, the recognition has grown that monopolistic or laissez-faire energy systems are unsustainable and require fundamental restructuring. This triggered substantial interest in academic research to analyse the performance of socio-technical systems organised around energy and to explore the role of energy governance that would enable the low-carbon transition (Bolton and Foxon 2015).

The traditional view that utility companies have to be the sole institutions that plan and operate all the energy production, transmission and distribution infrastructure is coming under ever closer scrutiny. An increasing number of initiatives have been taking place to establish municipal utilities (as opposed to national and private ones) and to create the conditions for the low-carbon energy transition in some developed countries (Blanchet 2015). Even where such tangible local energy ownership is yet to be established, especially in developing countries, local energy governance is already becoming instrumental in integrating sustainability considerations into local energy policy in contrast to the exclusively economic criteria often pursued by utility companies. Municipal energy policy has long been to ensure adequate service (electricity, heating) that meets energy demand at a reasonable service cost to its residents. Conventional energy policy typically tries to juggle such objectives based on operational efficiency (being economical by minimising costs, maximising service quality), affordability (e.g. service fees) and access (availability).

Energy use in cities, however, can be a substantial direct and indirect driver of GHG emissions and local air pollution. For this reason, contemporary thinking suggests that municipal energy planners also need to consider the demand side effects and should seek improvements in the urban energy system by adding potential climate and air pollution co-benefits to their palette of decision criteria. Such climate and pollution related objectives are often perceived to go against achieving regular energy objectives. In fact, climate co-benefits are not difficult to align with other benefits of energy system improvements if challenges in providing energy for the city are approached from a systemic point of view, where the overarching goal is to make the system viable in the long-run both from a local community and from an environmental perspective. For instance, being able to introduce energy-saving practices in a city is not only good for the environment, but may also lower the operating costs of the urban energy system, putting less burden on the taxpayers. On the other hand, being able to recover energy from the municipal waste, while creating climate co-benefits, may at the same time improve the community's energy self-reliance.

A successful urban energy transition rests on viable local energy governance that recognises institutional resources and burdens while steering strategic cooperation to overcome potential conflicts. At the same time, viable energy governance is also mindful of the nexus between energy and other sectors, especially those related to transport and waste spheres. The volume of fuel consumption and types of fuel choice inevitably affect the energy profile of a city. The energy profile of a city is also influenced by the methods of waste treatment – for example, energy recovery from waste and biomass content in waste-to-energy recovery. There is a need to demonstrate a framework that strategically manages energy transition over cross-sectional boundaries, through understanding institutional context and capacity.

From quantitative to qualitative tools for local energy governance

Climate co-benefit reductions in GHG emissions and local air pollutants are largely the result of a combination of two factors: (1) a shift in behaviour that generates energy consumption and (2) a shift in technologies used at the supply and/or demand side. Both energy-related behaviour (e.g. patterns of energy demand) and technology (e.g. what building materials, appliances, electric devices are used, what energy infrastructure is put in place, what sources of energy are used) are manifestations of choices made by individuals (citizens) and organisations (local authorities, organisations, businesses) that add up to create city-level patterns. In order to achieve societal (community) objectives, municipal energy policy should intend to shape these patterns of choices and in doing so they should rely on an array of strategies and corresponding policy measures that range from regulations, various forms of economic incentives, spending on infrastructure and technology, and the provision of information. These actions implemented by local authorities and stakeholders must rely on an understanding of what major driving factors affect energy-related behaviours and technology choices and how they may respond to various interventions. These conceptual links are depicted in Figure 10.1. The framework emphasises a practical policy logic in that it assumes, as a point of departure, that a range of policy options (measures) applicable to local-level energy policy can be identified as targeting various driving factors (leverage or intervention points) which will result in behavioural and technological changes and thus climate co-benefits.

Generally speaking, the purpose of decision-support tools in a framework like this is to offer practical models of these conceptual links. The practical models embodied in the tools translate the conceptual links into more concrete relationships so that decision-makers can evaluate how changes in one sub-system relate to potential changes in other sub-systems. Certainly, the conceptual links identified in Figure 10.1 – among them, targeted interventions, driving factors,

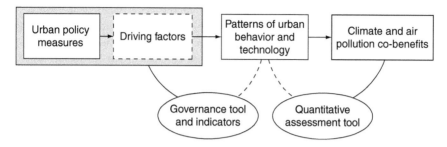

Figure 10.1 The co-benefits evaluation toolkit and the conceptual links.

behaviour, technology adoption and co-benefits – are a simplified model of the manifold complex interrelationships characterising the reality of these socio-technical systems. Decision-support tools as models of these links will always focus on a limited number of aspects of these relationships and thus will always need to be accepted as incomplete. Users will have to use their judgement in determining whether a particular tool and its underlying assumptions provide relevant answers to the scale and scope of the problem decision-makers face.

A further challenge in addition to the incompleteness of decision-support tools is that some relationships can be more readily captured in a practical model than others. The processes and dynamics of physical systems, for instance, can be translated into numerical terms using a range of equations specifying the relationships between the variables of interest. These specifications are typically based on empirical evidence established through research. Although parameters may change as the result of new discoveries and continuous refinement, the fundamental structure of the relationships are typically quite stable. Take, for instance, the calculation of the combined emissions from a changing mix of energy sources used in a city. If one has the adequate emission factors associated with each energy source and the proportion of the total energy supplied from each source, the differential emissions resulting from shifting around the propor-tions in the mix can be readily calculated (approximated).

In our simple framework of the local energy sector, quantitative decision-support tools, such as climate co-benefit calculators, are connecting the right-most two elements in Figure 10.1 as diagnostic tools. Climate co-benefits as outcomes are measured through a set of well-defined, quantifiable indicators, such as tonnes of emissions. The quantitative tool relates these outcomes to quantifiable input variables describing energy-related behaviour and technology. Scenarios assuming different levels of these input variables can be easily built and tested to see how co-benefit outcomes respond to these variations. The value of quantitative tools is two-fold. Not only do they offer a structured and thus replicable approach to approximate climate co-benefits, they also come pre-populated with some of the necessary data (in the form of parameters and options) for the convenience of users, sparing them from substantial research.

Unfortunately, quantitative tools cannot completely eliminate the burden of user input. While many physical model parameters may be adequate across a range of user contexts, input variables tapping into energy-related behaviour and technology are most certainly place specific. The relevance and quality of results will greatly depend on the accuracy of the user input. In other words, quantitative tools are very much prone to 'garbage in, garbage out'. In addition to data quality challenges, decision-makers relying on quantitative tools also need to face another, probably even trickier challenge. Quantitative tools are usually built to simply quantify the implications of changes in input parameters, such as aspects of energy-related behaviour or technology choices. They take those changes for granted and leave it to the user/modeller to understand what processes or interventions could trigger such changes in the model input parameters. Speaking in terms of our simple framework of the local energy sector, quantitative tools rarely model policy inputs and how they relate to driving factors but they rely on assumed policy outcomes captured in the form of altered patterns of behaviour and technology choices. Decision-makers can develop an idea of climate co-benefit implications of a range of 'what-if' scenarios but little will a quantitative tool teach them about what interventions are more likely to bring about certain scenarios and what implications they would have from a policy implementation point of view.

In our framework, we conceived of the Governance Tool as a qualitative tool connecting policy to behaviours and technology. In its decision-support function it is complementary to the quantitative assessment of climate co-benefits. As such there are Governance Tools for each of the sectors covered by the quantitative tools in Chapter 9, namely transport, waste and urban energy. Each tool has essentially the same structure and mode of operation, the only difference being the policies that are contained in the tool are, of course, relevant to the sector and will have different sensitivities to the context criteria.

Its purpose is to extend the analysis backwards to the origin of the estimated climate co-benefits and to help answer what interventions could/should be taken in order to achieve the desired level of co-benefits. Policy interventions can fundamentally differ in what makes them effective and applicable in a given urban setting. There is no single universal recipe for all city contexts. What intervention may very effectively work in one city can turn out to be a failure in another. This is because cities differ in many ways. Other than differences in geography, physical layout and structure, cities operate in different cultural, political, legislative, organisational and resource conditions. Policy measures are sensitive to these conditions, so evaluating the differential requirements of various policy options in a particular situation will help decision-makers better understand enabling factors and potential pain points in implementation. In this sense, the Governance Tool conceptually connects the policy domain to energy-related behaviour and technology patterns.

The structure of the Governance Tool

The current version of the Governance Tool contains data on 19 urban energy policy measures and their sensitivity to 12 aspects of the local policy context (or criteria), but the coverage of the tool can and should be expanded in both dimensions as new knowledge becomes available. The initial set of context criteria was chosen to represent the conditions that are critical to the successful implementation of urban energy measures. At the same time, however, their relevance may vary from city to city. For instance, in one city financial resources may be considered much more of a restrictive factor compared to creating political consensus, whereas in another city political consensus may be perceived more difficult to achieve compared to securing funding. Accordingly, the Governance Tool first requires that decision-makers assess how critical these criteria are relative to each other.

Based on this user input and following the method of the AHP, the tool calculates the weight of each criterion and these weights are then used to give various emphasis to the score the policy measures have on each of the 12 criteria. AHP is a structured technique to support decision-making in situations where options are evaluated on a range of criteria rather than a single criterion (Alonso and Lamata 2006). Multiple criteria often make it very difficult to choose an alternative that performs best in every aspect that decision-makers believe to be important for satisfying their overall goal(s). AHP decomposes the decision problem into a hierarchy of sub-problems (criteria), which can relate to any aspect of the decision problem regardless of whether it is precisely measurable or tentatively estimated. (In the case of our Governance Tool, AHP is structured to have 12 sub-problems which we label as context criteria or indicators, which represent qualitative judgements as to the sensitivity of decision alternatives [policy measures] to these conditions.)

After the hierarchy is set up, decision-makers evaluate the relative importance of each criterion, which leads to numerical weights or priorities. These weights are then used to assign a compound score to each decision alternative based on its relative ability to achieve the overall decision goal. These scores make it possible to compare alternatives in a single dimension and the Governance Tool then ranks policy measures based on their overall score, which reflects how challenging they may be to implement in the particular city. In addition to ranking policy measures, critical factors (context indicators) are highlighted. The Governance Tool also identifies which key energy variables are typically affected (targeted) by each policy measure and to what degree they are likely to change as a result of intervention.

The structure of the tool is depicted in Figure 10.2. White boxes represent parts of the tool which are visible to the user, either taking input or providing output. Grey boxes stand for the parts of the tool which are 'under the hood' and represent expert knowledge connecting user input to outputs.

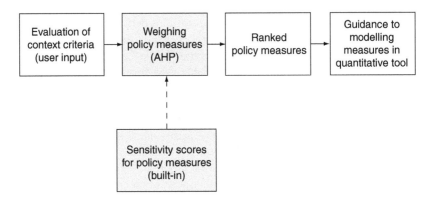

Figure 10.2 The structure of the Governance Tool.

Context criteria (context indicators)

The context criteria incorporated in the Governance Tool represent important local conditions for managing the energy system at the city level. In addition to their use as assessment criteria for planning a range of energy measures, they can also serve as context indicators during implementation providing feedback to decision-makers on changing conditions. In this latter usage, they can be developed into periodically measurable indicators. As criteria in the Governance Tool they are used in a qualitative way, only indicating whether a policy measure has low, medium or high sensitivity to a particular aspect of the local policy context. The 12 criteria were identified and chosen based on the existing literature relevant to the local governance and institution (Macário and Marques 2008; Bos and Brown 2014), and are briefly summarised below.

- **Lifestyle change.** Policy makers often focus on the most tangible aspects of taking action that are under their direct control – for instance, budget allocations, legislation and changing other formal rules of the game. It is easy to assume away the cultural and community context in which their strategies will be expected to work as intended. Some energy policy measures require that individuals (and organisations) embrace substantially different ways of organising their lives as it relates to using (and even generating) energy. If they are reluctant to change their attitudes, norms and routines, policy measures may not lead to satisfying outcomes (or at least not within the expected time frame). Understanding what factors of cultural dynamics play a role in changing the behaviour of the local community is crucial for policy measures that are especially dependent on cultural and lifestyle change. That understanding will help to identify complementary measures to make the transition happen as planned.

- **Public support and acceptance.** Decision-makers also need to consider whether a particular energy measure may create tension in the local community and hence require special attention to managing the introduction of the policy measure. Failing to make sure that the public accepts (and even supports) changes in energy system arrangements can have a substantial impact on whether intended outcomes are met or not. While the awareness-raising programmes may be typically welcomed by citizens, posing no special challenges to securing public support and acceptance, the collection of charges (or other fees and levies) may be a touchy issue in many locales.

- **Legal authority and legislation.** While our tool focuses on energy policy measures that can be typically implemented at the local level, there are certainly differences across cities as to which aspects of the energy sector (and connected domains) they have legal authority to rule and to what degree. For instance, in some cities their jurisdiction allows them to control the level of tax allowances and credits, while in some others it may be delegated to a higher level of government (state/country). Also, some energy policy measures may require extensive legislative action (e.g. formally passing new ordinances, council decisions), while others may require relatively little legal action. This context indicator shows how demanding a policy measure is in terms of legal authority and legislation.

- **Administrative structures and enforcement.** This criterion refers to the administrative and enforcement burden that a particular energy policy measure puts on local agencies (or stakeholders). For instance, introducing certain charges or subsidies may require setting up an administrative unit that keeps track of records and payment. Making sure that charges are actually paid moreover requires effective control and enforcement. On the other hand, an awareness-raising campaign about the benefits of solar PV, being an informational instrument, puts virtually no administrative or enforcement burden on authorities.

- **Openness and learning.** While policy measures may be more or less demanding in terms of necessary lifestyle change within the community, they also differ in the level of cultural change they require within the municipal administration (or more generally speaking the 'policy system'). Some policy measures may challenge generally agreed upon ideas, conventional thinking, norms and prevailing professional values (the status quo). Municipal administrations which are more open to such challenges and are willing and able to learn new ways of thinking will have a better chance at succeeding with such policy measures.

- **Expertise (management, planning and technical).** Putting policy measures into practice requires various forms (tacit and codified) and types of knowledge in several professional areas (e.g. planning, project management, engineering). This criterion focuses on one aspect very generally, that is, professional knowledge that can be acquired through formal training and education, and hence is believed to be relatively easy to transfer. Such knowledge is embodied in people (staff), their working relationships (the organisation) and is also contained in documents (e.g. plans, technical files and specifications) and the databases holding them.

- **Human resources.** While expertise more explicitly refers to professional knowledge available in the municipality, human resources emphasises more the quantitative aspect of staffing requirements that policy measures generate within the municipal organisation. For instance, purchase decisions (e.g. buying durable, eco-friendly supplies) may require much less staff time and no additional hiring necessary at all, while running a successful awareness-raising programme may call for extra staff time and hiring adequately trained personnel may even be required.

- **Financial resources.** Every policy measure has an associated cost, although not all types of costs are easy to express in monetary terms. This aspect refers to direct financial costs related to various forms of investment (e.g. into infrastructure, equipment) related to the implementation of a policy measure. As an example, installing a new energy recovery facility typically requires significantly more financing than promoting energy-efficient light bulbs through campaigns. Of course, financial costs are some function of the scale of the project. Here, we simplify the issue by assuming away the role of scale and just give a general indication of costliness.

- **Technology and infrastructure.** This criterion refers to the extent to which a certain policy measure is sensitive to the availability of physical infrastructure and technology necessary to make the policy option work successfully in practice. Administrative measures or informational instruments typically do not require advanced technology or expensive infrastructure, while energy generation and transmission do.

- **Horizontal coordination.** This criterion reflects the relative amount of local coordination necessary among various municipal departments, local agencies, service delivery organisations and stakeholders in order to successfully implement a policy measure. For instance, several municipal departments may be involved in planning and implementing a renewable energy programme for the city, including the ones responsible for public works, urban planning and building and economic development. Coordination often needs to cross organisational boundaries and may involve an array of (more or less autonomous) actors. In many cases, facility operators may not be under the direct control of the local government, which adds to the challenge of coordinated action. Horizontal coordination, to a great degree, rests on mutual trust among institutions and effective governance mechanisms.

- **Vertical coordination.** In addition to horizontal coordination, policy measures may also require coordination across various tiers of government (regional, state and federal). This may stem, for instance, from funding arrangements, resource allocations or legislative requirements. For example, there may be very little need for vertical coordination regarding an awareness-raising programme, but a major infrastructural investment like

the setting up of a power plant usually involves actors higher up in the government hierarchy (e.g. special authorities and agencies).
- **Consensus and commitment.** The effective implementation of policy measures is also sensitive to the degree of political consensus and commitment that can be forged in support of the measure. Consensus may be difficult to reach for policy measures that involve, for instance, great financial investment, a large amount of additional resources, uncertain or distant improvements. Consensus and commitment is also relatively difficult to get when a variety of potentially conflicting stakeholder interests are involved.

Policy measures

The Governance Tool has data on an initial set of 19 policy measures related to the urban energy system which are generally applicable to a wide range of country and city settings. These measures were chosen to be representative of several intervention points we identified based on our typology (Figure 10.3). As mentioned earlier, the Governance Tool is built on the view that the conceptual framework for energy measures corresponds to the Avoid-Shift-Improve (A-S-I) framework upon which this book is based. The measures (and the intervention points) can be divided into three sets depending on whether they seek to avoid (reduce) energy demands, shift from non-renewables to renewables, or improve energy efficiency in the system (Comodi *et al.* 2012).

Measures in the first group are primarily aimed at users (demand side). In our urban energy system perspective, this means households (residents), businesses (e.g. retailers, hotels, offices) and institutions (including schools and universities, and organisations of the local government). The second set of measures is targeted

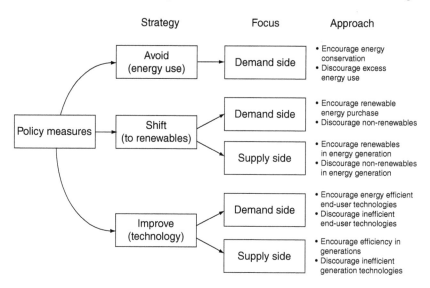

Figure 10.3 A typology of policy measures.

at both supply and demand sides. This includes incentives to increase the reliance on renewable energy. The actors involved in these activities can be private entities and public entities under the control of the municipality or some level of government. The third group of measures intend to improve energy efficiency both at the user-end and generation.

The list of 19 measures currently representing the default set built into the Governance Tool is of course by no means exhaustive. While recognising this as a potential limitation, our purpose was to offer reasonable coverage by including several plausible alternative measures for each intervention point. These measures are not mutually exclusive; in fact, some of them may work best if combined. As for 'vertical' linkage, the measures included for different intervention points actually require combination (pairing) to yield reasonable policy packages and outcomes.

Evaluation of context and policy measures

Based on the above concept, we developed the methodologies and guidelines for a series of energy indicators for urban co-benefits, emphasising self-examination of capacity to bring changes in the local energy policies. The tools analysis is subject to the degree of ability and resources of a sub-national government and the nature of its required policy change in the multiple policy categories.

The evaluation of context criteria

As mentioned earlier, the Governance Tool's first component is the 'Context Criteria'. This assessment allows the user to evaluate perceptions of how challenging the 12 context criteria are in the user's city. This assessment provides input to the calculation of weights that can be used in the comparison of policy alternatives. Of course, there is no universally applicable scale to measure the degree of challenge in these 12 domains; therefore, it must be stressed that this assessment exercise is strictly a matter of subjective judgement. The assessment of the context criteria can be done in one of two ways, currently implemented in two alternative versions of the Governance Tool. The first method is called ranking, while the second is pairwise comparison. While the former may be somewhat more intuitive, less cognitively demanding, the latter is reported to help users reflect and learn more about these initial conditions (Hajkowicz et al. 2010).

Ranking

In the ranking version, the user is asked to rate on how much challenge each criterion poses to municipal energy management (Figure 10.4). As the users evaluate, the tool automatically calculates weights.

	Not challenging at all	Extremely challenging	Rating
Lifestyle change			5
Public support & acceptance			5
Legal authority & control			5
Administrative structures & enforcement			5
Openness & learning			5
Expertise (planning, technical)			5

Figure 10.4 Sliders used for rating (partial screenshot of the Energy Governance Tool).

Pairwise comparison

In contrast to ranking, pairwise comparison expects users to make relative judgements as to which aspects of the local context would pose greater or lesser overall challenge to local energy policy development. Going pairwise means that each criterion has to be compared to all other criteria on a one-on-one basis. This is done in a matrix format (see Figure 10.5). Take an example where the user needs to compare 'lifestyle change' and 'public support & acceptance'. Which one is more challenging to control or improve in the city? Is one more challenging than the other? How much more? Users can evaluate these from the available judgement options.

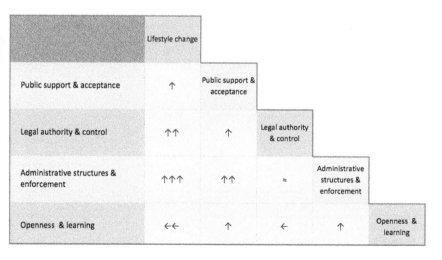

Figure 10.5 The pairwise comparison matrix (partial screenshot of the Energy Governance Tool).

Having four levels to express differences in challenge makes it possible to capture subtleties and obtain more accurate relative prioritisation among the 12 criteria. At the same time, it puts much greater burden on the users when going through the pairwise judgements compared to simply specifying which criterion is more challenging than the other. Processing 61 pairwise comparisons is not only demanding (of both time and concentration) but may also lead to inconsistencies in judgement after a point. To offer some feedback regarding the overall integrity of judgements contained in the matrix, the consistency ratio is reported.

Sensitivity profiles

The sensitivity of certain policy measures to the 12 aspects of local conditions included in the tool of course may be markedly different in various settings. Cities share a lot in common regardless of their location, yet they also differ in so many important aspects that they cannot be accounted for completely. The sensitivity scores incorporated in the tool therefore should be seen only as a general approximation based on expert opinion and experience reported in the energy management literature.

The sensitivity scores for each policy measure across the 12 context criteria are contained in tabular format, expressed on a four-point scale: not sensitive, low, medium and high sensitivity. A portion of the sensitivity table is shown in Figure 10.6. The sensitivity table is hidden by default as sensitivities are not meant to be altered by the user under normal circumstances.

Measure	Culture & community		Legal and
	Lifestyle change	Public support & acceptance	Legal authority & control
Subsidies/loans for retrofitting old buildings (to meet higher energy performance standards)	Low	Low	Low
Building codes for new construction (energy performance standards)	x	Medium	High
Standards for new municipal facilities (energy performance standards)	x	x	High
Standards for renovating city facilities (to meet higher energy performance standards)	x	Medium	High
Feed-in tariff	x	x	Medium
Net metering	Low	x	Medium
Tax credits for renewable energy installations (e.g. property tax & solar, geothermal)	x	Low	Medium
Subsidies/loans for investments in renewable energy (e.g. solar) by property owners	Low	Low	Low
Obligation of building owners to connect to district heating network	High	High	High

Figure 10.6 Sensitivity table (partial screenshot of the Energy Governance Tool).

Interpreting ranked measures

After providing the self-evaluation across the context criteria, the users are presented with a list of 'Ranked Measures' in which the policy measures are ranked on the basis of the overall score they receive as a result of the AHP calculations – that is, the combined weighted 'performance' score on each criteria (Figure 10.7). Policy measures listed lower down in the list will tend to have more critical issues identified for implementation. In the example, 'Standards for new municipal facilities' appears before 'Subsidies/loans for retrofitting old buildings', although the latter has five *moderate* and one *great* challenge, while the former has one *moderate*, two *great* challenges and one *substantial* challenge. This is due to the fact that 'Standards for municipal facilities' as a measure may score well under the average in other (non-critical) aspects, which leads to an overall lower score in spite of the four critical issues.

Through the presentation of the ranked measures, the Governance Tool provides policy makers with insight as to their potential to materialise policy development. It offers a holistic understanding about whether the decision-makers have sufficient local resources to bring changes. Judgement and population of the data on the Governance Tool is inevitably subjective, but would give a representation of the current local capacity and decisions, in relation to the alternative energy development and the degree of energy efficiency.

Potential uses of Governance Tools

There is ongoing discussion on how to address development issues simultaneously with climate change mitigation. The co-benefits approach aims to produce several different benefits from one particular policy, and the approach has been acknowledged in its Fourth Assessment Report of the IPCC (IPCC 2007). Climate co-benefits can be the primary motivation for developing countries to participate in international climate change action.

The co-benefits approach, however, has yet to be widely mainstreamed in international and domestic climate mitigation policy frameworks. There are some activities to mainstream co-benefits in the international climate mitigation framework by integrating the concept in its GHG accounting methodologies (Fransen 2009; Cheng 2010; Winkelman *et al.* 2011). These movements, however, have not yet progressed to become the sufficient force to drive the local decision-makers to scientifically evaluate the degree of co-benefits they may gain, through what policies, and how they prepare capacity to implement the policies.

Governance Tools, such as the one presented above for the energy sector, provide a useful framework for the assessment of institutional trajectories for positive policy transition. Through applying the analytical procedure, based on the tools, institutional capacity would be evaluated to identify the gap between current conditions and the required change to pursue a certain policy agenda. The assessment is important, as it can contribute to the institution to develop

Measure	Culture & Community		Legal and Institutions		Organization & Resources					Coordination		Political	Total Weighted Score
	Lifestyle change	Public support & acceptance	Legal authority & control	Administrative structures & enforcement	Openness & learning	Expertise (planning, technical)	Human resources	Financial resources	Technology & infrastructure	Horizontal coordination	Vertical coordination (across tiers)	Consensus & commitment	
Standards for new municipal facilities (energy performance standards)			***	*				***	**				1.415
Subsidies/loans for retrofitting old buildings (to meet higher energy performance standards)		*	*	*		*		***	*			*	1.522
Tax credits for renewable energy installations (e.g., property tax & solar, geothermal)			**	*		*		***	*		*		1.575
Net-metering			**	*		***			***			*	1.593
Feed-in tariff (FiT)		*	**	*		***			***		*	*	1.615
Building codes for new construction (energy performance standards)		*	***	*		***		*	*		*	*	1.653
Subsidies/loans for investments in renewable energy (e.g., solar) by homeowners/businesses		*	***	*		*		***	*		*		1.654
Obligation of building owners to connect to district heating network	*		***	*					***		*		1.662
Standards for renovating city facilities (to meet higher energy performance standards)		*	***	*		***		***	*				1.734
Local government investment into renewable energy generation facilities		*	*	*		***		***	***		*	*	1.997

Figure 10.7 Ranked policy measures (partial screenshot of the Energy Governance Tool).

paths for sustainable courses. Understanding organisational and institutional capacity can create a baseline against which future changes in institutional development may be benchmarked (Bos and Brown 2014).

The Governance Tools should be mindful of steering institutional transitions by generating organisational dynamics for transformative processes. Since the Governance Tool does not belong to any particular policy sphere in multilevel governance, its boundary-crossing capacity may give them specific importance at identifying the gaps and commonalities between different policy scopes in terms of organising, interpreting and linking different views and perceptions. The tool may help to build a network of commonly shared visions and values among different actors.

The Governance Tool for the energy sector in our example hosts a core set of context indicators and a core set of policy measures covering renewable energy and energy-efficiency development. Combined together, these two dimensions provide views on how many resources they have and/or they need to have more of to make progress in changing the local energy portfolio. This qualitative assessment framework was designed to be applied in conjunction with a quantitative energy assessment tool explained in Chapter 9 (pages 264–274), but it can also be a stand-alone self-assessment tool for local policy transition. Although the Governance Tool is meant to be used at the level of local government (city councils), it is not infeasible to assess national level capacity and decisions through this framework.

In general, these tools help to identify co-benefit-oriented policy measures which are more likely to be easily implemented in a particular city. They also help to highlight critical factors of their implementation. This alone, however, does not say anything about their potential to generate climate co-benefits. A measure that turns out to be marginally challenging to implement may only provide modest co-benefits. At the same time, a measure that poses great challenges may be found desirable for the substantial co-benefits it is expected to generate. It should be pointed out that the Governance Tool is intended to provide only an indication of the level of challenges for a set of policy measures rather than single out a 'best option'. The policy measures included in the tool are not mutually exclusive. Indeed, they are typically used in combination to yield reasonable results. For instance, awareness-raising measures will rarely work very effectively without measures that are intended to provide reasonable alternatives and incentives for changing behaviour and making desirable choices in technology.

Using the tool in and for local governance will always face concurrent challenge of reliability and validity. There is substantial deviation in understanding contextual capacities, which is only evaluated subjectively. Therefore, the Governance Tool can be infinitely questioned on its validity, because no evaluation is agreed by all the members of an institution. Quick adoption of the tool may only produce a self-assessment of the institutional status quo, and the incubation and implementation of the new policy measures can be left behind as a forgotten agenda.

The approach to developing qualitative tools proposed here also presents the need to create demand for the tool to be used as a mechanism to drive changes. Despite a proliferation of such indicators and tools, their tendency to sit unused on a shelf or in a computer suggests a lack of incentives to engage with them. 'Designing demand' for the indicators and tools is required, to incubate and deliver the changes in policy and practice. Addressing and implementing co-benefits policies is the ultimate goal of the Governance Tool, and there should be sufficient international advocacy to identify environmental co-benefits policies and their effects, in order for the local actors to seriously seek solutions.

Concluding remarks

The co-benefits concept is an approach for mainstreaming climate change issues at the local level. Generally speaking, the concept attempts to strengthen the policy making process so that each measure can intentionally realise multiple impacts at both the local and the global scale. By attempting to address both issues together it can be seen as a more coherent form of policy making which could also prove to be financially beneficial for locals and globally in the long term. Moreover, it is essential to encourage the implementation of climate-friendly measures in developing cities which are not obliged to reduce their carbon emissions but where much progress can be effectively made. In the context of urban sustainability, there have been several studies documenting such innovative practices around the world. However, given that most of those practices are to be of an incremental nature, it is challenging to assess the degree of contribution they made in tackling larger environmental problems or whether they have the potential to scale-up and stimulate systemic change in urban development processes.

The extent to which such an approach creates a difference remains questionable and a method to evaluate the co-benefits in the early stages of a long-term climate change strategy is still lacking. From this starting point, we focus on two environmental benefits that can be gained from sustainable urban measures: local environmental quality improvement and GHG emission reductions. In particular, this chapter provides a review of the initiatives to improve urban sustainability in cities and their potential for co-benefit and, based on these initiatives, proposes a framework to explore how the co-benefits approach may be adopted in the energy sector.

Although they cover a good range of energy strategies, they should not be understood as a comprehensive set of available policy measures by any means. They are rather representatives (or examples) of typical approaches which may actually have many variants and incarnations being implemented throughout the world. Another important implication is that the Governance Tool does not consider interaction effects. This means that the tool is not capable of indicating the simultaneous effects of several policy measures on the context criteria. Such a capability would involve working with substantially more assumptions and thus would potentially lead to even more uncertainty in estimates.

In addition, the Governance Tool assumes away the time dimension of implementing policy measures. Some measures may only lead to expected outcomes on longer timescales, while others can provide benefits in a relatively short term. Finally, the Governance Tool is based on qualitative data derived from expert judgements regarding the sensitivity of policy measures to selected local conditions and their potential impact on urban energy system variables. These expert judgements can, in principle, be justified and improved by supporting empirical data. However, such data may not be readily available for every policy measure and every criterion and for a particular geographical location.

In spite of all the limitations, the information offered by the Governance Tool can be useful in setting the direction of the urban energy sector and serve as a starting point for more elaborate analyses (with fewer limitations) of particular options, including more accurate estimates of costs and (co-)benefits. Existing frameworks and indicators exist for various aspects of local sustainability. While this chapter has demonstrated that these frameworks are useful for covering certain subjects related to national sustainability policies, they are not intended to focus on the energy governance aspects that may bring benefits to local and global communities. Existing guidelines are present to quantitatively assess the degree of renewable energy penetration and energy efficiency, but these are not intending to connect contextual potential and energy policy development.

The focus of the Governance Tool for the energy sector is to analyse institutional capacity for designing and implementing energy co-benefits policies through highlighting the variety of choices of energy governance at the local level. Energy issues in the urban context cannot simply be seen as just a matter of energy provision, meaning that urban energy policy is not separable from wider perspectives ranging from land-use planning, transport and waste management. This systematic view suggests that energy and its associated policies are an essential part of local development.

All these relevant dimensions have economic, social and environmental consequences which may have strong environmental and sustainability implications to cities. Thus they have to be considered in local energy policy making. By focusing on the specific challenges and tensions of governing energy on an urban scale, the Governance Tool intends to facilitate discourse among various interested parties not limited to academics and policy makers but especially local government so as to connect urban energy research more closely to the objectives and needs of local practitioners and policy makers to materialise co-benefits. Taken together, the Governance Tool here exhibits cities to be tangible locations of socio-technical change of energy systems, but also arenas of experimentation and learning around prospectus arrangement. It may be a way of learning and moving from the actual urban contexts worldwide to deliver environmental and sustainable outcomes.

Note

1 These tools were developed by the United Nations University Institute for Advanced Studies, available from http://urban.ias.unu.edu.

References

Alonso, JA and Lamata, MT 2006, 'Consistency in the analytic hierarchy process: A new approach', *International Journal of Uncertainty, Fuzziness and Knowledge-Based Systems*, vol. 14, no. 4, pp. 445–459.

Bai, X, McAllister, RR, Beaty, RM and Taylor, B 2010, 'Urban policy and governance in a global environment: Complex systems, scale mismatches and public participation', *Current Opinion in Environmental Sustainability*, vol. 2, no. 3, pp. 129–135.

Bhagavatula, L, Garzillo, C and Simpson, R 2013, 'Bridging the gap between science and practice: An ICLEI perspective', *Journal of Cleaner Production*, vol. 50, July, pp. 205–211.

Blanchet, T 2015, 'Struggle over energy transition in Berlin: How do grassroots initiatives affect local energy policy-making?', *Energy Policy*, vol. 78, March, pp. 246–254.

Bolton, R and Foxon, TJ 2015, 'Infrastructure transformation as a socio-technical process: Implications for the governance of energy distribution networks in the UK', *Technological Forecasting and Social Change*, vol. 90, Part B, pp. 538–550.

Bos, JJ and Brown, RR 2014, 'Assessing organisational capacity for transition policy programs', *Technological Forecasting and Social Change*, vol. 86, pp. 188–206.

Bulkeley, H and Betsill, MM 2003, *Cities and Climate Change: Urban Sustainability and Global Environmental Governance*, Routledge, London.

Cheng, C-C 2010, 'A new NAMA framework for dispersed energy end-use sectors', *Energy Policy*, vol. 38, no. 10, pp. 5614–5624.

Comodi, G, Cioccolanti, L, Polonara, F and Brandoni, C 2012, 'Local authorities in the context of energy and climate policy', *Energy Policy*, vol. 51, pp. 737–748.

Fransen, T 2009, *Enhancing Today's MRV Framework to Meet Tomorrow's Needs: The Role of National Communications and Inventories*, Working Paper, World Resources Institute, Washington, DC.

GIZ-ICLEI 2014, *Operationalizing the Urban NEXUS: Towards Resource-efficient and Integrated Cities and Metropolitan Regions*, GIZ-ICLEI, Bonn.

Gonzalez, EDRS, Sarkis, J, Huisingh, D, Huatuco, LH, Maculan, N, Montoya-Torres, JR and de Almeida, CMVB 2015, 'Making real progress toward more sustainable societies using decision support models and tools: Introduction to the special volume', *Journal of Cleaner Production*, vol. 105, Part C, pp. 1–13.

Hajkowicz, SA, McDonald, GT and Smith, PN 2010, 'An evaluation of multiple objective decision support weighting techniques in natural resource management', *Journal of Environmental Planning and Management*, vol. 43, no. 4, pp. 505–518.

Holden, M 2013, 'Sustainability indicator systems within urban governance: Usability analysis of sustainability indicator systems as boundary objects', *Ecological Indicators*, vol. 32, pp. 89–96.

IPCC 2007, *Climate Change 2007: Synthesis Report. Contribution of Working Groups I, II and III to the Fourth Assessment Report of the Intergovernmental Panel on Climate Change*, IPCC, Geneva.

IPCC 2014, *Climate Change 2014 – Impacts, Adaptation and Vulnerability: Regional Aspects*, Cambridge University Press, Cambridge.

Kousky, C and Schneider, SH 2003, 'Global climate policy: Will cities lead the way?', *Climate Policy*, vol. 3, no. 4, pp. 359–372.

Leck, H and Roberts, D 2015, 'What lies beneath: Understanding the invisible aspects of municipal climate change governance', *Current Opinion in Environmental Sustainability*, vol. 13, pp. 61–67.

Macário, R and Marques, cf. 2008, 'Transferability of sustainable urban mobility measures', *Research in Transportation Economics*, vol. 22, no. 1, pp. 146–156.

Moreno Pires, S, Fidélis, T and Ramos, TB 2014, 'Measuring and comparing local sustainable development through common indicators: Constraints and achievements in practice', *Cities*, vol. 39, pp. 1–9.

Winkelman, S, Helme, N, Davis, S, Houdashelt, M, Kooshian, C, Movius, D and Vanamali, A 2011, *MRV for NAMAs: Tracking Progress while Promoting Sustainable Development*, discussion draft, Center for Clean Air Policy, Washington, DC.

11 A systems approach for health/environment/climate co-benefits in cities

*Jose A. Puppim de Oliveira,
Christopher N.H. Doll, José Siri,
Magali Dreyfus, Hooman Farzaneh and
Anthony Capon*

Introduction

The collective pressure of human activities is affecting planetary systems (Rockström *et al.* 2009; Steffen *et al.* 2011), in large part through the transition of human populations to urban lifestyles (Hoornweg *et al.* 2011). This transition forms the backdrop for a range of imminent concerns relating to urban health and well-being and global environmental change. Some challenges, like climate change, obesity, and global biodiversity loss, are unprecedented in history and seem to increase inexorably, intractable to policy efforts at even the highest levels. Others, like urban air pollution, infectious disease outbreaks, or casualties from extreme events, involve phenomena for which the necessary tools for measurement, prediction, and policy action have long existed, as evidenced by their effective control over long periods, yet which evade preventive efforts in the modern urban context, particularly in the developing world. Policy resistance in such situations often reflects the lack of a systemic approach to the interconnected determinants of urban health, which in turn is intrinsically linked to deficits in governance.

Systems problems arise, in this setting, out of synergies between decision-making and the driving forces of modernization in complex urban environments. Such problems are best addressed through *systems approaches* designed to characterize and manage complexity while accounting for differing viewpoints and incentives among varied stakeholders, and acknowledging the distributed nature of knowledge and expertise. In particular, effective governance to improve health and well-being in cities requires an accurate and accessible evidence base and inclusive decision-making processes that are both streamlined and implementable across a range of urban contexts.

Although such problems are found in many domains, the focus here is on the interactions between climate change, urban health and well-being, and urban planning. This chapter examines the key role played by improved urban governance in facilitating the application of systems approaches to urban health. In particular, we argue that better recognition of the climate co-benefits in health (i.e. 'win–win' situations in which action to mitigate climate change also leads to improved health) would lead to an improvement in urban governance and allow for a more effective approach to health in cities. This is a particularly relevant context in which to apply systems approaches, since innovative solutions can be identified and implemented locally. This is critically important at the city scale (Capon *et al.* 2009), where decisions at higher levels can lag or are absent altogether.

In order to examine systems approaches to health/environment co-benefits in cities, this chapter provides a systematic discussion of the linkages between climate change, health and well-being, and governance in the urban context, collecting and summarizing relevant literature in these areas. We initially summarize the health impacts of climate change in cities and the general foundations of systems approaches. We then typify health/climate co-benefits in different urban sectors, consider the characteristics of systems thinking in the specific context of improvements in urban governance, and illustrate these concepts via a set of city-specific examples.

The impacts of climate change on health in cities

In general, climate effects on health can be categorized as primary – encompassing direct climatic environmental exposures; secondary – involving disruptions to ecosystems; or tertiary – involving social and economic disruptions driven by climate change (Butler and Harley 2010; McMichael 2014; Butler 2014).

At all scales, cities are at particular risk for adverse health outcomes from climate change (Bambrick *et al.* 2011). For one, cities concentrate people and infrastructure, leaving them more vulnerable to focal extreme climate events (e.g. hurricanes, droughts). Such events can affect cities directly or indirectly, through food supply chains, regional economic impacts, and other pathways. Given the necessity of water for human life and livelihoods, urban settlements are often coastal, and therefore often at high risk from sea-level rise or hydrological or geological events (McGranahan *et al.* 2007). Indeed, there is concern that sea-level rise will displace significant populations in the coming century (Nicholls *et al.* 2011), many of which will migrate to cities unprepared to absorb these new residents.

Moreover, because cities are where most people now live, they bear increased vulnerability in situations of local resource scarcity, such as droughts and famines, which impact their catchment areas. Issues of scarcity are, to some extent, offset by the greater connectivity urban areas enjoy compared to remote rural zones, but even well-connected cities can be overwhelmed by severe shortages, particularly in the developing world, where economic resources are insufficient to offset shortfalls. As with sea-level rise, scarcity-inducing events can also spur increases in migration (Obokata *et al.* 2014).

Attributes of the built environment in cities generate micro-environmental conditions that can generate unique risks in conjunction with climate change – for example, urban heat islands act synergistically with more frequent and intense heat waves to enhance health risks from thermal stress (Stone *et al.*

2010), and urban agriculture or green space can generate risk for vector-borne diseases (Klinkenberg *et al.* 2008; Stoler *et al.* 2009; Dongus *et al.* 2009), which may themselves undergo geographic expansion with a warming climate (Brisbois and Ali 2010). In a similar vein, the byproducts of urban activity (e.g. air pollution) can act in synergy with climatic factors to enhance health risks (e.g. allergic respiratory ailments) (D'Amato *et al.* 2013; De Sario *et al.* 2013).

The relationship between urbanization, urban metabolism, and climate change is, moreover, bidirectional – i.e. cities also affect climate, given that they are the origin of most resource demand and the location of most consumption. Cities may account for over 80 percent of global greenhouse gas emissions (Hoornweg *et al.* 2011). The impact of cities on climate change is one link in a reinforcing feedback chain that ultimately has major consequences for human health and well-being (Proust *et al.* 2012).

Inequity in impacts and resilience is a critical dimension of urban vulnerability to climate change. On a micro scale, slums and informal settlements, generally occupied by the poor, face disproportionately greater risks related to climate change (Tran *et al.* 2013) and health (Caiaffa *et al.* 2010). They are often unplanned, lacking both the infrastructure and the service base of wealthier neighborhoods. They are more frequently populated by recent migrants than are other areas, and may thus lack networks for social support. Moreover, they are often sited in areas that may, *a priori*, carry higher environmental risks (e.g. on floodplains or steep slopes).

More broadly, it is likely that impacts from climate change will most strongly affect developing-world regions – a particularly egregious asymmetry, given the vast imbalance in per capita emissions between high- and low-income countries and communities (Costello *et al.* 2009).

Systems approaches

It is increasingly recognized that complex problems of urban management and development require approaches that go beyond traditional norms in scientific inquiry and policy-making (Capon *et al.* 2009; Proust *et al.* 2012; ICSU 2011; Bai *et al.* 2012). This is particularly evident with respect to assuring urban health and well-being in the context of climate change. Conventional approaches often fail to achieve long-term objectives because they (a) focus on limited, siloed, or less-relevant aspects of the problem; (b) lack an effective interface between those responsible for constructing the evidence base and those that make decisions; (c) fail to account for adverse incentives on the part of either scientists or decision-makers in urban planning and management; or (d) fail to integrate insights and knowledge from these various domains (Haines *et al.* 2012). Systems approaches are designed to effectively address these concerns. We distinguish four main elements of such approaches, relating to analytic method, interdisciplinarity, transdisciplinarity, and scaling/bounding.

Analytic method

Traditional methods in epidemiology and other public health sciences tend to be reductive: that is, they focus on identifying the independent effects of individual variables. While there is no denying the historical value such work has brought to the study of health, or indeed its present utility in situations where causality is straightforward, reductive methods tend to fail in the face of complexity, such as seen in urban systems – for example, where feedback structures, dynamic decision-making processes, or threshold effects produce non-linear relationships.

Ever-more-intricate empirical statistical analyses of association have made substantial inroads in identifying complex causal relationships – for example, through the use of latent variable approaches, and multilevel and structural equation modeling[1] – yet most often such relationships are best identified through dynamical systems modeling approaches, broadly defined. Such approaches explicitly incorporate feedback structures, threshold effects and other nonlinearities, allowing for simulation, scenario testing, the identification of systemic leverage points, and optimization. They may also include individual-based or aggregate models, structured spatially or along network frameworks at multiple scales.

Interdisciplinarity

Beyond systems-based analytic methods, a key element of systems approaches is scientific and/or professional interdisciplinarity. A defining characteristic of urban systems is complexity, and the more complex the system, the less likely that any one practitioner – or set of researchers from a single disciplinary field – can accurately define the scope of the problem or the system in question. Interdisciplinarity involves integrating the disciplinary knowledge (i.e. concepts, methods, and principles) of practitioners from different fields to develop a shared, more complete understanding of a problem (Lawrence 2010).

Systems approaches thus necessarily involve not only teams of scientists from substantially different disciplinary backgrounds, but also urban design professionals – as well as methods for blending knowledge, identifying key commonalities and differences in understanding, harmonizing data design and collection, and recognizing valid systemic relationships (Newell and Proust 2012). In this regard, cognitive science can and should play a significant role; however, a substantial shift in attitudes on the part of scientists, planners, and ancillary communities (including funding agencies) is also needed.

Transdisciplinarity

Understanding how to resolve real-world problems goes well beyond identifying causes and effects *in vitro* or *in silico*. In particular, it requires understanding how incentive structures and the variable behavior of different stakeholders affect the feasibility of policy actions, and how dynamic changes in the system in response to policy can lead to new incentives for decision and policy-makers and the general population – and, no less, for the scientific community. Moreover, it involves translating new understandings of system behavior into actionable recommendations.

Tackling such questions involves transdisciplinarity – the incorporation of stakeholders beyond traditional science (or urban engineering and design, in this context) in defining systems, setting goals, and generally participating in the co-production of knowledge. This is necessary to provide an accurate understanding of feasibility and incentives, to sensitize scientists and urban planners to the political and policy context – and conversely, decision-makers to the evidence base – and to generate the will for sustained collective action. Effective transdisciplinary approaches also incorporate communities and citizens, and hence increase accountability among decision-making entities.

Scaling/bounding

One persistent issue with systems problems is the likelihood that both causes and effects will cross institutional, physical, or geographic decision-making boundaries. Such transboundary problems complicate effective short- and long-term control efforts in that decision-making entities often lack control of the causes of problems within their jurisdictions. Conversely, many of the consequences of their decisions may be felt outside their ambit. This is particularly true for cities, which drive environmental impacts over a much broader footprint than the urbanized zone and which are vulnerable to health consequences from processes occurring far beyond their borders.

Systems approaches address the multi-scale nature of systems problems by incorporating stakeholders from multiple geographic, disciplinary, and decision-making domains and by explicitly modeling multi-scale effects.

Co-benefits in cities: linking climate change and urban health across multiple sectors

The reduction of carbon emissions lies at the heart of current efforts to combat climate change, yet it also has consequences for urban health. Actions under this strategy broadly fall into two logical categories, namely shifting from carbon-intensive fuels to cleaner forms of energy and increasing energy efficiency.[2] While such efforts find their broadest expression in national-level energy policy, the complexity of the systems that give rise to carbon emissions leads to a diversity of implementations in different sectors and across different levels of governance.

Structural factors and policy options for tackling climate change also have local consequences for health. The overlapping effects allow for the identification of co-benefits between actions designed to reduce carbon emissions and consequent health outcomes. Climate co-benefits in health encompass win–win opportunities for simultaneously tackling climate change and improving health. Ideally, systems approaches can help identify synergies and trade-offs across sectors, yet the potential opportunities and benefits of applying such approaches in health promotion remain relatively undeveloped in practice (Paton *et al.* 2005). This section briefly outlines potential sectors where co-benefits for health are anticipated.

Transport (Chapter 2)

Urban transport affects health in various interconnected domains: respiratory and other ailments resulting from air pollution produced in the combustion of fuels; physical injury which may result from high speeds or traffic volumes or design characteristics of the built environment; stress and other factors affecting mental health that arise from features of transport or mobility, such as time spent commuting; and cardiovascular and other health risks arising from the increasingly sedentary nature of modern life – in part the result of planning decisions about transport which lead to a lack of physical activity. There is a growing body of evidence regarding the deleterious health effects arising from these various sources. Of these, physical inactivity, which has soared over the last few decades, appears to pose the greatest health risks, as it has a direct relation with obesity, diabetes, and cardiovascular disease. In a study comparing London and Delhi, 'active transport' (walking and cycling) offered the greatest health benefits in terms of Disability Adjusted Life Years (DALYs), by an order of 5–10 over switching to cleaner fuels alone, whilst a combination of both strategies was found to be even more beneficial (Woodcock *et al.* 2009).

Concern initially manifested over the relationship between urban transport and health in areas where widespread car use first proliferated (Frumkin 2002). Pendola and Gen (2007) reported a relationship between urban density and car use and between critically increased body-mass index (BMI) values for users who reported high levels of car use. Although the US has some of the highest obesity rates in the world, Day *et al.* (2013) also reported rapidly increasing levels of obesity linked to increased car use and low-density residential living in China. The complex of characteristics of modern urban organization which provide the conditions for physical inactivity in a population has been labeled the 'obesogenic urban form' (Swinburn *et al.* 1999; Townshend and Lake 2009).

Despite advances in vehicle technology, many cities in the world still experience unacceptable levels of air pollution. For example, Doll (2009) estimated that over three-quarters of a billion people are exposed to PM_{10} levels, exceeding even the least-stringent WHO pollution control guidelines in urban areas. Exposure to air pollution increases morbidity and mortality from respiratory illnesses and cardiovascular disease; in 2012, there were 3.7 million premature deaths related to outdoor air pollution (World Health Organization 2014). Many of these could be prevented by reducing dependence on private motor cars and shifting to clean public transport as well as active transport. Whilst necessary, such a shift is not sufficient and the integration of sustainable transport planning into the built environment is crucial. For example, the provision of walkable and cyclable areas is essential to ensure that gains from active transport are not offset by increased risk of collision with motorized vehicles.

Land use (Chapter 3)

The health benefits of sensibly planned urban areas, and particularly so-called 'green infrastructure' (EC 2012), are manifold. Green areas cool cities, countering the urban heat island effect, and filter the air of pollutants; they also act as locations where residents can exercise and engage in other outdoor activities. When sited as communal parks, village greens, and town squares, they can also foster a sense of community, social cohesion, and even build an appreciation of nature and environmental responsibility. Other types of green infrastructure such as wetlands or urban forests may also provide environmental co-benefits, such as water filtration and storm water regulation (EC 2012).

Tzoulas *et al.* (2007) cite a range of experimental and epidemiological studies and surveys which indicate benefits from green spaces, related to the innate need of humans for contact with nature for psychological well-being; among these are increased longevity, better self-reported health outcomes, greater relaxation levels, quicker recovery from stressful situations, and lessened aggression as a result of reduced fatigue. Bowler *et al.* (2010) systematically reviewed evidence of benefits from exposure to natural environments, finding overall improved levels of energy and decreased negative emotions such as anxiety, anger, fatigue, and sadness.

However, the positive benefits of green spaces cannot be generalized (Tzoulas *et al.* 2007); ecological changes in urban and peri-urban areas can, for example, affect the range of vector-borne diseases like Lyme disease and West Nile Virus. Planning in itself does not guarantee positive health outcomes. In Putrajaya, a planned city and the administrative capital of Malaysia, the desire to create an 'intelligent garden city' with green areas and water features combined with other aspects of urban governance resulted in some of the highest levels of dengue fever in Malaysia (Mulligan *et al.* 2012). For the greatest effect, planning must be embedded in a systems approach which accounts for systemic change and unintended consequences.

Urban energy (Chapter 5)

The chief health impact of the urban fuel cycle derives from incomplete combustion when fuel carbon is converted to health-damaging pollutants. About half of the world's households (mainly rural) use solid fuels (biomass and coal) for cooking and heating in simple devices that produce large amounts of air pollution (World Health Organization 2006). Although the use of biomass is lower in cities, poor populations in cities still use a range of fuels which cause adverse health effects.

In developing countries, significant health co-benefits can be achieved by replacing existing inefficient indoor and outdoor cooking systems with increased-efficiency, low-emission stoves and also by improving the energy efficiency of appliances in buildings, which would result in substantial health benefits through the reduction of respiratory infection and adult heart and lung disease. Using such methodologies, a case study in Delhi showed that a five-year program to introduce low-emission cooking and high-efficiency ventilation systems could prevent around one million premature deaths, particularly from cardiovascular mortality and chronic obstructive pulmonary disease (estimate by author).

Impacts can also be made on the demand side of the energy equation. Improving ventilation performance in an attempt to reduce energy demand not only reduces air-flow from outdoor air pollution but also reduces fossil fuel consumption in power plants, which has an indirect effect on health protection in cities. Distributed power generation through multiple micro generation facilities is expected to play an increasingly important role in cities, and such new modes, in tandem with energy generation from renewable resources, are seen as critical for meeting GHG reduction targets – although this is not only an urban issue. Changing methods of electricity generation to reduce greenhouse gas emissions, particularly by reducing the use of coal, would reduce particulate air pollution (PM_{10} and $PM_{2.5}$), which can harm health. Mitigating climate change via intervention in the urban energy system thus presents excellent opportunities for improving public health through reductions in acute respiratory infections, tuberculosis, chronic bronchitis, and lung cancer (Smith 1990).

Poorly constructed and maintained houses are more likely to be inhabited by people with low incomes and this too has an indirect effect on health (Liddell and Morris 2010). Developing methods for retrofitting low-income apartments and single-room occupancies that achieve energy savings and simultaneous indoor air quality improvements can make residents more resilient to increasing energy prices and improve their health. Table 11.1 gives some examples of specific strategies required for climate change mitigation and adaptation along with health co-benefits in the context of improved construction.

Improved governance as a component of systems approaches

Traditional approaches to dealing with urban development and health are largely dissociated one from the other. For example, decisions about short- or long-term investments in development of water and sewage infrastructure rarely involve consultation with health specialists, departments, or ministries. The same is true for transportation and land use. Conversely, health departments rarely involve stakeholders in urban development in investment decisions for health infrastructure or services.

Strengthening governance through the application of systems approaches could help realize the health co-benefits of a low-carbon urban development path and lead to improved management of both climate change and health. This alignment of different development needs would improve the effectiveness and efficiency of urban interventions in both sectors (Puppim de Oliveira *et al.* 2013).

Table 11.1 Strategies for climate change mitigation and adaptation with health co-benefits in buildings

Adaptation/mitigation tactic	Environmental outcomes	Health co-benefits
Green roofs	Carbon sequestration, water retention, energy conservation, reduced greenhouse gas emissions, UHI mitigation	Reduce temperature-related illnesses and respiratory illnesses, increase thermal comfort, increase contact with nature, increase food security
Increase albedo	Reduce energy use and greenhouse gas emissions, UHI mitigation	Reduce temperature-related illnesses and respiratory illnesses, increase thermal comfort
LEED building compliance	Increase energy efficiency of buildings, reduce energy use and greenhouse gas emissions	Reduce temperature-related illnesses and respiratory illnesses, positive aspects of increased natural light in workplace
Home insulation	Increase energy efficiency of buildings, reduce energy use and greenhouse gas emissions	Increase thermal comfort, reduce heat-related illnesses and respiratory illnesses
Solar panels and water heaters	Reduce energy use and greenhouse gas emissions, reduce fossil fuel extraction	Reduce heat-related illnesses and respiratory illnesses

Governance in urban areas

Good governance provides a favorable context for sustainable development (Kemp and Parto 2005), and may particularly influence the social determinants of health (Burris *et al.* 2007). For example, increase in citizen participation in urban investments through participatory budgeting has had positive impacts on public health, including reduction in health inequalities (Caiaffa *et al.* 2010). Many of the investments chosen by communities in their areas addressed the underlying causes of urban health problems, such as lack of sanitation.

Against this backdrop, three areas under the broad framework of governance offer promise for innovative thinking and more effective outcomes for health: understanding the urban context; engaging and organizing stakeholders; and ensuring effectiveness.[3] We analyze those areas and provide examples from different contexts.

Understanding the context

Improving governance through systems approaches requires a sufficiently complete overview of the context within which health – or lack thereof – arises. In fact, although climate change is a global phenomenon, its impacts depend to a large extent on local conditions (Moensch *et al.* 2011). It is thus critical to understand local vulnerability – 'the degree to which a system is susceptible to, and unable to cope with, adverse effects of climate change' (IPCC 2007, p. 89). Vulnerability itself is determined by a system's exposure, sensitivity ('the degree to which a system is affected, either adversely or beneficially, by climate variability or climate change') (IPCC 2007, p. 86), and adaptive capacity ('the whole of capabilities, resources and institutions of a country or region to implement effective adaptation measures') (IPCC 2007, p. 76).

Systems thinking offers a way to identify opportunities for action, and in some cases to identify potential co-benefits of sectoral policies. Perspectives from both natural and social sciences are helpful in highlighting sources of vulnerability. Thorough analysis also requires mapping of urban actors and their powers and interactions, as well as influential policies and institutions. To fully comprehend vulnerability in urban settings, the knowledge of local dwellers is also key, as they experience and notice changes on the ground. Collaboration between scientists, other urban actors, and local populations – i.e. inter- and transdisciplinarity – is therefore a first step in the process of adapting and reforming systems that assure urban health and well-being (see Box 11.1).

Identifying, engaging and organizing stakeholders

Systems approaches to urban health issues call for participatory and inclusive decision-making processes (ICSU 2011), which can identify co-benefits that might otherwise be overlooked in a more sectoral, top-down approach. This requires involving all stakeholders in a given city, including communities and citizens, public authorities, businesses, and even external actors, such as funding agencies. Two steps can set the stage for effective participatory processes: first, empower citizens through awareness-raising activities and establish common interest groups to prepare participation; second, facilitate dialogue and collaboration between urban actors.

Empowering people is especially important for the poorest segment of the population, which is also often the most vulnerable to the impacts of climate change on health. For instance, lack of tenure rights and access to essential

---

Box 11.1 Participatory processes to fight dengue in Yogyakarta, Indonesia

In 2000, in Yogyakarta, Indonesia, following a dengue outbreak, policy-makers adopted a participatory approach to decision-making. In particular, researchers undertook an eco-bio-social investigation based on interviews with community groups. First, they met with households to collect data. Then, local community leaders, decision-makers and city department officers in charge of water supply and waste management worked together to identify and implement interventions, such as sanitation and covering water sources. This community-level participatory process has improved awareness and yielded positive results in the fight against dengue (Katz et al. 2012; Tana et al. 2012).

services experienced by slum dwellers affects their livelihoods and health. Gathering people in groups of shared interests raises their profile. People are thus easier to reach and capacity-building schemes can be tailored to their needs. It is then important to design policy processes in such a way as to ensure that these different groups meet and are heard. This can ease the acceptance of norms later on and thus increase their legitimacy (Bernstein 2004). At the same time, a multi-stakeholder approach is also relevant within governments to overcome sectoral barriers. In fact, some sectoral activities may generate co-benefits across sectors (see Box 11.2).

Ensuring the effectiveness of decisions, norms, and governance frameworks

From a systems perspective, one aspect of better governance is the implementation of the policies and enforcement of the agreements and norms adopted through participatory and other decision-making processes. Decision-makers should be held accountable and citizens informed of activities undertaken to that end. In addition, mechanisms to enforce those 'negotiated' laws and regulations – for instance, judicial proceedings – are a key complementary tool to make sure that policy-makers and individuals' duties and rights are upheld.

In this regard, the rights-based approach is a conceptual framework used by development agencies to promote the empowerment of people through their capacity to know and claim the protection of human rights. In the urban context, citizens demand the provision of basic services such as waste management, clean water availability, and education. These then become standards that public authorities have to meet. Against this background, judges may have to protect citizens from interventions by the public and private sectors, such as land evictions, when they have an impact on health and well-being (Emmel and D'Souza 1999) (see Box 11.3).

Box 11.2 Networking community groups for health in Rio de Janeiro, Brazil

In 2004, in Rio de Janeiro, a network of community groups (the Network of Healthy Communities) representing over 1.3 million people was founded. The groups are various and represent different interests such as religious, cultural, or human rights groups. The network works directly with the local Centre for Health Promotion. This representation of the interests of diverse groups of city inhabitants to a public authority has allowed the direct presentation and prioritization of local needs. The various stakeholders slowly formed a partnership and undertook development programs, tackling health-related issues such as prevention of diseases and poor nutrition (Barten *et al.* 2011). The Network is a good example of a social initiative where poor populations organize themselves in a collective and participatory way to influence public policy and strive for better conditions of life in disadvantaged settings, like the favelas (Becker *et al.* 2007).

Box 11.3 The role of the judicial system in urban health governance in Delhi, India

In India, the Supreme Court has associated the right to life, enshrined in the Constitution, with the right to live in a healthy environment. Public interest litigation (PIL) allows those whose fundamental rights have been violated to bypass ordinary legal proceedings and address the Supreme Court directly (Rajamani 2007; Dreyfus 2013). Environmental groups and activist lawyers soon understood the opportunities inherent in this legal mechanism. On this basis, several PILs were filed in the 1980s to draw attention to the high level of air pollution in Delhi and its impacts on health. The Center for Science and Environment (CSE) published a book (Sharma and Roychowdhury 1996) highlighting an estimated 10,000 people per year (more than one an hour) were dying prematurely due to air pollution in Delhi (Faiz and Sturm 2000), and a recent analysis suggests this figure continues to rise (Nagpure *et al.* 2014). As vehicular pollution accounts for 64 percent of the total pollution load in Delhi (Rajamani 2007; CPCB 1995), the Court made decisions ordering the governments of the National Capital Territory of Delhi and the Union of India to enforce existing environmental legislation. It also supported the establishment of a permanent Environment Pollution (Prevention and Control) Authority for the National Capital Region. The Court also issued more technical orders, such as the conversion of the entire bus fleet to compressed natural gas, a clean fuel, within three years (Rajamani 2007). Studies showed that the norms adopted as a consequence of the Court's activity have had a beneficial effect on air quality in Delhi for some time. In particular the level of suspended particulate matters has decreased by 26 percent (Rajamani 2007; CSE 2006).

Discussion and conclusions

Systems approaches are an essential element of improved governance geared towards dealing more effectively with the complex interactions between environmental change and urban health. Good governance could facilitate a co-benefits perspective and strengthen decision-making and implementation of urban development interventions. Although progress towards these goals will be gradual, we propose five steps to facilitate this transition.

First, there is a need for improving understanding and coordination among different sectors. Cities are highly complex environments, yet they are still largely managed in the form of discrete departments. Pincetl (2010) traces the co-development of disciplines, institutions, and administrative structures (notably the planning profession, civil engineering, and the National Water Quality Association) during urban expansion in the United States around the turn of the twentieth century to mitigate the worst aspects of urbanization and create what Melosi (1999) termed the sanitary city. Whilst this seemed an appropriate way to plan for growing cities, it is becoming clear that the interactions of many of these elements cannot be effectively managed. The city divisions of health, transport, planning, and environment are derived from a variety of different intellectual traditions, which, while (usually) competent for their given remit, generally address any emergent urban problem using the tools most comfortable to their practitioners. This runs the risk of creating gaps in coverage of important issues, or worse, generating internecine conflict when attempting to implement cross-cutting strategies aimed at addressing an emergent problem. Paralysis may ensue, with poor coordination or even competition between these fragmented governance frameworks. We must therefore create the institutional mechanisms and incentives to enable these sectors to effectively work together.

Second, we need to think about the design of service providers and reforms carried forward, particularly in recent decades, which have aggravated the problems described in the previous paragraph. Trends in public management, such as corporatization and privatization of certain public services, can exacerbate cross-sectoral problems, as results-based organizations are reluctant or unwilling to share resources or information with other organizations, implying, as this does, higher costs or loss of competitive advantage (McDonald 2014). Designing services in such a way that providers can be held accountable to the public and are prepared to work together would allow for a more systematic approach to issues of climate change and urban health.

Third, we should make greater efforts to bring together different civil society stakeholders in the decision-making process. Civil society is capable of merging various knowledge systems and perspectives over the same issue. For example, participatory initiatives could identify the main concerns and likely reactions of local populations towards potential urban interventions, as happened in the case of participatory budgeting in Belo Horizonte, Brazil (Caiaffa *et al.* 2010). Broad and open consultations about short- and long-term development plans could help to incorporate other views and information in development pathways, leading to improved decision-making and possibly to increases in co-benefits.

Fourth, systems approaches are not silver bullets capable of resolving all problems with a single policy. Transport, energy, and land-use planning often complement each other but their health effects can be quite different. For example, green areas, which are considered good for city ambience, exercise, and mental health, must not come at the expense of an expansive urban form with increased reliance on high levels of personal transit, nor should they provide conditions for the spread of vector-borne diseases. The inherent complexity of these issues underscores the fact that no single policy is a panacea. However, there are generally too many plans, with not enough thought given to coordination and implementation. We highlight the need for systems approaches as a means to better integrate sectors and that seeking out co-benefits can facilitate such integration.

Fifth, in moving towards systems approaches in urban health, tools that explicitly and quantitatively estimate health co-benefits can improve sectoral integration and decision-making (Doll and Balaban 2013). However, to move beyond the modeling stage, consideration needs to be given to how such measures can be implemented at the city scale. Critically, we must move beyond the siloed thinking that exists across sectors and urban governance. Training policy-makers in simple systems thinking and systems interactions will be beneficial; however, ultimately there needs to be a change in the incentive structure in governance that rewards addressing urban issues from a systemic rather than a sectoral standpoint.

Acknowledgements

This chapter is a modified version of a paper published in the Brazilian Journal *Cadernos de Saude Publica*. It is reprinted here under the creative commons license.

- Puppim de Oliveira, Jose A., Doll, Christopher, Siri, José G., Dreyfus, Magali, Farzaneh, Hooman and Capon, Anthony G. (2015). 'Urban governance and the systems approach to health/environment co-benefits in cities', *Cadernos de Saude Publica*, vol. 31, no. 1, pp. 25–38.

Notes

1 Hovmand (2003), for example, explores circumstances under which structural equation modeling can represent non-linear and feedback relationships, comparing them with equivalent systems dynamics modeling techniques.
2 Avoiding activities which create emissions entirely constitutes another plausible logical category, but reducing consumption is rarely a priority of national energy policies.
3 These three areas are inspired by the work of Mayers *et al.* (2013), yet the original authors separated 'engaging' and 'organizing'. We have addressed them jointly, as they often overlap – as acknowledged in the primary work.

References

Bai, X, Nath, I, Capon, A, Hasan, N and Jaron, D 2012, 'Health and wellbeing in the changing urban environment: Complex challenges, scientific responses, and the way forward', *Current Opinion in Environmental Sustainability*, vol. 4, no. 4, pp. 465–472.

Bambrick, HJ, Capon, AG, Barnett, GB, Beaty, RM and Burton, AJ 2011, 'Climate change and health in the urban environment: Adaptation opportunities in Australian cities', *Asian Pacific Journal of Public Health*, vol. 23, no. 2, pp. 67S–79.

Barten, F, Akerman, M, Becker, D, Friel, S, Hancock, T, Mwatsama, M, Rice, M, Sheuya, S and Stern, R 2011, 'Rights, knowledge, and governance for improved health equity in urban settings', *Journal of Urban Health*, vol. 88, no. 5, pp. 896–905.

Becker, D, Edmundo, KB, Guimarães, W, Vasconcelos, MS, Bonatto, D, Nunes, NR and Baptista, AP 2007, 'Network of healthy communities of Rio de Janeiro – Brazil', *International Journal of Health Promotion and Education*, vol. 14, no. 2, pp. 101–102.

Bernstein, S 2004, 'Legitimacy in global environmental governance', *Journal of International Law and International Relations*, vol. 1, no. 1–2, pp. 139–166.

Bowler, DE, Buyung-Ali, LM, Knight, TM and Pullin, AS 2010, 'A systematic review of evidence for the added benefits to health of exposure to natural environments', *BioMed Central Public Health*, vol. 10, p. 456.

Brisbois, BW and Ali, SH 2010, 'Climate change, vector-borne disease and interdisciplinary research: Social science perspectives on an environment and health controversy', *EcoHealth*, vol. 7, no. 4, pp. 425–438.

Burris, S, Hancock, T, Lin, V and Herzog, A 2007, 'Emerging strategies for healthy urban governance', *Journal of Urban Health*, vol. 84, supp. 1, pp. 154–163.

Butler, CD (ed.) 2014, *Climate Change and Global Health*, Centre for Agriculture and Biosciences International, Oxfordshire, UK.

Butler, CD and Harley D 2010, 'Primary, secondary and tertiary effects of eco-climatic change: The medical response', *Postgraduate Medical Journal*, vol. 86, no. 1014, pp. 230–234.

Caiaffa, WT, Nabuco, AL, Friche, AA and Proietti, FA 2010, *Urban Health: Global Perspectives, Urban Health and Governance model in Belo Horizonte, Brazil*, John Wiley & Sons, New York.

Capon, AG, Synnott, ES and Holliday, S 2009, 'Urbanism, climate change and health: Systems approaches to governance', *New South Wales Public Health Bull*, vol. 20, no. 1–2, pp. 24–28.

Central Pollution Control Board (CPCB) 1995, *Pollution Statistics 1993–1994*, Central Pollution Control Board, India.

Centre for Science and Environment (CSE) 2006, *Leapfrog Factor: Clearing the Air in Asian Cities*, Centre for Science and Environment, New Delhi, India.

Costello, A, Abbas, M, Allen, A, Ball, S, Bell, S, Bellamy, R, Friel, S, Groce, N, Johnson, A, Kett, M, Lee, M, Levy, C, Maslin, M, McCoy, D, McGuire, B, Montgomery, H, Napier, D, Pagel, C, Patel, J, Antonio, J, Puppim de Oliveira, JA, Redclift, N, Rees, H, Rogger, D, Scott, J, Stephenson, J, Twigg, J, Wolff, J and Patterson, C 2009, 'Managing the health effects of climate change', *Lancet and University College London Institute for Global Health Commission, The Lancet*, vol. 373, no. 9676, pp. 1693–1733.

D'Amato, G, Baena-Cagnani, CE, Cecchi, L, Annesi-Maesano, I, Nunes, C, Ansotegui, I, D'Amato, M, Liccardi, G, Sofia, M and Canonica, WG 2013, 'Climate change, air pollution and extreme events leading to increasing prevalence of allergic respiratory diseases', *Multidisciplinary Respiratory Medicine*, vol. 8, no. 1, pp. 12.

Day, K, Alfonzo, M, Chen, Y, Guo, Z and Lee, KK 2013, 'Overweight, obesity, and inactivity and urban design in rapidly growing Chinese cities', *Health Place*, vol. 21, pp. 29–38.

De Sario, M, Katsouyanni, K and Michelozzi, P 2013, 'Climate change, extreme weather events, air pollution and respiratory health in Europe', *European Respiratory Journal*, vol. 42, no. 3, pp. 826–843.

Doll, CNH 2009, *Spatial Analysis of The World Bank's Global Urban Air Pollution Dataset*, e-book, International Institute for Applied Systems Analysis, Laxenburg, Austria, viewed 30 April 2016, www.iiasa.ac.at/Admin/PUB/Documents/IR-09-033.pdf.

Doll, CNH and Balaban, O 2013, 'A methodology for evaluating environmental co-benefits in the transport sector: Application to the Delhi metro', *Journal of Cleaner Production*, vol. 58, pp. 61–73.

Dongus, S, Nyika, D, Kannady, K, Mtasiwa, D, Mshinda, H, Gosoniu, L, Drescher, AW, Fillinger, U, Tanner, M, Killeen, GF and Castro, MC 2009, 'Urban agriculture and Anopheles habitats in Dar es Salaam, Tanzania', *Geospatial Health*, vol. 3, no. 2, pp. 189–210.

Dreyfus, M 2013, 'The Judiciary's role in environmental governance, the case of Delhi', *Environmental Policy and Law*, vol. 43, no. 3, pp. 162–174.

Emmel, ND and D'Souza, L 1999, 'Health effects of forced evictions in the slums of Mumbai', *The Lancet*, vol. 354, no. 9184, p. 1118.

European Commission (EC) 2012, *The Multifunctionality of Green Infrastructure*, European Commission, Brussels, Belgium.

Faiz, A and Sturm, PJ 2000, 'New directions: Air pollution and road traffic in developing countries', *Atmospheric Environment*, vol. 34, no. 27, pp. 4745–4746.

Frumkin, H 2002, 'Urban sprawl and public health', *Public Health Reports*, vol. 117, no. 3, pp. 201–217.

Haines, A, Alleyne, G, Kickbusch, I and Dora, C 2012, 'From the Earth Summit to Rio+20: Integration of health and sustainable development', *The Lancet*, vol. 379, no. 9832, pp. 2189–2197.

Hoornweg, D, Sugar, L and Gómez, CLT 2011, 'Cities and greenhouse gas emissions: Moving forward', *Environment and Urbanization*, vol. 23, no. 1, pp. 207–227.

Hovmand, PS 2003, *Structural Equation Modeling: Applications in Ecological and Evolutionary Biology, Analyzing Dynamic Systems: A Comparison of Structural Equation Modeling and System Dynamics Modeling*, e-book, Cambridge University Press, United Kingdom, Cambridge, viewed 29 April 2016, http://dx.doi.org/10.1017/CBO9780511542138.010.

Intergovernmental Panel on Climate Change (IPCC) 2007, *Glossary Fourth Assessment Report*, Intergovernmental Panel on Climate Change, Geneva, Switzerland.

International Council for Science (ICSU) 2011, *Report of the ICSU Planning Group on Health and Wellbeing in the Changing Urban Environment: A Systems Analysis Approach*, International Council for Science, Paris, France.

Katz, R, Mookherji, S, Kaminski, M, Haté, V and Fischer, JE 2012, 'Urban governance of disease', *Administrative Sciences*, vol. 2, no. 2, pp. 135–147.

Kemp, R, and Parto, S 2005, 'Governance for sustainable development: Moving from theory to practice', *International Journal of Sustainable Development*, vol. 8, no. 1–2, pp. 12–30.

Klinkenberg, E, McCall, P, Wilson, MD, Amerasinghe, FP and Donnelly, MJ 2008, 'Impact of urban agriculture on malaria vectors in Accra, Ghana', *Malaria Journal*, vol. 7, p. 151–162.

Lawrence, RJ 2010, 'Deciphering interdisciplinary and transdisciplinary contributions', *Transdisciplinary Journal of Engineering and Science*, vol. 1, no. 1, pp. 111–116.

Liddell, C and Morris, C 2010, 'Fuel poverty and human health: A review of recent evidence', *Energy Policy*, vol. 38, no. 6, pp. 2987–2997.

Mayers, J, Morrison, E, Rolington, L, Studd, K and Turrall, S 2013, 'Improving governance of forest tenure: A practical guide', *Forest Carbon Asia, other publications*, viewed 30 April 2016, www.forestcarbonasia.org/other-publications/improving-governance-forest-tenure-practical-guide/.

McDonald, D (ed.) 2014, *Rethinking Corporatization and Public Services in the Global South*, Zed Books, London.

McGranahan, G, Balk, D and Anderson, B 2007, 'The rising tide: Assessing the risks of climate change and human settlements in low elevation coastal zones', *Environment and Urbanization*, vol. 19, no. 1, pp. 17–37.

McMichael, AJ, 2014, *Climate Change and Global Health*, Centre for Agriculture and Biosciences International, Oxfordshire, UK.

Melosi, M 1999, *The Sanitary City: Urban Infrastructure in America from Colonial Times to the Present*, The Johns Hopkins University Press, Baltimore.

Moensch, M, Tyler, S and Lage, J 2011, *Catalyzing Urban Climate Resilience: Applying Resilience Concepts to Planning Practice in the ACCCRN Program*, ISET-International, Boulder, US.

Mulligan, K, Elliott, SJ and Schuster-Wallace, C 2012, 'The place of health and the health of place: Dengue fever and urban governance in Putrajaya, Malaysia', *Health Place*, vol. 18, no. 3, pp. 613–620.

Nagpure, AS, Gurjar, BR and Martel, JC 2014, 'Human health risks in national capital territory of Delhi due to air pollution', *Atmospheric Pollution Research*, vol. 5, no. 3, pp. 371–380.

Newell, B and Proust, K 2012, *Introduction to Collaborative Conceptual Modelling*, e-book, Australian National University, Canberra, Australia, viewed 29 April 2016, https://digitalcollections.anu.edu.au/handle/1885/9386.

Nicholls, RJ, Marinova, N, Lowe, JA, Brown, S, Vellinga, P, de Gusmão, D, Hinkel, J and Tol, RSJ 2011, 'Sea-level rise and its possible impacts given a "beyond 4°C world" in the twenty-first century', *Philosophical Transactions of the Royal Society A*, vol. 369, no. 1934, pp. 161–181.

Obokata, R, Veronis, L and McLeman, R 2014, 'Empirical research on international environmental migration: A systematic review', *Population and Environment*, vol. 36, no. 1, pp. 111–135.

Paton, K, Sengupta, S and Hassan, L 2005, 'Settings, systems and organization development: The Healthy Living and Working Model', *Health Promotion International*, vol. 20, no. 1, pp. 81–89.

Pendola, R and Gen, S 2007, 'BMI, auto use, and the urban environment in San Francisco', *Health and Place*, vol. 13, no. 2, pp. 551–556.

Pincetl, S 2010, 'From the sanitary city to the sustainable city: Challenges to institutionalising biogenic (nature's services) infrastructure', *Local Environment: The International Journal of Justice and Sustainability*, vol. 15, no. 1, pp. 43–58.

Proust, K, Newell, B, Brown, H, Capon, A, Browne, C, Burton, A, Dixon, J, Mu, L and Zarafu, M 2012, 'Human health and climate change: Leverage points for adaptation in urban environments', *International Journal of Environmental Research and Public Health*, vol. 9, no. 6, pp. 2134–2158.

Puppim de Oliveira, JA, Doll, CNH, Kurniawan, TA, Geng, Y, Kapshe, M and Huisingh, D 2013, 'Promoting win–win situations in climate change mitigation, local environmental quality and development in Asian cities through co-benefits', *Journal of Cleaner Production*, vol. 58, pp. 1–6.

Rajamani, L 2007, 'Public interest environmental litigation in India: Exploring issues of access, participation, equity, effectiveness and sustainability', *Journal of Environmental Law*, vol. 19, no. 3, pp. 293–321.

Rockström, J, Steffen, W, Noone, K, Persson, A, Chapin, FS, Lambin, EF, Lenton, TM, Scheffer, M, Folke, C, Schellnhuber, HJ, Nykvist, B, de Wit, CA, Hughes, T, van der Leeuw, S, Rodhe, H, Sörlin, S, Snyder, PK, Costanza, R, Svedin, U, Falkenmark, M, Karlberg, L, Corell, RW, Fabry, VJ, Hansen, J, Walker, B, Liverman, D, Richardson, K, Crutzen, P and Foley, JA 2009, 'A safe operating space for humanity', *Nature*, vol. 461, no. 7263, pp. 472–475.

Sharma, A, and Roychowdhury, A 1996, *Slow Murder: The Deadly Story of Vehicular Pollution in India*, Centre for Science and Environment, New Delhi, India.

Smith, K 1990, 'Risk transition and global warming', *Journal of Energy Engineering*, vol. 116, no. 3, pp. 178–188.

Steffen, W, Persson, A, Deutsch, L, Zalasiewicz, J, Williams, M, Richardson, K, Crumley, C, Crutzen, P, Folke, C, Gordon, L, Molina, M, Ramanathan, V, Rockström, J, Scheffer, M, Joachim Schellnhuber, H and Svedin, U 2011, 'The anthropocene: From global change to planetary stewardship', *Ambio*, vol. 40, no. 7, pp. 739–761.

Stoler, J, Weeks, JR, Getis, A and Hill, AG 2009, 'Distance threshold for the effect of urban agriculture on elevated self-reported malaria prevalence in Accra, Ghana', *American Journal of Tropical Medicine* and *Hygiene*, vol. 80, no. 4, pp. 547–554.

Stone, B, Hess, JJ, Frumkin, H, Steffen, W, Persson, A, Deutsch, L, Zalasiewicz, J, Williams, M, Richardson, K, Crumley, C, Crutzen, P, Folke, C, Gordon, L, Molina, M, Ramanathan, V, Rockström, J, and Scheffer, M 2010, 'Urban form and extreme heat events: Are sprawling cities more vulnerable to climate change than compact cities?', *Environmental Health Perspectives*, vol. 118, no. 10, pp. 1425–1428.

Swinburn, B, Egger, G and Raza, F 1999, 'Dissecting obesogenic environments: The development and application of a framework for identifying and prioritizing environmental interventions for obesity', *Preventive Medicine*, vol. 29, no. 6, pt 1, pp. 563–570.

Tana, S, Umniyati, S, Petzold, M, Kroeger, A and Sommerfeld, J 2012, 'Building and analyzing an innovative community-centered dengue-ecosystem management intervention in Yogyakarta, Indonesia', *Pathogens and Global Health*, vol. 106, no. 8, pp. 469–478.

Townshend, T and Lake, AA 2009, 'Obesogenic urban form: Theory, policy and practice', *Health Place*, vol. 15, no. 4, pp. 909–916.

Tran, KV, Azhar, GS, Nair, R, Knowlton, K, Jaiswal, A, Sheffield, P, Mavalankar, D and Hess, J 2013, 'A cross-sectional, randomized cluster sample survey of household vulnerability to extreme heat among slum dwellers in Ahmedabad, India', *International Journal of Environmental Research and Public Health*, vol. 10, no. 6, pp. 2515–2543.

Tzoulas, K, Korpela, K, Venn, S, Yli-Pelkonen, V, Ka mierczak, A, Niemela, J and James, P 2007, 'Promoting ecosystem and human health in urban areas using Green Infrastructure: A literature review', *Landscape and Urban Planning*, vol. 81, no. 3, pp. 167–178.

Woodcock, J, Edwards, P, Tonne, C, Armstrong, BG, Ashiru, O, Banister, D, Beevers, S, Chalabi, Z, Chowdhury, Z, Cohen, A, Franco, OH, Haines, A, Hickman, R, Lindsay, G, Mittal, I, Mohan, D, Tiwari, G, Woodward, A and Roberts, I 2009, 'Public health benefits of strategies to reduce greenhouse-gas emissions: Urban land transport', *The Lancet*, vol. 374, no. 9705, pp. 1930–1943.

World Health Organization 2006, *Fuel for Life: Household Energy and Health*, viewed 30 April 2016, www.who.int/indoorair/publications/fuelforlife/en/.

World Health Organization 2014, *7 Million Premature Deaths Annually Linked to Air Pollution*, viewed 30 April 2016, www.who.int/mediacentre/news/releases/2014/air-pollution/en/.

Index

Page numbers in *italics* denote tables, those in **bold** denote figures.

For Product Safety Concerns and Information please contact our EU
representative GPSR@taylorandfrancis.com
Taylor & Francis Verlag GmbH, Kaufingerstraße 24, 80331 München, Germany

www.ingramcontent.com/pod-product-compliance
Ingram Content Group UK Ltd.
Pitfield, Milton Keynes, MK11 3LW, UK
UKHW021622240425
457818UK00018B/691